D1399326

Sovereign Debt and the
Financial Crisis

Sovereign Debt and the Financial Crisis

Will This Time Be Different?

Edited by

Carlos A. Primo Braga

Gallina A. Vincelette

THE WORLD BANK
Washington, D.C.

ISBN: 978-0-8213-8483-1
eISBN: 978-0-8213-8543-2
DOI: 10.1596/978-0-8213-8483-1

Cover images
Image Source/Getty Images; Benson HE, 2010 Used under license from Shutterstock.com; Andre Blais, 2010 Used under license from Shutterstock.com

Cover design
Ruth: Edelman Integrated Marketing

Library of Congress Cataloging-in-Publication data has been applied for.

In memory of our colleague Dana Weist

Contents

Foreword

This volume on managing sovereign debt in the context of the financial crisis is extremely timely. Governments—especially governments in many affluent countries—will be heavily engaged over the next five years in reducing their fiscal deficits and managing large public debt portfolios.

Managers of sovereign debt shoulder enormous responsibilities in securing funding, structuring debt portfolios to best meet cost and risk objectives, and meeting other debt management goals, such as developing an efficient domestic market for government securities and managing the government's contingent liabilities. Government debt managers manage what is usually the largest debt portfolio in the country and the largest liability on the government's balance sheet. These portfolios can contain risky exposures, including significant proportions of foreign currency–linked and short-term debt. Because they represent the government in negotiating, structuring, and executing transactions, debt managers also carry important reputational responsibilities and risk for the government.

Government debt managers have faced many challenges over the past 10 years. Around the middle of the decade, the global economy grew at its most rapid rate in 40 years. Fiscal positions steadily improved; in several advanced countries, government debt managers faced the prospect of managing a contracting stock of public debt and debated the merits of maintaining a sizable and liquid government bond market. Governments in many emerging market countries extended their yield curves, as foreign investors increased their currency and interest rate exposure and domestic institutions invested more in government securities following reforms to the pension and insurance sectors. These governments also increased the maturity of their debt portfolios and reduced the proportion of foreign currency–denominated debt.

The recent financial crisis originated in the advanced countries. It demonstrated how all of the elements that form the Basel II pillars, including market discipline, could fail in a G-7 economy, creating economic instability on a global scale. The crisis markedly increased the complexity of the challenges confronting government debt managers. Fiscal positions rapidly deteriorated, competition for funding dramatically increased, governments were forced into new roles, and well-established policy frameworks were soon tested by the markets.

Long-serving fiscal management frameworks that were based on medium-term policy settings and nominal anchors—such as golden rules, deficit- and debt-to-GDP targets, and fiscal responsibility legislation—were overwhelmed, as was the carefully designed signaling and transmission architecture that separated fiscal, monetary, financial, and debt management policies. Policy signals started to blur when governments became guarantors and investors of last resort and took on ownership interests outside their traditional risk habitat and risk tolerance. At a time when the funding needs of governments and corporations increased, many emerging market issuers found themselves locked out of the global capital market for extended periods or were able to access the market only for restricted amounts and for short maturities at much higher spreads than before the crisis.

Challenging times lie ahead for government debt managers. Funding costs are likely to increase as the competition for savings intensifies and governments strengthen their banking systems and continue their structural reforms. Many governments have taken over quasi-public and private sector debt obligations and provided a range of guarantees and other contingent undertakings that will need to be monitored and managed by budget teams and government debt managers.

Fortunately, nations are much better equipped to manage these responsibilities than they were 15 years ago. They have absorbed the lessons from the 1998/99 Asian crisis and subsequent contagion, and they have made impressive progress in strengthening governance arrangements and developing sound debt management strategies that reflect the government's cost and risk preferences. Governments have also improved their monitoring and assessment of risk and performance by investing heavily in the human capital and management information systems needed for sound government debt management. All of this experience will be needed in navigating the path ahead.

Graeme Wheeler
Former Managing Director of Operations and
former Treasurer and Vice President
World Bank
Former Treasurer of the Debt Management Office
Government of New Zealand

Acknowledgments

In addition to the individual authors, this volume benefited from the input and support of many people, to whom we are very grateful. We would especially like to thank Otaviano Canuto, Vice President of the Poverty Reduction and Economic Management (PREM) Network at the World Bank, for his support for this project.

We greatly appreciate the input from the participants and speakers at the Sovereign Debt and Financial Crisis conference held in Tunis, Tunisia, March 29–30, 2010, co-organized by the World Bank and the African Development Bank, as well as the related conference in Washington, DC, held June 9, 2010. We extend our gratitude to the discussants and the chairs of the two events, many of whom contributed to this book. Special thanks go to Nicole P. F. Bollen, Maria Cannata, Jaime Coronado, Carlo Cottarelli, Claire Cheremetinski, E. Whitney Debevoise, Thomas A. Duvall, Anna Gelpern, Indermit Gill, Marcelo Giugale, Garth Greubel, Herve Joly, Jürgen Kaiser, David A. Kihangire, Aart Kraay, Nkosana D. Moyo, Baba Yusuf Musa, Aloysius Uche Ordu, Raphael Otieno, Godfred Awa Eddy Penn, Brian Pinto, Yvonne Quansah, Arindam Roy, Raed Safadi, Marie-Ange Saraka-Yao, Gerry Teeling, Graeme Wheeler, and Donna Yearwood, who provided valuable insights and suggestions during the two conferences.

The editors and the authors would also like to thank Sudharshan Canagarajah, Arindam Chanda, Anna Gelpern, Jan Gottschalk, Ivailo Izvorski, Thor-Jurgen Greve Loberg, Jennifer Keller, Mizuho Kida, Naoko Kojo, Auguste Tano Kouame, Aart Kraay, Eduardo Ley, Anne-Marie Leroy, Otavio Medeiros, Michael Pomerleano, Juan Pradelli, Mona Prasad, Maurizio Ragazzi, Frederico Gil Sander, Raju Singh, Michael Tomz, and Sona Varma for their invaluable comments during the review process of the manuscript for this book.

Duane Chilton, Detre Dyson, Ivana Ticha, and Debbie Sturgess, from the World Bank's Economic Policy and Debt Department, provided superb assistance in organizing the two events on Sovereign Debt and the Financial Crisis. We are also grateful for the excellent cooperation with the

African Development Bank in organizing the conference in Tunis. Barbara Karni, Janet Sasser, Sidra Rehman, and Stephen McGroaty were instrumental in the editing and production of this volume. We would like to acknowledge the financial support of the Debt Management Facility, which was essential in making this book a reality.

This book is dedicated to the memory of Dana Weist, a friend, mentor, and guide to many who contributed to this book and many more besides. We will remember her for her beauty, grace, wisdom, and energy.

Contributors

Faisal Ahmed is an economist in the Monetary and Capital Markets Department at the International Monetary Fund.

Phillip R. D. Anderson is acting director of the Banking and Debt Management Department at the World Bank Treasury.

Luca Bandiera is an economist in the Economic Policy and Debt Department of the Poverty Reduction and Economic Management Network at the World Bank.

Dimitri Bellas is an economics student at HEC Paris and ENSAE Paris and a consultant at the Organisation for Economic Co-operation and Development.

Hans J. Blommestein is a head of the Bond Market and Public Debt Management Unit of the Organisation for Economic Co-operation and Development.

Mehmet Caner is a professor of economics at North Carolina State University.

Daniel Cohen is a professor of economics at the Ecole Normale Supérieure in Paris and vice president of the Paris School of Economics, which he co-founded.

Jesús Crespo Cuaresma is a professor of economics at the Vienna University of Economics and Business.

Mansoor Dailami is the manager of the Emerging Global Trends Team in the Development Prospects Group at the World Bank.

Udaibir S. Das is an assistant director in the Monetary and Capital Markets Department at the International Monetary Fund.

Dörte Dömeland is a senior economist in the Economic Policy and Debt Department of the Poverty Reduction and Economic Management Network at the World Bank.

Edgardo Favaro is a lead economist in the Economic Policy and Debt Department of the Poverty Reduction and Economic Management Network at the World Bank.

Eduardo Fernández-Arias is a principal advisor to the Research Department at the Inter-American Development Bank.

Boris Gamarra is a senior economist in the Resource Mobilization Department of the Concessional Finance and Global Partnerships Vice-Presidency of the World Bank.

Sudarshan Gooptu is the sector manager in the Economic Policy and Debt Department of the Poverty Reduction and Economic Management Network at the World Bank.

Thomas Grennes is a professor of economics at North Carolina State University.

Leonardo Hernández is a lead economist in the Economic Policy and Debt Department of the Poverty Reduction and Economic Management Network at the World Bank.

Fritzi Koehler-Geib is an economist in the Economic Policy Group of the Latin American Region at the World Bank.

Ying Li is a consultant in the Economic Policy and Debt Department of the Poverty Reduction and Economic Management Network at the World Bank.

Yuefen Li is the head of the Debt and Development Finance Branch at the United Nations Conference on Trade and Development.

Lili Liu is a lead economist in the Economic Policy and Debt Department of the Poverty Reduction and Economic Management Network at the World Bank.

William O'Boyle is a consultant in the Economic Policy and Debt Department of the Poverty Reduction and Economic Management Network at the World Bank.

Rodrigo Olivares-Caminal is a sovereign debt expert in the Debt and Development Finance Branch at the United Nations Conference on Trade and Development.

Ugo Panizza is the chief of the Debt and Finance Analysis Unit in the Division on Globalization and Development Strategies at the United Nations Conference on Trade and Development.

Michael G. Papaioannou is a deputy division chief in the Sovereign Asset and Liability Management Division of the Monetary and Capital Markets Department at the International Monetary Fund.

Christoph G. Paulus is a professor of law at the Humboldt-Universität zu Berlin.

Guilherme Pedras is a technical assistance advisor in the Monetary and Capital Markets Department at the International Monetary Fund.

Iva Petrova is an economist in the Fiscal Affairs Department at the International Monetary Fund.

Juan Pradelli is an economist in the Economic Policy and Debt Department of the Poverty Reduction and Economic Management Network at the World Bank.

Abha Prasad is a senior debt specialist in the Economic Policy and Debt Department of the Poverty Reduction and Economic Management Network at the World Bank.

Carlos A. Primo Braga is the director of the Economic Policy and Debt Department in the Poverty Reduction and Economic Management Network at the World Bank.

Anderson Caputo Silva is a senior debt specialist in the Global Capital Markets Development Department of the Financial and Private Sector Development Vice-Presidency at the World Bank.

Tihomir Stučka is an economist in the Economic Policy and Debt Department of the Poverty Reduction and Economic Management Network at the World Bank.

Vivek Suri is a lead economist in the Poverty Reduction and Economic Management Sector of the East Asia and Pacific Region at the World Bank.

Jay Surti is an economist in the Monetary and Capital Markets Department at the International Monetary Fund.

Eriko Togo is a senior economist in the Economic Policy and Debt Department of the Poverty Reduction and Economic Management Network at the World Bank.

Cécile Valadier is an economist at the Agence Française de Développement.

Ralph Van Doorn is an economist in the Economic Policy and Debt Department of the Poverty Reduction and Economic Management Network at the World Bank.

Antonio Velandia-Rubiano is a lead financial officer in the Banking and Debt Management Department at the World Bank Treasury.

Gallina A. Vincelette is a senior economist in the Economic Policy and Debt Department of the Poverty Reduction and Economic Management Network at the World Bank.

Michael Waibel is a British Academy postdoctoral fellow at the Lauterpacht Centre for International Law and Downing College at the University of Cambridge.

Dana Weist was a consultant in the Economic Policy and Debt Department of the Poverty Reduction and Economic Management Network at the World Bank.

Mark L. J. Wright is an assistant professor of economics at the University of California, Los Angeles.

Abbreviations

$	All dollar amounts are U.S. dollars unless otherwise indicated.
BIS	Bank for International Settlements
BMA	Bayesian model averaging
BOT	Buoni Ordinari del Tesoro
CAC	collective action clause
CAIC	Comisión para la Auditoría Integral del Crédito Público
CARICOM	Caribbean Community
CPI	consumer price index
CPIA	Country Policy and Institutional Assessment
CRC	*chambres regionales des comptes* (regional chambers of accounts)
DeMPA	Debt Management Performance Assessment
DMF	Debt Management Facility
DMO	debt management office
DRF	Debt Reduction Facility
DSA	Debt Sustainability Analysis
DSF	Debt Sustainability Framework
ECCU	Eastern Caribbean Currency Union
EMBI	Emerging Markets Bond Index
EMBIG	Emerging Markets Bond Index Global
EPFR	Emerging Portfolio Fund Research
EU	European Union
FCL	flexible credit line
FDI	foreign direct investment
GDF	Global Development Finance (database and publication)
GDP	gross domestic product
GNI	gross national income
HIPC	Heavily Indebted Poor Countries (Initiative)
ICSID	International Centre for Settlement of Investment Disputes
IDA	International Development Association
ILLR	international lender of last resort
IMF	International Monetary Fund

LCU	local currency unit
LLR	lender of last resort
M&A	merger and acquisitions
MDRI	Multilateral Debt Relief Initiative
MFC	most favored creditor
MTDS	Medium-Term Debt Management Strategy
OECD	Organisation for Economic Co-operation and Development
PIP	posterior inclusion probability
PMG	pooled mean group
PPG	public and publicly guaranteed
PRGF	Poverty Reduction and Growth Facility
QEDS	Quarterly External Debt Statistics
RIC	risk inflation criterion
SAR	Special Administrative Region (China)
S&P	Standard & Poor's
SDR	Special Drawing Rights
SDRM	Sovereign Debt Restructuring Mechanism
SDT	Sovereign Debt Tribunal
TARP	Troubled Asset Relief Program
TIA	Trust Indenture Act
VaR	value at risk
WEO	World Economic Outlook (database and publication)

Introduction

Carlos A. Primo Braga and Gallina A. Vincelette

The financial crisis of 2008 has rekindled interest in sovereign debt crises among policy makers and scholars.[1] History shows that lending booms typically end in busts, with the beneficiaries of debt in the upswing often forced to default or reschedule their debts in the downswing (Sturzenegger and Zettelmeyer 2006). The impact of the first financial crisis of the 21st century on capital flows to developing countries and the signs of stress in debt markets of several European countries in the first half of 2010 raise the inevitable question, Are we about to witness a new generation of sovereign debt crises?

This book addresses this question. It adopts an integrated approach by drawing on both theoretical research and experience from professionals involved in technical assistance in this area. It documents recent improvements in macroeconomic policies and debt management practices—which to a large extent explain the resilience of developing and emerging economies—and identifies challenges ahead and areas that require special attention from policy makers.

The Financial Crisis and Sovereign Debt

The financial crisis, which intensified in the last quarter of 2008, came on the heels of the food and fuel crises and grew into a global economic crisis—the Great Recession. The crisis was "nurtured" by global macroeconomic imbalances, lax monetary policies in the developed world, an asset price bubble associated with excess investment in real estate, poor corporate governance of the financial system, and regulatory failures.

At the epicenter of the crisis were the most sophisticated financial systems in the world, in which investors held complex financial instruments and relied on high levels of leveraging. The crisis spread far beyond its origins, however. Since September 2008, continuous shocks have been transmitted through trade and finance channels, with almost no country being unaffected. Emerging and developing economies experienced significant

1

capital outflows, as financial institutions withdrew liquid investment to shore up their balance sheets in developed economies. Global export volumes collapsed (declining by roughly 25 percent between April 2008 and January 2009), and the prices of commodities in some cases fell by 50 percent or more.

Countries around the world took aggressive measures to address the impact of the financial crisis. The most notable policy actions included the easing of monetary policies, the recapitalization of financial systems, the bailout of the household and corporate sectors, the overhaul of financial regulatory systems, and the launching of fiscal stimulus packages. Most central banks significantly lowered their policy interest rates, with several approaching the zero lower-bound constraint. Many central banks also adopted aggressive balance sheet policies, including credit policies that affected interbank and nonbank credit markets and the purchase of government bonds and foreign currency–denominated securities.

In addition to these monetary actions, governments adopted countercyclical fiscal policies. Fiscal deficits in advanced economies, which stood at about 1.1 percent of GDP in 2007, jumped to 8.8 percent in 2009 and are projected to fall only slightly, to about 8.4 percent, in 2010. Emerging economies, which were in fiscal equilibrium in 2007, registered deficits of 4.9 percent of GDP in 2009, with a forecast for 2010 at 3.9 percent (IMF 2010).

These government interventions have led to an increased supply of sovereign debt, with implications for growth and debt sustainability outlooks in both mature and developing economies. In industrial countries, sovereign debt has risen significantly: in 2008, the net sovereign borrowing needs of the United Kingdom and the United States were five times larger than the average of the preceding five years (2002–07). In advanced economies as a whole, government debt to GDP ratios are expected to reach 110 percent by 2015—an increase of almost 40 percentage points over precrisis levels (IMF 2010). Many middle-income countries also witnessed a deterioration of their debt positions, although the trends are not as dramatic as those of advanced economies. In low-income countries, in 2009–10 the present value of the public debt to GDP ratio has deteriorated by 5–7 percentage points compared with precrisis projections (IDA and IMF 2010). Forty percent of low-income countries either are already in debt distress or face a high risk of falling into debt distress.

In sum, the economic boom fostered by the growing indebtedness of the private sector came to a halt when the asset bubble burst. Governments stepped in to avoid the collapse of the financial sector, forestall credit contraction, and sustain aggregate demand. This is not the first time financial cycles have led to asset bubbles with international implications, but not since the Great Depression has the recession been so severe. It is true that most developing economies have shown remarkable resilience in "navigating" these external shocks. There is no denying, however, that these shocks will increase the challenges they face in financing their development needs.

The magnitude of public liabilities incurred and the uncertainty surrounding the exit from unprecedented discretionary fiscal stimulus programs have become sources of concern about a future crisis. Moving forward, governments will have to regain the confidence of markets while introducing regulatory reforms that clamp down on excessive risk taking. Balancing these goals is a difficult task that is complicated by the fact that current fiscal imbalances put policy makers in a corner: they are damned if they introduce fiscal austerity programs (which slow the nascent recovery) and damned if they fail to address the growing debt burden, which may reduce market confidence and raise the fear of a "debt trap," with medium-term growth implications. The recent stress in debt markets in some Euro Area countries is a testament to the lingering concern that despite massive government efforts, the economic crisis is still unfolding and sovereign debt markets need close monitoring.

This book examines the implications of the financial crisis for sovereign debt in emerging and developing economies. It is structured around four main themes:

- Understanding the forces affecting sovereign defaults, the valuation of sovereign debt, and the economic cost of large public debts
- Assessing the impact of the recent global economic crisis on debt in different groups of countries
- Drawing lessons from and exploring new ideas for debt restructuring
- Presenting relevant public debt management experiences in the context of financial crises.

Part I: A New Wave of Sovereign Debt Crises?

Since September 2008, global financial conditions have been volatile and risks associated with rising sovereign debt burdens and sovereign debt downgrades have increased. Despite its unprecedented consequences for government finances, however, the ongoing global financial crisis has not yet triggered a wave of sovereign defaults. Is this time different? Are policy makers in a better position to recognize ex ante signs of debt distress? More broadly, what are the implications of increasing debt levels on economic growth?

In chapter 1, Daniel Cohen and Cécile Valadier explore the determinants of debt distress in order to understand what makes the ongoing crisis different from previous debt crises. Using an updated database of 126 countries for the period 1970–2007, they confirm the results of other studies that find that differences in the probability of sovereign debt distress are explained largely by debt burdens and institutional quality indicators.

Put differently, countries with low external debt levels are better able to cope with deteriorating conditions in international financial markets. The authors observe that many developing countries with records of default did not default during the recent crisis because their debt burdens were much more manageable this time around. Cases of distress occurred largely in heavily exposed European countries, countries involved in war or internal conflicts, and countries with fragile institutions.

Luca Bandiera, Jesús Crespo Cuaresma, and Gallina A. Vincelette reach similar conclusions regarding the level of indebtedness as an important predictor of defaults in chapter 2. Because emerging market economies have historically been more vulnerable to debt crises than higher-income countries, the authors focus on a sample of 46 emerging market economies spanning 25 years. They find that countries with different levels of indebtedness also have different characteristics: on average, countries with external debt below 50 percent of gross national income (GNI) grow their economies faster and have lower inflation than countries with higher levels of external debt; they also achieve primary fiscal surpluses. These countries are also typically less open (and therefore less exposed to shock from external demand), run lower current account deficits, and have higher levels of reserves than more indebted emerging market countries.

For the entire sample, the authors find that the probability of default is robustly associated only with the level of indebtedness. The quality of policies and institutions are also good predictors of default episodes in emerging market countries with levels of external debt below 50 percent of GNI. For emerging markets with debt that exceeds 50 percent of GNI, macroeconomic stability plays a significant role in explaining differences in default probabilities.

The first two chapters of this book revisit past sovereign debt crises to understand how to better recognize the signs of trouble ex ante. Chapter 3, by Mehmet Caner, Thomas Grennes, and Fritzi Koehler-Geib, observes the dynamics of surging public debt to assess the effect of public liabilities on economic growth. Does a tipping point in public debt exist beyond which a country's economic growth suffers? What is the quantitative impact of public debt on economic growth if debt stays above the threshold for an extended period of time?

The authors estimate public debt to GDP thresholds based on an annual data set of 99 developing and developed economies for 1980–2008. They find that if the average public debt to GDP ratio remains above 77 percent in the long run, each additional percentage point increase in the ratio costs 0.017 percentage point of annual real growth. The effect is even more profound in emerging markets, where the debt to GDP threshold is 64 percent. In these countries, the loss in annual real growth with each additional percentage point in public debt amounts to 0.02 percentage point. Although temporary deviations from the threshold in the context of short-term fiscal stabilization policies may be appropriate, surpassing these thresholds for extended periods could slow economic growth for years.

Because large increases in the level and funding costs of government debt can cause real economic losses, it is important to study the factors that may affect the valuations of sovereign debt. During the current global financial crisis, governments provided massive support to the domestic financial systems and launched large fiscal stimulus packages. Governments' balance sheet risks increased in the form of wider sovereign bond spread in both advanced and emerging market countries. Indeed, sovereign yields exhibited an unprecedented degree of volatility in 2010, particularly among higher-debt, lower-rated sovereigns (see, for example, Caceres, Guzzo, and Segoviano 2010).

Chapter 4, by Dimitri Bellas, Michael G. Papaioannou, and Iva Petrova, unveils the drivers behind sovereign bond spreads. Using quarterly data spanning the past decade, the authors demonstrate an important dichotomy. In the long run, macroeconomic fundamentals, such as debt and debt-related variables, trade openness, and a set of risk-free rates, primarily determine sovereign bond spreads. In the short run, however, it is the degree of financial stability in a country that plays the key role in the valuation of sovereign debt.

In chapter 5, Mansoor Dailami analyzes the channels through which sovereign default risks affect the determination of corporate bond yield spreads in emerging markets. He argues that rising sovereign risks represent a major source of policy concern and market anxiety because of the hidden dynamics between sovereign and corporate debt, which could create a negative feedback loop once investors lose confidence in the government's ability to use public finances to stabilize the economy or provide a safety net to corporations in distress. Using a database covering corporate and sovereign bond issues on global markets between 1995 and 2009, Dailami finds that investors' perceptions of sovereign debt problems in emerging markets translate into higher costs of capital for private corporate issuers. A key policy recommendation from this analysis is that measures are needed to improve creditworthiness at the sovereign level before investor fears spill over to and adversely affect private firms' cost of and access to foreign capital.

Part II: How Has the Crisis Affected Debt?

The global financial crisis has depressed economic activity and reduced confidence in the prospects for growth almost everywhere in the world. What are the implications of the crisis for sovereign debt and the overall financial positions of developing and emerging market countries? How well positioned, with respect to economic and institutional fundamentals, are these countries to weather the effects of the crisis? Will poor indebted countries require new rounds of debt relief because of the financial crisis?

Chapter 6, by Leonardo Hernández and Boris Gamarra, addresses the last question for a group of 31 IDA-only African countries, several of which are in fragile debt situations. Using the debt sustainability analyses undertaken for these countries by the World Bank and the International Monetary Fund (IMF) as of end-September 2009, the authors study the potential adverse effects of the ongoing financial crisis on countries' debt burden indicators as a function of the depth and length of the crisis (measured by the impact of the crisis on exports revenues) and the terms at which a country can obtain financing to muddle through the crisis. The analysis underscores the importance of concessional financing for these countries, especially if the crisis proves to be a protracted one.

Many middle-income countries are facing high financing requirements, making them particularly susceptible to market sentiment. In chapter 7, Ralph Van Doorn, Vivek Suri, and Sudarshan Gooptu examine whether middle-income countries can restore their pre-2008 macroeconomic space or contain further deterioration in the medium term. Through illustrative scenarios, they show that some countries have limited room to maneuver unless they embark on sizable fiscal adjustments and may need more time to do so than current projections seem to suggest.

Small vulnerable economies are among the most indebted countries in the world. In chapter 8, Edgardo Favaro, Dörte Dömeland, William O'Boyle, and Tihomir Stučka investigate the effect of the crisis on 46 small states with various income levels. They find that the impact of the crisis was more severe among small states with higher external exposure and among exporters of natural resource–based products than in small states with lower levels of international integration. The chapter concludes that imprudent fiscal management has led to high levels of public debt in many small states, wiping out the decline in debt to GDP ratios achieved in the early 2000s and leaving them with debt ratios that will adversely affect their capacity to provide basic public goods and to encourage new investment and economic growth. Managing the higher levels of public debt in an uncertain economic environment will be a significant challenge for these small states going forward.

Output collapse and related revenue losses have been the key factors driving debt surges in developed countries (IMF 2010b). Chapter 9, by Edgardo Favaro, Ying Li, Juan Pradelli, and Ralph Van Doorn, analyzes this issue in the context of the recent financial difficulties in Europe. The authors argue that countries can be clustered into two groups according to the main determinants of the current account deficits within the area. In some countries, high public sector deficits are driving the current account disequilibrium; in others, the private sector and the high and persistent savings-investment gap explain the disequilibrium. The policy challenge ahead is to reduce these imbalances by generating current account surpluses in deficit countries so that they can repay their debts. The difficulty is that in the current financial environment, an external surplus can be achieved only through expenditure-reducing measures, which have a poor record of success at reversing significant real exchange rate misalignments and are likely to reduce output in the short run.

Part III: Are New Mechanisms for Debt Restructuring Needed?

Against the background of increasing stresses in debt markets, revisiting the options for sovereign debt restructuring has attracted renewed attention. The chapters in part III examine the legal and economic principles underlying the debt-restructuring process with the aim of reducing the risk and cost of sovereign defaults. Given that there is no structured way for managing sovereign defaults and effectively enforcing sovereign debt contracts, what are the policy options for dealing with defaults by sovereigns? Can explicit contingent contracts between investors and sovereigns be designed that provide incentives for borrowers to remain solvent? What lessons can be learned from previous episodes of sovereign defaults? Can institutions be established that improve information and foster commitment?

Sovereign debts are costly and difficult to restructure. The process is often delayed by creditor holdouts, refusal to reveal private information, the inability of countries to commit to a restructuring agreement, and political economy problems in the defaulting country. These factors affect the efficiency of restructuring ex post; they also affect borrowing strategies and default incentives ex ante.

Chapter 10, by Yuefen Li, Rodrigo Olivares-Caminal, and Ugo Panizza, discusses how the recent financial and economic crisis has affected the evolution of instruments and options for restructuring debt. The authors examine a sample of 56 developing and emerging economies, complemented by a detailed study of four recent default episodes. They find that three factors are important for understanding defaults: the presence of large external debt shocks, the practice of overborrowing by the private and public sectors, and the existence of contentious debt contracts.

The authors discuss policy options at the national and international levels for mitigating the probability of future debt crises. They encourage governments to avoid overborrowing and to move to contingent debt contracts. They argue that in the absence of mechanisms for resolving sovereign defaults, orderly workout procedures should be developed to deal with sovereign defaults. They express support for the development of a set of universally agreed upon principles for responsible sovereign lending and borrowing.

Chapter 11, by Lili Liu and Michael Waibel, unveils the challenges of rapidly increasing subnational debt for sovereigns and discusses the legal and institutional principles underpinning debt restructuring at the subnational level. Regulatory frameworks across countries for subnational insolvency share central features. Fiscal rules, or ex ante regulation, contain the risk of subnational defaults; ex post regulation typically allocates default risk while providing breathing space for orderly debt restructuring and fiscal adjustment. The authors caution against unregulated subnational borrowing and encourage countries to develop regulatory frameworks for market-based subnational financing systems.

Chapter 12, by Mark L. J. Wright, examines the restructuring mechanisms for sovereign debt to private creditors. He presents new empirical results on the differences in private sovereign debt-restructuring outcomes across debtor countries in different regions and at different levels of development. Using data on 90 defaults and 73 renegotiations between 1989 and 2004, he finds that both the time taken to complete a private debt restructuring and the size of creditor losses are greater for low-income countries, in particular in Sub-Saharan Africa, than in middle-income countries. Despite private creditor "haircuts" averaging about 38 percent, poor countries tend to exit defaults more indebted to private creditors than when they entered.

The chapter reviews recent theoretical research on the process of sovereign debt restructuring to private creditors and assesses the policy options available to both debtor and creditor governments. It argues that although recent theory can explain the magnitude of delays observed in the data, it has less to say about which aspects of the debt-restructuring process lead to large increases in indebtedness to private creditors in low-income countries. The author recognizes the advantages of supranational mechanisms such as the Debt Reduction Facility (DRF) for IDA-only countries to deal with collective action problems.[2]

Every international financial crisis exposes the lack of established mechanisms for fast and efficient resolution of sovereign disputes. Various proposals have been formulated to overcome this shortcoming. Common elements among these proposals include a fair forum for negotiation, a standstill clause, and clauses that limit the ability of disgruntled minority bondholders to file lawsuits against creditor nations. Chapters 13 and 14 discuss alternatives to the status quo in dealing with sovereign defaults.

In chapter 13, Christoph G. Paulus argues for a pragmatic approach to predictable and reliable procedures for debt restructuring. He suggests establishing a sovereign debt tribunal within a highly respected international institution that is not a creditor or potential creditor to sovereigns. Under his proposal, the announcement of a default by a sovereign would be enough to trigger arbitration. The tribunal could initiate and decide cases only upon prior contractual agreement to arbitration; parties not accepting agreement of such arbitration clause would not be subject to the tribunal's jurisdiction.

Chapter 14, by Eduardo Fernández-Arias, explores alternatives for solving sovereign debt repayment difficulties, tailored to country-specific circumstances. The author endorses recent efforts by international financial institutions such as the Flexible Credit Line offered by the IMF and arrangements for financing options through Stand-by Arrangements or Extended Facilities. But he argues that the absence of an international bankruptcy system may delay the call for needed debt rescheduling and curtail bridge financing in cases where rescheduling is already taking place. The author promotes the establishment of a comprehensive international lender-of-last-resort framework to address both liquidity and solvency problems. The novelty of his proposal lies in bringing debt restructuring into such an integrated international system.

Both of the proposals presented in chapters 13 and 14 offer new elements for institutional structures at the supranational level to deal with sovereign repayment difficulties. Both require coordinated political action at the international level. As illustrated by the debate in 2001–03 over the Sovereign Debt-Restructuring Mechanism (SDRM) developed by IMF staff, implementation of a statutory approach to debt restructuring is not easy (see Rieffel 2003 and Krueger 2002). Whether sovereigns would be willing to reopen this debate in view of the financial crisis remains unclear. At the national level, however, sovereign debtors can improve the stability of their financial systems by (among other things) strengthening their debt management institutions.

Part IV: Managing Public Debt in Crises

Given the rapid buildup of government liabilities around the world and the strong interlinkages between sovereign risk and international capital markets, concerns about the possibility of a new wave of sovereign debt crises have reemerged. Although unexpected shocks are, by definition, beyond the control of any individual country, policy makers in both developing and advanced economies can benefit from prudent public debt management in shaping their borrowing strategies with a view to cushioning the effects of external shocks. How have countries responded to this challenge so far? What policy options have different countries chosen for dealing with elevated debt burdens?

Chapter 15, by Udaibir S. Das, Michael Papaioannou, Guilherme Pedras, Jay Surti, and Faisal Ahmed, explores explicitly the relationship between financial stability and the management of public debt. The linkage between government finances and financial stability is symmetric through the cycle. In an upswing, the quality of financial institutions' exposure to the government is high, as it carries low default, extension, and liquidity risk. During a downswing, maintenance of the asset quality of the government's liabilities becomes critical in containing adverse developments in the real and financial sectors. The authors suggest that debt managers and policy makers analyze the implications of debt management strategies on the balance sheet of their government, the economy, and the financial system.

Sound debt management practices can support effective countercyclical policy. Elements of such practices include maintaining manageable public debt stock, targeting rational movements in asset prices during booms, creating a liability structure for public debt that sustains low levels of refinancing risk for the sovereign through the cycle, and securing the sovereign's ability to issue the necessary volume of debt at a reasonable cost in a downswing. Countries that follow such principles in debt management are better positioned to cushion shocks and to implement countercyclical fiscal policy.

Indeed, as chapter 16, by Phillip R. D. Anderson, Anderson Caputo Silva, and Antonio Velandia-Rubiano, discusses, improved macroeconomic and public debt management in emerging market economies over the past decade explain why, despite its scale, the global financial crisis has not yet resulted in a sovereign debt crisis for these countries. The authors review the improvements in macroeconomic fundamentals and the composition of public debt portfolios in emerging market economies before the crisis and conclude that the policies and strategies pursued by governments provided them with a buffer when the crisis hit. Nevertheless, with the international capital markets effectively closed for more than three months and domestic borrowing in many cases affected by extreme risk aversion, government debt managers were required to adapt their strategies to these rapidly changing circumstances. The chapter asserts that government debt managers will need to consider how they can increase the resilience of their public debt portfolios for the uncertain times that lie ahead.

Chapter 17, by Dana Weist, Eriko Togo, Abha Prasad, and William O'Boyle, examines the challenges that debt managers in low-income countries face in the current environment. Cost and risk characteristics of financing options have changed dramatically since 2007. In view of the greater uncertainty, coping with the challenges of the past two years will require a reevaluation of existing debt management strategies in these countries, with a focus on mitigating risks.

Chapter 18, by Hans J. Blommestein, provides an overview of debt management strategies pursued by developed countries. The chapter details the changes made by Organisation for Economic Co-operation and Development (OECD) countries to meet the surge of government borrowing needs under tougher issuance conditions. By presenting the pros and cons of debt management decisions such as greater use of syndicated loans, greater reliance on short-term debts, and greater frequency of issuance and ad hoc issuance, this chapter illustrates the rapidly changing conditions faced by debt managers.

* * *

This book identifies and analyzes the significant challenges faced by governments trying to strike the right balance between reinforcing financial stability and reaping the benefits of resource reallocation at the global level. Improved debt management, financial regulatory standards, and surveillance can all play important roles in curtailing excessive risk taking and fostering stability in domestic and international financial markets.

As the analyses in this book illustrate, it is not easy to predict with certainty whether the financial crisis will evolve into a systemic sovereign debt crisis. But the cautionary words of Polonius that "borrowing dulls the edge of husbandry" continue to ring true. Adapted to current circumstances, they could read "excessive borrowing creates disincentives to good policies."[3] It is hoped that this volume will contribute to better policy making, particularly better debt management practices.

Notes

1. See, for example, Herman, Ocampo, and Spiegel (2010); Reinhart and Rogoff (2009); Sturzenegger and Zettelmeyer (2006); and the comprehensive review of the literature provided by Panizza, Sturzenegger, and Zettelmeyer (2009).

2. For a discussion of the DRF, see Gamarra, Pollock, and Primo Braga (2009).

3. The editors thank Aart Kraay for the reference and the creative translation of *Hamlet* Act 1, Scene 3, Line 81.

References

Caceres, Carlos, Vincenzo Guzzo, and Miguel Segoviano. 2010. "Sovereign Spreads: Global Risk Aversion, Contagion or Fundamentals?" IMF Working Paper 10/120, International Monetary Fund, Washington, DC.

Gamarra, Boris, Malvina Pollock, and Carlos A. Primo Braga. 2009. "Debt Relief to Low-Income Countries: A Retrospective." In *Debt Relief and Beyond: Lessons Learned and Challenges Ahead*, ed. Carlos A. Primo Braga and Dörte Dömeland, 11–34. Washington, DC: The World Bank.

Herman, Barry, Jose A. Ocampo, and Shari Spiegel, eds. 2010. *Overcoming Developing Country Debt Crises*. Oxford, UK: Oxford University Press.

IDA (International Development Association) and IMF (International Monetary Fund). 2010. "Preserving Debt Sustainability in Low-Income Countries in the Wake of the Global Crisis." http://www.imf.org/external/np/pp/eng/2010/040110.pdf.

IMF (International Monetary Fund). 2010. *Fiscal Monitor: Navigating the Fiscal Challenges Ahead*. Washington, DC: IMF.

Krueger, Anne O. 2002. *A New Approach to Sovereign Debt Restructuring*. Washington, DC: International Monetary Fund.

Panizza, Ugo, Federico Sturzenegger, and Jeromin Zettelmeyer. 2009. "The Economics and Law of Sovereign Debt and Default," *Journal of Economic Literature* 47 (3): 651–98.

Reinhart, Carmen M., and Kenneth S. Rogoff. 2009. *This Time Is Different: Eight Centuries of Financial Folly.* Princeton, NJ: Princeton University Press.

Rieffel, Lex. 2003. *Restructuring Sovereign Debt: The Case for Ad Hoc Machinery.* Washington, DC: Brookings Institution Press.

Sturzenegger, Federico, and Jeromin Zettelmeyer. 2006. *Debt Defaults and Lessons from a Decade of Crises.* Cambridge, MA: The MIT Press.

Part I

A New Wave of Sovereign Debt Crises?

1

The Sovereign Debt Crisis That Was Not

Daniel Cohen and Cécile Valadier

In a famous Sherlock Holmes story, the clue to the drama lay in the fact that the dog did not bark. During the most recent financial crisis, none of the usual suspects—the "serial defaulters" of previous sovereign debt crises, namely, Brazil, Indonesia, Mexico, and Thailand—ran into trouble.

What explains their performance? We offer the simplest answer: the so-called serial defaulters were much better managed this time. Before the crisis, their debt ratios had fallen substantially, allowing them to move down the ladder of risk. In a very straightforward manner, they learned the lessons of the previous crises and were able to smooth the outcome of one of the most formidable financial crises of all time.

In order to quantify this result, we first revisit the history of the sovereign crises of the past 40 years. We show that neither the serial defaulter nor the "global crisis" theories of sovereign crises explain much. Sovereign debt crises are related to the level of indebtedness, which accounts for about half the risk factor we compute in this chapter. Half the remaining risk is related to the quality of governance of the country, as captured by the Country Policy and Institutional Assessment (CPIA) index, which indirectly measures the ability of countries to weather external shocks. On both fronts, most of the countries that were at the center of previous crises are now out of the danger zone.

Historically, world credit shocks accounted for the smallest share of risk of the factors of risk we quantify—about 7 percent of overall risk over the past 40 years. The recent crisis is exceptional. Indeed, the effect of world credit shocks on the risk factor during the recent crisis was as great as the effects of all other sources of risk combined in earlier episodes. Because of these shocks, many countries that would have fallen into the lowest risk categories had the world shock been "normal" found themselves in high-risk categories.

Two conflicting forces are at work today: low debt and bad financing conditions. Extrapolating from previous default events, bad financing should dominate. As of early 2010, however, low debt appeared to have the upper hand. While waiting for the financing situation to improve, can countries build on their low debt bases to avoid the increase in risk associated with the current financing situation?

Forty Years of Sovereign Debt Crises

In this section, we draw lessons from past debt crises to shed light on what is currently happening. We start by presenting our sample and the variables of interest for the analysis.

Database on Debt Distress Events

Our database includes annual data on 126 countries for the period 1970–2007. We use a slightly modified version of Kraay and Nehru's (2004) database, which we extended through 2007. A country is said to experience a debt crisis in a year if one of the following conditions holds:

- The sum of its interest and principal arrears on long-term debt outstanding to all creditors exceeds 5 percent of the total debt outstanding. Countries that are unable to service their external debt need not necessarily fall into arrears; they can obtain balance of payments support from the International Monetary Fund (IMF) as well as debt rescheduling or debt reduction from the Paris Club.
- The country receives debt relief from the Paris Club. We exclude events such as Heavily Indebted Poor Countries (HIPC) Initiative exits (completion points), because they usually indicate that a country's performance has improved.
- The country receives substantial balance of payment support from the IMF in the form of Stand-By Arrangements or Extended Fund Facilities. The amount of financing a member can obtain from the IMF (its access limit) is based on its quota. Currently, a member can borrow up to 100 percent of its quota annually and 300 percent cumulatively. However, access may be higher in exceptional circumstances. We define as exceptional support by the IMF the event in which a country actually uses more than 50 percent of its quota in one year. Kraay and Nehru (2004) look at all events in which the IMF extended resources to a country in excess of 50 percent of its quota, regardless of whether the support was actually used. Our definition includes only instances of actual debt distress, defined here as defaults that were avoided thanks to IMF support.

Historical Statistics on Debt Distress Events

The unconditional probability that a country in the database experienced a debt crisis in any given year was 37 percent. One plausible explanation for this high figure is that some countries are driving the mean up (the "serial defaulters" theory [Reinhart, Rogoff, and Savastano 2003]). Another is that there are years in which all countries experience a crisis (the "global crisis" theory). Investigation of both possibilities reveals that neither convincingly explains the whole story of debt crises.

We define the number of years in which a country is considered to be in debt distress as the number of years in which at least one of the three indicators cited above is positive between 1970 and 2007 (figure 1.1). The picture here, confirmed below by econometric checks, seems to be that we cannot really identify two groups of countries, one with a high default rate and one with a very low default rate.

We also investigate the extent to which debt crises are influenced by global events (such as the Volcker shock of the early 1980s or the contagion effects of the Thai crisis of the late 1990s) in a given year, creating a time profile of the debt crisis. These data reveal that there is a gradual increase in the number of reported defaults up to the early 1990s, followed by a decline (figure 1.2).

On average, a given country in our sample is in debt distress one-third of the time (11.6 years out of 38 years). In a given year, on average, one-third

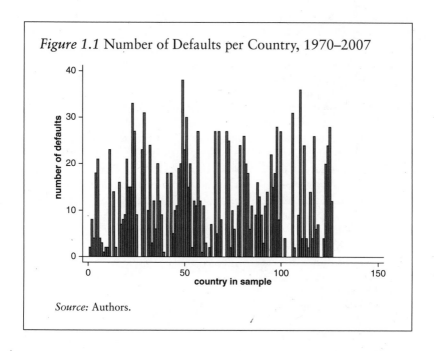

Figure 1.1 Number of Defaults per Country, 1970–2007

Source: Authors.

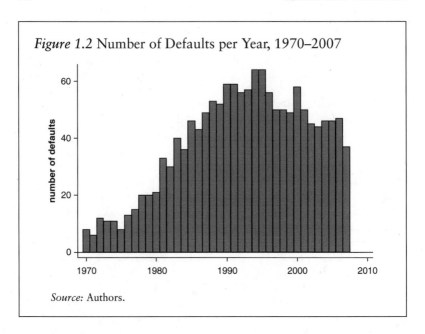

Figure 1.2 Number of Defaults per Year, 1970–2007

Source: Authors.

of the countries (38.5 out of 126) are in debt distress. The detailed percentiles are shown in table 1.1.

In order to see whether these average numbers are hiding significant heterogeneity across years, we exclude years in which more than 52 countries were in a debt crisis (the fourth quartile). Doing so reduces the mean annual probability of a debt crisis only slightly, from 37 percent to 32 percent. We then exclude countries that spent more than 20 years in a debt crisis—"serial defaulters"—in order to see if they are responsible for the high unconditional default rate in our sample. Doing so reduces the mean annual probability of a debt crisis to 24 percent.

We examine whether other measures could corroborate the "serial defaulters" or "global shocks" theories by looking at countries with and without market access. A country is defined as a market-access borrower in a given year if total net flows in the form of bonds and commercial bank loans to the public sector are positive. Although there is a difference in the unconditional probability of default in market-access countries (27 percent) and non-market-access countries (43 percent), the apparent difference is actually a difference in the length of their crises, as we show below. We then look at years of global crises, proxied by years in which there is a recession in the United States. The data reveal no significant difference between the average probabilities of debt crises in years of recession (33 percent) and other years (38 percent).

Table 1.1 Summary Statistics on Default Events

Percentile	Number of years in which a given country is in debt distress	Number of countries in debt distress in a given year
10	0	11
25	2	20
50	10	46
75	20	52
100	27	59

Source: Authors.
Note: The median number of years during which a given country in our sample is considered to be in debt distress is 9.5. In a given year, the median number of countries considered to be in debt distress is 45.5. Entries in the table have been rounded.

A New Definition of Debt Distress Events

One critical problem with these raw statistics is that they do not distinguish between ongoing and new crises. The high number of debt distress occurrences actually reflects the fact that several consecutive years of crisis appear as different events.

In order to address this problem, we construct a new debt distress classification that counts distress episodes as years in which a country experiences a debt crisis following three years of no crisis. We define normal times as a year without crisis preceded by three years without crisis. This classification allows us to identify "real" debt distress episodes. Doing the same for normal times allows us to treat events of crisis and noncrisis symmetrically in our econometric estimations and to control for covariates in $t - 2$, knowing for sure that a country is not in a debt crisis (to avoid simultaneity problems).

Kraay and Nehru (2004) redefined debt distress events to correct for the fact that multiple years of distress are not independent observations. They start by eliminating all episodes that last less than three years; they then eliminate all distress episodes that are preceded by periods of distress in any of the three previous years. They define normal times as nonoverlapping periods of five consecutive years in which none of the three indicators of debt distress is observed. This procedure allows them to identify 94 episodes of debt distress and 286 normal time episodes over the period 1970–2001.

Their definition leads to a very high unconditional default probability of slightly more than 20 percent in their sample. We depart from their methodology for two main reasons. First, we do not want to treat default events (cells of at least three years in Kraay and Nehru) and normal times (cells of five years in Kraay and Nehru) asymmetrically, as they do, because we want to be able to infer annual default probabilities from our statistical analysis. Second, as all covariates are taken in $t - 2$ with respect to the first year of a cell, it may be that such observations are measured during a crisis before a normal times episode, which could bias the estimation. With our definition, all covariates are measured in normal times, as both default and normal years are preceded by three years without default.

It is possible that we include too many nondefault events, which we define as one-year events, implicitly assuming that normal years are independent observations when they may not be. We take comfort in the fact that our default probability is still quite high (6.9 percent a year), with respect to common measures of default probability such as spreads, suggesting that conditional on experiencing three years without default, there is still a substantial risk of defaulting in the fourth year. Out of 1,863 episodes in our database, we identify 128 sovereign debt crises and 1,735 "normal" periods (figure 1.3). Most countries experience at most one or two episodes of debt distress. Only a few countries suffered debt distress episodes more than twice: The Gambia, Ghana, Grenada, Turkey, and Uruguay experienced three debt crises, and Kenya experienced four. Similarly, only a few peaks emerged, in the early 1980s and 2000s (figure 1.4), with no rising trends of the sort shown in figure 1.2. Using this stricter definition of debt distress, we find no significant difference between the probabilities of unconditional default in countries with and without market access. On the whole, comparison of the two databases seems to show

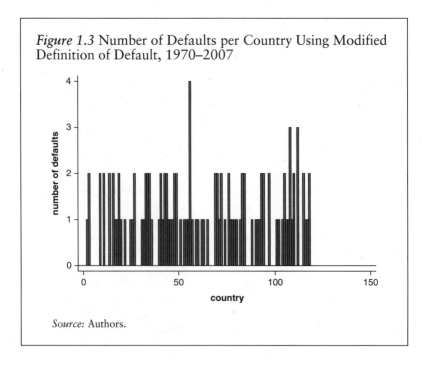

Figure 1.3 Number of Defaults per Country Using Modified Definition of Default, 1970–2007

Source: Authors.

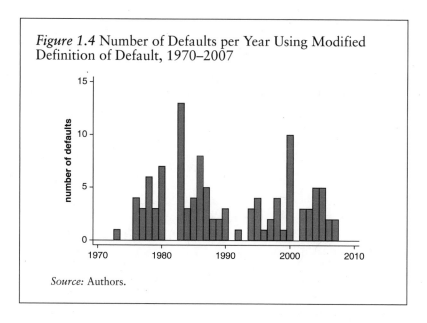

Figure 1.4 Number of Defaults per Year Using Modified Definition of Default, 1970–2007

Source: Authors.

that countries experience long episodes of debt distress and that neither the serial defaulters theory nor the global crisis theory seems to entirely explain the data patterns.

Debt Crises, Currency Crises, and Banking Crises

Using this new definition of debt crises, we look at currency crises and systemic banking crises to see how they correlate with debt crises. We follow the definitions of Laeven and Valencia (2008) to identify both currency and banking crises. A country is said to experience a currency crisis in a given year if the exchange rate with respect to the U.S. dollar falls more than 30 percent and the rate of depreciation is at least 10 percent greater than that of the previous year. (The second condition is designed to weed out countries constantly experiencing high inflation rates that are not experiencing a currency crisis.)

In order to measure exchange rate depreciation, Laeven and Valencia use the percent change of the end-of-period official nominal bilateral dollar exchange rate from the World Economic Outlook (WEO) database of the IMF. For countries that meet the criteria for several continuous years, they use the first year of each five-year window to identify a currency crisis (figure 1.5). This definition yields 179 currency crises during the period 1970–2007 for our sample of countries. These episodes also include large devaluations by countries that adopt fixed exchange rate regimes.

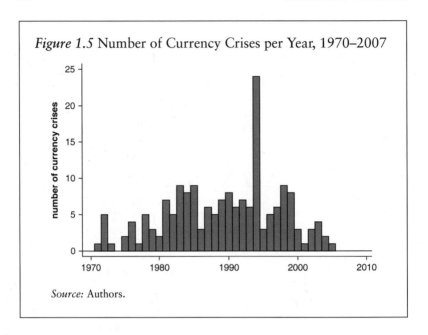

Figure 1.5 Number of Currency Crises per Year, 1970–2007

Source: Authors.

Laeven and Valencia (p. 7) define systemic banking crises as follows:

> In a systemic banking crisis, a country's corporate and financial sectors experience a large number of defaults and financial institutions and corporations face great difficulties repaying contracts on time. As a result, nonperforming loans increase sharply and all or most of the aggregate banking system capital is exhausted. This situation may be accompanied by depressed asset prices (such as equity and real estate prices) on the heels of run-ups before the crisis, sharp increases in real interest rates, and a slowdown or reversal in capital flows.

Using this definition, we identify 106 systemic banking crises in our sample of countries over the period 1970–2007 (figure 1.6).

Following Laeven and Valencia, we define a twin crisis in year t as a debt (currency) crisis in year t, combined with a currency (banking) crisis during $[t-1, t+1]$. We define a triple crisis in year t as a debt crisis in year t, combined with a currency crisis during $[t-1, t+1]$ and a banking crisis during $[t-1, t+1]$. We identify 36 simultaneous sovereign and currency crises, 19 simultaneous sovereign and banking crises, 40 simultaneous currency and banking crises, and 10 triple crises (see annex table 1A.1). The sample includes 128 debt crises.

These results indicate that debt crises are not usually correlated with other kinds of crises but are rather crises of their own. When we change the observation window from $[t-1, t+1]$ to $[t-2, t+2]$, quite a substantial expansion of the range of observation, we identify 49 simultaneous sovereign

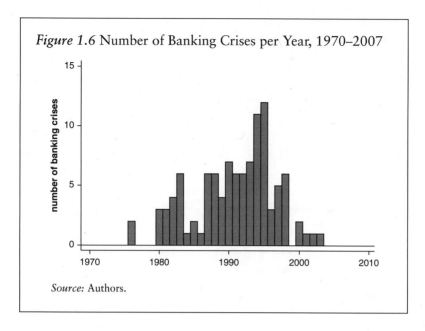

Figure 1.6 Number of Banking Crises per Year, 1970–2007

Source: Authors.

and currency crises, 24 simultaneous sovereign and banking crises, and 54 simultaneous currency and banking crises. The number of triple crises rises to 17 events, but the figure still remains low relative to the overall number of sovereign debt crises.

Sovereign Risk Categories and Sources of Risk

Once the debt distress events properly delimited, we compute in this section the historical default probabilities of the countries in our sample. Using a limited number of core explanatory variables, we are able to identify the underlying risk factor to this probability and to analyze how it has recently evolved.

Macroeconomic Determinants of Debt Crises

The literature on the determinants of debt defaults usually estimates the contribution of various explanatory variables to the probability of a debt crisis using the following model:

$$P\ (y_{ct} = 1) = G\ (\beta' X_{ct}),$$

in which y_{ct} is a dummy variable equal to 1 when country c experiences a debt crisis at time t and 0 otherwise. X_{ct} is a vector of explanatory variables, β is the vector of estimated coefficients, and G is usually taken as the cumulative distribution function of the logistic distribution (logit estimation).

We run a logit regression to explain the risk of a debt crisis by the following variables: logarithm of debt to GDP, total debt service over exports, GDP per capita, the country's CPIA index, and a year-fixed variable that measures the spread between the yield of U.S. corporate bonds rated Baa by Moody's and the yield on 10-year U.S. Treasury bonds as a proxy for worldwide financial shocks. In our regressions, we measure each of the covariates two years before the debt distress event, in order to mitigate the potential simultaneity bias, except for the Baa U.S. corporates spread, which measures current financial conditions (table 1.2).

As expected, all key variables are highly significant. Income is clearly a proxy for many hidden variables, such as risks (domestic or external) other than those captured by the CPIA index. In order to test the serial defaulters' hypothesis more formally, we tried to include several dummy variables that were equal to 1 when the country had defaulted at least one time in the past 30, 20, or 10 years. None of these dummies entered significantly in the regression.

Table 1.2 Determinants of Default

Variable	Debt distress = 1
ln (debt/GDP)	0.523***
	(0.199)
Total debt service/exports	3.943***
	(0.795)
Real GDP per capita	−0.379***
	(0.148)
CPIA index	−0.577***
	(0.181)
Baa-rated U.S. corporates spread	0.611***
	(0.236)
Intercept	0.718
	(1.12)
Number of observations	1,159
Pseudo R^2	0.0987
Prob > chi^2	0

Source: Authors.
Note: Standard errors are shown in parentheses.
*** Significant at the 1% level.

Classification of Countries into Categories

The fitted values of the logit regression presented in table 1.2 allow us to rank all events (defaults and normal periods) in our database based on their default probabilities. We classify countries into five categories (A, B, C, D, and E) corresponding to the five quintiles of risk (table 1.3). We use a discontinuous classification in order to convey more easily than with a continuous ranking the extent to which a country changes from one risk category to another or remains at the same level of risk.

The median defaulter is in category D, with a default probability of 10.6 percent; the median nondefaulters are in category C, with a default probability of about 5 percent. About 25 percent of nondefaulters stand in category D, and about the same number of defaulters are in category B.

In order to assess the stability of each group, we analyze how many defaulters at time t changed category over the course of the three previous years. We are able to compute estimated probabilities at time t for 81 of 88 debt distress events (some covariates are missing for 7 events) and for 77 events at time $t - 3$.

The bulk of defaulters (60 of 75) were in categories D or E at the time of their default and were already in a risky category three years earlier (44 of 75) (table 1.4). A number of C countries became D or E category countries during the three years before their default. The most striking change comes from the 11 of the 16 countries in category C that turned into category E countries at the time of the crisis. Between $t - 3$ and t, the distribution of our sample of defaults, which was evenly spread at $t - 3$ among categories C, D, and E, skewed toward the E category at time t.

Table 1.3 Risk Category Definitions and Number of Default and Nondefault Events, by Category

Category	Probability of sovereign default (percent)	Number of default events	Number of nondefault events
A	Less than 2.5	4	227
B	2.5–4.4	10	222
C	4.4–7.1	16	216
D	7.1–11.3	16	216
E	More than 11.3	42	190
Total		88	1,071

Source: Authors.

Table 1.4 Dynamics of Risk Categories

		1	2	3	4	5	
		A_{t-3}	B_{t-3}	C_{t-3}	D_{t-3}	E_{t-3}	Total
1	Defaulters A_t	0	0	0	2	0	2
2	Defaulters B_t	4	0	1	1	0	6
3	Defaulters C_t	0	1	2	3	1	7
4	Defaulters D_t	1	4	2	4	1	12
5	Defaulters E_t	0	5	11	10	22	48
	Total	5	10	16	20	24	75

Source: Authors.

Note: Table should be read as follows: line 2—out of six defaulters in class B at the time of their default, four were in class A, one was in class C, and one was in class D at time $t - 3$; column 2—among defaulters at time t, 10 were in risk category B at time $t - 3$. Among these, one ended up in category C, four in category D, and five in category E at the time of default.

In only 10 cases was an event of default the result of a strong deterioration of the risk index (defaulters in category A or B at time $t - 3$ ending up in category D or E at time t).[1] Among countries that defaulted while belonging to category C at time t, 4 of 7 had been in category D or E.

This anecdotal evidence is inconsistent with the view of Dale, Merton, and Bodie (2007) that risks can accumulate gradually and then suddenly erupt into a full-blown crisis as a result of nonlinearities. For Merton, random changes in financial flows and market prices cause uncertainty about the value of a country's assets and liabilities. At some point, this uncertainty could cause the total value of assets to decline to below the level of promised payments on the debt, causing distress or default. It is hard to see how stochastic volatility such as that induced by simple Brownian motion could by itself explain the eruption of crises, however, as in continuous time there should always be room for adjustment before the crisis.

Country Risk over the Past 40 Years

The median country in our sample belongs to category B and exhibits an exposure to risk of about 5 percent a year. This seemingly low number is in fact very high, as it means that the probability of not defaulting over a 40-year period is estimated to be just 14 percent. Indeed, only nine countries in our sample (Botswana, Colombia, Fiji, Lao People's Democratic Republic [PDR], Lesotho, Malaysia, Nepal, Papua New Guinea, and Samoa) never defaulted.

Sources of Risk

Four factors stand out in our estimations of the likelihood of a debt distress episode:

- Debt and debt service
- GDP per capita
- Governance quality (as measured by the CPIA index)
- World shock (Baa-rated Treasury Bond spread).

We denote as z the risk index corresponding to the linear combination of these risk factors weighted by the coefficients of the baseline regression. The default probabilities we estimate are simply $G(z)$, in which G is the cumulative distribution function of the logistic distribution. The z factor has the merit of being additive, as far as the cause of risk is concerned. As a result, we can measure the weight of a particular factor on the probability of risk through its direct influence on z and then compare that weight with the weight of other factors.

In order to measure the influence of each variable on the default probability, we compute the average value of each variable (weighted by its coefficient in the regression) for each risk category for each observation in our regression sample (table 1.5). (For the z index and its decomposition for each of the 88 default episodes, see annex table 1A.2.)

The bulk of the discrepancy between the high risk (score −1.5 in the aggregate) and the low risk (score −4.1) comes directly from the debt variable, which explain 46 percent of the gap. The CPIA index comes second, explaining another 25 percent of the gap between the best and worst performers. GDP explains 14 percent of the gap, and the world shock explains 7 percent.

Some variables have a strong influence on the risk factor—and ultimately on default probabilities—in all risk categories. Other variables

Table 1.5 Sources of Risk (z Factor), by Risk Category

Variable	A	B	C	D	E
Debt + debt service	−0.5	−0.2	0.05	0.3	0.8
Governance quality	−2.3	−2.1	−1.9	−1.8	−1.6
GDP per capita	−3.2	−3.1	−3.0	−2.9	−2.8
World shock	1.2	1.3	1.3	1.3	1.4
Intercept	0.7	0.7	0.7	0.7	0.7
z	−4.1	−3.4	−2.8	−2.4	−1.5

Source: Authors.

Table 1.6 Contribution of the Risk Factors to Default Probability, by Risk Category

Variable	A	B	C	D	E
x = debt + debt service	0.06	0.08	0.10	0.12	0.18
x = governance quality	0.10	0.12	0.14	0.15	0.18
x = GDP per capita	0.13	0.14	0.15	0.17	0.18
x = world shock	0.15	0.17	0.17	0.17	0.18
z	0.02	0.03	0.06	0.08	0.18

Source: Authors.

vary across risk categories. This fact restores the relevance of institutional variables without diminishing that of debt burdens.

To calculate the corresponding probabilities of default, we perform the following exercise (see table 1.6). We take the average values of each variable for class E countries as a numeraire and compute the role of each factor in explaining the overall risk. We measure the degree to which the risk declines when we change the average of each of the five variables in E to the average in group A, B, C, and D (table 1.6). More precisely, in this table we compute for each cell $P(xi + vE)$, where $xi + vi = zi$. All x, v and z are averaged over i = A, B. . .E. This procedure allows us to measure the contribution of each factor to total risk. It shows, for example, that the risk of default falls from 18 percent to 6 percent if the average ratio of debt in the highest-risk group (E) falls to that of the lowest-risk group (A).

Assessing Sovereign Risk Today

What are the looming risks of sovereign default today? To answer this critical question, we start by analyzing the risk categories sovereign countries belong to.

Current Risk Categories

We classify countries in one of our five categories, using predictors based on data lagged by two years (table 1.7). We have data on the covariates in 2007 on only 48 countries. For the other 67 countries, we conduct a risk analysis based on the latest values available. As the data show, the distribution of countries over risk categories has not changed much over the past 40 years. Most countries are still in categories D and E.

The debt risk factor decreased considerably for all categories of countries. In 2009 category C countries had the same debt risk index as category A countries did over the previous 40 years (−0.5). The GDP risk factor

Table 1.7 Number of Countries
in Each Risk Category, 2009

Risk category	Number of countries
A	5
B	10
C	17
D	46
E	37
Total	115

Source: Authors.

plays a greater role now than it used to for all categories of risk (a country in category E in 2009 has a GDP risk index almost equal to the index of a category C country in the previous 40 years). The governance risk factor is at about the same level in 2009 and during the 40 years of the sample.

Apart from the amelioration of the risk factor associated with higher levels of GDP per capita and lower levels of debt, the biggest change is the huge increase in the world shock risk factor, which rose from 1.2 to 2.5 (table 1.8). Risk is now driven almost entirely by the world shock factor, as proxied by the high spread on Baa-rated U.S. corporate in 2009.

Current Sources of Risk

The risk classification for all of the countries in our sample as of 2009 (or latest information available) reveals that most countries have withstood the crisis (annex table 1A.3). The world shock factor explains a great deal of the risk classification for countries as of 2009.

As the financial crisis has now largely passed, we also show the risk category into which countries would fall if the world shock factor were set equal to its early 2010 level (average of daily spreads for January, February, and March) (table 1.9). Between 2009 and 2010, most countries moved to lower risk categories.

Half of the 20 countries in categories D or E in 2010 are not experiencing an ongoing debt crisis. These countries are Belize, Eritrea, Guinea-Bissau, Kazakhstan, Lao PDR, Lebanon, Mauritania, Niger, Samoa, and the Solomon Islands (table 1.10). The main risk factor for most of these countries lies with the debt level. For Belize, Guinea-Bissau, Kazakhstan, and Samoa, the weight of the debt factor is very high compared with historical averages for category D and E countries. For Eritrea and the Solomon Islands, the main risk factor is per capita GDP growth.

Table 1.8 Sources of Risk (*z* Factor), 2009

Variable	A	B	C	D	E
Debt + debt service	−0.8	−0.7	−0.5	−0.2	0.6
Governance quality	−2.6	−2.3	−2.1	−2.1	−1.9
GDP per capita	−3.6	−3.5	−3.4	−3.2	−3.0
World shock	2.5	2.5	2.5	2.5	2.5
Intercept	0.7	0.7	0.7	0.7	0.7
z	−3.9	−3.3	−2.8	−2.3	−1.1

Source: Authors.

Table 1.9 Distribution of Countries across Risk Categories with World Shock Factor Set at First Quarter 2010 Level

Risk category	Number of countries
A	21
B	47
C	27
D	5
E	15

Source: Authors.

Table 1.10 Risk Factors for Category D and E Countries as of First Quarter 2010

Country	Debt factor	Governance	GDP	World shock	Intercept	z
Belize	2.6	−1.7	−3.5	1.6	0.7	−0.3
Eritrea	−0.1	−1.4	−2.4	1.6	0.7	−1.7
Guinea-Bissau	2.0	−1.5	−2.5	1.6	0.7	0.3
Kazakhstan	1.9	−2.1	−3.7	1.6	0.7	−1.6
Lao PDR	0.6	−1.8	−3.0	1.6	0.7	−1.8
Lebanon	0.7	−1.7	−3.4	1.6	0.7	−2.1
Mauritania	0.7	−1.9	−3.0	1.6	0.7	−1.9
Niger	0.3	−1.9	−2.6	1.6	0.7	−1.9
Samoa	1.5	−2.2	−3.3	1.6	0.7	−1.8
Solomon Islands	−0.3	−1.6	−2.7	1.6	0.7	−2.3

Source: Authors.

New Debt Distress Events in 2008/09

Because of lack of information on arrears on principal or interest payments for 2008 and 2009, we look only at the other two indicators to identify recent episodes of debt distress. In 2008 six countries borrowed from the IMF through Stand-By Arrangements or Extended Fund Facilities in excess of 50 percent of their quota (Georgia, Latvia, Liberia, Pakistan, the Seychelles, and Ukraine). In 2009, 10 countries did so (Armenia, Belarus, Bosnia, the Dominican Republic Mongolia, Romania, Angola, Maldives, the Seychelles, and Sri Lanka). In 2008 five countries benefited from debt relief from the Paris Club that was not related to the HIPC Initiative (the Republic of Congo, Djibouti, Guinea, Liberia, and Togo). In 2009 three countries benefited from such assistance (Comoros, Côte d'Ivoire, and the Seychelles).

If we use our previous definition of a debt crisis (a debt distress event preceded by three years without crisis), only 9 of these 21 debt distress events represent new debt crises (Armenia 2009, Belarus 2009, Bosnia and Herzegovina 2009, Maldives 2009, Mongolia 2009, Pakistan 2008, Romania 2009, Sri Lanka 2009, and Ukraine 2008). All of the other episodes represent ongoing crises. Recategorizing these countries using the 2010 world shock factor moves all of them into less risky categories (table 1.11).

Table 1.11 Risk Categories of Countries Facing New Debt Distress

Country	Estimated annual distress probability (2009)	Risk category using 2009 world shock factor	Risk category using 2010 world shock factor
Armenia	0.04	B	A
Belarus[a]	0.04	B	A
Bosnia and Herzegovina	0.08	D	B
Maldives	0.08	D	B
Mongolia	0.09	D	B
Pakistan	0.08	D	B
Romania[a]	0.10	D	B
Sri Lanka	0.09	D	B
Ukraine[b]	0.10	D	C

Source: Authors.
Note: Table includes countries that experienced new episodes of debt distress in 2008 or 2009.
a. CPIA 2006 used for projection.
b. CPIA 2005 used for projection.

Not surprisingly, most of the countries in table 1.11, including six of the nine Eastern European countries, were in risky categories two years before their crises. The fact that six out of nine are Eastern European countries is reminiscent of the Russian crisis of 1998, when Russia defaulted with almost no debt. The new underlying factor at work here is the world crisis. Based on current spreads, all of the countries in table 1.11 would fall into the two lowest-risk categories.

Concluding Remarks

The financial crisis of 2008–09 was the worst crisis since the Great Depression. Although its magnitude was such that most countries should have been in dire difficulties, few countries defaulted. The straightforward explanation of why the effects were not more severe is that many countries, even among sovereign defaulters, were much better managed than they had been in previous crisis episodes. Most of the most vulnerable countries lacked access to financial markets, which insulated them from world turbulence.

A group of countries, most of them in Eastern Europe, did experience financial stresses. Pakistan, which experienced very tense relations with its neighbors, and Sri Lanka, which was engaged in a civil war, also entered into debt distress. All of these countries were undergoing domestic turbulence, which is probably poorly evaluated by standard CPIA methods.

Annex

Table 1A.1 Sovereign, Currency, and Banking Crises, by Country, 1970–2007

Country	Year	Sovereign and currency crises	Sovereign and banking crises	Currency and banking crises	Triple crises
Algeria	1994	✓			
Argentina	1981			✓	
	2000		✓		
	2002			✓	
Armenia	1994			✓	
Azerbaijan	1994			✓	
Belarus	1994			✓	
Bolivia	1980	✓			

Table 1A.1 (continued)

Country	Year	Sovereign and currency crises	Sovereign and banking crises	Currency and banking crises	Triple crises
Brazil	1983	✓			
	1998	✓			
Bulgaria	1996			✓	
Cameroon	1987		✓		
	1994			✓	
Central African Republic	1994			✓	
Chile	1982			✓	
	1983	✓			
Congo, Dem. Rep. of	1976	✓			
	1983			✓	
	1994			✓	
Costa Rica	1981	✓			
Dominican Republic	2003			✓	
	2004	✓	✓		✓
Ecuador	1982			✓	
	1983	✓	✓		✓
	1999			✓	
	2000	✓			
Egypt, Arab Rep. of	1979			✓	
El Salvador	1990		✓		
Gambia, The	2003	✓			
Georgia	1992			✓	
Ghana	1983	✓	✓	✓	✓
	2001	✓			

(continued next page)

Table 1A.1 *(continued)*

Country	Year	Sovereign and currency crises	Sovereign and banking crises	Currency and banking crises	Triple crises
Guatemala	1986	✓			
Guinea-Bissau	1981	✓			
	1994			✓	
Haiti	2004	✓			
Indonesia	1997	✓	✓		✓
	1998			✓	
Jamaica	1978	✓			
Jordan	1989	✓	✓	✓	✓
Kazakhstan	1998	✓			
Kenya	1992	✓	✓		✓
	1993			✓	
Lebanon	1990			✓	
Malaysia	1998			✓	
Mauritania	1984		✓		
Mexico	1982			✓	
	1983	✓			
	1995			✓	
Morocco	1980	✓	✓		✓
	1981			✓	
Mozambique	1987			✓	
Nicaragua	1979	✓			
	1990			✓	
Niger	1983		✓		
Peru	1983		✓		
Philippines	1983			✓	
	1984	✓	✓		✓
	1998			✓	
Romania	1991		✓		

Table 1A.1 (continued)

Country	Year	Sovereign and currency crises	Sovereign and banking crises	Currency and banking crises	Triple crises
Russian Federation	1998			✓	
São Tomé and Principe	1986	✓			
	1992			✓	
Sierra Leone	1989			✓	
Sri Lanka	1977	✓			
Thailand	1997	✓	✓		✓
	1998			✓	
Togo	1994			✓	
Tunisia	1991		✓		
Turkey	1978	✓			
	1995	✓			
	2000	✓	✓		✓
	2001			✓	
Ukraine	1998			✓	
Uruguay	1983	✓			
	2002		✓		
Venezuela, R. B. de	1985	✓			
	1990	✓			
	1994			✓	
Vietnam	1988	✓			
Yemen, Rep. of	1995			✓	
Zambia	1996			✓	
Zimbabwe	1983	✓			

Source: Authors.

Table 1A.2 Default Events and Sources of Risk, by Country,
1970–2007

Country	Year	Default probability	Risk class	z	Debt factor	Country factor	World shock factor
Argentina	1983	0.18	E	−1.50	1.39	−5.10	1.50
	2000	0.12	E	−2.03	1.85	−6.03	1.43
Bangladesh	1981	0.14	E	−1.80	−0.08	−3.73	1.30
Benin	1983	0.10	D	−2.14	−0.34	−4.03	1.50
	2000	0.09	D	−2.31	0.18	−4.64	1.43
Bolivia	1980	0.38	E	−0.51	1.78	−4.38	1.37
	2004	0.10	D	−2.17	0.84	−5.03	1.30
Brazil	1983	0.29	E	−0.89	2.00	−5.10	1.50
	1998	0.09	D	−2.27	0.86	−5.05	1.20
Burkina Faso	1987	0.15	E	−1.72	−0.18	−3.60	1.34
Burundi	1998	0.61	E	0.44	2.27	−3.74	1.20
Cameroon	1987	0.13	E	−1.88	0.69	−4.62	1.34
	2005	0.06	C	−2.76	0.41	−4.97	1.08
Cape Verde	1988	0.06	C	−2.69	−0.04	−4.58	1.21
Chile	1983	0.27	E	−0.97	2.17	−5.36	1.50
Comoros	1987	0.30	E	−0.85	0.43	−3.34	1.34
Congo, Rep. of	1986	0.34	E	−0.66	1.01	−4.05	1.66
Costa Rica	1981	0.07	C	−2.59	1.04	−5.64	1.30
Côte d'Ivoire	1981	0.08	D	−2.49	0.45	−4.96	1.30
Djibouti	1994	0.07	C	−2.63	−0.15	−4.13	0.94
Dominica	2005	0.04	B	−3.11	0.48	−5.40	1.08
Dominican Republic	1983	0.17	E	−1.57	0.31	−4.10	1.50
Ecuador	1983	0.31	E	−0.82	1.52	−4.56	1.50
	2000	0.18	E	−1.50	0.96	−4.61	1.43
Egypt. Arab Rep. of	1984	0.12	E	−1.99	0.73	−4.50	1.06
El Salvador	1990	0.13	E	−1.88	0.30	−4.01	1.11
Ethiopia	1991	0.48	E	−0.07	1.41	−3.39	1.19

Table 1A.2 (continued)

Country	Year	Default probability	Risk class	z	Debt factor	Country factor	World shock factor
Gambia, The	1982	0.14	E	−1.83	−0.05	−4.39	1.90
Ghana	1983	0.14	E	−1.79	0.03	−4.04	1.50
	1996	0.10	D	−2.19	0.93	−4.82	0.98
	2001	0.14	E	−1.78	0.57	−4.86	1.79
Grenada	1981	0.04	B	−3.10	−0.52	−4.60	1.30
	1985	0.10	D	−2.24	0.16	−4.40	1.28
Guatemala	1986	0.15	E	−1.71	0.13	−4.23	1.66
Guinea-Bissau	2005	0.27	E	−0.97	1.24	−4.01	1.08
Haiti	1986	0.10	D	−2.15	−0.17	−4.37	1.66
Honduras	1979	0.07	C	−2.64	0.29	−4.42	0.77
	2004	0.05	C	−2.97	0.09	−5.08	1.30
India	1982	0.08	D	−2.44	−0.77	−4.29	1.90
Indonesia	1997	0.06	C	−2.71	0.93	−5.28	0.93
Jordan	1989	0.04	B	−3.20	0.91	−5.87	1.03
Kazakhstan	1998	0.02	A	−4.06	−0.85	−5.12	1.20
Kenya	1980	0.08	D	−2.45	0.08	−4.62	1.37
	1992	0.18	E	−1.49	1.29	−4.71	1.20
	2000	0.11	D	−2.10	0.14	−4.40	1.43
	2004	0.09	D	−2.34	0.23	−4.59	1.30
Kyrgyz Republic	2002	0.26	E	−1.05	1.30	−5.02	1.95
Macedonia, FYR	2000	0.04	B	−3.29	−0.05	−5.39	1.43
Madagascar	1981	0.11	D	−2.12	−0.47	−3.66	1.30
Malawi	1980	0.14	E	−1.83	0.53	−4.45	1.37
	2001	0.23	E	−1.23	0.78	−4.52	1.79
Mauritania	1980	0.30	E	−0.85	0.78	−3.72	1.37
	1984	0.23	E	−1.22	0.95	−3.94	1.06
Mauritius	1985	0.04	B	−3.12	0.59	−5.71	1.28

(continued next page)

Table 1A.2 (continued)

Country	Year	Default probability	Risk class	z	Debt factor	Country factor	World shock factor
Mexico	1983	0.17	E	−1.57	1.22	−5.01	1.50
Moldova	2003	0.16	E	−1.62	0.75	−4.77	1.68
Morocco	1980	0.13	E	−1.88	0.56	−4.53	1.37
Nicaragua	1979	0.06	C	−2.71	0.28	−4.49	0.77
	1983	0.28	E	−0.94	1.51	−4.68	1.50
Niger	1983	0.26	E	−1.06	0.85	−4.13	1.50
Nigeria	1986	0.39	E	−0.44	1.06	−3.87	1.66
Pakistan	1981	0.20	E	−1.40	0.22	−3.64	1.30
	1999	0.17	E	−1.62	0.98	−4.68	1.36
Panama	1985	0.03	B	−3.48	0.20	−5.68	1.28
Peru	1983	0.22	E	−1.26	1.77	−5.24	1.50
Philippines	1984	0.17	E	−1.62	1.46	−4.86	1.06
Romania	1991	0.04	B	−3.12	−1.24	−3.79	1.19
Rwanda	1994	0.08	D	−2.49	0.31	−4.46	0.94
Senegal	1980	0.10	D	−2.18	0.05	−4.31	1.37
Seychelles	1990	0.07	D	−2.54	0.08	−4.45	1.11
Solomon Islands	1995	0.06	C	−2.70	−0.10	−4.31	1.00
	2002	0.13	E	−1.90	−0.06	−4.50	1.95
Somalia	1981	0.13	E	−1.93	0.07	−4.02	1.30
Sri Lanka	2005	0.02	A	−3.74	−0.02	−5.52	1.08
Swaziland	2005	0.02	A	−4.16	−0.78	−5.18	1.08
Thailand	1981	0.04	C	−3.08	0.03	−5.13	1.30
	1997	0.02	A	−3.99	0.19	−5.82	0.93
Togo	2000	0.12	E	−2.00	0.26	−4.41	1.43
Tonga	2003	0.06	C	−2.80	−0.29	−4.92	1.68
Tunisia	1987	0.06	C	−2.67	0.70	−5.43	1.34
	1991	0.06	C	−2.75	0.69	−5.34	1.19

Table 1A.2 (continued)

Country	Year	Default probability	Risk class	z	Debt factor	Country factor	World shock factor
Turkey	1995	0.06	C	−2.74	0.44	−4.89	1.00
	2000	0.05	C	−2.86	0.42	−5.42	1.43
Uganda	1986	0.19	E	−1.43	0.56	−4.37	1.66
Uruguay	1983	0.03	B	−3.43	−0.21	−5.43	1.50
	1998	0.03	B	−3.41	−0.04	−5.29	1.20
	2002	0.06	C	−2.67	0.63	−5.96	1.95
Zimbabwe	1983	0.04	B	−3.19	−0.72	−4.69	1.50

Source: Authors.

Table 1A.3 Risk Classification of Countries, 2009 and 2010

Country	World shock factor set at 2009 level	World shock factor set at 2010 level
Albania	C	B
Angola[a]	D	C
Argentina	D	B
Armenia	B	A
Azerbaijan	A	A
Bangladesh	D	B
Belarus[a]	C	A
Belize	E	E
Benin	D	B
Bolivia	D	C
Bosnia and Herzegovina[a]	D	B
Botswana	A	A
Brazil	D	B
Bulgaria	D	B
Burkina Faso	E	C
Burundi[a]	E	E

(continued next page)

Table 1A.3 (continued)

Country	World shock factor set at 2009 level	World shock factor set at 2010 level
Cambodia	D	C
Cameroon	D	B
Cape Verde	C	A
Chile	A	A
China	B	A
Colombia	D	B
Congo, Rep. of[a]	E	C
Costa Rica	B	A
Côte d'Ivoire	E	D
Croatia	E	C
Djibouti[a]	E	C
Dominica	E	C
Dominican Republic[a]	C	B
Ecuador	E	C
Egypt, Arab Rep. of	C	B
El Salvador	C	B
Eritrea	E	E
Ethiopia	D	B
Fiji	B	A
Gabon	D	B
Gambia, The[a]	E	E
Georgia[a]	B	A
Ghana	D	B
Grenada[a]	D	B
Guatemala	C	A
Guinea[a]	E	D
Guinea-Bissau	E	E
Guyana	E	C

Table 1A.3 (continued)

Country	World shock factor set at 2009 level	World shock factor set at 2010 level
Haiti	E	C
Honduras	C	B
India	C	B
Indonesia	D	B
Iran, Islamic Rep. of	B	A
Jamaica	E	C
Jordan	D	B
Kazakhstan	E	E
Kenya	D	B
Kyrgyz Republic	E	C
Lao PDR	E	E
Latvia	E	E
Lebanon	E	D
Lesotho	E	C
Liberia[a]	E	E
Macedonia, FYR	D	C
Madagascar	D	C
Malawi	E	C
Malaysia	A	A
Maldives[a]	D	B
Mali	D	C
Mauritania	E	E
Mauritius	B	A
Mexico	B	A
Moldova	E	C
Mongolia[a]	D	B
Morocco	D	B
Mozambique	D	B

(continued next page)

Table 1A.3 (continued)

Country	World shock factor set at 2009 level	World shock factor set at 2010 level
Nepal	D	C
Nicaragua	E	C
Niger	E	E
Nigeria	B	A
Pakistan[a]	D	B
Panama	C	B
Papua New Guinea	E	C
Paraguay	D	B
Peru	D	B
Philippines	D	C
Poland	D	B
Romania	D	B
Russian Federation	C	A
Rwanda	D	B
Samoa	E	E
São Tomé and Principe[a]	E	E
Senegal	D	B
Seychelles[a]	E	E
Sierra Leone[a]	D	B
Solomon Islands	E	D
South Africa	A	A
Sri Lanka[a]	D	B
St. Kitts and Nevis	D	B
St. Lucia	C	A
St. Vincent and the Grenadines	D	B
Sudan[a]	E	D
Swaziland	C	A
Tajikistan	D	B

Table 1A.3 (continued)

Country	World shock factor set at 2009 level	World shock factor set at 2010 level
Tanzania	D	C
Thailand	B	A
Togo[a]	E	E
Tonga	D	B
Tunisia	D	B
Turkey	E	C
Turkmenistan	D	B
Uganda	C	B
Ukraine[a]	D	C
Uruguay	D	B
Vanuatu	C	B
Venezuela, R. B. de	C	B
Vietnam	C	B
Yemen, Rep. of	E	C
Zambia	D	B

Source: Authors.
a. Country was in debt crisis in 2010.

Note

1. Nonlinear events (that is, a sudden deterioration of the risk index) occurred in Cameroon (1981), Costa Rica (1981), The Gambia (1982), Grenada (1981), India (1982), Tunisia (1987), Turkey (2000), Uruguay (1983, 2002), and Zimbabwe (1983).

References

Dale, G., R. Merton, and Z. Bodie. 2007. "New Framework for Measuring and Managing Macrofinancial Risk and Financial Stability." NBER Working Paper 13607, National Bureau of Economic Research, Cambridge, MA.

Kraay, A., and V. Nehru. 2004. "When Is External Debt Sustainable?" World Bank Policy Research Working Paper 3200, Washington, DC.

Laeven, L., and F. Valencia. 2008. "Systemic Banking Crises: A New Database." IMF Working Paper 08/224, International Monetary Fund, Washington, DC.

Reinhart, C., K. Rogoff, and M. Savastano. 2003. "Debt Intolerance." NBER Working Paper 9908, National Bureau of Economic Research, Cambridge, MA.

2

Unpleasant Surprises: Determinants and Risks of Sovereign Default

Luca Bandiera, Jesús Crespo Cuaresma,
and Gallina A. Vincelette

After a period of high growth and macroeconomic stability, emerging market countries entered the current global financial crisis in a better position than in past crises. Many emerging market countries, especially in East Asia and Latin America, substantially reduced their debt, consolidated their fiscal position, and accumulated a buffer of reserves. Still, many countries in Eastern and Central Europe and Central Asia have been severely affected by the crisis, as a result of their exposure to foreign financing and the global slowdown in growth in 2009.

The strength of their initial position allowed many emerging market countries to implement countercyclical fiscal policy to offset the effect of stagnating external demand on their economies and protect the poor. These sizable fiscal interventions, as well as tight financing conditions, pose threats to debt sustainability. Growing debt levels and the uncertainty surrounding the exit from discretionary fiscal stimulus have become a major source of concern about a future debt crisis. As the literature on debt crisis suggests, absent improvement in their fiscal balances, emerging market countries may face a higher risk of default on their obligations than mature economies, a risk that may be exacerbated by tighter debt markets and the financing needs of higher-income countries.

Econometric models with a strong ability to predict sovereign defaults are needed so that individual countries can react as effectively as possible. This chapter identifies the determinants of sovereign default that are robust to model uncertainty using Bayesian model averaging (BMA) techniques.

Using BMA techniques, this chapter suggests that the level of indebtedness with respect to available reserves is the best predictor of default episodes for the entire sample of 46 emerging market countries.[1] However, countries with high levels of debt (defined as total external debt that exceeds 50 percent of GDP, the median of the sample) reduce their probability of default by maintaining a stable macroeconomic environment (proxied by low inflation rates). Countries with low levels of debt have a lower unconditional probability to default than countries with high levels of debt. Low-debt countries further reduce their default probability by improving their institutional environment and the quality of their policies.

Model-averaged estimates outperform any other model in predicting out-of-sample sovereign default episodes. These results are consistent with the recent literature on default episodes, which shows that a limited number of macroeconomic variables are sufficient to predict reasonably well episodes of default, that indebtedness and inflation are the most important predictors of default episodes, and that the recurrence of default episodes could be the symptom of more deeply rooted country characteristics, such as the quality of their policies and institutions. The results presented here find that for emerging market countries with high total gross external debt, macroeconomic stability becomes key to debt sustainability (see also Reinhard and Rogoff 2010).

The chapter is structured as follows. The next section reviews key findings in the literature on the determinants of sovereign defaults. The following section presents the data set for 46 emerging market countries, as well as stylized empirical facts related to debt default. The third section isolates robust determinants of default episodes among variables representing macroeconomic fundamentals, liquidity and solvency risks, and the quality of policies and institutions. The last section draws conclusions and presents policy recommendations.

Empirical Determinants of Sovereign Default

Most empirical models of sovereign default start by identifying sovereign defaults based on some definition (which is not necessarily consistent across studies) and build binary dependent variable models (generally logit or probit models) to assess the statistical significance of different potential determinants of debt crises. Although differences in the choice of explanatory variables are wide, in general empirical sovereign default models tend to include determinants that can be clustered into differentiated groups (table 2.1).

Country-specific macroeconomic fundamentals mirroring the effectiveness of economic policy and developments in the real economy tend to

Table 2.1 Variables and Samples Used in Selected Empirical Studies on Determinants of Sovereign Default

Reference	Variables		Sample
Detragiache and Spilimbergo (2001)	Short-term debt	Concessional share of debt	Annual data on 69 countries, 1971–98
	Debt coming due	Multilateral share of debt	
	Foreign exchange reserves	Interest rates	
	Total debt to GDP ratio	Overvaluation	
	Commercial share	Openness	
Catão and Sutton (2002)	Terms of trade	Total external debt service to export ratio	Annual data on 25 emerging markets, 1970–2001
	Real interest rate on U.S. bonds	Foreign exchange reserves to debt ratio	
	Government balance over GDP	Openness	
	Real effective exchange rate	Volatility of fiscal policy	
	Short-term debt	Volatility of terms of trade	
	Foreign exchange control index	Volatility of money base coverage	
	Real GDP growth	Volatility of capital control	
Kruger and Messmacher (2004)	Proportion of new financing needs	Current account deficit to GDP	Annual data on 42 countries, 1970–2001
	GDP growth	Debt to exports	

(continued next page)

Table 2.1 (*continued*)

Reference	Variables		Sample
	Change in growth rate of terms of trade	Long-term debt service to reserves ratio	
	Export growth	Long-term debt service to GDP ratio	
	U.S. three-month interest rate	Short-term debt to reserves ratio	
	Foreign debt to GDP ratio		
Kraay and Nehru (2006)	Present value of debt to exports ratio	Rule of law	Data on 94 crisis episodes in low-income countries, 1970–2001
	Debt service to revenues ratio	Depreciation	
	Debt service to reserves ratio	Terms of trade growth	
	CPIA rating	GDP per capita	
	GDP growth	Inflation	
Pescatori and Sy (2007)	Openness	Short-term debt over reserves ratio	Several samples, 1975–2002
	Overvaluation	GDP growth	
	Total debt to GDP ratio	Inflation	
Tomz and Wright (2007)	GDP (Hodrick-Prescott filtered)		Annual data on 106 countries, 1820–2004

Source: Authors' compilation.
Note: CPIA = Country Policy and Institutional Assessment (World Bank).

be included as potential determinants of the probability of default. These variables include GDP growth, current account developments, fiscal and monetary policy variables, and measures of real exchange rate misalignment. Measures of the quality of countries' policies and institutions are also widely used to assess the effects of soft factors, such as institutions, corruption, and governance, that are not directly captured by macroeconomic variables.

In addition, measures of external solvency and liquidity, which proxy a country's repayment capability, are systematically included. Among these covariates, the extent and composition of external debt play a privileged role as an explanatory variable.

External shocks are also represented in the set of determinants by such variables as the U.S. real interest rate. The effect of external developments on country-specific default probabilities can be thought of as mediated by the degree of external exposure of a given economy, which justifies the inclusion of trade and financial openness measures in debt default models.

The robustness analysis presented here uses representative variables of each of these groups in order to evaluate their relative importance in the framework of model uncertainty. The analysis also includes debt management variables, to account for the importance of the structure and characteristics of the existing external debt portfolio and the terms of new borrowing to estimate default probabilities. These variables include the effective interest rate and the average time to maturity of the portfolio, both defined below.

Data and Stylized Facts

The database used here mirrors a large subset of the variables in Manasse, Roubini, and Schimmelpfennig (2003) and Fioramanti (2008).[2] It contains annual information on 16 variables, which cover representative regressors from the thematic groups defined above (table 2.2). We construct an unbalanced panel of 46 emerging market countries for the period 1980–2004.

The dependent variable is a binary variable taking a value of one if a country is defined to be in default in a given year. A country is defined to be in a debt crisis in a given year if it is classified by Standard & Poor's as being in default or if it receives a large nonconcessional International Monetary Fund (IMF) loan (defined as in excess of 100 percent of the country's IMF quota). The default episodes are listed in Standard & Poor's (2004); nonconcessional loans are drawn from the IMF's International Financial Statistics database. The definition of a country in default used here corresponds to the criterion used in Manasse, Roubini, and Schimmelpfennig (2003) to identify debt crises.

The regressor side includes proxies for the most important determinants of sovereign defaults considered in the literature, as cited in table 2.1. Data

Table 2.2 Descriptive Statistics
(percent, except where otherwise indicated)

Variable	Full sample					External debt/gross national income < 0.5					External debt/gross national income > 0.5				
	Mean	Median	Maximum	Minimum	Std. Dev.	Mean	Median	Maximum	Minimum	Std. Dev.	Mean	Median	Maximum	Minimum	Std. Dev.
Sovereign default	0.48	0.00	1.00	0.00	0.50	0.36	0.00	1.00	0.00	0.48	0.58	1.00	1.00	0.00	0.49
CPIA (index)	3.80	3.78	6.00	2.05	0.72	3.87	3.80	6.00	2.11	0.71	3.73	3.75	6.00	2.05	0.72
Current account as percentage of foreign direct investment	-366.14	-117.80	31,614.29	-34,771.29	3,299.79	-373.74	-115.40	31,614.29	-34,588.25	3,275.93	-359.04	-119.88	21,485.71	-34,771.29	3,328.24
Current account as percentage of gross national income	-2.19	-2.38	18.52	-17.49	4.71	-1.86	-2.04	9.87	-10.21	3.24	-2.49	-3.18	18.52	-17.49	5.74
Current account as percentage of reserves	-34.67	-26.47	998.98	-530.20	94.45	-32.37	-24.41	151.62	-460.49	60.75	-36.82	-29.93	998.98	-530.20	117.61
Effective interest rate	5.43	5.04	21.19	0.09	2.34	5.64	5.33	13.44	2.11	1.95	5.24	4.84	21.19	0.09	2.64
Average maturity (years)	16.66	15.50	385.40	0.00	17.73	16.37	13.50	385.40	0.00	25.07	16.93	16.80	34.70	0.00	5.34
External debt as percentage of gross national income	58.44	51.32	253.21	4.13	36.25	31.29	31.86	49.82	4.13	10.97	83.82	71.73	253.21	50.05	33.11

External debt as percentage of reserves	799.56	513.22	8,399.82	44.79	962.08	450.09	322.83	2,281.43	44.79	370.25	1,126.17	737.59	8,399.82	135.48	1,201.78
GDP growth	3.48	4.00	16.10	–13.40	4.47	4.06	4.30	15.20	–12.90	4.26	2.95	3.60	16.10	–13.40	4.61
Inflation rate	51.93	9.30	11,749.60	–30.30	538.70	39.31	10.90	2,075.80	–1.40	183.58	63.72	7.95	11,749.60	–30.30	728.48
Openness (exports + imports in % of GDP)	77.94	64.38	436.51	15.47	50.70	58.90	52.86	212.08	15.47	31.53	95.73	75.74	436.51	29.16	58.28
Overvaluation (deviation from real exchange trend)	41.21	40.35	95.00	0.00	17.28	41.80	39.68	95.00	15.18	16.49	40.67	40.94	78.45	0.00	18.00
Primary deficit as percentage of gross national income	0.54	0.23	21.70	–20.02	4.46	–0.05	–0.08	7.71	–10.54	2.89	1.10	0.70	21.70	–20.02	5.49
Short-term debt as percentage of reserves	114.40	64.88	2,399.83	0.94	199.08	70.47	46.68	610.47	0.94	74.30	155.46	81.25	2,399.83	4.81	261.06
Short-term debt as percentage of total external debt	15.02	12.95	65.06	0.83	10.13	16.78	15.40	65.06	1.61	10.63	13.38	10.96	61.14	0.83	9.36
U.S. Treasury Bill rate	5.37	5.07	14.08	1.61	2.19	5.21	5.02	14.08	1.61	2.16	5.53	5.41	14.08	1.61	2.22
Number of observations/countries			503/46					261/39					242/35		

Source: Authors.

Note: CPIA = Country Policy and Institutional Assessment (World Bank).

on the explanatory variables come from the IMF's World Economic Outlook and International Financial Statistics databases and the World Bank's
Global Development Finance database. The Country Policy and Institutional Assessment (CPIA) was obtained from the World Bank.[3]

Two debt management variables—the effective interest rate and the
average time to maturity of the portfolio—are obtained from Global
Development Finance. Each represents a different cost and relates to risks
that debt managers are expected to minimize. The effective interest rate—
calculated as interest rate payments in year t, divided by the stock of debt
at the end of $t - 1$, or the average interest payment per unit of debt—
represents a classical measure of the cost of servicing the existing debt
portfolio. An increase in this variable signals a higher cost for existing debt
and elevated pressure on the fiscal balance.

The average time to maturity measures the average time of rolling over
the existing portfolio. A shortening of this indicator suggests that the portfolio is being rolled over more frequently and is therefore more exposed
to refinancing shocks. This variable refers to new debt, and it captures the
marginal costs of debt accumulation.

Countries are divided into two subsamples (see table 2.2). A country
belongs to the low debt-level group in years in which it has a level of total
external debt over gross national income (GNI) below 50 percent, which is
roughly the median value of this variable over the full data set. It belongs
to the high debt-level group in years in which it has debt ratios above
50 percent of GNI. Countries in the high debt-level group are almost
twice as likely to default on their external debt as low debt-level countries.
Average external debt to GNI ratios are 31 percent for low-debt countries
and 84 percent for high-debt countries. On average, countries with lower
debt grow a full 1 percentage point more and have a third of the inflation
rates of countries with debt to GNI ratios above 50 percent. This observation is consistent with the recent literature (Reinhart and Rogoff 2010).
On average, countries with debt below 50 percent of GNI post a small
primary surplus; countries with higher debt burdens run primary deficits.
This result reinforces the empirical finding that fiscal surpluses are key to
reducing public debt in emerging market countries (Gill and Pinto 2005).
The quality of policies and institutions (measured by the World Bank
CPIA rating) is marginally better in countries with lower levels of debt.

Countries with more debt are also more open than countries with debt to
GNI ratios of less than 50 percent. In high-debt countries, the average level
of openness is twice that of less indebted countries. More indebted countries
have larger current account deficits. They also tend to be less covered against
default episodes, because their reserve coverage is lower with respect to their
total external debt, short-term liabilities, and current account deficits.

Data in the sample do not highlight significant differences in debt risk
indicators. On average, no substantial differences are found in the interest
rate on external debt or the maturity profile, although two outliers in the
low-debt group (Paraguay in 1998, with an average maturity of 91 years,

and Romania in 2002, with an average maturity of 385 years) distort this subsample. Countries with lower levels of external debt do tend to have larger shares of short-term debt, suggesting that they are more exposed to rollover risk but also more capable of rolling over a larger portion of debt than countries with higher levels of external debt. To a certain degree, the maturity structure of external debt is endogenous, as high-debt countries with a higher default probability may find themselves excluded from short-term borrowing markets.

Unveiling the Robust Determinants of Debt Default under Model Uncertainty

The descriptive statistics in table 2.2 paint a clear picture of the differential characteristics of defaulting countries. A full-fledged econometric analysis is needed to identify robust predictors of sovereign default risk.

Assessing Model Uncertainty

The usual econometric approach used to assess default determinants is to start by defining a binary variable (y) that takes the value of 1 at default periods ($y = 1$) and 0 in the rest of the sample ($y = 0$). Assume that there is a set of variables $X = \{x_1, \ldots, x_k\}$ that comprises K variables that have been proposed as potential explanatory factors for triggering debt default. In principle, any combination of these variables may be considered as regressors in a model. Let X_k denote a group of $k \leq K$ variables from the set X. A typical model explaining default with this group of covariates is given by

$$P(y = 1|\mathbf{X}_k) = F(\mathbf{X}_k\beta), \qquad (2.1)$$

where $F(z)$ will typically be a logistic function ($1 - F(z) = (1 + e^z)^{-1}$), leading to a logit model, or the Gaussian distribution function ($F(z) = \Phi(z)$), leading to a probit model. Once $F(z)$ has been chosen, a model is defined by a list of included variables. Thus, 2^K possible models can be considered (each model is denoted as M_j, for $j = 1 \ldots 2^K$). BMA estimates of a parameter of interest in this setting can be obtained by weighting each (model-specific) estimate of the parameter with the posterior probability of the model it comes from and summing over the whole model space, which comprises all 2^K specifications:

$$P(\beta_s \,|\, y) = \sum_{m=1}^{2^K} P(\beta_s \,|\, y, M_m) P(M_m \,|\, y). \qquad (2.2)$$

The posterior model probability is a function of the prior probability of the model and its marginal likelihood, so that $P(M_k|y) \propto P(y|M_k)P(M_k)$. A choice needs to be made on the prior probability over the model space, as well as over the parameters of each specific model. A flat prior probability over models is the preferred choice in the literature, leading to a 0.5 prior probability of inclusion for each of the K variables considered. However, this choice of model space prior leads to a mean prior model size of $K/2$ and assigns relatively high prior probability to models that may be considered "too large" for many econometric applications. Ley and Steel (2009) propose using a hyperprior on model size and show that their approach leads to more robust inference when applying BMA.

Raftery (1995), Kass and Raftery (1995), and Clyde (2000) propose using Laplace approximations for determining posterior model probabilities, which simplifies the computational burden for limited dependent variable models considerably. The Bayes factor comparing two models ($B_{jk} = P(y \mid M_j)/P(y \mid M_k)$) can thus be approximated using the Bayesian information criterion (Schwarz 1978) as

$$-2\log B_{jk} \approx BIC_k - BIC_j,$$

where BIC_i is the Bayesian information criterion of model i. Different penalties for the inclusion of new parameters in the model can be achieved by changing BIC by the risk inflation criterion (RIC) (Foster and George 1994) or the Akaike information criterion (Akaike 1973). In these cases, we depart from the purely Bayesian case and average over models using weights that are justified using non-Bayesian approaches to inference but that have often been used in BMA exercises (see Clyde 2000 for a theoretical discussion and applications). We use the RIC approximation to compute weights for the different specifications that form the model space.

The BMA technique allows statistics such as the posterior inclusion probability of the different potential determinants of debt default to be computed. This statistic—the sum of the posterior probability of models including a given variable—can be interpreted as the probability that this variable belongs to the true model determining default. The posterior inclusion probability is routinely interpreted as the robustness of a variable as a determinant of the phenomenon under investigation. Weighted averages of the parameter estimates and its variance are interpreted as the estimated effect of the covariate and its precision once the model's uncertainty has been taken into account. The method is thus able to deliver a full account of the relative importance of the different mechanisms put forward in the literature, as well as estimates of the size of their effect. In particular, the method allows the explanatory variables to be ordered in terms of their robustness as predictors of default episodes.

Robust Determinants of Sovereign Default

We use the BMA setting described above using the RIC approximation[4] and a Markov Chain Monte Carlo Model Composition (MC³) method (Madigan and York 1995) to compute the posterior probability of the different model specifications in our model space.[5] All variables are lagged one year, in order to impose a causal structure in the models and avoid, to a certain extent, endogeneity problems. The results show the posterior inclusion probability (PIP) for each variable; the ratio of the posterior mean to the posterior standard deviation of the parameter associated with each of the covariates (PM/PSD, a measure of the precision of the estimate); and the model-averaged marginal effect of each variable (table 2.3).

The data set includes multiyear periods of debt-servicing difficulties, which implies a high degree of persistence in the dependent variable. Although estimates based on binary dependent variable models with country-fixed effects are theoretically feasible in the setting of BMA, the computational costs are high. For this reason, we retain the pooled structure of the data and jointly explain differences across countries and in time. As many of the potential explanatory variables are also persistent over time, the momentum of debt service problems can be partly assessed by the dynamics of covariates. Alternatively, the data set may be collapsed as a summary of sustained default and nondefault episodes, as in Kraay and Nehru (2006). After compressing the data to such episodes, the number of observations is too small to allow for a reasonable model averaging analysis: defining debt stress periods as lasting more than five years leads to fewer than 40 usable observations.

The results presented in table 2.3 indicate that for the entire sample, a single variable—the size of external debt as a percentage of reserves—achieves both a high posterior inclusion probability and a high degree of precision in the estimation of its effect. The associated model-averaged parameter is positive, as expected, implying that access to liquidity decreases the probability of sovereign default. For all other variables, the PIPs are below 0.5 (the benchmark given by the expected value of the prior inclusion probability), the precision of the estimation is too small to consider them robust determinants of sovereign default, or both.

BMA estimates for countries with high and low debt levels in our sample indicate possible threshold effects in terms of the robustness of default determinants. For country/years in the low-debt subsample, debt defaults episodes are more likely the larger is the external debt as a percentage of reserves and the poorer the quality of policies and institutions, as measured by the CPIA index.[6] For countries with higher levels of debt, the CPIA index loses robustness as a predictor of default in terms of posterior inclusion probability. For these countries, inflation and indebtedness are robustly and positively associated with a higher probability of default.

This result is in line with the results of Reinhart, Rogoff, and Savastano (2003), who also single out indebtedness and macroeconomic stability (proxied by inflation) as the most significant determinants of sovereign defaults. However, our sample selection highlights that indebtedness and

Table 2.3 Model Averaging Results

Variable	Full sample			External debt/gross national income < 0.5			External debt/gross national income > 0.5		
	PIP	PM/PSD	MEFF	PIP	PM/PSD	MEFF	PIP	PM/PSD	MEFF
External debt as percentage of reserves	1.0000	7.7958	0.0005	1.0000	5.0431	0.0008	1.0000	4.6676	0.0001
CPIA index	0.2362	−0.5058	−0.0232	0.9838	−2.9691	−0.1928	0.0019	0.0232	0.0000
GDP growth	0.2335	−0.5018	−0.0035	0.0043	−0.0501	0.0000	0.0020	−0.0278	0.0000
Short-term debt as percentage of total external debt	0.0205	−0.1263	−0.0001	0.1642	−0.3970	−0.0015	0.0013	0.0189	0.0000
Openness	0.0071	−0.0714	0.0000	0.0013	0.0076	0.0000	0.0038	−0.0479	0.0000
Overvaluation	0.0051	−0.0602	0.0000	0.0026	0.0049	0.0000	0.2003	−0.4513	−0.0004
External debt as percentage of gross national income	0.0040	0.0457	0.0000	0.0520	−0.2091	−0.0004	0.0043	0.0503	0.0000
Inflation rate	0.0037	0.0455	0.0000	0.0008	0.0087	0.0000	1.0000	3.5289	0.0029
Effective interest rate	0.0036	−0.0500	−0.0071	0.0018	−0.0185	0.0000	0.0009	−0.0134	0.0000

Short-term debt as percentage of reserves	0.0035	-0.0424	0.0000	0.0539	-0.2118	-0.0001	0.0014	0.0133	0.0000
U.S. Treasury Bill rate	0.0023	0.0280	0.0000	0.0016	-0.0043	0.0000	0.0016	0.0243	0.0000
Current account as percentage of reserves	0.0013	-0.0163	0.0000	0.0012	-0.0263	0.0000	0.0036	-0.0453	0.0000
Primary deficit	0.0012	0.0183	0.0000	0.0593	-0.2233	-0.0016	0.0041	0.0496	0.0000
Current account as percentage of foreign direct investment	0.0011	-0.0190	0.0000	0.1751	-0.4155	0.0000	0.0006	0.0061	0.0000
Current account as percentage of gross national income	0.0010	0.0197	0.0000	0.0018	0.0299	0.0001	0.0020	-0.0295	0.0000
Effective maturity	0.0006	0.0137	0.0000	0.0009	0.0131	0.0000	0.0130	0.0961	0.0000

Source: Authors.

Note: CPIA = Country Policy and Institutional Assessment (World Bank); MEFF = model-averaged marginal effect; PIP = posterior inclusion probability; PM = posterior mean (mean of the posterior distribution of the corresponding parameter); PSD = posterior standard deviation (standard deviation of the posterior distribution of the corresponding parameter). Variables were ordered by PIP in the full sample. Results were obtained from 10,000 replications of the MC^3 procedure after a burn-in phase of 10,000 replications.

inflation are systematically relevant only for the subsample of countries characterized by a relatively high level of debt. In countries with lower debt levels, concentrating on improvements in quality of policies and institutions is more relevant to avoid defaults. Low-debt countries have lower inflation on average, which creates a lower level of dispersion.

In a group of countries whose macroeconomic variables are more stable, soft factors related to the institutional framework become relevant as predictors in episodes of default. The debt management variables introduced, which proxy for debt costs and rollover risk of the portfolio, are not robustly associated with the probability of default.

Several robustness checks were run to ensure that the results hold when outliers are excluded and reduced sets of covariates are used.[7] Excluding the two observations with outlying values for the maturity variable leaves the results unchanged. We then exclude total external debt over GNI as a potential determinant while leaving the variables based on short-term debt as part of the variables under study. The results of the BMA analysis then point toward a robust positive effect of the overall level of short-term debt over GNI and a robust negative effect of the variable measuring the share of short-term debt in total external debt. This implies that the size of the short-term debt variable matters but that countries with a higher share of long-term debt are more prone to defaulting, an effect that is probably related to the exclusion of highly indebted countries from short-term debt markets.

Model Averaging and Out-of-Sample Predictive Ability for Sovereign Default

To determine whether exploiting model uncertainty can lead to improvements in the out-of-sample predictions of the probability of sovereign default, we conduct a simple out-of-sample forecasting exercise, structured as follows. Using data up to 1994, we obtain model-averaged predictions of the default probabilities for the countries in our sample for 1995, which are computed as weighted averages of single-model predictions using posterior model probabilities as weights. In parallel the predictions of the model with the highest posterior probability are saved, in order to compare the model-averaged results with those that would have been obtained if model selection had been used instead of averaging. We add the observation corresponding to 1995 to the estimation period and obtain predictions for 1996. We then repeat this procedure until the end of the sample is reached.

We evaluate the quality of the predictions by transforming the probability forecasts into "alarms" signaling the occurrence of default. For this purpose, we need to delimit the probability threshold that defines alarms for probability predictions above that value. Following the empirical literature on early warning systems (see Berg, Borensztein, and Pattillo 2004),

Table 2.4 Prediction Results

Item	BMA prediction	Best model prediction
Value of loss function	0.303	0.329
Cut-off probability threshold	0.362	0.357
Correct alarms as percentage of total alarms	0.800	0.725
Correct nonalarms as percentage of quiet periods	0.595	0.617

Source: Authors.
Note: Results are based on out-of-sample predictions for the period 1995–2004 (337 observations). BMA = Bayesian model averaging.

we define a simple loss function of the policy maker as the sum of wrongly predicted crises as a share of total crisis periods and wrongly predicted "quiet periods" as a share of total quiet periods. Using this loss function, which implies that the policy maker cares equally about type I and type II errors concerning sovereign default predictions, we estimate the probability threshold defining alarms as the level of probability that minimizes the loss function over the prediction period.[8] We estimate this threshold for both the set of predictions based on BMA and those emanating from the single best specifications (in terms of posterior probability). The results indicate that BMA methods improve the predictive ability of single models (table 2.4). Model-averaged predictions do particularly well at improving the share of correct alarm signals, albeit at the cost of a small reduction in the share of correctly predicted quiet times. Our results thus suggest that methods that use quantifications of model uncertainty to aggregate predictions of single models should be added to the instruments policy makers use to anticipate and measure potential sovereign default risks.

The improvement is relatively modest with respect to the best model, partly because the posterior mass over the model space is highly concentrated on a small number of models. This "supermodel effect" is related to the priors used in the analysis (see Feldkircher and Zeugner 2009). The use of a hyperprior structure over parameters should improve mixing among models, although it would increase the computational burden enormously.

Conclusions

Using a database spanning 25 years for 46 emerging market countries, we use BMA techniques to determine the set of robust determinants of debt default. A first look at the data indicates that countries with different levels of indebtedness have different characteristics. On average, countries with external debt below 50 percent of GNI (roughly the median of this variable in our sample), grow more rapidly and have lower inflation than countries with higher levels of external debt; they also achieve primary surpluses. Because they are also less open, these countries are less exposed to shocks from external demand, run lower current account deficits, and hold higher levels of reserves than more indebted countries.

For the entire sample, the probability of default is robustly associated only with the level of indebtedness. For countries with debt to GNI ratios below 50 percent, the quality of their policies and institutions also becomes relevant. In countries with external debt above 50 percent of GNI, inflation and indebtedness are positively associated with a higher probability of debt default. The importance of the institutional settings and quality of policies fades away for countries with higher levels of debt.

Variables representing debt costs and rollover risk do not appear robust as predictors of debt default. This result confirms the view in the literature that only a few macroeconomic and institutional quality variables are necessary to predict defaults (Kraay and Nehru 2006). It also implies that more analysis is necessary to determine the importance of debt management in decreasing the probability of default.

The results show that model averaging improves the out-of-sample predictive ability for debt crises and that such techniques should become part of the set of instruments used by policy makers to assess sovereign default risk. Further improvements may be realized by using a fully Bayesian approach to obtain model-averaged results, using the results by Albert and Chib (1993) in the framework of BMA. This improvement is straightforward from an analytical point of view but may be computationally costly.

Notes

1. The sample included the following countries: Algeria; Argentina; Bolivia; Brazil; Chile; China; Colombia; Costa Rica; Cyprus; Czech Republic; the Dominican Republic; Ecuador; Egypt, Arab Rep. of; El Salvador; Estonia; Guatemala; Hungary; India; Indonesia; Israel; Jamaica; Jordan; Kazakhstan; Latvia; Lithuania; Malaysia; Mexico; Morocco; Oman; Pakistan; Panama; Paraguay; Peru; the Philippines; Poland; Romania; Russian Federation; Slovak Republic; South Africa; Thailand; Trinidad; Tunisia; Turkey; Ukraine; Uruguay; and Venezuela, R. B. de.

2. We are very grateful to Marco Fioramanti for kindly sharing his data set with us.

3. The CPIA rates countries on a scale from 1 to 6, with higher values indicating better quality policies and institutions.

4. The BIC approximation was also used, leading to qualitatively similar results.

5. The model space in our application contains more than 65,000 models. Although this is a tractable size, we decided to reduce computing time by using the MC^3 sampler to evaluate the model space. Doing so allowed us to estimate less than

a third of the models in the full model space (10,000 models after 10,000 runs in the burn-in phase).

6. Kraay and Nehru (2006) find that the marginal effect of the CPIA on the probability of default is much larger in low-income than in middle-income countries. BMA point estimates of the marginal contribution of the CPIA in emerging market countries are consistent with the previous finding. For low-debt emerging market countries, the quality of policies and institutions appears to be a stronger determinant of default than for the whole sample of middle-income countries considered by Kraay and Nehru (2006), suggesting that for low-debt emerging market countries, the level of indebtedness is not the only piece of information that markets consider.

7. The results of the robustness checks are not presented in detail here. They are available from the authors upon request.

8. The loss function could place more weight on crisis events that are not correctly predicted when true (type II errors), as policy makers may find it unacceptable to miss a crisis. Doing so, however, could lead to raising too many red flags when they are not needed. For this reason, we chose to minimize types I and II errors equally.

References

Akaike, H. 1973. "Information Theory and an Extension of the Maximum Likelihood Principle." In *Second International Symposium on Information Theory*, ed. N. Petrov and F. Csaki, 267–81. Budapest: Academiai Kiado.

Albert, J., and S. Chib. 1993. "Bayesian Analysis of Binary and Polychotomous Response Data." *Journal of the American Statistical Association* 88 (422): 669–79.

Berg, A., E. Borensztein, and C. A. Pattillo. 2004. "Assessing Early Warning Systems: How Have They Worked in Practice?" IMF Working Paper 04/52, International Monetary Fund, Washington, DC.

Catão, L., and B. Sutton. 2002. "Sovereign Defaults: The Role of Volatility." IMF Working Paper 02/149, International Monetary Fund, Washington, DC.

Clyde, M. 2000. "Model Uncertainty and Health Effect Studies for Particulate Matter." *Environmetrics* 11: 745–63.

Detragiache, E., and A. Spilimbergo. 2001. "Crises and Liquidity: Evidence and Interpretation." IMF Working Paper 01/2, International Monetary Fund, Washington, DC.

Feldkircher, M., and S. Zeugner. 2009. "Benchmark Priors Revisited: On Adaptive Shrinkage and the Supermodel Effect in Bayesian Model Averaging." IMF Working Paper No. 09/202, International Monetary Fund, Washington, DC.

Fioramanti, M. 2008. "Predicting Sovereign Debt Crises Using Artificial Neural Networks: A Comparative Approach." *Journal of Financial Stability* 4 (2): 149–64.

Foster, D. P., and E. I. George. 1994. "The Risk Inflation Criterion for Multiple Regression." *Annals of Statistics* 22: 1947–75.

Gill, I., and B. Pinto. 2005. "Public Debt in Developing Countries: Has the Market-Based Model Worked?" In *Managing Economic Volatility and Crises: a Practitioner's Guide*, ed. J. Aizenman and B. Pinto. Cambridge: Cambridge University Press.

Kass, R. E., and A. E. Raftery. 1995. "Bayes Factors." *Journal of the American Statistical Association* 90: 773–95.

Kraay, A., and V. Nehru. 2006. "When Is External Debt Sustainable?" *World Bank Economic Review* 20 (3): 341–65.

Kruger, M., and M. Messmacher. 2004. "Sovereign Debt and Financing Needs." IMF Working Paper 04/53, International Monetary Fund, Washington, DC.

Ley, E., and M. F. Steel. 2009. "On the Effect of Prior Assumptions in Bayesian Model Averaging with Applications to Growth Regression." *Journal of Applied Econometrics* 24 (4): 651–74.

Madigan, D., and J. York. 1995. "Bayesian Graphical Models for Discrete Data." *International Statistical Review* 63: 215–32.

Manasse, P., N. Roubini, and A. Schimmelpfennig. 2003. "Predicting Sovereign Debt Crises." IMF Working Paper 03/221, International Monetary Fund, Washington, DC.

Pescatori, A., and A. N. S. Sy. 2007. "Are Debt Crises Adequately Defined?" IMF Staff Papers 54 (2): 306–37.

Raftery, A. E. 1995. "Bayesian Model Selection in Social Research." *Sociological Methodology* 25: 111–96.

Reinhart, C. M., and K. S. Rogoff. 2009. *This Time Is Different: Eight Centuries of Financial Folly.* Princeton, NJ: Princeton University Press.

———. 2010. "Growth in a Time of Debt." NBER Working Paper 15639, National Bureau of Economic Research, Cambridge, MA.

Reinhart, C. M., K. S. Rogoff, and M. Savastano. 2003. "Debt Intolerance." *Brookings Papers on Economic Activity*, Brookings Institution, Washington, DC.

Schwarz, G. 1978. "Estimating the Dimension of a Model." *Annals of Statistics* 6: 461–64.

Standard & Poor's. 2005. "2004 Transition Data for Rated Sovereigns." Standard & Poor's.

Tomz, M., and M. L. J. Wright. 2007. "Do Countries Default in 'Bad Times'?" FRB of San Francisco Working Paper 2007-17, Federal Reserve Bank of San Francisco. http://www.frbsf.org/publications/economics/papers/2006/wp07-17bk.pdf.

3

Finding the Tipping Point: When Sovereign Debt Turns Bad

Mehmet Caner, Thomas Grennes, and Fritzi Koehler-Geib

Public debt has increased substantially for countries at all income levels as a result of the current global economic crisis. Historical evidence indicates that increases in debt persist for years following financial crises (Reinhart and Rogoff 2010; Scott 2010). In addition, projections of standard measures of public debt relative to GDP for the next 30 years indicate that debt levels are unsustainable for many countries (Cecchetti, Moharty, and Zampolli 2010). Taking account of the implicit public debt associated with social security, medical care, and contingent liabilities would reveal a substantially magnified debt problem (Cecchetti, Moharty, and Zampolli 2010).

The increase in public debt has raised concerns over whether it is starting to hit levels at which it might slow economic growth. Does such a "tipping point" exist? How strong would the growth impact be if debt surpassed the threshold? What would happen if debt stayed at elevated levels for an extended period of time?

According to Reinhart and Rogoff (2010), the answer to the first question is "yes." Using histograms summarizing evidence from 44 developed and developing economies, they find a threshold of 90 percent central government debt to GDP, after which the real growth rate declines. This threshold has received considerable attention in the press, which has referred to it as a "tipping point" (Pozen 2010). The threshold has practical significance because the United States and many other countries either have reached this point or are projected to reach it soon and remain above it for years.

If debt thresholds exist, there are theoretical and empirical reasons why they might vary by country income. Debt may play out differently in low-income countries, because of less developed domestic financial markets; a different degree of openness (Frankel and Romer 1999; Levine and Renelt 1992); and different institutions (Acemoglu and others 2003; Alfaro and Volosovych 2008). Debt levels in low-income countries may also have different implications for growth through the inflation channel. Governments in countries without well-developed bond markets have resorted to monetizing government debt by selling bonds to their central banks. As a result, empirical studies have found a connection between fiscal deficits and inflation in low-income countries but no systematic connection in high-income countries (Catão and Terrones 2005; Pattillo, Poirson, and Ricci 2002).

This chapter analyzes thresholds in long-term average public debt to GDP ratios and the differential impact of debt on long-term GDP growth below and above such a threshold. It relies on estimates first introduced by Hansen (1996, 2000) and takes into account country characteristics such as initial GDP, inflation, and trade openness.

The analysis contributes to the literature by providing an econometrically rigorous analysis of the impact of long-run average public debt to GDP ratios on long-run average growth rates. It differs from the literature in three significant ways. First, the literature focuses primarily on the nexus between external debt and growth (see, for example, Cordella, Ricci, and Ruiz-Arranz 2010; Pattillo, Poirson, and Ricci 2002, 2004). In contrast, this chapter analyzes the nexus between total public debt and growth. Second, other studies (Cordella, Ricci, and Ruiz-Arranz 2010; Pattillo, Poirson, and Ricci 2002, 2004; and Reinhart and Rogoff 2010) investigate the short-run effect of external debt on growth. In contrast, this analysis emphasizes the long-run relationship. Third, this analysis uses a different methodology to provide the core findings. In contrast to previous studies, which relied on spline functions (Cordella, Ricci, and Ruiz-Arranz 2010; Pattillo, Poirson, and Ricci 2002, 2004) or histograms (Reinhart and Rogoff 2010), this analysis relies on the threshold estimation techniques developed by Hansen (1996, 2000).[1]

The chapter is organized as follows. The next section describes the data. The second section describes the methodology. The third section presents the results. The last section provides some concluding remarks.

Data

The analysis is based on a data set of 101 countries (75 developing and 26 developed), consisting of annual observations for the period 1980–2008 (countries are listed in annex A). By including a large group of both developing and developed countries, this data set improves on previous data sets.[2]

Table 3.1 Data Sources

Variable	Time series	Data source
Real GDP growth	GDP (constant 2000 dollars)	World Development Indicators (World Bank)
Public debt	General government, gross debt GDP (current dollars)	World Economic Outlook (IMF)
Openness	Imports of goods and services (current dollars) Exports of goods and services (current dollars) GDP (current dollars)	World Development Indicators (World Bank)
Inflation	Consumer price index	World Economic Outlook (IMF)
Initial GDP	GDP per capita in 1970 (constant 2000 dollars)	World Development Indicators (World Bank)

Source: Authors.

The main variables are gross public debt, GDP growth, and a set of control variables known to influence economic growth (table 3.1).[3] Public debt is measured as the ratio of general government gross debt to GDP. When considering the debt-growth nexus, debt at all levels of government is relevant, because it influences the government's ability to engage in growth-enhancing potentially countercyclical policies. The average debt to GDP ratio was 67.1 percent for the entire sample (59.9 percent for high-income countries). Average GDP growth was 3.8 percent for the entire sample (2.6 percent for high-income countries).

We consider inflation, trade openness, and initial GDP as control variables. The inflation variable is self-explanatory. Trade openness is calculated as the sum of imports and exports of goods and services relative to GDP. Initial GDP is calculated as the logarithm of per capita GDP in 1970. A date before the start of the time period is chosen to ensure the absence of endogeneity.

Methodology

The main results of the analysis draw on a threshold least squares regression model following Hansen (1996, 2000). We also use pooled least squares regressions, to relate our findings to those of Reinhart and Rogoff (2010). The description of the methodology here focuses on the threshold estimation technique (we do not account for potential endogeneity in the regressions).

Threshold estimation is used because it is superior to other techniques that have been used to estimate a nonlinear function. It allows one to identify the threshold level, its significance, the coefficients of the different regimes, and their significance simultaneously from the data based on a solid theory.

Threshold Regression Model

The specification of the threshold least squares regression model is as follows:

$$Y_i = \beta_{0,1} 1_{\{X_i \leq \lambda\}} + \beta_{0,2} 1_{\{X_i > \lambda\}} + \beta_{1,1} X_i 1_{\{X_i \leq \lambda\}} + \beta_{1,2} X_i 1_{\{X_i > \lambda\}}$$

$$+ \beta_{2,1} W_i 1_{\{X_i \leq \lambda\}} + \beta_{2,2} W_i 1_{\{X_i > \lambda\}} + u_i, \tag{3.1}$$

where 1 represents an indicator function that takes the value of one when the event inside happens and zero when it does not; Y represents the long-run average real growth rate; X represents the long-run average public debt to GDP ratio; W represents control variables; and i is a country index. The unknown threshold value λ as well as the coefficients $\beta_{0,1}$ through $\beta_{2,2}$ are estimated with the threshold least squares method of Hansen (2000). Equation 3.1 can be rewritten in two equations, in which the first represents the regime below the threshold and the second represents the regime above the threshold:

$$Y_i = \beta_{0,1} + \beta_{1,1} X_i + \beta_{2,1} W_i + u_i, \quad if \quad X_i \leq \lambda$$

$$Y_i = \beta_{0,2} + \beta_{1,2} X_i + \beta_{2,2} W_i + u_i, \quad if \quad X_i > \lambda.$$

A more specific methodology would be to set thresholds on selected control variables. Here, however, we start from a more general specification with two separate regimes, as described in equation (3.1).

Test for Threshold

We test for a threshold in the relationship between the long-run average public debt to GDP ratio (1980–2008) and long-run average growth to verify the model in equation (3.1). The null hypothesis is that the slope coefficients and intercepts are identical in the two regimes. In equation (3.1) this means that by using a heteroskedasticity-consistent Lagrange multiplier test (Hansen 1996), we test the following null hypothesis:

$$H_0: \beta_{0,1} = \beta_{0,2}, \beta_{1,1} = \beta_{1,2}, \beta_{2,1} = \beta_{2,2}. \tag{3.2}$$

If there is no threshold, expression (3.2) will not be rejected, and a simple least squares model can be estimated. If there is a threshold effect, equation (3.1), including the unknown threshold value of λ, is estimated. Bootstrap p-values are used for this purpose, because they can replicate the asymptotic distribution, as Hansen shows (1996).

Results

Overall, the results suggest that thresholds exist in the relationship between the long-run average public debt to GDP ratio and long-run GDP growth. They suggest that it is crucial to take into account initial GDP, that the threshold level differs for developing and developed economies, and that the cost of surpassing the debt threshold is high over time.

A note of caution concerns the potential endogeneity of long-run average debt. Because we focus here on the relation between long-run average debt and long-run GDP growth, we cannot use the instrumental variable threshold technique of Caner and Hansen (2004), which relies on short-run averages as instruments. Short-run average debt can be used to address a different research question, which we will tackle through panel data analysis in a future project.

We address potential endogeneity by adding initial debt/GDP (1980) to the estimations to control for omitted variables bias and reverse causality. The results remain qualitatively the same with the same threshold values and small changes of the coefficients in the two regimes.

Debt Threshold for All Countries

The first main result is that the threshold level of the average long-run public debt to GDP ratio on GDP growth is 77.1 percent for the entire sample of 79 countries (initial GDP data were not available for 22 countries) (table 3.2). If debt surpasses this level, each additional percentage point in the ratio of public debt to GDP costs the economy 0.0174 percentage point in annual average real growth. This effect is highly significant and quantitatively important. Below this threshold, additional debt increases growth (the estimated coefficient is 0.065). This result is consistent with the idea that at moderate debt levels, a higher public debt to GDP ratio may actually imply that credit constraints are looser and the economy has more resources available for investment.

The results are derived from the model in equation (3.1), first developed by Hansen (1996), when equation (3.2) is rejected. We control for the (logarithm of) initial (1970) GDP per capita, inflation, and trade openness. The test statistic for the Lagrangean multiplier test is 14.21. Because the limit is nonstandard but recoverable by a bootstrap procedure (Hansen 1996), the p-value from 1,000 bootstrap replications is 0.093, significant at the

Table 3.2 Threshold Regression Results under Different
Threshold Debt Levels

Variable	Regime 1 (debt ≥ 77 percent)		Regime 2 (debt < 77 percent)	
	Slope	Standard error	Slope	Standard error
Log initial GDP per capita (1970)	0.00006*	0.00001	0.0002*	0.0001
Trade openness	0.0454*	0.0078	–0.0007	0.0012
Inflation	0.0012	0.0007	–0.0244	0.0164
Debt/GDP	–0.0174*	0.0010	0.0653*	0.0128

Source: Authors.

Note: Dependent variable is real average GDP growth. R^2 is 0.985 for the first regime, 0.987 for the second. There are 12 countries in the first regime and 67 in the second. The 95 percent confidence interval for the debt to GDP ratio is [–0.0195, –0.0154] in regime 1 and [0.0402, 0.0905] in regime 2, based on the likelihood ratio test in Hansen (2000). The 95 percent confidence interval for the threshold estimate is [0.770574, 0.770574].

* Significant at the 5 percent level using standard normal critical values, as in Hansen (2000).

10 percent level. The coefficients on inflation are insignificant. Trade has a positive effect on the growth under the high-debt regime, possibly because more credit is available for trade. Initial GDP per capita coefficients are significant and much higher in low-debt than high-debt regimes.

Debt Threshold Excluding Initial GDP

The second main result is that it is crucial to include initial GDP in the estimations. Repeating the estimations but omitting initial GDP significantly changes the threshold value. The estimated threshold for the debt to GDP ratio is 97.6 percent (table 3.3). The impact is small but highly significant and positive.

The results are derived from a Lagrangean multiplier test of equation (3.2). The test statistic for the Lagrangean multiplier test is 12.75, with a bootstrap p-value from 1,000 bootstrap replications of 0.097, significant at the 10 percent level. The country sample covers all 99 countries.

Debt Thresholds in Developing and Developed Economies

The third main result is that the threshold differs substantially for developing and developed economies. Repeating the estimations for the subsample of developing countries yields a debt to GDP threshold of 64 percent.

Table 3.3 Threshold Regression Results under Different
Threshold Debt Levels, Excluding Initial GDP

Variable	Regime 1 (debt ≥ 97.6 percent of GDP)		Regime 2 (debt < 97.6 percent of GDP)	
	Slope	Standard error	Slope	Standard error
Trade openness	0.00007*	0.00001	–0.0005*	0.0001
Inflation	0.0027*	0.0003	–0.0091	0.0103
Debt/GDP	–0.0147*	0.0007	0.0805*	0.0069

Source: Authors.

Note: Dependent variable is real average GDP growth. R^2 is 0.976 for the first regime and 0.969 for the second. There are 11 countries in the first regime and 88 in the second. The 95 percent confidence interval for the debt to GDP ratio is [–0.0173, –0.0130] in regime 1 and [0.0688, 0.0946] in regime 2. Estimations are based on the likelihood ratio test in Hansen (2000). The 95 percent confidence interval for threshold estimate is [0.9074, 1.0441].

* Significant at the 5 percent level using standard normal critical values, as in Hansen (2000).

Moreover, the negative impact of debt exceeding this threshold is slightly greater than in the full set of countries (coefficient is –0.020 compared with –0.017 for the entire sample). We would have liked to repeat the exercise for the sample of developed countries only, but the small number (26) of countries made doing so impossible. The difference between the threshold for the full sample and the threshold for developing countries suggests that as a group, developing countries encounter growth rate problems at a lower debt to GDP level.

The results, based on a Lagrangean multiplier test of equation (3.2), reveal the existence of a threshold (table 3.4). The coefficient for the Lagrangean multiplier test is 18.66; the bootstrap p-value is 0.002. The sample size of developing countries is 55 (reduced by lack of data on initial GDP for some countries). Coefficients on the control variables show the expected signs. Interestingly, the coefficient on trade openness is positive for high-debt regimes, which is understandable, but negative for low-debt regimes, possibly because of trade barriers.

Growth Costs of Exceeding the Debt Threshold

The fourth main result is that the impact of the public debt to GDP ratio exceeding the threshold level is costly in terms of GDP growth (table 3.5). The most extreme case is Nicaragua, where the average annual real growth rate could have been 4.7 percent higher had debt been at the 64 percent debt threshold for developing countries. High indebtedness was responsible for

Table 3.4 Threshold Regression Results for Developing Countries

Variable	Regime 1 (debt ≥ 64 percent of GDP)		Regime 2 (debt < 64 percent of GDP)	
	Slope	Standard error	Slope	Standard error
Log initial GDP per capita (1970)	0.0249*	0.0015	0.0034	0.0024
Trade openness	0.0002*	0.0001	–0.0015*	0.0007
Inflation	0.0008*	0.0004	–0.0086	0.0311
Debt/GDP	–0.0203*	0.0039	0.0739*	0.0093

Source: Authors.

Note: Dependent variable is real average GDP growth. R^2 is 0.98 for both regimes. There are 16 countries in the first regime and 40 in the second regime. The 95 percent confidence interval for the debt to GDP ratio is [–0.0312, –0.0088] in regime 1 and [0.0491, 0.0965] in regime 2. These results are based on the likelihood ratio test in Hansen (2000). The 95 percent confidence interval for the threshold estimate is [0.6335, 0.8524].

* Significant at the 5 percent level using standard normal critical values, as in Hansen (2000).

Table 3.5 Estimated Forgone Growth as a Result of Exceeding the Debt Threshold, by Country

Country	How high growth could have been if the debt to GDP ratio had been at the threshold level (percent real average growth rate)	Annual percentage point loss in real GDP growth	Cumulated loss over 28 years (percentage point loss in real GDP growth)
Angola	3.2	1.2	62.8
Belgium	2.7	0.6	18.4
Bolivia	2.4	0.1	1.6
Bulgaria	2.5	0.6	16.7
Burundi	2.6	0.8	24.3
Canada	3.1	0.4	11.6
Congo, Rep. of	5.0	1.0	32.7

Table 3.5 (continued)

Country	How high growth could have been if the debt to GDP ratio had been at the threshold level (percent real average growth rate)	Annual percentage point loss in real GDP growth	Cumulated loss over 28 years (percentage point loss in real GDP growth)
Côte d'Ivoire	2.1	1.2	41.1
Croatia	1.5	0.2	6.0
Ecuador	3.0	0.1	1.5
Greece	2.2	0.0	0.5
Guinea	4.0	0.4	13.0
Hungary	1.8	0.1	3.2
Indonesia	6.8	1.3	45.2
Italy	2.1	0.4	10.9
Jamaica	2.0	0.2	5.1
Japan	2.9	0.6	18.6
Jordan	5.1	0.1	2.3
Lao PDR	6.8	0.8	33.0
Latvia	2.5	0.1	3.1
Lebanon	5.2	0.4	11.7
Madagascar	2.4	0.5	15.3
Mali	3.3	0.2	5.2
Nicaragua	6.6	4.7	264.6
Nigeria	3.4	0.2	4.7
Philippines	3.2	0.0	1.2
Sierra Leone	3.1	1.0	33.0
Singapore	7.3	0.4	13.0
Tanzania	5.0	0.2	6.3

Source: Authors' calculations.

Note: The public debt to GDP threshold applied is 77 percent for developed economies and 64 percent for developing countries.

an annual loss of 4.7 percentage points of real GDP growth, equivalent to a 264 percent loss over the 28 years of the study. This example illustrates the high costs of persistent violations of debt threshold levels.

Comparison of Results with Results of Reinhart and Rogoff

We compare our findings with those of Reinhart and Rogoff (2010) by running simple pooled least squares regressions for subsamples below and above the threshold they suggest. In the pooled regressions, we find a regime switch at the 90 percent debt to GDP ratio, as indicated by Reinhart and Rogoff's analysis based on histograms. However, repeating the pooled regressions with a debt threshold of 60 percent also shows a regime switch. These results illustrate that their methodology does not deliver clear threshold levels. Moreover, given the demonstrated importance of controlling for initial GDP, the use of histograms or pooled regressions can be only indicative and must be interpreted with care. At least over longer periods, public debt can become detrimental to growth at lower levels of debt.[4]

We pool observations on GDP growth and government debt to GDP ratios for the same 20 industrial countries as Reinhart and Rogoff. We then run simple pooled least squares (with heteroskedasticity-corrected errors) for two sets of countries. The first set contains countries with debt levels of at least 90 percent (table 3.6). The second includes countries with debt ratios below 90 percent. We compare the slope coefficients for the government debt to GDP ratios for the two sets of regressions. The result allows a more precise comparison of countries above and below the threshold than Reinhart and Rogoff. As Reinhart and Rogoff (2010) suggest, there is a regime switch at the 90 percent debt to GDP ratio.[5]

We extend this simple exercise by also considering a 60 percent public debt to GDP ratio. The first set of observations corresponds to debt ratios above 60 percent, and the second group is for debt ratios below 60 percent. The difference between slope coefficients for the two groups is small compared with the 90 percent threshold. However, in these regressions there is a regime switch at the threshold level, with the impact of debt on GDP turning negative above.

Table 3.6 GDP Growth and Debt Ratio

Debt ratio	Slope	Standard error	t-test	p-value
≥ 90 percent	−0.0137	0.0065	−2.10	0.038
< 90 percent	0.0012	0.0055	0.23	0.819
≥ 60 percent	−0.0091	0.0037	−2.43	0.016
< 60 percent	−0.0057	0.0089	−0.03	0.519

Source: Authors.

Concluding Remarks

This analysis provides an analytical foundation for the debt-growth relationship by formally testing for the existence of a threshold and estimating the threshold value while controlling for other important variables that influence growth. The threshold value is sensitive to the inclusion of income per capita, and it decreases when high-income countries are excluded from the sample.

The main findings are that the threshold level of the average long-run public debt to GDP ratio on GDP growth is 77 percent for the full sample and 64 percent for the subsample of developing countries. Surpassing these thresholds is costly for countries, which forgo GDP growth if debt exceeds the threshold for an extended period.

The analysis of debt thresholds can be informative, but threshold levels should be interpreted with caution. Our analysis is based on long-term averages over nearly 30 years, so that temporary deviations from the average need not have important negative effects on growth. If a country's debt ratio exceeds the threshold for a year or two because of a recession, its long-term growth need not suffer (Scott 2010). The existence of debt thresholds need not preclude short-term fiscal stabilization policy (Leeper and Bi 2010). If debt explosions move debt ratios above the threshold and keep them there for decades, however, economic growth is likely to suffer.

Annex: Countries Covered

Table 3A.1 Countries Covered, by Type

Economy type	Countries
Developing economy (75)	Algeria; Angola; Argentina; Bangladesh; Benin; Bolivia; Brazil; Bulgaria; Burkina Faso; Burundi; Cameroon; Chad; Chile; China; Colombia; Congo, Rep. of; Costa Rica; Côte d'Ivoire; Croatia; Dominican Republic; Ecuador; Egypt, Arab Rep. of; El Salvador; Estonia; Ethiopia; Ghana; Guatemala; Guinea; Haiti; Honduras; Hungary; India; Indonesia; Jamaica; Jordan; Kenya; Lao PDR; Latvia; Lebanon; Lithuania; Madagascar; Malaysia; Mali; Mexico; Morocco; Nicaragua; Niger; Nigeria; Pakistan; Panama; Papua New Guinea; Paraguay; Peru; the Philippines; Poland; Romania; Russian Federation; Rwanda; Senegal; Sierra Leone; Singapore; the Slovak Republic; Slovenia; South Africa; Sri Lanka; Tanzania; Thailand; Togo; Tunisia; Turkey; Uganda; Ukraine; Uruguay; Venezuela, R. B. de; Vietnam

(continued next page)

Table 3A.1 (continued)

Economy type	Countries
Developed economy (26)	Australia; Austria; Belgium; Canada; the Czech Republic; Denmark; Finland; France; Germany; Greece; Iceland; Ireland; Italy; Japan; Korea, Rep. of; the Netherlands; New Zealand; Norway; Portugal; the Slovak Republic; Slovenia; Spain; Sweden; Switzerland; the United Kingdom; the United States

Source: Authors.

Notes

The authors thank Rodrigo Chaves and Zafer Mustafaoglu for very helpful comments and support and Gallina A. Vincelette for very helpful suggestions.

1. Cordella, Ricci, and Ruiz-Arranz (2010) also estimate threshold regressions. These result are not used for the main message of their paper.

2. Reinhart and Rogoff (2010) analyze 20 developed countries; other studies focus exclusively on developing countries. See, for example Pattillo, Poirson, and Ricci (2002, 2004) and Cordella, Ricci, and Ruiz-Arranz (2010), each of which analyzes more than 60 countries.

3. Real GDP growth is calculated in constant 2000 dollars.

4. We use a shorter period of time than Reinhart and Rogoff (2010) and general government debt rather than central government debt.

5. The simple pooled regression does not control for any other economic variables that affect growth or test for the existence of a threshold. The results should therefore be interpreted with caution.

References

Acemoglu, Daron, Simon Johnson, James Robinson, and Yunyong Thaicharoen. 2003. "Institutional Causes and Macroeconomic Symptoms: Volatility, Crises and Growth." *Journal of Monetary Economics* 50 (1): 49–123.

Alfaro, L., and V. Volosovych. 2008. "Why Doesn't Capital Flow from Rich to Poor Countries? An Empirical Investigation." *Review of Economics and Statistics* 90 (2): 347–68.

Buiter, Willem. 2010. "Public Debt Explosions in Developed Nations." March, Citi Investment Research, New York, NY.

Caner, Mehmet, and Bruce Hansen. 2004. "Instrumental Variable Estimation of a Threshold Model." *Econometric Theory* 20: 813–43.

Catão, Luis A. V., and Marco Terrones. 2005. "Fiscal Deficits and Inflation." *Journal of Monetary Economics* 52 (3): 529–54.

Cecchetti, Stephen, M. S. Moharty, and Fabrizio Zampolli. 2010. "The Future of Public Debt: Prospects and Implications." Paper presented at the International Research Conference hosted by the Bank of India, February 12, in Delhi.

Cordella, Tito, Luca A. Ricci, and Marta Ruiz-Arranz. 2010. *Debt Overhang or Debt Irrelevance: Revisiting the Debt Growth Link.* IMF Staff Paper, International Monetary Fund, Washington, DC.

Frankel, Jeffrey, and David Romer. 1999. "Does Trade Cause Growth?" *American Economic Review* 89 (3): 379–99.

Hansen, B. E. 1996. "Inference When a Nuisance Parameter Is Not Identified under the Null Hypothesis." *Econometrica* 64 (2): 413–30.

———. 2000. "Sample Splitting and Threshold Estimation." *Econometrica* 68 (3): 575–603.

Leeper, Eric, and Bi Huitxin. 2010. "Sovereign Debt Risk and Fiscal Policy in Sweden." NBER Working Paper 15810, National Bureau of Economic Research, Cambridge, MA.

Levine, Ross, and David Renelt. 1992. "A Sensitivity Analysis of Cross-Country Growth Regressions." *American Economic Review* 82 (4): 942–63.

Pattillo, Catherine, Helene Poirson, and Luca Ricci. 2002. "External Debt and Growth." IMF Working Paper 02/69, International Monetary Fund, Washington, DC.

———. 2004. "What Are the Channels through Which External Debt Affects Growth?" IMF Working Paper 04/15, International Monetary Fund, Washington, DC.

Pozen, R. 2010. "The US Public Debt Hits Its Tipping Point." *Boston Globe*, February 23.

Reinhart, Carmen, and Kenneth Rogoff. 2009. *This Time Is Different: Eight Centuries of Financial Folly.* Princeton, NJ: Princeton University Press.

———. 2010. "Growth in a Time of Debt." *American Economic Review* 100 (2): 573–78.

Reinhart, Carmen, Kenneth S. Rogoff, and Miguel A. Savastano. 2003. "Debt Intolerance." *Brookings Papers on Economic Activity* 1: 1–74.

Scott, Andrew. 2010. "The Long Wave of Government Debt." *Vox*, March 11.

4

Determinants of Emerging Market Sovereign Bond Spreads

Dimitri Bellas, Michael G. Papaioannou, and Iva Petrova

During the current global financial crisis, sovereign bond spreads for both developed and emerging market economies widened dramatically. This deterioration has been attributed to the adverse impact of both large public interventions in support of domestic financial systems and fiscal stimulus packages, which led to rapidly growing public debt and balance sheet risks. Countries with large debt stocks and unsound banking sectors were affected the most.

These developments have prompted renewed interest in the determination of sovereign bond spreads. This chapter sheds light on this topic by investigating the short- and long-run effects of fundamental (macroeconomic) and temporary (financial market) factors on sovereign bond spreads.

Many studies have examined the relationship between sovereign bond spreads and various macroeconomic indicators and variables (see, for example, Baldacci, Gupta, and Mati 2008; Eichengreen and Mody 1998; Kamin and Kleist 1999; and Min 1998). These studies examine whether debt and fiscal variables, reserves, GDP growth, and interest rates of various maturities play an important role in explaining sovereign bond spreads. Although they find some empirical regularities, especially in the case of specific countries or regions and for certain time horizons, they by no means settle the debate over the stable and significant determinants of sovereign bond spreads.

An extension of these studies is the identification of short- and long-term causes of sovereign bond spreads with a dynamic error correction model (examples include Dell'Aricia, Goedde, and Zettelmeyer 2000; Ferrucci 2003; and Goldman Sachs 2000). Ferrucci (2003) concludes that markets take into account macroeconomic fundamentals when pricing sovereign risk. The external debt to GDP ratio, the degree of openness, the ratio of amortizations to reserves, and the ratio of the current account to GDP are all significantly correlated with sovereign spreads; the interest payments to external debt ratio and the fraction of short-term external debt are also correlated with sovereign spreads, albeit more weakly. Ferucci also finds that nonfundamental factors play an important role, as suggested by the strong empirical relationship between sovereign spreads and external factors such as global liquidity conditions and U.S. equity prices.

Researchers have also examined financial sector and crisis-related determinants of sovereign bond spreads. Ebner (2009) finds significant differences in government bond spreads in Central and Eastern Europe during crisis and noncrisis periods. According to his work, market volatility, political instability or uncertainty, and global factors explain the rise in spreads during crisis periods, when macroeconomic variables lose some of their importance. Dailami, Masson, and Padou (2008) propose a framework in which the probability of default is a nonlinear function of the risk-free rate (U.S. Treasuries), implying that the U.S. interest rate alone is not a sufficient explanation of the spread level. Interactions with the severity of the debt dynamics, global liquidity conditions, the appetite for risk, and shock indicators are also important, and a distinction has to be made between crisis and noncrisis periods.

Mody (2009) investigates the links between sovereign bond spreads in euro countries and financial vulnerability. He finds that financial fragility (measured by the ratio of the equity index of the country's financial sector to the overall equity index) is strongly correlated with spread changes. Between the time the euro was introduced and July 2007, for example, markets considered the probability of sovereign default to be negligible. Following the onset of the crisis, sovereign spreads in euro countries rose, as investors sought risk-free assets. After the rescue of Bear Stearns, in March 2008, a differentiation in spreads across countries emerged, caused mainly by differences in the prospects of the domestic financial sector. Differences widened in September 2008 (when Lehman Brothers failed), as some countries paid an increased penalty for high public debt to GDP ratios.

A related topic that has received considerable attention is the relationship between sovereign spreads and default risk. Sovereign bond spreads are widely considered a comprehensive measure of a country's overall risk premium, stemming from market, credit, liquidity, and other risks. Caceres, Guzzo, and Segoviano (2010) model sovereign spreads on joint probabilities of distress, extracted from credit default swap spreads, controlling for global risk aversion and macroeconomic fundamentals. Their approach helps assess the extent to which the large fluctuations in euro sovereign spreads reflect changes in global risk aversion and the rise in country-specific risk. The results show that early in the crisis, the surge in global risk aversion was a significant factor influencing sovereign spreads. Recently, country-specific factors have started playing a more important role.

Our model extends the Ferrucci (2003) framework by incorporating a financial stress index, which attempts to capture the state of a country's financial health. Doing so allows us to better explain movements of emerging market sovereign spreads relating to financial vulnerabilities, as well as the short- versus long-term implications of financial crises. Our findings indicate that financial sector vulnerabilities, measured by the Emerging Markets Financial Stress Index developed by staff of the International Monetary Fund (IMF), appear to be a crucial factor in explaining movements in spreads in the short run. This finding is consistent with the view that financial crisis periods may adversely affect the ability of sovereign issuers to service their debt, which is reflected in the premium on their bond yields. In the long run, macroeconomic factors that affect a country's liquidity and sustainability and thus its debt repayment capacity, as well as political risk, are significant determinants of emerging market sovereign bond spreads, a result that is consistent with previous studies.

The chapter is organized as follows. The first section explains the theoretical framework and the variables used. The second section presents the calibrated model, selected variables, and the data. The third section outlines the estimation methods based on a static fixed-effects model and the pooled mean group approach. The fourth section discusses the results. The last section presents some concluding remarks.

Methodological Framework

We propose a model of sovereign borrowing that formalizes the consumption choice of a small open economy. The economy smoothes its consumption path over time by borrowing from abroad when domestic resources are scarce and paying back its debt when resources are abundant. In this setting foreign lenders focus on the ability of the economy to generate enough foreign exchange resources to service its external obligations and its government's ability to generate enough domestic resources to purchase the foreign exchange required for servicing its external obligations. We formalize this framework by enhancing Ferrucci (2003).

The starting point of our analysis is the simple relationship between the probability of default p on emerging market sovereign bonds and the risk-free interest rate of equal maturity r (the U.S. Treasuries rate). Specifically, based on the overarching assumption that the expected return of an emerging market sovereign bond (interest rate i) should yield the same return as U.S. Treasuries $1 + r = (1 + i)(1 - p) + 0 \cdot p$, we adjust the probability of default to factor in the possibility that the country may be facing financial distress, during which default would be more likely

$$1 + r = (1 + i_t)\,(1 - p \cdot I_t) + 0 \cdot p \cdot I_t, \tag{4.1}$$

where I_t is a financial stress index. We assume that the financial stress index takes values greater than 0 such that $1 - pI_t > 0$ in the short run and 1 in the long run, implying that in the short run, extraneous financial conditions could ameliorate or amplify the probability of default. For example, a high distress period, such as the ongoing financial crisis, could temporarily increase the probability of sovereign default, which would raise domestic interest rates in order to restore parity with the risk-free interest rate. In the long run, the probability of default is constant and determined solely by macroeconomic fundamentals, as shown below.

The spread over U.S. Treasuries can be written as

$$S_t = i_t - r = \left(\frac{1+r}{1-p \cdot I_t}\right) - 1 - r = (1+r)\left(\frac{1}{1-p \cdot I_t} - 1\right)$$

$$= (1+r)\frac{p \cdot I_t}{1-p \cdot I_t}. \tag{4.2}$$

We assume that markets close access to financing for two periods if a sovereign defaults. Therefore, the government will be able to finance its funding needs through debt issuance each period only if it is current on its debt payments during that period and did not default during the previous period. Given that primary public spending (G_t) and interest payments on the existing external debt stock (iD_t) are financed by tax revenues (T_t) and debt issuance $(D_t + 1 - D_t)$ if the government has financial market access, the government budget constraint in period t is given by

$G_t \leq T_t + D_{t+1} \ \forall t \in N, t > 0$ with probability $p \cdot I_{t-1}$ that the government defaulted during the previous period and

$G_t + (1 - pI_t)(1 + i)D_t \leq T_t + (1 - pI_t)D_{t+1} \ \forall t \in N, t > 0$ with probability $1 - p \cdot I_{t-1}$ that the government did not default during the previous period; and probability $1 - p \cdot I_t$ that the government is not in default during the current period.

The maximization problem for this small open economy is

$$Max \ U_0 = \sum_{t=0}^{T} \beta^t u(C_t)$$

subject to

$$G_0 = T_0 + D_1$$

$$G_t + (1 - p \cdot I_{t-1})(1 - p \cdot I_t)(1 + i_t)D_t \leq T_t + [p \cdot I_{t-1} + (1 - p \cdot I_{t-1})$$
$$(1 - p \cdot I_t)]D_{t+1}, t > 0$$

$$Y_t = C_t + G_t$$

$$T_t = f(Y_t)$$

$$Y_t = (1 + g)Y_{t-1},$$

where U_0 is an intertemporal welfare function depending on consumption (C_t), and β is the discount factor.

The first two constraints are government budget constraints. For simplicity, we assume that all external debt is public. The third constraint is the usual accounting identity, equating total domestic output (Y_t) to the sum of private and government consumption. The last two equations in the formulation are required to close the model and define tax revenues as a function of output and the evolution of output over time (which for simplicity is assumed to be exogenous).

In this setup, the solution to the maximization problem should satisfy $G_0 = T_0 + D_1$ in period $t = 0$ and

$$G_t + (1 - p \cdot I_{t-1})(1 - p \cdot I_t)(1 + i_t)D_t = T_t + [p \cdot I_{t-1} + (1 - p \cdot I_{t-1})$$
$$(1 - p \cdot I_t)]D_{t+1}, \, t > 0 \, .$$

In the steady state,

$$\left((1-p)^2 i - p\right)D = T - G \text{ and } \left(r(1-p) - p^2\right) = \frac{T - G}{D} \, . \tag{4.3}$$

Using equation (4.2), we can express p as a function of s:

$$p = \frac{s}{s + (1 + r)}, \tag{4.4}$$

in which the probability of default and the sovereign bond spread increase jointly. The long-run solution of equation (4.3) then implies the following:

- If the ratio of fiscal balance to domestic output, $(T-G)/Y$, increases, p and s should decrease (that is, a stronger fiscal position should decrease both the probability of sovereign default and the sovereign spread).
- A higher debt to GDP ratio is associated with a higher probability of default and wider sovereign bond spreads.
- If the stock of debt is greater than the fiscal deficit, an increase in the risk-free interest rate (r) should lead to a higher probability of sovereign default and larger sovereign bond spreads. Given that this condition is almost always satisfied, it is safe to conclude that the risk-free interest rate and the sovereign bond spreads are positively correlated.[1]

These three relationships determine the expected theoretical signs of $(T-G)/Y$, D/Y, and r, p, and s in the long run. We look at p and s as functions of $(T-G)/Y$, D/Y, and r. In the short run, the spread is also affected by the financial stress index, with higher values of the index implying a wider spread.

Variable Selection and Data

We use the following variables to explain the spread levels:

- External debt/GDP
- Interest payments on external debt/reserves
- Short-term debt/reserves
- External debt amortization/reserves
- Fiscal balance/GDP
- Trade openness
- Current account balance/GDP
- Financial fragility (financial stress index)
- Risk-free rate (U.S. 3-month Treasury Bill and 10-year government bond yield).

Macroeconomic Variables

Our theoretical framework indicates the selection of fundamental factors, such as the risk-free rate (r), the stock of debt (D), gross domestic product (Y), and the fiscal balance $(T - G)$, as the main determinants of sovereign bond spreads. In addition, liquidity and sustainability indicators need to be included in order to assess a country's capacity to repay its debt. Liquidity indicators measure issuers' ability to fulfill their current obligations. Notably, the stock of international reserves plays a role by providing a buffer of foreign liquidity that could be used to repay debt.[2] We therefore include (as ratios to reserves) external debt amortization, interest payments, and the amount of short-term debt, which—together with the fiscal balance and the current account balance—characterize the country's gross financing needs. We expect these variables to have a positive impact on sovereign spreads, with greater financing needs implying greater compensation for risk.

External solvency is linked to a sustainable level of external indebtedness and factors that affect it, such as the current account balance and trade openness (proxied by the ratio of exports plus imports to GDP). In particular, a low degree of openness can affect the trade surplus and therefore increase the probability of external default. Therefore, we expect both the current account and trade openness to have negative signs.

Financial Fragility and Crisis Periods

Employing only macroeconomic fundamentals to explain spreads, without incorporating political and crisis considerations, does not adequately capture debt dynamics and the probability of default (and therefore the effect on spreads). Using zero-one binary variables often used in econometric work (see Mody 2009) does not always provide a good measure of intensity of stress and often ignores the ambiguity of "near-miss" events, such as the emerging market sell-off in June 2006, which increased price volatility in countries with large current account deficits but had just minor macro-economic implications. We therefore use the Emerging Markets Financial Stress Index developed by Balakrishnan and others (2009), which provides a high-frequency measure of stress in emerging economies. The components of the index include the following:

- The exchange market pressure index, which increases as the exchange rate depreciates or international reserves decline
- Default risk measures (sovereign bond spreads)
- The banking sector beta, based on the standard capital asset pricing model, computed over a 12-month rolling window (a beta higher than 1 indicates that banking stocks move more than proportionately with the overall stock market, suggesting that the banking sector is riskier than the market as a whole)
- Stock price returns, calibrated such that falling equity prices correspond to increased market stress
- Time-varying stock return volatility, wherein higher volatility captures heightened uncertainty.

In all estimations, we modify the financial stress index by excluding its sovereign bond spread component, in order to avoid endogeneity problems. Higher values of this index indicate greater distress.

Political instability has been found to undermine the issuers' credibility and increase default probability (Baldacci, Gupta, and Mati 2008). Adding a measure of political risk would thus widen sovereign bond spreads.

Data Description

The data set covers 14 countries between the first quarter of 1997 and the second quarter of 2009. The dependent variable is the secondary market spread, as provided by JP Morgan's Emerging Markets Bond Index (EMBI). This spread is measured by an index that includes sovereign and quasi-sovereign (guaranteed by the sovereign) instruments that satisfy certain liquidity criteria in their trading. The spread of an instrument (bond) is calculated as the premium paid by an emerging market over a U.S. government bond with comparable maturity features. A country's spread index is then calculated as the average of the spreads of all bonds that satisfy the inclusion criteria, weighted by the market capitalization of the instruments. One of the benefits of such an index is that the time series are continuous, without breaks as bonds mature.

The right-hand-side variables of the model comprise country-specific macroeconomic fundamentals and external liquidity indicators, as well as political risk and financial stress indices (table 4.1). We used several

Table 4.1 Description of the Variables

Variable	Description	Unit	Frequency	Interpolation	Source
Spreads	Secondary market spreads, calculated as premium paid over U.S. government bond with comparable features	Basis points	Quarterly	No	Bloomberg (JP Morgan EMBIG Index), Ferrucci (2003)
GDP	Nominal GDP, in current prices	Dollars	Quarterly	No	Haver Statistics database; *International Financial Statistics* (IMF 2009b)
External debt	Stock of external debt	Dollars	Annual	Yes	*Global Development Finance* (World Bank 2009)
Public debt	Stock of public debt to GDP	Percent	Annual	Yes	*World Economic Outlook* (IMF 2009c)
Short-term debt	Short-term external debt	Dollars	Annual	Yes	*Global Development Finance* (World Bank 2009)
Interest	Interest payments on external debt	Dollars	Annual	Yes	*Global Development Finance* (World Bank 2009)
Reserves	Stock of international reserves, excluding gold	Dollars	Quarterly	No	*International Financial Statistics* (IMF 2009b)
Amortization	Principal repayments on external debt	Dollars	Quarterly	No	*International Financial Statistics* (IMF 2009b)
Fiscal balance	Fiscal balance to GDP	Percent	Quarterly	No	*International Financial Statistics* (IMF 2009a)

Current account	Current account balance	Dollars	Quarterly	No	International Financial Statistics (IMF 2009b)
Openness	Exports + imports/GDP	Percent	Quarterly	No	International Financial Statistics (IMF 2009b)
Political risk index	Total political risk score (0–100), evaluating a range of factors relating to political stability and effectiveness; higher score indicates greater political risk	Index	Quarterly	No	The Economist Intelligence Unit (2009)
Financial stress index	Standard components: exchange market pressure index (which depends on exchange rate and change in reserves); sovereign spreads (excluded); banking sector beta stock returns; stock return volatility	None	Quarterly	No	Balakrishnan and others (2009)
U.S. 3-month Treasury Bill	U.S. 3-month Treasury Bill rate	Percent	Quarterly	No	Federal Reserve
U.S. 10-year government bond	U.S. 10-year government bond rate	Percent	Quarterly	No	Federal Reserve

Source: Authors' compilation.

sources, including the IMF's International Financial Statistics database, the IMF Global Data Source, the Haver Statistics database, and the World Bank database, to compile the series.

Simple summary statistics of the variables (figure 4.1 and table 4.2) reveal that EMBI spreads are highly positively correlated with the ratios of external debt (public and private) to GDP and public debt (external and domestic) to GDP. Interest payments to reserves, short-term debt to reserves, and, to a lesser extent, amortization to reserves also appear to have a positive correlation with EMBI spreads, as do the indices of political risk and financial stress. The fiscal balance and the current account are not highly correlated with the spreads and are likely to appear insignificant in the estimations. The ratios of external and public debt have a very high positive correlation (0.8). To minimize replication, we present the results using the ratio of total external debt, for which we have longer series. The three liquidity measures—short-term debt, interest payments, and amortization to reserves—are also highly correlated, suggesting that they should be used in the estimations one at a time.

Calibration and Model Estimation

As in Ferrucci (2003) and Dailami, Masson, and Padou (2008), we use the pooled mean group (PMG) estimator of Pesaran, Shin, and Smith (1995, 1999) to capture the structure of the quarterly frequency data. The PMG estimator distinguishes short-term from long-term parameters of the model and allows the short-term parameters to vary across countries while keeping long-term elasticities constant. Using such a model instead of static fixed-effects estimators has several benefits: the dynamic aspect of the model controls for possible cointegration; the model imposes commonality on the long-run coefficients without restricting the short-term coefficients, which is more plausible economically; and the separation of long-term and short-term views allows the specificity of some variables across countries in the short term to be taken into account. Baltagi and Griffin (1997) and Boyd and Smith (2000) show that pooled estimators have desirable properties and may outperform their heterogeneous counterparts. They find that pooled models tend to produce more plausible estimates even for panels with relatively long time series and that they offer overall superior forecast performance. This estimation method is appropriate for frameworks in which cross-country variation is needed in the short-term dynamics but commonality is needed in the long run, assuming that an equilibrium (steady state) is reached. These assumptions seem consistent with the nature of the problem.

Figure 4.1 Determinants of EMBI Spreads

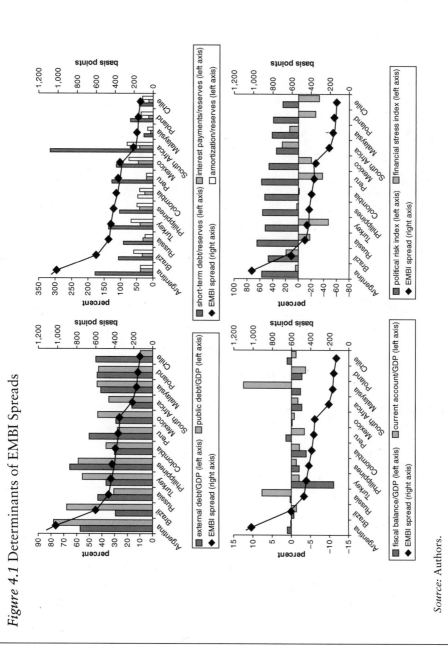

Source: Authors.

Table 4.2 Summary Statistics, by Country

Variable mean	Argentina	Brazil	Bulgaria	Chile	Colombia	Malaysia	Mexico	Peru	Philippines	Poland	Russian Fed.	South Africa	Turkey	Venezuela, R. B. de	All countries Mean	All countries Observations
Spread	1,017	746	602	465	444	419	393	380	367	353	214	169	156	136	410	988
External debt/GDP	0.567	0.292	0.870	0.446	0.302	0.407	0.289	0.500	0.653	0.437	0.433	0.164	0.369	0.433	0.490	1,363
Public debt/GDP	0.781	0.676	0.408	0.097	0.366	0.435	0.434	0.275	0.591	0.428	0.309	0.344	0.554	0.416	0.515	785
Short-term debt/reserves	1.765	1.061	1.071	0.425	0.463	0.282	1.134	1.253	1.037	0.705	0.903	3.157	1.372	0.506	1.168	1,204
Interest payments/reserves	0.381	0.319	0.284	0.132	0.239	0.073	0.451	0.192	0.405	0.134	0.299	0.410	0.393	0.245	0.317	1,204
Amortization/reserves	0.381	0.596	0.288	0.325	0.400	0.163	0.741	0.189	0.492	0.356	0.229	0.801	0.675	0.282	0.445	1,339
Fiscal balance/GDP	0.010	-0.006	-0.008	0.012	-0.038	-0.022	0.000	0.014	-0.021	-0.027	0.003	-0.026	-0.109	0.006	-0.016	928
Current account/GDP	0.000	-0.011	-0.076	-0.011	-0.020	0.123	-0.006	-0.033	-0.012	-0.036	0.076	-0.016	-0.019	0.018	-0.006	1,046
Political risk index	56.8	46.6	44.4	24.4	51.8	40.0	45.1	57.2	55.4	39.0	64.6	33.4	51.1	66.5	52.5	899
Openness	0.063	0.173	0.935	0.509	0.269	1.765	0.114	0.289	0.755	0.598	0.482	0.434	0.309	0.106	0.399	1,046
Financial stress index	0.036	0.191		-0.324	-0.009	0.135	-0.200	-0.382	0.017	-0.263	-0.171	0.251	-0.466	-0.094	-0.094	565
U.S. 3-month Treasury Bill rate															0.039	1,404

Pairwise correlation	1	2	3	4	5	6	7	8	9	10	11	12	13
Spread between U.S. 10-year and 3-month rates												0.018	1,404
U.S. 10-year government bond yield												0.057	1,404
EMBI spread	1.0												
External debt/GDP	0.3	1.0											
Public debt/GDP	0.4***	0.8***	1.0										
Short-term debt/reserves	0.4***	0.1***	0.1***	1.0									
Interest payments/reserves	0.4***	0.1***	0.1	0.7***	1.0								
Amortization/reserves	0.2***	0.0	0.0	0.5***	0.8***	1.0							
Fiscal balance/GDP	-0.1**	0.0	-0.1***	-0.1***	-0.2***	-0.2***	1.0						
Current account/GDP	0.0	-0.1***	-0.1	-0.1*	0.0	0.0	0.0	1.0					
Political risk index	0.6***	0.3***	0.4***	0.1***	0.3***	0.1**	0.0	0.2***	1.0				
Openness	-0.4***	0.1***	-0.2***	-0.1***	-0.2***	-0.2***	-0.1***	0.2***	-0.4***	1.0			
Financial stress index	0.3***	0.0	0.0	0.1	0.2***	-0.1	-0.1*	-0.1***	0.0	-0.1*	1.0		
U.S. 3-month Treasury Bill rate	0.0	0.0	0.0	0.2	0.2	0.0	0.0	0.0	0.0	-0.1***	-0.1	1.0	
Spread between U.S. 10-year and 3-month rates	0.2***	0.0*	0.1**	0.1***	0.0	0.0	-0.1*	0.0	0.0	-0.1*	0.1**	-0.6***	1.0
U.S. 10-year government bond yield	0.3***	0.1**	0.0	0.3***	0.3***	0.0	0.0	0.0	0.1*	-0.2***	0.0	0.8***	0.8***	0.0

Source: Authors.

Note: EMBI = Emerging Markets Bond Index.

*** Significant at the 1% level; ** significant at the 5% level; * significant at the 10% level.

Many researchers have used the basic log model, which is

$$\log s_{it} = \alpha + \sum_{j=1}^{J} \beta_j x_{jit} + \varepsilon_{it}. \tag{4.6}$$

Because of the time series dimension of the panel data set, it is likely that the correct model includes lagged dependent variables, which would bias the standard fixed-effects estimation. If we assume that the parameters vary across countries, we can use the following dynamic panel representation of the model:

$$\log s_{it} = \mu_i + \lambda_i \log s_{it-1} + \sum_{j=1}^{J} \gamma_{1ji} x_{jit} + \sum_{j=1}^{J} \gamma_{2ji} x_{jit-1} + u_{it}.$$

By rearranging, we get the error correction equation, which is

$$\Delta \log s_{it} = \phi_i \left[\log s_{it-1} - \alpha_i - \sum_{j=1}^{J} \beta_{ji} x_{jit} \right] - \sum_{j=1}^{J} \gamma_{2ji} \Delta x_{jit} + u_{it},$$

where $\phi_i = -(1 - \lambda_i) \ \alpha_i = \dfrac{\mu_i}{1 - \lambda_i} \ \beta_{ji} = \dfrac{\gamma_{1ji} + \gamma_{2ji}}{1 - \lambda_i}$

(this representation of the model applies to both stationary and I(1) series). The term in brackets is the long-term relationship between the spread s and the vector X of the explanatory variables, with β_{ij} representing the long-run elasticity of variable j and country i. The assumption of long-run commonalities requires that these elasticities not vary across countries, which means that for all i, $\beta_{ij} = \beta_j$. The equation to estimate is therefore

$$\Delta \log s_{it} = \phi_i \left[\log s_{it-1} - \alpha_i - \sum_{j=1}^{J} \beta_j x_{jit} \right] - \sum_{j=1}^{J} \gamma_{2ji} \Delta x_{jit} + u_{it}. \tag{4.7}$$

Discussion of Results

We use two different approaches to estimate the coefficient: the fixed-effects model for estimation of equation (4.6) and the PMG model for estimation of equation (4.7). In general, the estimation methods show some important regularities for the determinants of sovereign bond spreads.

Fixed-effects Model

The benchmark specification of the estimation of equation (4.6) (specification 2 in table 4.3) includes all variables. Specifications (3)–(7) exclude certain variables (liquidity indicators, interest rates) that were found to be collinear. Specification 1 is provided as a comparison with the benchmark to demonstrate the impact of adding the financial stress index to the estimations. The benchmark specification is satisfactory in terms of explanatory power (R^2 of 0.76), sign, and significance level. All coefficients except the fiscal balance and the current account are highly statistically significant. All coefficients except debt to reserves and debt amortization have the expected (negative) signs.

The sum of all liquidity indicators is positive, however, suggesting that in general, greater financing needs relative to liquid resources increase sovereign bond spreads. This implication is confirmed by specifications (3)–(5), in which the three liquidity indicators used one at a time have positive signs, and two of them (short-term debt to reserves and interest payments to reserves) are highly significant.

U.S. Treasury rates have the greatest impact on EMBI spreads. In particular, a 1 percentage point increase in the 3-month Treasury Bill rate increases EMBI spreads by about 4 percentage points; a 1 percentage point increase in the term spread between the 10-year U.S. government bond and the 3-month Treasury Bill increases spreads by 7 percentage points. Therefore, both U.S. policy conditions and the slope of the yield curve affect emerging market bond spreads.

The financial stress index is also highly significant and positively correlated with the spread level, indicating that the idiosyncratic financial environment in a country can affect the financing conditions of the sovereign. A substantial drop in the coefficient of determination (R^2) is observed when the estimation excludes the index (5 percent), suggesting that the variable plays an important role in explaining the spread level.

This set of estimations indicates that the fiscal balance is not consistently statistically significant across all specifications, as suggested by the theoretical framework. Not all of these findings conform with those of previous studies, which find that local factors play a much less important role than external factors in determining spreads on international sovereign bonds. However, an increase in the ratio of debt to GDP by 1 percentage point increases spreads by about 3.5 basis points. Provided the increase in the debt ratio is caused by a higher fiscal deficit, its impact is already factored in. Specifications in which interest payments are excluded show significant coefficients for the fiscal balance, suggesting a colinearity impact.

Pooled Mean Group Model

The PMG method, which allows short-run parameters to vary across countries, is used to estimate equation (4.7).[3] The estimated long-term

Table 4.3 Fixed-Effects Estimation

Coefficient	(1)	(2)	(3)	(4)	(5)	(6)	(7)
External debt/GDP	3.485*** (0.166)	3.369*** (0.184)	3.099*** (0.194)	3.235*** (0.169)	2.944*** (0.163)	3.430*** (0.184)	3.462*** (0.174)
Short-term debt/reserves	-0.202** (0.081)	-0.206** (0.09)	0.238*** (0.073)			-0.216** (0.090)	-0.222** (0.089)
Interest payments/reserves	3.174*** (0.314)	2.797*** (0.318)		1.717*** (0.214)		2.964*** (0.312)	2.772*** (0.318)
Amortization/reserves	-0.466*** (0.140)	-0.555*** (0.139)			0.0736 (0.102)	-0.578*** (0.139)	-0.527*** (0.138)
Fiscal balance/GDP	-0.927** (0.423)	-0.285 (0.414)	-0.935** (0.441)	-0.363 (0.423)	-0.872** (0.405)	-0.358 (0.415)	-0.362 (0.412)
Current account/GDP	-1.202*** (0.452)	-0.003 (0.583)	-0.166 (0.633)	-0.066 (0.597)	-0.352 (0.592)	-0.127 (0.584)	-0.02 (0.584)
Political risk index	0.011*** (0.004)	0.017*** (0.004)	0.02** (0.004)	0.016*** (0.004)	0.024*** (0.004)	0.017*** (0.004)	0.017*** (0.004)
Openness	-1.983*** (0.228)	-1.682*** (0.306)	-1.618*** (0.329)	-1.820*** (0.311)	-1.056*** (0.266)	-1.812*** (0.303)	-1.755*** (0.303)

	(1)	(2)	(3)	(4)	(5)	(6)	(7)
Financial stress index		0.078*** (0.0101)	0.093*** (0.0108)	0.082*** (0.0103)	0.120*** (0.00878)	0.078*** (0.0101)	0.077*** (0.0101)
U.S. 3-month Treasury Bill rate	2.128 (2.350)	5.001** (2.335)	11.67*** (2.398)	6.681*** (2.351)	10.62*** (2.269)	0.166 (1.142)	
Spread between U.S. 10-year and 3-month rate	3.833 (3.067)	7.281** (3.072)	13.31*** (3.252)	8.567*** (3.133)	14.90*** (3.213)		
U.S. 10-year government bond yield							4.212* (2.277)
Constant	4.242*** (0.252)	3.882*** (0.264)	3.567*** (0.284)	3.827*** (0.267)	3.329*** (0.251)	4.176*** (0.235)	3.952*** (0.260)
Number of observations	532	438	438	438	512	438	438
R^2	0.716	0.763	0.719	0.751	0.709	0.760	0.762
Number of countries	14	12	12	12	12	12	12

Source: Authors.

Note: The dependent variable is the log of the EMBI spreads. Standard errors are in parentheses. EMBI = Emerging Markets Bond Index.

*** Significant at the 1% level; ** significant at the 5% level; * significant at the 10% level.

coefficients are compared with the coefficients obtained with the fixed effects. The long-run relationship between the variables is significant

$\left(\dfrac{1}{N} \displaystyle\sum_{j=1}^{N} \phi_i \neq 0 \right)$, implying that the spread level cannot be explained only by

short-term variations (table 4.4).

For the PMG estimations, specification (2), containing all selected variables, shows several important differences with the fixed effects. First, the fundamental variables (the debt ratio and the current account ratio), the liquidity indicators (summing to a positive effect), and the political risk index are significant in the long run but not the short run. As expected, these variables determine the steady-state level of the sovereign bond spreads. The long-run coefficients of the 3-month U.S. Treasury Bill rate and the term spread between the 10-year U.S. bond and the 3-month Treasury Bill rate continue to be positive, but they are significant in specification (significant only in specifications (3)–(5), in which the liquidity variables are included one at a time. The long-run coefficient of the degree of openness is also significant in the long run (with a negative sign) only in specifications (3)–(5).

Second, openness and the financial stress index are the only variables whose short-term coefficients are significant in specification (2). Concerning openness, the results show interesting dynamics between the short and the long run. Although openness is associated with better economic performance and therefore lower sovereign spreads in the long run, it brings about substantial volatility in the short run, which puts pressure on the sovereign's financing conditions. The financial stress index is significant only in the short run. As suggested by the theoretical framework, it thus has no effect on the steady-state conditions, implying that the volatility experienced in stock market returns and the foreign exchange market has only a short-lived impact on sovereign spreads. The high error correction coefficient indicates that about 46 percent of the adjustment to the steady state takes place each period.

Overall, these model specifications point toward a strong long-term relationship between emerging market sovereign bond spreads and macroeconomic fundamentals such as debt and debt-related variables, trade openness, risk-free rates, and political risk. However, part of the variation in sovereign bond spreads—notably in the short run—seems to be explained by the financial health of the country, as proxied by the financial stress index. This effect likely reflects the fact that financial difficulties are assumed to increase the probability of default and, consequently, sovereign bond spreads. These results are consistent with findings in other studies, in particular Ferrucci (2003).

Concluding Remarks

This chapter analyzes the short- and long-term relationship between emerging market sovereign bond spreads and a set of macroeconomic and

Table 4.4 Pooled Mean Group Estimation

Coefficient	(1)	(2)	(3)	(4)	(5)	(6)	(7)
Long-term coefficient							
External debt/GDP	3.310***	2.793***	4.175***	2.380***	1.680**	3.490***	2.929***
	(0.360)	(0.476)	(0.514)	(0.596)	(0.681)	(0.403)	(0.414)
Short-term debt/reserves	−0.974***	−0.900***	0.481***			−1.142***	−0.870***
	(0.166)	(0.221)	(0.165)			(0.229)	(0.234)
Interest payments/reserves	6.252***	6.591***		3.620***		6.177***	6.289***
	(0.632)	(0.743)		(0.764)		(0.654)	(0.745)
Amortization/reserves	−1.267***	−1.465***			−1.417***	−1.241***	−1.279***
	(0.231)	(0.238)			(0.394)	(0.258)	(0.249)
Fiscal balance/GDP	3.677***	4.141***	3.059***	4.228***	6.314***	2.743***	3.393***
	(1.014)	(1.122)	(1.057)	(1.322)	(2.142)	(1.033)	(1.012)
Current account/GDP	−4.100***	−4.762***	−2.592**	−3.744***	−5.604***	−4.802***	−4.503***
	(0.925)	(1.102)	(1.172)	(1.272)	(2.092)	(0.991)	(1.035)
Political risk index	0.029***	0.029***	0.040***	0.033***	0.009	0.038***	0.026***
	(0.006)	(0.006)	(0.009)	(0.009)	(0.012)	(0.007)	(0.007)
Openness	−1.005**	−0.463	−1.889***	−1.931***	−2.007***	−0.793*	−1.003**
	(0.390)	(0.524)	(0.490)	(0.592)	(0.734)	(0.469)	(0.457)
Financial stress index		0.003	−0.001	−0.005	0.039	−0.013	−0.004
		(0.017)	(0.023)	(0.021)	(0.032)	(0.018)	(0.017)

(continued next page)

95

Table 4.4 (continued)

Coefficient	(1)	(2)	(3)	(4)	(5)	(6)	(7)
U.S. 3-month Treasury Bill rate	4.051 (3.620)	2.023 (3.800)	23.40*** (4.497)	23.16*** (4.541)	17.18** (7.451)	0.427 (1.797)	
Spread between U.S. 10-year and 3-month rate	8.157* (4.429)	7.045 (4.665)	16.71*** (6.311)	24.34*** (6.279)	24.72** (10.43)		
U.S. 10-year government bond rate							4.092 (3.941)
Error correction (phi)	-0.425*** (0.069)	-0.463*** (0.078)	-0.308*** (0.060)	-0.338*** (0.058)	-0.219*** (0.038)	-0.450*** (0.072)	-0.460*** (0.073)
Short-term coefficient							
External debt/GDP	2.097* (1.156)	2.248* (1.359)	1.634 (1.062)	2.540** (1.158)	1.493 (1.553)	2.307* (1.315)	1.515 (1.347)
Short-term debt/reserves	0.795 (0.667)	1.343* (0.757)	0.0458 (0.632)			1.626** (0.791)	1.521** (0.730)
Interest payments/reserves	-4.753 (4.288)	-8.726* (4.980)		-3.259 (3.662)		-9.115* (4.825)	-8.865* (5.114)
Amortization/reserves	0.795 (0.788)	1.345 (0.924)			1.292* (0.682)	1.185 (0.933)	1.302 (0.900)
Fiscal balance/GDP	-0.158 (0.472)	0.0174 (0.470)	0.802 (0.503)	0.693 (0.541)	-0.162 (0.387)	0.255 (0.435)	0.224 (0.470)

	(1)	(2)	(3)	(4)	(5)	(6)	(7)
Current account/GDP	1.825*	1.296	0.985	1.030	0.647	1.498*	1.181
	(1.091)	(1.208)	(1.201)	(1.251)	(0.813)	(0.886)	(1.289)
Political risk index	-0.008	-0.008	-0.012	-0.006	-0.002	-0.01*	-0.005
	(0.007)	(0.007)	(0.007)	(0.008)	(0.006)	(0.005)	(0.005)
Openness	1.288	1.457**	2.475***	2.603***	2.177**	1.908**	1.356
	(0.856)	(0.639)	(0.819)	(0.888)	(0.928)	(0.801)	(0.896)
Financial stress index		0.018***	0.024***	0.025***	0.024***	0.017***	0.018***
		(0.005)	(0.006)	(0.005)	(0.006)	(0.005)	(0.005)
U.S. 3-month Treasury Bill rate	-3.539	-3.320	-8.850**	-10.95***	-3.464	0.893	
	(3.606)	(4.474)	(3.781)	(4.147)	(2.863)	(2.956)	
Spread between U.S. 10-year and 3-month rate	-4.622**	-4.197	-5.755***	-7.413***	-4.273**		
	(1.909)	(2.948)	(2.154)	(2.462)	(1.941)		
U.S. 10-year government bond rate							-3.027
							(2.452)
Constant	1.279***	1.423***	0.630***	0.849***	1.167***	1.253***	1.546***
	(0.231)	(0.251)	(0.217)	(0.197)	(0.200)	(0.224)	(0.259)
Number of observations	517	425	425	425	499	425	425
Number of countries	14	12	12	12	12	12	12

Source: Authors.

Note: The dependent variable is the log of the EMBI spreads. Standard errors are in parentheses. EMBI = Emerging Markets Bond Index.

*** Significant at the 1% level; ** significant at the 5% level; * significant at the 10% level.

financial stress variables, using EMBI secondary market spreads. To determine the choice of variables, we introduce a framework that helps us form certain priors. We use a fixed-effects model and a dynamic model, the PMG estimation technique, which allows us to distinguish short- from long-term effects. We allow the short-run parameters to vary across countries, which is appropriate given the clustered short-term nature of the data. The results are satisfactory in terms of sign, significance, and explanatory power.

In particular, the regressions suggest that in the short run, financial volatility is a more important determinant of spreads than fundamental indicators. The short-term coefficient of the financial stress index appears to be highly significant in all estimations, while the short-term coefficients of fundamental variables are less robust. This is an innovative result that extends the findings of Mody (2009) and other researchers who use dummy variables for crisis periods to show the correlation between financial volatility and sovereign spreads.

Our findings confirm that in the long run, fundamentals are significant determinants of emerging market sovereign bond spreads. However, other factors, such as political instability, corruption, and asymmetry of information, may also affect the spread level, given their potential impact on the ability of governments to repay their bondholders. In this regard, we show that political risk is an important long-term determinant of sovereign bond spreads.

Notes

The views expressed in this chapter are those of the authors and should not be attributed to the International Monetary Fund, its Executive Board, or its management.

1. None of the countries included in the empirical analysis violated this condition during the period covered by the study.

2. We omitted some variables used in the literature. More complex models include external competitiveness indicators, such as exchange rates (Bordo, Meissner, and Weidenmier 2009; McGee 2005), which affect trade activity and fiscal sustainability. Our model includes a trade-related indicator—trade, defined as the ratio of the sum of exports and imports and GDP—as a proxy for competitiveness. Because many indebted emerging market economies are commodity exporters, other studies use an index of commodity prices. We approximate this activity by openness and GDP.

3. Fisher-type unit root tests (Dickey-Fuller and Phillips-Perron), which are appropriate for unbalanced panel data, reject the unit root hypothesis at the 5 percent level for all variables. Pesaran, Shin, and Smith (1999) show that consistency and asymptotic normality of the PMG estimator are established under standard conditions given stationarity.

References

Balakrishnan, R., S. Danninger, S. Elekdag, and I. Tytell. 2009. "The Transmission of Financial Stress from Advanced to Emerging Economies." IMF Working Paper 09/133, International Monetary Fund, Washington, DC.

Baldacci, E., S. Gupta, and A. Mati. 2008. "Is It (Still) Mostly Fiscal? Determinants of Sovereign Spreads in Emerging Markets." IMF Working Paper 08/259, International Monetary Fund, Washington, DC.

Baltagi, H. B., and J. M. Griffin. 1997. "Pooled Estimators vs. Their Heterogeneous Counterparts in the Context of Dynamic Demand for Gasoline." *Journal of Econometrics* 77 (2): 303–27.

Bordo, M. D., C. M. Meissner, and M. D. Weidenmier. 2009. "Identifying the Effects of an Exchange Rate Depreciation on Country Risk: Evidence from a Natural Experiment." *Journal of International Money and Finance* 28 (6): 1022–44.

Boyd, D., and R. Smith. 2000. *Some Econometric Issues in Measuring the Monetary Transmission Mechanism, with an Application to Developing Countries.* Birkbeck College Discussion Paper in Economics 15, University of London.

Caceres, C., V. Guzzo, and M. Segoviano. 2010. "Sovereign Spreads: Global Risk Aversion, Contagion or Fundamentals?" IMF Working Paper 10/120, International Monetary Fund, Washington, DC.

Dailami, M., P. R. Masson, and J. J. Padou. 2008. "Global Monetary Conditions versus Country-Specific Factors in the Determination of Emerging Market Debt Spreads." *Journal of International Money and Finance* 27 (8): 1325–36.

Dell'Ariccia, G., I. Goedde, and J. Zettelmeyer. 2000. "Moral Hazard in International Crisis Lending: A Test." IMF Working Paper 02/181, International Monetary Fund, Washington, DC.

Ebner, A. 2009. "An Empirical Analysis on the Determinants of CEE Government Bond Spreads." *Emerging Market Review* 10 (2009): 97–121.

The Economist Intelligence Unit. 2009. Country Risk Model (various issues). London. https://eiu.bvdep.com/version-2010728/cgi/template.dll?product=105&user=ipaddress.

Eichengreen, B., and A. Mody. 1998. "What Explains Changing Spreads on EM Debt: Fundamentals or Market Sentiment?" NBER Working Paper 6408, National Bureau of Economic Research, Cambridge, MA.

Ferrucci, G. 2003. "Empirical Determinants of Emerging Market Economies' Sovereign Bond Spreads." Bank of England Working Paper 205, London.

Goldman Sachs. 2000. "A New Framework for Assessing Fair Value in EMs' Hard Currency Debt." Global Economics Paper 45, New York.

IMF (International Monetary Fund). 2009a. *Global Development Statistics.* Washington, DC: International Monetary Fund.

————. 2009b. *International Financial Statistics.* Washington, DC: International Monetary Fund.

————. 2009c. *World Economic Outlook.* Washington, DC: International Monetary Fund.

Kamin, S. B., and K. Kleist. 1999. "The Evolution and Determinants of EM Credit Spreads in the 1990s." International Finance Discussion Paper 653, Bank for International Settlements, Basel.

McGee, C. D. 2005. "Sovereign Bond Market with Political Risk and Moral Hazard." *International Review of Economics & Finance* 16 (2): 186–201.

Min, H. G. 1998. "Determinants of EM Bond Spread: Do Economic Fundamentals Matter?" World Bank Working Paper in International Economics, Trade, and Capital Flows 1899, Washington, DC.

Mody, A. 2009. "From Bear Stearns to Anglo Irish: How Eurozone Sovereign Bond Spreads Related to Financial Sector Vulnerability." IMF Working Paper 09/108, International Monetary Fund, Washington, DC.

Pesaran, M. H., Y. Shin, and R. P. Smith. 1995. "Estimating Long-Run Relationships from Dynamic Heterogeneous Panels." *Journal of Econometrics* 68 (1):
79–113.

———. 1999. *Pooled Mean Group Estimation of Dynamic Heterogeneous
Panels*. ESE Discussion Paper, Edinburgh School of Economics, University of
Edinburgh.

World Bank. 2009. *Global Development Finance*. Washington, DC: World Bank.

5

Sovereign Debt Distress and Corporate Spillover Impacts

Mansoor Dailami

At a time when rising sovereign credit risk in highly indebted developed economies represents a major source of policy concern and market anxiety, drawing attention to the corporate debt problems that may loom ahead is not only a call for a more systematic approach to debt management. It is also an opportunity to highlight the hidden dynamics between sovereign and corporate debt that could create a negative feedback loop if investors lose confidence in the government's ability to use public finances to stabilize the economy or provide a safety net for corporations in distress. Although such sovereign credit events are rare, with global financial markets still unsettled and public finances stretched to the limit in many countries, their likelihood is rising, even in countries with seemingly manageable external debt profiles. Under such circumstances, markets' assessment of public and private credit risk takes on a completely different dynamic than during normal times, when markets' belief in a government's power of taxation and spending provides a cushion against macroeconomic shocks. Understanding such market dynamics is thus crucial in formulating mitigating policy support measures before investor fear sets in that could have adverse consequences for private firms' access to foreign capital.

This chapter investigates the degree to which heightened perceptions of sovereign default risk during times of market turmoil—gauged by the widening of bond market spreads beyond a critical threshold—influence the determination of corporate bond yield spreads in emerging markets. Using a new database that covers nearly every emerging market corporate and sovereign entity that issued bonds on global markets between 1995 and 2009 (4,441 transactions, amounting to $1.46 trillion), I develop an empirical methodology to analyze whether sovereign risk is priced into corporate bond spreads, controlling for specific bond attributes and common global risk factors. I model emerging corporate bond spreads as incorporating three risk premiums: corporate default, home-country sovereign debt distress, and compensation for the fact that emerging bond market spreads vary systematically with global business cycles and with global financial market conditions.

Covering 59 countries and encompassing virtually all major emerging market crises of the past two decades,[1] the data set is sufficiently rich to allow a more rigorous investigation of the link between sovereign and corporate credit risk than has been possible to date. The unique nature of each crisis hitting emerging markets over the past two decades provides an additional degree of variance that allows identification of underlying economic mechanisms and channels. A common string running through all of these episodes has been intense risk aversion and the consequent widening of bond spreads as investors have sold off emerging market assets in response to perceived local or global risk factors.

The rest of the chapter is organized as follows. The next section highlights the growing importance of corporate debt in the external financial profile of emerging market economies and provides estimates of corporate debt refinancing coming due in the next few years. The following section presents a two-period model of corporate bond price valuation in the presence of sovereign risk to motivate the empirical analysis and reports the main results and findings. The last section concludes with a discussion of policy recommendations and key issues warranting future research and attention.

The Growing Importance of Emerging Market Corporate Debt

The increasing engagement of corporations from developing countries in global investment and finance has been a defining feature of financing of development in the first decade of the 21st century. As sovereign demand for external financing declined in the majority of developing countries in the years leading up to the crisis of 2008–09, market attention shifted to the corporate sector, which offered a new generation of emerging market credit and equity products. In many respects, the market for emerging market credit has shifted toward the corporate sector (encompassing both private and public entities, such as state-owned banks and public enterprises), with implications for access to finance, debt sustainability, and long-term investment and growth. In the decade leading up to the 2008–09 crisis, the emerging market corporate bond market evolved into a robust, versatile, and active market offering considerable foreign funding opportunities across major currencies and jurisdictions to many blue-chip companies based in Latin America, Asia, and the Middle East. From 2002 to the end of 2007, 727 privately owned emerging market companies tapped international bond markets to raise a total of $336.7 billion of foreign debt capital. Easy financing conditions also facilitated access to the international syndicated loan market, with 1,584 emerging market private firms going to overseas markets to raise a total of $640.4 billion of foreign-currency credit through 2,595 loans. Total foreign capital raised through bonds and syndicated loans during this period amounted to $977 billion, up from $222 billion between 1999 and 2001 (figure 5.1). Many companies borrowed primarily to finance oil and gas or banking operations or to fund aggressive cross-border merger and acquisition (M&A) deals. Multinational companies based in emerging markets undertook more than 857 cross-border acquisition deals worth $107 billion in 2008, up from 239 such deals in 2000 worth $12 billion (Dailami 2010).

Private sector borrowing in emerging markets grew during 2002–07 at a much faster pace than public sector borrowing, surging to account

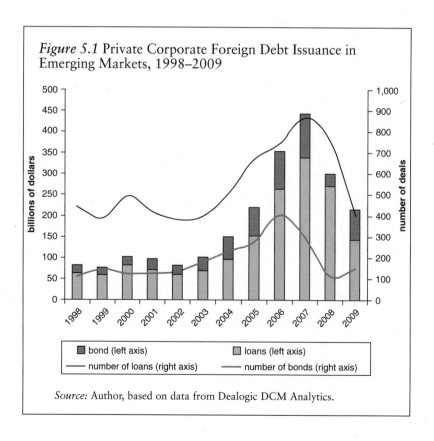

Figure 5.1 Private Corporate Foreign Debt Issuance in Emerging Markets, 1998–2009

Source: Author, based on data from Dealogic DCM Analytics.

for 69 percent of total emerging market borrowings by 2007 (figures 5.2 and 5.3). As emerging market corporate borrowers are predominantly large private sector firms in the banking, infrastructure, and mining industries with high growth potential, their access to overseas markets not only underpins long-term growth and competitiveness, it also affords policy makers greater scope to allocate domestic resources to high-priority areas, such as investments in rural areas or small businesses, without crowding out the corporate sector.

Emerging market private firms' large exposure to foreign-currency debt, built up mostly during the boom years of 2002–07, has important implications for both debt sustainability and the design of international institutional arrangements for corporate debt restructuring and liability management. For much of the postwar era, sovereign financing was the quintessential feature of emerging market finance, generating a body of market practice, credit risk assessment standards, international institutional arrangements for debt restructuring and dispute resolution, and national and international policy and regulatory concerns. The shift in the market pattern from public to private debt in emerging market finance will inevitably bring to the fore a new set of policy challenges, as well as the need to develop appropriate metrics to measure and evaluate private corporate risk exposure and default probability. At the same time, several

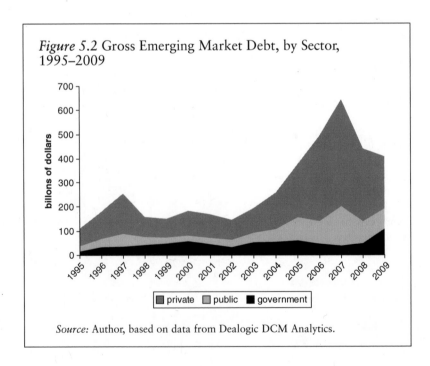

Figure 5.2 Gross Emerging Market Debt, by Sector, 1995–2009

Source: Author, based on data from Dealogic DCM Analytics.

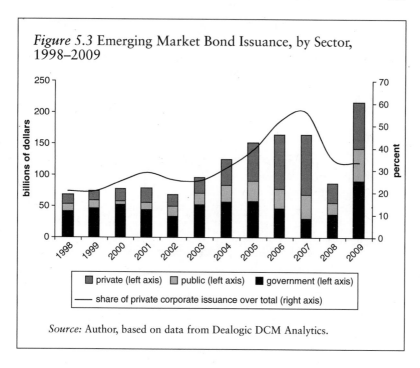

Figure 5.3 Emerging Market Bond Issuance, by Sector, 1998–2009

Legend:
- private (left axis)
- public (left axis)
- government (left axis)
- share of private corporate issuance over total (right axis)

Source: Author, based on data from Dealogic DCM Analytics.

distinctive features of the 2008–09 financial crisis—the severity of the global business downturn, the scale of banks' credit contraction, the precipitous drop in local equity markets, and the global nature of the crisis— could imply a more arduous and extended debt-restructuring cycle than was experienced following the 1997–98 East Asian crisis.

Effect of the Crisis on the Emerging Market Corporate Sector

Having been hard hit by the credit crunch and global recession, can the emerging market corporate sector regain its past momentum to become the dominant source of issuance in global bond markets? In countries with economies battered by a dramatic decline in exports and slumping local equity markets where authorities were pursuing tight domestic monetary policy while simultaneously allowing local currencies to depreciate to fend off external shocks, the corporate sector has borne the combined impacts of the global financial crisis and recession since 2008. In these countries, the financial crisis hit the emerging market corporate sector hard. The share of private corporate sector debt in total emerging market bond issuance that had peaked at 76 percent in the second quarter of 2007 fell to about 14 percent in the first quarter of 2009. In contrast, the share of sovereign debt issuance has increased sharply since the crisis. Relative to spreads on emerging market sovereign bonds, spreads on foreign-currency emerging market corporate bonds spiked to much higher levels at the outset of the crisis and remained much wider even after March 2009, when spreads on sovereign debt began to narrow. In the fourth quarter of 2008, emerging market corporations were virtually locked out of international bond markets (figure 5.4).

Refinancing Needs

Corporations based in emerging markets now face the challenge of servicing their substantial debt obligations in an environment of sluggish global growth, high currency volatility, shrinking bank credit, and intensified competition from sovereign borrowers in advanced economies. Of the key drivers of emerging market corporate bond issuance volume in the next few years, the need to refinance a large volume of foreign-currency debt coming due will be the strongest. About $892 billion of emerging market corporate debt is due to mature in the bond and bank loan markets between 2010 and 2013, of which about 80 percent originated from the syndicated loan market.

Given the fragility of the international banking industry, a full rollover of emerging market bank loans seems unlikely, leaving bond markets to absorb a portion of such loans. Several factors—including rating status, other available financing options (including those in equity markets), and

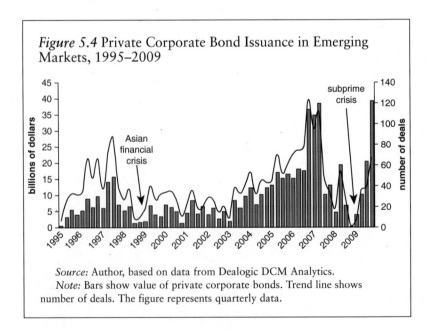

Figure 5.4 Private Corporate Bond Issuance in Emerging Markets, 1995–2009

Source: Author, based on data from Dealogic DCM Analytics.
Note: Bars show value of private corporate bonds. Trend line shows number of deals. The figure represents quarterly data.

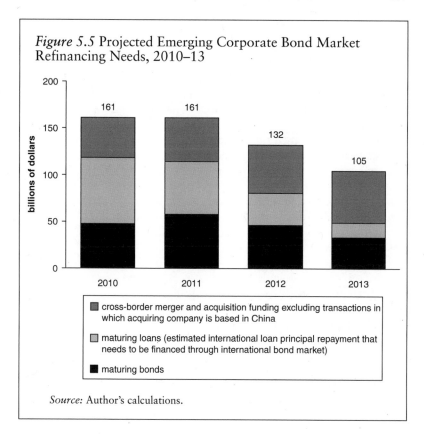

Figure 5.5 Projected Emerging Corporate Bond Market Refinancing Needs, 2010–13

Source: Author's calculations.

loan-specific characteristics and covenant clauses—will dictate the volume of maturing loans that makes its way into bond markets. Assuming 25 percent of private corporate borrowers decide to refinance in bond markets, issuance volumes originating from this source would be on the order of $71 billion in 2010, $57 billion in 2011, and $34 billion in 2012.

Pursuit of cross-border M&A as part of multinational companies' growth and expansion strategies is also expected to contribute to the rebound in emerging market corporate bond issuance in the coming years. Detailed data on the payments of M&A deals involving emerging market companies are not disclosed, but such deals can be funded through cash, share swaps, or credit. It can be assumed that firms in emerging markets, with the major exception of state-owned Chinese firms, rely on bond markets to fund their transactions. The estimated amount of new issuances arising from demand for cross-border M&A is projected to be $43 billion in 2010, $47 billion in 2011, and $52 billion in 2012 (figure 5.5).

Determinants of Emerging Market Corporate Debt Spreads in the Presence of Sovereign Risk

Standard corporate bond valuation models of structural and reduced-form types dominate the literature in corporate finance in advanced countries (see, for example, Black and Cox 1976; Duffie and Singleton 1999; Jarrow and Turnbull 1995; Longstaff and Schwartz 1995; Merton 1974). These models treat sovereign debt as a risk-free asset that is traded in capital markets based on interest rate risks rather than credit risks. Accordingly, corporate bond prices depend on idiosyncratic risk factors specific to the issuing company, with public debt playing an indirect role to the extent that it is believed to affect the term structure of interest rates. With concerns over sovereign creditworthiness assumed away, there was, thus, little need to pay attention to or explicitly model the link between sovereign and corporate credit risk in the pricing of corporate bonds in advanced countries.

In emerging markets—as in highly indebted advanced countries—the question of how sovereign credit risk affects corporate sector borrowing in international markets commands explicit attention, as sovereign credit risk has been an inherent characteristic feature of the asset class that has affected how investors have come to conduct trade and form views on market developments. From its inception in the early 1990s, the emerging sovereign bond market has been viewed and priced as a risky asset, comparable in many ways to the U.S. high-yield bond asset class. The market's advent, in the early 1990s, is traced to the conversion of problem bank loans into collateralized marketable bond instruments under the Brady plan. Thus, a key priority in research on the determinants of corporate credit spreads in emerging markets is the question of how sovereign risk perceptions are likely to shape the terms of corporate access to international capital markets.

Higher sovereign credit risk spills over to the corporate side through three channels. The first is the possibility of reduced liquidity, as growing market concerns about a country's sovereign debt lead to a drop in risk appetite across all debt issuers in a country. In turn, investors' perception of greater systemic sovereign risk translates into higher risk premiums, which must be added to the price of corporate securities offered on overseas markets. Because the pricing of corporate bonds is typically based on the sovereign curve and sovereign debt bears primarily macroeconomic risks, a structural link exists between sovereign and corporate bonds. This link is reinforced in emerging market economies by limited liquidity in the emerging market asset class in general and in corporate assets in particular. Furthermore, this mechanism is likely to operate in emerging markets with large corporate external debt refinancing needs. It is particularly likely among borrowing companies refinancing from the international banking market, where despite significant easing since the collapse of Lehman

Brothers in September 2008, liquidity conditions remain highly vulnerable to bank balance sheet and funding pressures. With as much as $951 billion of emerging market corporate debt maturing over 2010–14, the risk posed by reduced liquidity is serious and warrants attention, especially in Europe, whose banks hold the lion's share of emerging market corporate external debt.

The second mechanism through which sovereign credit risk can spill over to the corporate side relates to fiscal space and the fact that highly indebted governments have less scope to use fiscal policy to provide a cushion for corporate borrowers to fall back on in an environment of constrained credit. In practice, this may mean that debt-distressed governments are limited in their ability to offer the guarantees that are generally required for major corporate debt restructurings.[2]

A third mechanism is fiscal adjustment in countries with high levels of government debt, which can lead to substantial spillover effects from sovereign to corporate debt, as tight fiscal policy can have negative real economy consequences that adversely affect corporate earnings and profitability. Within the corporate sector, banking is most susceptible to sovereign stress, as banks' funding costs rise with sovereign spreads because of the perception that domestic banks hold a large volume of government securities and that government guarantees are worth less in an environment of sovereign stress.

The fact that most firms in emerging markets tapping international debt markets are large and relatively highly leveraged raises the possibility that corporate debt distress could also spill over to the sovereign side, as (financial and nonfinancial) corporations in distress may require government support, either directly or indirectly, through government involvement in the process of corporate debt restructuring and workouts. Although corporate default in emerging economies was relatively contained during the financial crisis, the large volume of external corporate debt outstanding and its complex profile remain a source of worry and concern.

Analytical Framework

To illustrate how sovereign risk can affect the corporate bond market, I begin with a highly simplified model of corporate bond price valuation in a two-period model that incorporates both corporate and sovereign risk. The approach is in the spirit of the Merton (1974) structural model, with the added complexity that the firm's cash flows are contingent not only on its own investment in real assets but also on the financial health of its home country government. In the presence of sovereign risk, investors' assessment of the firm's securities depends on both the firm's specific factors and the probability that the sovereign runs into financial problems that bear on the firm's ability and capacity to service its debt obligations in a timely manner.

Consider a firm issuing a bond with a face value of F dollars at time $t = 0$ to finance a project with a random cash flow of X dollars (in foreign-currency equivalence) to be realized at time 1. I define X to include the liquidation value of assets net of operating costs. The debt contract is a fixed obligation that promises to pay D (which includes interest and principal) at time $t = 1$. To incorporate sovereign risk, I define a random variable Z, which takes, for simplicity, two values: 0 with probability p, indicating that the sovereign is in financial distress, and 1 with probability $1 - p$, indicating that the sovereign is solvent. In the case of sovereign distress, the firm's ability to service its debt obligation in a timely manner is adversely affected by a combination of factors—an economywide downturn, the tightening of external liquidity conditions, exchange rate depreciation or controls—that can translate into a downward shift in the firm's cash flow distribution.

With this setup, the payoff to bond holders, $\tilde{Y}$, will be a function of both sovereign and corporate risks:

$$\tilde{Y} = g(\tilde{X}, D, \tilde{Z}) = \begin{cases} \min(D, \tilde{X}) \, if \ Z = 1 \\ \alpha \min(D, \tilde{X}) \, if \ Z = 0, \end{cases} \tag{5.1}$$

where $0 < \alpha \le 1$, and $\min(D, \tilde{X}) = \begin{cases} D \ if \ \tilde{X} \ge D \\ \tilde{X} \ if \ \tilde{X} < D. \end{cases}$ $\tag{5.2}$

In the general case, in which X (project cash flow) and Z are not independent, conditional distributions are not identical. Furthermore, I assume that the conditional distributions of $\tilde{X}$ given $\tilde{Z}$ are normal, with means μ_1, μ_2 and variances σ_1^2, σ_2^2. Thus, the expected return to bondholders can be expressed as follows:

$$E(\tilde{Y}) = p\alpha \left\{ \int_0^D x f_1(x|z = 0) dx + D \int_D^\infty f_1(x|z = 0) dx \right\}$$
$$+ (1 - p) \left\{ \int_0^D x f_2(x|z = 1) dx + D \int_D^\infty f_2(x|z = 1) dx \right\},$$
$$\tag{5.3}$$

where $f_1(x)$ and $f_2(x)$ are the conditional density probability functions of $\tilde{X}$ under the two scenarios of $Z = 0$ and $Z = 1$. Equation (5.3) describes the expected value of the return to bond holders as a weighted average of the expected values calculated separately for the cases in which the government is or is not in distress, with the weights reflecting the respective probabilities of such events.

Under the assumption that creditors are risk neutral, the market price of corporate debt V is the present value of $E(\tilde{Y})$, discounted at the international risk-free rate of interest, r:

$$V = \frac{E(\tilde{Y})}{1 + r}. \tag{5.4}$$

To assess how corporate bond prices depend on sovereign default risk, I simulate equation (5.4) for different parameter values (see figure 5.6). I assume that the share of foreign currency loan paid back in the case of country default (α) is 60 percent, that the corporate cash flow under the two scenarios of whether the government is in financial distress or not follows conditional normal distribution displayed in figure 5.7, and that the standard deviation is 25 percent and increases by 30 percent if the country defaults. The payment obligation was obtained by applying an interest rate of 7.5 percent to the debt face value of 100. Raising the probability of sovereign default from 2.8 percent (corresponding to a credit default swap spread of 120 basis points) to 23.8 percent (corresponding to a credit default swap spread of 820 basis points) results in a 9 percent decrease in the corporate bond price.

Econometric Methodology and Specification

When pricing emerging market bond securities issued internationally, investors take into account many risk factors. They generally make a distinction between bonds issued by public sector entities (government and government-owned companies) and those offered by private borrowers. They also take into account factors such as the state of the home country macroeconomy, global financial market conditions, and bond- and

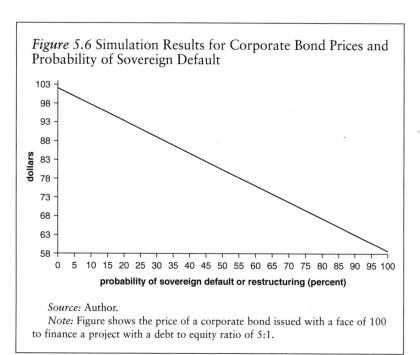

Figure 5.6 Simulation Results for Corporate Bond Prices and Probability of Sovereign Default

Source: Author.

Note: Figure shows the price of a corporate bond issued with a face of 100 to finance a project with a debt to equity ratio of 5:1.

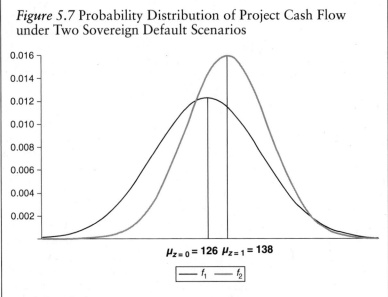

Figure 5.7 Probability Distribution of Project Cash Flow under Two Sovereign Default Scenarios

$\mu_{z=0} = 126$ $\mu_{z=1} = 138$

— f_1 — f_2

Source: Author.
Note: f_1 = conditional density probability distribution of corporate cash flow when $z = 0$, which refers to the government's being in financial distress; f_2 = conditional density probability distribution of corporate cash flow when $z = 1$, which refers to the government's being solvent.

firm-specific factors (maturity, currency of denomination, jurisdiction, covenants, sector, and the fact that corporate ratings are often subject to sovereign ceilings). Reflecting the influence of such factors, investors typically attach a higher risk premium to private than public bond instruments.

Formally, the analysis of the relationship between sovereign and corporate risk centers on the following set of regressions specifying sovereign and corporate bond spreads at issuance as a function of offering terms; currency of denomination; industry; and various macroeconomic, financial, and institutional control variables for each issuer's home country, as well as global financial and business cycle conditions. Sovereign spreads are given by

$$Y_{s,ijt} = \alpha_{s,j} + \beta'_s X_{jt} + \psi'_s V_t + \gamma'_s Z_i. \tag{5.5}$$

Corporate spreads are given by the equation

$$Y_{c,ijt} = \alpha_{c,j} + \beta'_c X_{jt} + \psi'_c V_t + \gamma'_c Z_i + \delta'_c W, \tag{5.6}$$

where the subscripts s and c refer to sovereign and corporate; ijt refers to bond i issued in country j at time t; X_{jt} denotes systematic (macroeconomic) factors; V_t denotes global risk factors; Z_i denotes bond-specific features; and W denotes firm-specific characteristics.

The econometric analysis of correlation risk between emerging market private corporate borrowers and their home sovereigns is based on a sample of 4,441 bond issuances denominated in U.S. dollars or euros offered by the government, public corporations, and private corporations in 59 emerging economies between 1995 and 2009.[3] The sample represents a wide cross-section of issues by country, industry, and bond attributes, including maturity, amount, coupon, rating, and applicable law and jurisdiction (table 5.1). Total capital raised amounted to $1.4 trillion, 80 percent of it in dollar-denominated bonds and the rest in euro-denominated bonds. Sovereign bonds (bonds issued by governments, government agencies, and public corporations whose payments are guaranteed explicitly by governments) account for 60 percent of total issuance volume but only 40 percent of deals, reflecting their much larger deal size.

Several other differences between emerging market sovereign and private corporate bonds deserve attention. Sovereign bonds tend to be larger, carry lower at-issue spreads, and have longer maturities than private corporate bonds, for two main reasons. First, corporate entities face higher information barriers and greater market constraints than sovereigns, which benefit from membership in multilateral financial institutions and from the state-centric nature of the international economic order. Second, even locally creditworthy firms may be constrained by a variety of factors. Corporate ratings are often subject to sovereign ceilings, corporate assets are not easily amenable to collateralization in international debt markets, swap markets for credit derivatives are better developed and more liquid for emerging sovereigns than for corporates, and private corporate borrowers' relations and interactions with foreign creditors are shaped largely by economic considerations whereas sovereigns' relations are driven by a mix of politics and economics.[4]

Estimation Results

I begin by estimating equations (5.5) and (5.6) separately, in order to establish empirically the structural differences between private and sovereign bond markets in emerging market economies. The dependent variable in both sets of equations is the at-issue spread, quoted in basis points and measured as the offering spread over the yield of a maturity-matched U.S. Treasury security or, in the case of a euro issue, a comparable German Bunds obligation. The primary data sources on spreads at issuance are Dealogic DCM Analytics and Bloomberg; I filled in data gaps by estimating spreads at issuance, using information available on yield to maturity or coupon (1,622 transactions). Using offerings' at-issue bond yield spreads has the advantage of better reflecting the state of investors' sentiment and

Table 5.1 Summary Statistics for Emerging Market Sovereign and Corporate Bonds Issued, 1995–2009

Issuer	Number of issuances	Total volume raised (US$ billions)	In dollars	In euros	Average amount (US$ millions)	Average spread (basis points)	Average maturity (years)	Average rating
Sovereign	1,711	866.6	649.2	217.4	506.5	283.5	9.1	BBB–
Government	949	577.9	410.2	167.7	608.9	339.9	9.8	BB+
Public corporation	762	288.7	239	49.7	378.9	213.3	7.2	BBB+
Private corporation	2,730	596.7	537	59.6	218.6	310.7	6.5	BBB–
Total	4,441	1,463.3	1,186.3	277	329.5	300.2	7.3	BBB–

Source: Author.

views; it has the drawback of introducing the problem of endogeneity of issuance timing—that is, in bad times, borrowers may decide to postpone or cancel issuance. A borrower's decision to come to the market to raise capital is rarely an accident of fate; it is typically the product of a deliberate process of balancing the costs and benefits involved. Success in raising capital depends on an array of factors, including the deal structure, distribution, marketing, jurisdiction and governing law, and the timing of coming to the market. Getting each of these factors right is important, because there are considerable reputational costs associated with an unfavorable market reaction, as illustrated by the drying up of emerging market debt issuance in the fourth quarter of 2008.

To capture common local and global systematic risk factors, I include data on the macroeconomic, institutional, and financial market development of each issuer's home country, along with data on international interest rates, which I match by month, quarter, or year with the issue from a variety of sources. I also control for the state of global investor sentiment to account for common shocks affecting both private and public bond markets. I use the bond issuers' general industry group, as defined by Dialogic DCM Analytics, to control for the sector. The results are reported in tables 5.2 and 5.3.

Table 5.2 Determinants of Emerging Market Sovereign Bond Spreads

Variable	(1)	(2)	(3)
Local macroeconomic variables			
GDP growth rate	−8.34	−7.19	−7.56
	(0.000)***	(0.000)***	(0.000)***
GDP per capita	−4.82	−3.44	−4.50
	(0.000)***	(0.002)***	(0.000)***
Inflation	131.59	137.73	140.15
	(0.010)***	(0.007)***	(0.005)***
Private credit/GDP	−0.61	−0.49	−0.51
	(0.167)	(0.266)	(0.248)
Fiscal balance/GDP	−1.08	−2.39	−1.36
	(0.493)	(0.132)	(0.382)
Exports/GDP	1.08	1.84	1.42
	(0.169)	(0.019)**	(0.069)*
Foreign bank claims/GDP	1.45	1.50	1.36
	(0.066)*	(0.058)*	(0.083)*

(continued next page)

Table 5.2 (continued)

Variable	(1)	(2)	(3)
Country credit risk rating index	15.55 (0.000)***	15.87 (0.000)***	15.28 (0.000)***
Country financial crisis dummy			80.73 (0.000)***
Global factors			
U.S. 10-year Treasury bond yield (basis points)	−0.20 (0.003)***	−0.16 (0.018)**	−0.18 (0.005)***
U.S. 10-year Treasury-bond yield minus U.S. 2-year Treasury-bond yield (percent)	17.79 (0.001)***	15.30 (0.007)***	17.82 (0.001)***
Volatility[a]	42.64 (0.000)***		38.76 (0.000)***
World industrial production index (percentage year-on-year growth)		−9.487 (0.000)***	
Bond attributes			
Euro-denominated bond	−6.05 (0.576)	−6.98 (0.519)	−6.96 (0.515)
Log (maturity)	−4.73 (0.463)	−6.39 (0.320)	−2.90 (0.650)
Log (value)	−6.94 (0.108)	−7.81 (0.070)*	−5.60 (0.190)
Floating rate notes	−94.10 (0.000)***	−95.66 (0.000)***	−93.13 (0.000)***
Guarantee	22.39 (0.106)	15.41 (0.266)	25.82 (0.060)*
Eurobond	0.63 (0.952)	1.92 (0.855)	0.24 (0.982)
Rule 144A	−6.44 (0.523)	−3.09 (0.760)	−6.50 (0.515)
Nonnegative pledge issuer	10.57 (0.211)	11.99 (0.158)	10.73 (0.199)
Bond rating at launch	13.87 (0.000)***	13.54 (0.000)***	14.02 (0.000)***

Table 5.2 *(continued)*

Variable	(1)	(2)	(3)
Number of observations	1,087	1,087	1,087
R-squared	0.71	0.71	0.72

Source: Author.

Note: Figures in parentheses are *p*-values. Country effects are not reported.

a. The volatility indicator is derived from a common factor analysis of several variables: VIX to measure equity market volatility; volatility of major currencies exchange rates; volatility of commodity price indices (agricultural, energy, and industrial metals); and TED spreads, as described in Dailami and Masson (2009).

*** Significant at the 1% level; ** significant at the 5% level; * significant at the 10% level.

Table 5.3 Determinants of Emerging Market Private Corporate Bond Spreads

Variable	(1)	(2)	(3)
Local macroeconomic variables			
GDP growth rate	−11.34	−8.73	−10.48
	(0.000)***	(0.000)***	(0.000)***
GDP per capita	−0.68	0.60	−0.39
	(0.581)	(0.629)	(0.752)
Inflation	199.40	213.02	200.96
	(0.016)**	(0.010)**	(0.015)**
Private credit/GDP	0.00	−0.06	−0.01
	(0.994)	(0.920)	(0.983)
Fiscal balance/GDP	−0.65	−2.65	−1.10
	(0.725)	(0.158)	(0.554)
Exports/GDP	2.02	2.54	2.07
	(0.045)**	(0.012)**	(0.040)**
Foreign bank claims/GDP	1.02	1.47	1.04
	(0.353)	(0.179)	(0.342)
Country credit risk rating index	17.89	16.06	17.32
	(0.000)***	(0.000)***	(0.000)***
Country financial crisis dummy			58.8410
			(0.004)***
Global factors			
U.S. 10-year Treasury-bond yield (basis points)	−0.29	−0.26	−0.31
	(0.000)***	(0.002)***	(0.000)***

(continued next page)

Table 5.3 (continued)

Variable	(1)	(2)	(3)
U.S. 10-year Treasury-bond yield minus 2-year Treasury-bond yield (percent)	24.03 (0.001)***	25.80 (0.000)***	23.41 (0.001)***
Volatility[a]	43.79 (0.000)***		42.05 (0.000)***
World industrial production index (percentage year-on-year growth)		−11.00 (0.000)***	
Bond attributes			
Euro-denominated bond	−15.51 (0.355)	−17.60 (0.294)	−15.91 (0.341)
Log (maturity)	8.81 (0.158)	8.39 (0.179)	9.13 (0.143)
Log (value)	−31.52 (0.000)***	−32.25 (0.000)***	−31.25 (0.000)***
Floating rate notes	−114.39 (0.000)***	−116.15 (0.000)***	−112.26 (0.000)***
Guarantee	17.53 (0.090)*	18.85 (0.069)*	17.52 (0.090)*
Eurobond	−0.29 (0.981)	4.30 (0.727)	1.86 (0.880)
Rule 144A	33.19 (0.001)***	35.36 (0.000)***	34.02 (0.001)***
Nonnegative pledge issuer	35.05 (0.000)***	36.14 (0.000)***	34.74 (0.000)***
Bond rating at launch	26.02 (0.000)***	26.12 (0.000)***	26.65 (0.000)***
Sector			
Finance	−34.75 (0.003)***	−32.57 (0.005)***	−35.21 (0.002)***
Oil and gas	−52.54 (0.003)***	−56.29 (0.001)***	−54.30 (0.002)***
Mining	−90.20 (0.003)***	−99.04 (0.001)***	−87.77 (0.004)***
Utility and energy	−75.03 (0.003)***	−68.22 (0.007)***	−72.33 (0.004)***

Table 5.3 (continued)

Variable	(1)	(2)	(3)
Number of observations	1,427	1,427	1,427
R-squared	0.65	0.64	0.65

Source: Author.
Note: Figures in parentheses are *p*-values. Country effects are not reported.
   a. The volatility indicator is derived from a common factor analysis of several variables: VIX to measure equity market volatility; volatility of major currencies exchange rates; volatility of commodity price indices (agricultural, energy, and industrial metals); and TED spreads, as described in Dailami and Masson (2009).
   *** Significant at the 1% level; ** significant at the 5% level; * significant at the 10% level.

The results confirm the view that the emerging sovereign bond market is different from the private corporate market in many respects that go beyond differences in bond attributes such as size, maturity, currency of denomination, and ratings. Controlling for such attributes, sovereign bonds are more responsive to changes in local macroeconomic conditions than private corporate bonds. This result is consistent with the argument of Dittmer and Yuan (2008) that sovereign bonds bear only macroeconomic risks whereas corporate bonds are driven by both macroeconomic and firm-specific risk factors.

The results reported in table 5.3 suggest the importance of bond-specific characteristics, domestic macroeconomic factors, and global risk factors to the price of emerging market corporate bonds. First, local macroeconomic factors affect investors' perceptions largely through their assessment of corporate profitability and cash flows, which depend on local economic conditions such as growth performance, inflation, degree of trade openness, and access to local finance. Of particular interest is the role of domestic growth on foreign investors' perception of corporate risk. The estimation results reveal that investors attach considerable importance to prospects for economic growth in the home country of companies whose securities they are considering purchasing. In contrast, inflation in the home country increases bond spreads by making the issuer's domestic operations more risky.

Second, emerging private firms based in countries with a well-developed banking system (that is, a high ratio of private credit to GDP) pay significantly less to issue debt. These results confirm anecdotal evidence and previous findings that local financial development plays a major role in facilitating access to global capital markets for emerging market firms.

Third, the level of economic development, measured by per capita income, is of the right sign, indicating that countries with greater economic development pay less for foreign capital. One possible explanation for this result is that it is possible that per capita income may serve as a proxy for a country's institutional development and related corporate governance and transparency indicators. All indicators of global factors are statistically significant and of the right sign.

Spillover Impacts from the Sovereign to the Corporate Sector

To estimate the spillover from the sovereign to the private corporate side, I define a set of country-specific crisis dummies to identify episodes of sovereign debt distress:

$$I_{jt} = \begin{cases} 1 & \text{if country } j\text{'s secondary sovereign spreads at} \\ & \text{time } t \geq \text{a critical threshold} \\ 0 & \text{otherwise.} \end{cases}$$

My approach in relying on market-based credit spreads rather than the occurrence of default to identify episodes of sovereign debt distress is consistent with the recent literature on the costs of sovereign default (Das, Papaioannou, and Trebesch 2010; Trebesch 2009). This literature recognizes that although emerging market borrowers have experienced several episodes of severe debt-servicing difficulties and market turmoil over the past two decades, the incidence of sovereign default, particularly on bond market obligations, has been rare (Pescatori and Sy 2004). Over the past decade, which saw waves of financial, banking, and currency crises, only 14 foreign currency sovereign defaults occurred in developing countries.[5]

One reason why sovereign foreign debt–servicing difficulties in emerging market economies have not resulted in default has to do with the advent and growth of the emerging market bond market in the 1990s, which has afforded borrowers in distress broader options for taking preemptive measures through debt restructuring and improved liability management (debt buybacks and swaps) to avoid the heavy costs of default (Medeiros, Ramlogan, and Polan 2007; Mendoza and Yue 2008). Improved domestic macroeconomic conditions in debtor countries, along with reforms in sovereign bond contracts and documentation in international capital markets, such as the shift in adopting collective actions clauses in sovereign bond contracts under New York State law, have contributed to reducing the incidence of default on foreign currency debt obligations. Another reason why defaults have been rare relates to the efforts undertaken by emerging sovereign borrowers to improve their external debt profiles through liability management and the buyback and retirement of Brady bonds.[6]

I use secondary market bond spreads to capture sovereign debt–servicing problems, because sovereign debt distress can express itself in a broad range of policy and official rescue outcomes and credit ratings are backward looking. I define episodes of debt distress as occurring when a sovereign borrower's bonds trade at spreads of at least 1,000 basis points over comparable U.S. Treasury securities. This definition captures the periods in which Standard & Poor's classified countries as being in selective default (table 5.4).

I run a set of regressions with interactions between the systematic component of sovereign spreads (estimated from equation [5.5]) and the country-specific crisis dummies using

$$Y_{c,ijt} = \alpha_{c,j} + \beta'_c X_{jt} + \psi'_c V_t + \gamma'_c Z_i + \delta'_c W + \theta SSR_{jt} + \eta(SSR_{jt} \times I_t), \quad (5.7)$$

where $SSR_{jt} = \hat{\alpha}_{s,j} + \hat{\beta}'_s X_{jt}$.

The estimated coefficient for sovereign systematic risk (SSR) is positive and statistically significant, even with the presence of domestic macroeconomic variables in the equation explaining the determinants of private corporate bond market spreads in emerging economies. Interacting SSR with the country crisis dummy variable provides a measure of the degree to which sovereign risk affects private external borrowing capital costs during times of sovereign debt distress and financial crises. In all equations reported in table 5.5, the estimated coefficient is positive and significant.

Table 5.4 Sovereign Selective Default Episodes and Spreads on Foreign-Currency Bond Markets

Country	Secondary market spread (basis points)	Selective default date	Emergence date	Time in selective default (months)
Argentina	5,320	November 6, 2001	June 1, 2005	43.0
Dominican Republic	616	February 1, 2005	June 29, 2005	5.0
Ecuador	3,654	December 15, 2008	June 15, 2009	6.0
Russian Federation	2,537	January 27, 1999	December 8, 2000	22.0
Uruguay	929	May 16, 2003	June 2, 2003	1.0
Venezuela, R. B. de[a]	446	January 18, 2005	March 3, 2005	1.5
Average	2,250			13.0

Sources: Default information is from Standard & Poor's 2010; sovereign spreads are from J.P. Morgan EMBI Global.

a. In the case of República Bolivariana de Venezuela, there was a debate among credit agencies at the time. Evidently, investors did not react to the Standard & Poor's downgrade.

Table 5.5 Spillover Effects from Sovereign to Private Corporate Sector

Variable	(1)	(2)	(3)
Sovereign systematic risk (*SSR*)	0.97 (0.067)*	0.74 (0.000)***	0.78 (0.000)***
SSR*country crisis dummy	0.10 (0.026)**	0.12 (0.011)**	0.11 (0.015)**
Local macroeconomic variables			
GDP growth rate	−3.474 (0.477)		
GDP per capita	2.83 (0.207)		
Inflation	69.12 (0.532)		
Private credit/GDP	0.49 (0.383)		
Fiscal balance/GDP	1.32 (0.573)		
Exports/GDP	1.78 (0.842)		
Foreign bank claims/GDP	0.21 (0.878)		
Country credit risk rating index	−0.43 (0.340)		
Global factors			
U.S. 10-year Treasury-bond yield (basis points)	−0.31 (0.000)***	−0.38 (0.000)***	−0.39 (0.000)***
U.S. 10-year Treasury-bond yield minus 2-year Treasury-bond yield (percent)	23.24 (0.001)***	22.86 (0.000)***	16.77 (0.006)***
Volatility[a]	43.21 (0.000)***		48.532 (0.000)***
Bond attributes			
Euro-denominated bond	−16.15 (0.335)	−15.24 (0.365)	−12.16 (0.465)

(continued next page)

Table 5.5 (continued)

Variable	(1)	(2)	(3)
Log (maturity)	9.12	7.62	8.84
	(0.143)	(0.226)	(0.156)
Log (value)	–31.37	–30.91	–30.24
	(0.000)***	(0.000)***	(0.000)***
Floating rate notes	–113.09	–115.45	–112.58
	(0.000)***	(0.000)***	(0.000)***
Guarantee	17.43	13.01	11.04
	(0.092)*	(0.208)	(0.280)
Eurobond	0.94	12.11	5.94
	(0.939)	(0.321)	(0.624)
Rule 144A	33.43	36.34	32.69
	(0.001)***	(0.000)***	(0.001)***
Nonnegative pledge issuer	34.58	32.97	31.59
	(0.000)***	(0.000)***	(0.001)***
Bond rating at launch	26.50	25.42	26.03
	(0.000)***	(0.000)***	(0.000)***
Sector			
Finance	–35.29	–37.79	–39.55
	(0.002)***	(0.001)***	(0.001)***
Oil and gas	–54.21	–54.74	–56.16
	(0.002)***	(0.002)***	(0.001)***
Mining	–88.36	–99.50	–90.30
	(0.004)***	(0.001)***	(0.003)***
Utility and energy	–73.32	–75.03	–76.83
	(0.004)***	(0.003)***	(0.002)***
Country effects (not reported here)			
Number of observations	1,427	1,427	1,427
R-squared	0.65	0.63	0.64

Source: Author.

Note: Figures in parentheses are *p*-values.

a. The volatility indicator is derived from a common factor analysis of several variables: VIX to measure equity market volatility; volatility of major currencies exchange rates; volatility of commodity price indices (agricultural, energy, and industrial metals); and TED spreads, as described in Dailami and Masson (2009).

*** Significant at the 1% level; ** significant at the 5% level; * significant at the 10% level.

Concluding Remarks

In the corporate world, the ability of a borrower to access international capital markets and the terms at which capital can be raised depend not only on the creditworthiness of the borrower but also on investors' views and risk perceptions of the country in which the borrower is domiciled. For corporate borrowers in advanced countries, country risk has not traditionally been important, given their governments' high credit-rating status and the associated perceived institutional strength of rule of law, transparency, and corporate governance considerations. In contrast, for private corporate borrowers in emerging economies, sovereign default risk remains critical in determining the cost of capital.

This chapter explores how debt distress can potentially affect the costs of private corporate external borrowing in emerging market economies by using primary bond market spreads that reflect more accurately the actual cost of capital to emerging borrowers than the more commonly used secondary market spreads. It develops an analytical framework for thinking about the correlation between sovereign and corporate credit risk and provides tentative evidence on the size of additional capital costs private borrowers bear in times of sovereign debt distress.

The sources of such a correlation vary from country to country. One important source could be the fact that both the firm and its home government operate in the same domestic macroeconomic and global environment. As a result, periods of economic downturns that heighten the firm's probability of default also worsen the government's fiscal situation and hence its capacity to service its debt. A second source is the fact that the government's ability to provide emergency support to private firms in distress is compromised when its own credit quality is in question. A third source could be that in many countries, local banks hold a large volume of government securities on their books, which erodes their ability to provide finance to private firms in times of high sovereign default risk.

An important policy recommendation emerging from the analysis relates to the need for improving sovereign creditworthiness before investor fears set in that could lead to a panicky sell-off in sovereign debt. Econometric evidence presented in this chapter confirms that investors' perceptions of sovereign debt problems in an emerging economy translate into higher costs of capital for that country's private corporate issuers, with the magnitude of such costs increasing once the sovereign bonds trade at spreads exceeding 1,000 basis points. This result reinforces the need for paying greater attention to the domestic costs of sovereign default in the ongoing debt sustainability work promoted by major international financial institutions. It also highlights the salience of the domestic growth costs of sovereign debt in explaining the feasibility of sovereign debt over the theories of reputation and punishments pioneered by the influential works of Eaton and Gersovitz (1981) and Bulow and Rogoff (1989).

Notes

The author thanks Jamus Jerome Lim and Marcelo Giugale for useful discussions and Sergio Kurlat and Yueqing Jia for research assistance.

1. The past two decades have not been short on emerging market crises. Mexico's Tequila crisis of 1994–95, brought on by the devaluation of the peso; the 1998 Russian Gosudarstvennye Kratkosrochnye Obyazatel'stva (GKO) default, a sovereign debt crisis; and the 1997–98 East Asian crisis, which began as a balance of payments crisis under a fixed exchange rate regime in Thailand all led to significant disruption in global financial markets. The 2002 economic crisis in Brazil and external debt problems in Turkey, both directly related to the market's perception of political risk associated with general elections in these countries, also had negative effects on global markets. The 2008–09 global financial crisis was unique not only in its scope but in the fact that it originated in core financial markets and reverberated to emerging countries through a liquidity squeeze and flight to safety.

2. An example is the case of Naftogaz, in Ukraine. As part of its debt restructuring, Naftogaz offered to exchange its $500 million loan participation notes due September 30, 2009, with new notes (with a five-year maturity) backed by an unconditional and irrevocable sovereign guarantee.

3. The 59 countries are Argentina, Azerbaijan, Bahrain, Belarus, Brazil, Bulgaria, Chile, China, Colombia, Costa Rica, Croatia, the Czech Republic, the Dominican Republic, Ecuador, the Arab Republic of Egypt, El Salvador, Estonia, Georgia, Ghana, Guatemala, Hungary, India, Indonesia, Jamaica, Jordan, Kazakhstan, Kenya, the Republic of Korea, Kuwait, Latvia, Lebanon, Lithuania, Malaysia, Mexico, Mongolia, Morocco, Nigeria, Oman, Pakistan, Panama, Peru, the Philippines, Poland, Qatar, Romania, the Russian Federation, Saudi Arabia, the Slovak Republic, Slovenia, South Africa, Sri Lanka, Thailand, Trinidad and Tobago, Turkey, Ukraine, the United Arab Emirates, Uruguay, República Bolivariana de Venezuela, and Vietnam.

4. My analysis also takes into account the empirical literature on the determinants of credit yield spreads, which emphasizes the benchmark status of sovereign debt in analyzing the spillover effect between sovereign and corporate bonds (Dittmer and Yuan 2008; Yuan 2005).

5. The defaults occurred in Argentina, Belize, the Dominican Republic, Ecuador, Grenada, Indonesia, Paraguay, Russia, the Seychelles, and República Bolivariana de Venezuela (Standard & Poor's 2009).

6. A country could also face market turmoil and reversal of capital flows not because of its own fault but because of contagion effects and covariation of bond prices across the emerging-market asset class (Dailami and Masson 2009).

References

Black, Fischer, and John C. Cox. 1976. "Valuing Corporate Securities: Some Effects of Bond Indenture Provisions." *Journal of Finance* 31 (2): 351–67.

Bulow, Jeremy, and Kenneth Rogoff. 1989. "Sovereign Debt: Is to Forgive to Forget?" *American Economic Review* 79 (1): 43–50.

Dailami, Mansoor. 2010. "Finding a Route to New Funding." *Credit Magazine.*

Dailami, Mansoor, Paul Masson, and Jean Jose Padou. 2008. "Global Monetary Conditions versus Country-Specific Factors in the Determination of Emerging Market Debt Spreads." *Journal of International Money and Finance* 27: 1325–36.

Dailami, Mansoor, and Paul R. Masson. 2009. "Measures of Investor and Consumer Confidence and Policy Actions in the Current Crisis." World Bank Policy Research Working Paper WPS 5007, World Bank, Washington, DC.

Das, Udaibir S., Michael G. Papaioannou, and Christoph Trebesch. 2010. "Sovereign Default Risk and Private Sector Access to Capital in Emerging Markets." IMF Working Paper 10/10, International Monetary Fund, Washington, DC.

Dittmer, Robert F., and Kathy Yuan. 2008. "Do Sovereign Bonds Benefit Corporate Bonds in Emerging Markets?" *Review of Financial Studies* 21 (5): 1983–2014.

Duffie, D., and K. Singleton. 1999. "Modeling Term Structures of Defaultable Bonds." *Review of Financial Studies* 12 (4): 687–720.

Eaton, Jonathan, and Mark Gersovitz. 1981. "Debt with Potential Repudiation: Theoretical and Empirical Analysis." *Review of Economic Studies* 48 (2): 289–309.

Jarrow, Robert, and Stuart Turnbull. 1995. "Pricing Derivatives on Financial Securities Subject to Credit Risk." *Journal of Finance* 50 (1): 53–86.

Longstaff, F., and E. Schwartz. 1995. "A Simple Approach to Valuing Risky Fixed and Floating Rate Debt." *Journal of Finance* 50 (3): 789–820.

Medeiros, Carlos I., Parmeshwar Ramlogan, and Magdalena Polan. 2007. "A Primer on Sovereign Debt Buybacks and Swaps." IMF Working Paper 07/58, International Monetary Fund, Washington, DC.

Mendoza, Enrique G., and Vivian Z. Yue. 2008. "A Solution to the Disconnect between Country Risk and Business Cycle Theories." NBER Working Paper 13861, National Bureau of Economic Research, Cambridge, MA.

Merton, Robert C. 1974. "On the Pricing of Corporate Debt: The Risk Structure of Interest Rates." *Journal of Finance* 29: 449–70.

Pescatori, Andrea, and Amadou N. R. Sy. 2004. "Debt Crises and the Development of International Capital Markets." IMF Working Paper 04/44, International Monetary Fund, Washington, DC.

Standard & Poor's. 2010. "Sovereign Defaults and Rating Transition Data, 2009 Update." March.

Trebesch, Christoph. 2009. "The Cost of Aggressive Sovereign Debt Policies: How Much Is the Private Sector Affected?" IMF Working Paper 09/29, International Monetary Fund, Washington, DC.

Yuan, Kathy. 2005. "The Liquidity Service of Benchmark Securities." *Journal of the European Economic Association* 3 (5): 1156–80.

Part II

The Effects of the Crisis on Debt

6

Debt Sustainability and Debt Distress in the Wake of the Ongoing Financial Crisis: The Case of IDA-Only African Countries

Leonardo Hernández and Boris Gamarra

The ongoing financial crisis differs from previous crises that have affected developing countries in recent decades. In particular, it originated in the developed world, in sharp contrast to the debt crisis of the early 1980s, the Tequila Crisis of 1994, and the Asian Crisis of 1997–98, to name just a few. It is also 1 of 4 of the past 122 recessions that included a credit crunch, a housing price bust, and an equity price bust (Claessens, Kose, and Terrones 2008), which implies a more protracted recovery. Finally, it occurred at a time when developing countries had, on average, stronger fundamentals than in previous crisis episodes, as a result of having pursued sound monetary and fiscal policies in previous years.

As a result of these factors, most developing countries were not severely affected during the first (that is, financial) phase of the crisis. Only a few countries were affected during this phase, most of them Eastern European and Central Asian countries whose banking systems were directly or indirectly exposed (through their headquarters) to the same toxic assets as banks in Europe and the United States or countries that had enjoyed a period of rapid expansion and a real estate bubble in their domestic markets. Developing countries in general were not severely affected during the first phase of the crisis, except for a short-lived liquidity squeeze that was resolved by aggressive interventions by central banks around the world.

Developing countries have been affected by the sharp fall in export volumes and commodity prices during the second phase of the crisis, which resulted from the decline in aggregate demand in the developed world. Indeed, global trade and commodity prices fell significantly in late 2008 (figures 6.1 and 6.2). In addition, private capital flows to developing countries, in particular debt flows, fell sharply from their peak in 2007 (figure 6.3). Some developing countries have also been affected by a significant decline in remittances since 2008 (figure 6.4), which deepened in 2009 as a result of increased unemployment in the developed world.[1] Official development assistance flows are also expected to decline as a result of the recession in developed countries. In sum, most developing countries have been affected mainly by a sharp drop in exports, private and official capital flows, and remittances rather than by the financial dimensions of the crisis. This is particularly so for low-income countries, which largely escaped the shocks transmitted through the financial channel because of their limited integration into global financial markets.

This chapter analyzes the potential deterioration in low-income countries' external debt burden indicators as a result of the fall in exports caused by the ongoing crisis. The analysis uses the Debt Sustainability Framework (DSF) adopted by the World Bank and the International Monetary Fund

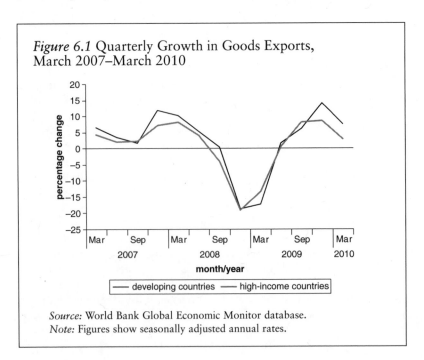

Figure 6.1 Quarterly Growth in Goods Exports, March 2007–March 2010

Source: World Bank Global Economic Monitor database.
Note: Figures show seasonally adjusted annual rates.

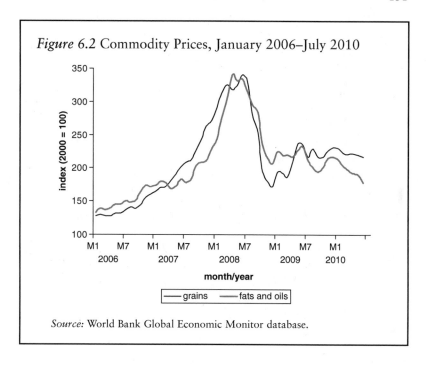

Figure 6.2 Commodity Prices, January 2006–July 2010

Source: World Bank Global Economic Monitor database.

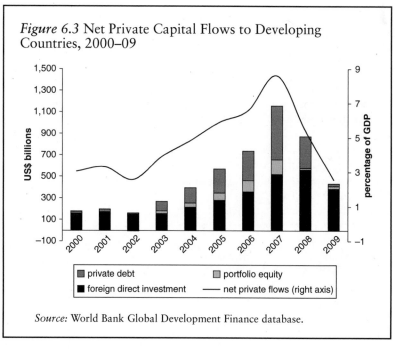

Figure 6.3 Net Private Capital Flows to Developing Countries, 2000–09

Source: World Bank Global Development Finance database.

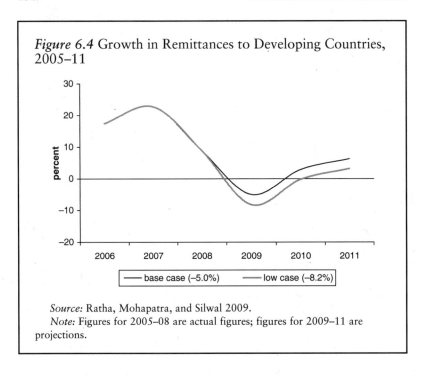

Figure 6.4 Growth in Remittances to Developing Countries, 2005–11

Source: Ratha, Mohapatra, and Silwal 2009.
Note: Figures for 2005–08 are actual figures; figures for 2009–11 are projections.

(IMF) for low-income countries, which projects key macroeconomic variables (exports, GDP, government revenues, and so forth) and indebtedness over a 20-year horizon. The behavior of countries' debt burden indicators affects their risk ratings (low, moderate, and high risk or in debt distress) and conditions countries' access to concessional sources of finance. The five debt burden indicators considered under the DSF are the present value of debt to exports ratio, the present value of debt to GDP ratio, the present value of debt to government revenues ratio, the debt service to exports ratio, and the debt service to government revenues ratio (see annex 6C). The analysis is carried out by simulating the effects of different exports shocks on countries' indebtedness after countries borrow to smooth out the effects of the crisis.

The chapter's main conclusion is that it is critical to ensure continuous access to concessional (soft) financing for these countries, as the probability of debt distress rises significantly when financing conditions tighten. Alternatively, the adjustment in fiscal policy, including policies governing social expenditures and investment, required to avoid defaults is deemed unfeasible under tougher financial conditions. The need for soft financing becomes more acute if the global crisis proves to be a protracted one. However, access to such financing does not preclude the need for fiscal adjustments in a few cases in order to avoid a default.

The chapter is organized as follows. The first section describes several simulation exercises and provides relevant methodological information. The second section analyzes the results of the exercises for a typical low-income country and for the group of 31 low-income countries in the sample. The last section provides some concluding comments.

Methodology

This section describes step by step how simulations were made using the DSF. It describes the sample of 31 countries and then explains the types of shocks that countries suffer.

Sample

The sample comprises 31 African countries that are eligible for assistance from the International Development Association for which a Debt Sustainability Analysis (DSA) was available by end-July 2009.[2] The simulations are built so that the crisis hits all countries in 2009. Debt burden indicators are projected—and compared with respect to each template's baseline—for 2009–27.

Although the effects of the crisis through exports began to be felt more intensively in most low-income countries in 2009, the fact that DSAs performed at different dates are used implies that the baseline scenario against which our projections are compared could be too optimistic for all but eight of the countries in our sample.[3] For the other 23 countries, the actual deterioration of the debt burden indicators (and the associated risk of debt distress that results from comparing such indicators to the indicative policy-dependent thresholds) could be lower than projected in the simulation exercises, because the size of the shocks and the associated change in indebtedness are proportional to the baseline whereas the thresholds are constant.[4]

Shocks: Depth, Length, and Transmission to the Rest of the Economy

The simulations are based on different assumptions regarding the depth and length of the shock to exports (table 6.1).[5] With respect to the baseline year (2009), we simulated export declines of 10, 20, and 30 percent. We assume that after the initial decline in exports, countries could take two, four, six, or eight years to return to the levels projected under the DSA baseline. We assume that the return to the DSA baseline levels is linear.

Shocks are ranked ex ante according to a severity index, defined as the cumulative loss (deviation) in exports with respect to the DSA baseline (table 6.2). The severity index for a 30 percent shock lasting two years is

Table 6.1 Depth and Duration of Export Shocks

Depth of shock (percent)	Length of shock (years)	Annual recovery (percent)
10	2, 4, 6, 8	5.0, 2.5, 1.67, 1.25
20	2, 4, 6, 8	10.0, 5.0, 3.33, 2.5
30	2, 4, 6, 8	15.0, 7.5, 5.0, 3.75

Source: Authors.
Note: The depth of the shock is the percentage deviation from the 2009 baseline. The length of the shock is the number of years until the export level projected under the DSA baseline is reached. The annual recovery is the percentage-point deviation from the baseline corresponding to the length of the shock.

Table 6.2 Severity Index of Shocks to Exports

Shock type	Depth of shock	Length of shock	Severity index (cumulative percentage loss with respect to DSA baseline)
902	10	2	15
904	10	4	25
802	20	2	30
906	10	6	35
908	10	8	45
702	30	2	45
804	20	4	50
806	20	6	70
704	30	4	75
808	20	8	90
706	30	6	105
708	30	8	135

Source: Authors.
Note: The shock type comprises two numbers: the first two digits (90, 80, and 70) indicate the level of exports after the shock as a percent of the baseline. The second (2, 4, 6, and 8) indicates the number of years until exports return to the levels projected under the DSA baseline.

45 (30 percent loss the first year and 15 percent loss the second), the same as the index for a 10 percent shock lasting eight years.

We consider two alternatives in analyzing the impact of the shocks on a country's debt burden indicators. Under the first alternative, the decline in exports is compensated for by an increase in domestic absorption, so that it does not adversely affect aggregate output (that is, unemployment is unaffected), as assumed in some of the stress tests built in the DSA template.[6]

It occurs, for instance, if the government buys all the production that firms are unable to export (in order to keep resources fully employed) or if firms build up their inventories (which could be more easily done in the case of nonperishable commodities, such as diamonds or copper). Under the second alternative the decline in exports is not compensated for and therefore has an effect on aggregate output and on unemployment. The second alternative—with transmission to GDP—is more realistic and will differ from the first proportionally to the share of exports to GDP. Debt burden indicators expressed in percentage of GDP and government revenues will deteriorate even further under the second alternative.[7]

To the extent that countries implement fiscal stimulus packages to partially offset the effect of the crisis on GDP, these alternatives provide lower and upper bounds on the actual effect of the crisis on countries' debt burden indicators.

Adjustment to Shocks: Marginal Financial Conditions

Countries could adjust to the crisis by severely constraining aggregate expenditures (that is, reducing imports). Not smoothing the export shock would impose a heavy burden on the population, however. To avoid a sharp adjustment in consumption and investment, it would be desirable to allow for an increase in indebtedness, to the extent that it does not lead to a more severe adjustment later on, which would be the case if the country falls into debt distress and eventually defaults.

To assess the impact of increased indebtedness on a country's risk of debt distress under each of the 12 shocks shown in table 6.2, we project debt burden indicators assuming that there is no reduction in absorption (that is, that the country borrows $1 for every $1 not received from exports).[8] The deterioration in debt burden indicators depends on the financial conditions under which the new debt is contracted. We analyze the impact of contracting new debt under four sets of terms (table 6.3).

The conditions under which low-income countries could obtain financing are arbitrarily chosen. They are likely to be more stringent than they had been, however, because of the increasing scarcity of concessional

Table 6.3 Terms under Which New Debt Is Contracted

Financial conditions index	Interest rate (percent)	Maturity (years)	Grace period (years)
FC10	0.75	40	10
FC20	2.25	10	5
FC30	5.25	10	0
FC40	10.25	5	0

Source: Authors.

financing caused by the crisis. In contrast to the case discussed earlier, the assumption of a 1:1 substitution of new debt for exports unequivocally provides an upper-bound estimate of the real effect of the crisis on the deterioration of countries' debt burden indicators, as countries probably borrow to only partly compensate for the fall in export proceeds.

Measuring the Impact of Shocks

We assess the impact of the shocks and new borrowing on the set of countries considered in this analysis using three measures: the number of breaches, the average deviation from the threshold, and the maximum distance from the threshold. For a given country, the number of breaches is equal to the number of years in the projection period (2009–27) in which the relevant indicative debt threshold is breached. Consecutive breaches are counted separately; thus, a country could have up to 19 breaches. For the complete set of countries, the indicator is equal to the sum of the number of breaches across countries. The average deviation from the threshold for a given country corresponds to the average deviation from the relevant indicative threshold (as a percentage of the threshold), calculated for the years in which breaches of the thresholds are observed. For the complete set of countries, the indicator equals the sum of the averages across countries. The maximum distance from the threshold for a given country is equal to the maximum distance from the relevant indicative threshold (as a percentage of the threshold) over the entire projection period. For the complete set of countries, this indicator is equal to the sum of the maximum distances across countries.

The three complementary measures are calculated for each of the five debt burden indicators used in the DSF. The number of breaches provides an indication of how protracted the effect of the shock is; the average deviation and maximum distance from the threshold indicate how deep the impact of the shock is. Therefore, it better proxies the effect on the country's probability of debt distress.

Results

This section examines the extent to which different combinations of exports shocks and financing conditions affect countries' indebtedness and their associated risk of debt distress assessments. The analysis uses the three measures described in the preceding paragraph.

Debt Burden Indicators for a Typical Country in the Sample

Annex 6A illustrates the impact of the assumed shocks and new borrowing on the debt burden indicators for a typical country in the sample. For presentational purposes, the figures in the analysis correspond to an assumed

20 percent drop in exports with transmission to GDP (that is, with adverse effects on unemployment), which represents an upper bound on the actual effect on countries. (The results for other cases are qualitatively the same and are available upon request from the authors.) We also discuss the average results for all 12 export shocks under different borrowing conditions.[9]

One (expected) result is that, for given borrowing conditions, debt burden indicators deteriorate monotonically with the duration (severity) of the export shock. This result stems from the fact that a longer-lasting (deeper) shock forces a country to incur additional borrowing to smooth out the effects of the crisis on domestic absorption, something that has a monotonic adverse effect on both solvency and liquidity indicators (see graphs on the right side of all five figures in annex 6A).

Less stringent borrowing conditions also imply a smoother adjustment of debt burden indicators (that is, debt burden indicators deteriorate less initially under less stringent financial conditions but also return to the original (baseline) level more slowly than under tougher borrowing conditions). This implies that when debt burden indicators breach their corresponding indicative thresholds, they tend to stay above such values for a longer period under less stringent borrowing conditions (table 6.4), because the repayment period is shorter under the more stringent new borrowing conditions. The underlying relationship is not perfectly monotonic, however, because the higher interest rate assumed for new borrowing with shorter maturity—as well as the behavior of the corresponding debt burden indicator under the baseline scenario—also influences the number of times the relevant threshold (which is constant) is crossed.

Table 6.4 Average Number of Episodes across 12 Export Shocks under Different Financial Conditions

Indicator	Number of episodes in baseline	FC10 (0.75, 40, 10)	FC20 (2.25, 10, 5)	FC30 (5.25, 10, 0)	FC40 (10.25, 5, 0)
Present value of debt to GDP	5	18	17	11	9
Present value of debt to exports	0	12	13	6	4
Present value of debt to government revenues	0	0	8	5	3
Debt service to exports	0	0	10	7	5
Debt service to government revenues	0	0	0	7	5

Source: Authors.
Note: Numbers in parentheses in the column headings indicate the interest rate, maturity, and grace period, respectively.

Present value–based indicators are nonlinear transformations of debt service payments (whose behavior is better captured by debt service indicators). For this reason, these indicators do not exhibit a monotonic deterioration with the tightening of new borrowing conditions. Such a monotonic relationship is observed in the case of both debt service–based indicators (that is, the debt service to exports ratio and the debt service to government revenues ratio), as shown in annex figures 6A.4 and 6A.5.

In addition to higher interest rates, tighter new borrowing conditions convey a shorter repayment period. As a result, debt burden indicators return more quickly to the original (baseline) level, assuming countries manage to "survive" the shorter, albeit harder, period caused by the tighter financial conditions. The deterioration of the debt burden indicators underlying the results shown in table 6.4 is significant (in the baseline scenario only one indicator breaches the threshold on five occasions over the 19 years of projections), but it does not provide a clear or complete picture of the possibility of a country falling into debt distress. Such a picture is better captured by the distance (in percentage points) from the threshold when the threshold is breached. The results from the simulations are shown in annex 6A (for a 20 percent export shock) and summarized in tables 6.5 and 6.6 (for all export shocks).

It is clear from tables 6.5 and 6.6 that even under relatively lenient financial conditions (that is, FC20), the probability of debt distress rises relative to the baseline, implying that fiscal adjustment may be unavoidable in some cases. On average, the probability of debt distress increases significantly—the only

Table 6.5 Average Deviation from Threshold across All 12 Export Shocks under Different Financial Conditions

Indicator	Percentage points above threshold in baseline	FC10 (0.75, 40, 10)	FC20 (2.25, 10, 5)	FC30 (5.25, 10, 0)	FC40 (10.25, 5, 0)
Present value of debt to GDP	1.8	21	29	29	25
Present value of debt to exports	0	16	31	17	11
Present value of debt to government revenues	0	0	27	31	13
Debt service to exports	0	0	3	5	8
Debt service to government revenues	0	0	0	6	12

Source: Authors.
Note: Numbers in parentheses in the column headings indicate the interest rate, maturity, and grace period, respectively.

Table 6.6 Maximum Deviation from Threshold: Mean across
All 12 Export Shocks under Different Financial Conditions
(percentage points)

Indicator	Percentage points above threshold in baseline	FC10 (0.75, 40, 10)	FC20 (2.25, 10, 5)	FC30 (5.25, 10, 0)	FC40 (10.25, 5, 0)
Present value of debt to GDP	4.3	29	48	49	43
Present value of debt to exports	0	22	47	31	19
Present value of debt to government revenues	0	0	46	44	19
Debt service to exports	0	0	3	8	14
Debt service to government revenues	0	0	0	8	21

Source: Authors.
Note: Numbers in parentheses in the column headings indicate the interest rate, maturity, and grace period, respectively.

indicator that breaches the threshold under the baseline scenario increases by a factor of about 10—and almost monotonically with the tightening of financial conditions (monotonically for the case of the debt service to exports and debt service to revenues indicators). These observations indicate that on average across all shocks, the possibility of a country not being able to meet its financial obligations in subsequent years after a shock (as measured by the average or maximum deviation in percentage points from the different thresholds) is significantly higher than in the baseline scenario.

The same conclusion emerges when looking at the figures in annex 6A, which show that debt burden indicators deteriorate initially much more under the more stringent new borrowing conditions, although they tend to stay higher for shorter periods. As indicated in annex figures 6A.4 and 6A.5, however, the initial deterioration could be large enough that countries are not able to "survive" under the tighter financial conditions and would therefore be forced into default before making it to the later stages of the crisis. This conclusion does not appear as neat in the case of the present value indicators because of the nonlinearity referred to above. For an assessment of the effects of the different shocks in the short run, however, liquidity indicators appear more relevant than present value indicators, because they assess the possibility of a country not being able to meet its financial obligations each year after a shock occurs.

An alternative way of looking at the same issue is to ask how large a reduction in domestic absorption is needed to ensure that countries muddle through the crisis without defaulting on their debt. The size of the adjustment needs to be much larger, albeit shorter, in the case of tighter financial conditions, implying that cuts in social services or public investment will need to be much larger and perhaps unfeasible.

The severity of shocks, assessed (ex post) by the deterioration in debt burden indicators, does not always result in exactly the same ordering as indicated in table 6.2 (compare the left-hand panels in annex figures 6A.1–6A.5). This is so because of the nonlinear transformation in the present value calculations, the projected trajectory of the indicators under the DSA baseline, and the interaction between the severity of the shock (depth and length) and the cost at which the country obtains financing.

Debt Burden Indicators for the Full Sample

This analysis for the 31 countries as a group compares the aggregate measures under different assumptions with the same measures under the baseline scenario. The figures in annex 6B show the pattern of these aggregate measures for the various export shocks and financial conditions. The same results are presented averaged across the different export shocks in tables 6.7–6.9 for the entire sample. For presentational purposes, we examine the case with transmission to GDP (that is, the case in which the drop in exports causes unemployment). Other results are available upon request from the authors. The severity of shocks assessed (ex post) by the

Table 6.7 Average Number of Episodes across All 12 Export Shocks under Different Financial Conditions, Entire Sample

Indicator	Number of episodes in baseline	FC10 (0.75, 40, 10)	FC20 (2.25, 10, 5)	FC30 (5.25, 10, 0)	FC40 (10.25, 5, 0)
Present value of debt to GDP	113	166	184	162	147
Present value of debt to exports	145	192	214	196	185
Present value of debt to government revenues	78	102	114	105	97
Debt service to exports	26	32	50	91	121
Debt service to government revenues	27	32	47	74	88

Source: Authors.
Note: The number in each cell corresponds to the sum over all countries.
In columns 3–6, this sum is averaged for the different shocks. Numbers in parentheses in the column headings indicate interest rate, maturity, and grace period, respectively.

Table 6.8 Average Deviation from Threshold across All 12 Export Shocks under Different Financial Conditions, Entire Sample

Indicator	Percentage points above threshold in baseline	FC10 (0.75, 40, 10)	FC20 (2.25, 10, 5)	FC30 (5.25, 10, 0)	FC40 (10.25, 5, 0)
Present value of debt to GDP	242	317	368	381	378
Present value of debt to exports	1,488	1,901	2,061	2,114	2,118
Present value of debt to government revenues	1,245	1,522	1,704	1,799	1,806
Debt service to exports	20	34	36	63	144
Debt service to government revenues	46	50	50	93	205

Source: Authors.

Note: The number in each cell corresponds to the sum of each country's average deviation from the threshold. In columns 3–6, this sum is averaged for the different shocks. Numbers in parentheses in the column headings indicate interest rate, maturity, and grace period, respectively.

deterioration in the different debt burden indicators does not yield exactly the same ordering as in table 6.2.

Overall, as expected, debt burden indicators deteriorate with a deepening of the crisis, given the new borrowing conditions. For a given export shock, the indicators deteriorate with a tightening of the new borrowing conditions, albeit not monotonically (see annex 6B). Especially when the crisis deepens under tighter financial conditions, for the liquidity indicators the corresponding measures reach values that are several times larger than in the DSA baseline scenario. The probability of debt distress in the short run, as assessed by the debt service to exports and debt service to revenues ratios, deteriorates almost monotonically and significantly with the tightening of financial conditions. Indeed, in some cases, the (maximum or average) distance from the threshold reaches values several times the baseline levels (tables 6.8 and 6.9; see annex figures 6B.2 and 6B.3). The same argument presented earlier regarding the size of the fiscal adjustment needed to ensure the service of the external government debt under tighter financial conditions applies here.

It is important to analyze the difference in results when the drop in exports causes unemployment with that in which it does not (that is, cases with and without transmission to GDP). In the case of no transmission to

Table 6.9 Maximum Deviation from Threshold: Mean across
All 12 Export Shocks under Different Financial Conditions,
Entire Sample

Indicator	Percentage points above threshold in baseline	FC10 (0.75, 40, 10)	FC20 (2.25, 10, 5)	FC30 (5.25, 10, 0)	FC40 (10.25, 5, 0)
Present value of debt to GDP	508	653	730	766	774
Present value of debt to exports	2,522	3,469	3,704	3,801	3,847
Present value of debt to government revenues	2,462	2,936	3,183	3,311	3,347
Debt service to exports	34	66	72	115	251
Debt service to government revenues	107	116	122	183	365

Source: Authors.
Note: The number in each cell corresponds to the sum of each country's average
deviation from the threshold. In columns 3–6, this sum is averaged for the different
shocks. Numbers in parentheses in the column headings indicate interest rate,
maturity, and grace period, respectively.

GDP, we assume that production remains constant, either because firms
increase their inventories, the government buys and stores the products
that are not exported, or both. The differences between the cases with and
without transmission are not very large: in only a few cases is the difference larger than 10 percent, and the largest difference is about 20 percent
(table 6.10). Despite the small magnitude, we believe it is more relevant
(realistic) to analyze the case with transmission to GDP.

Risk Assessments under Different Exports Shocks and Financial Conditions

In this section, we analyze the potential deterioration in countries' risk
rating assessments for different combinations of assumptions on exports
shocks and new borrowing. We do so by looking separately at the three
measures defined above for each country and comparing them against the
baseline scenario. The risk rating used here differs radically from that used
in the World Bank–IMF DSF. We classify countries at risk of debt distress
based on the criteria shown in table 6.11.

In contrast to the DSF, which looks at a country's behavior across all
five debt burden indicators, we assess risk based on each of the five debt

Table 6.10 Maximum Difference in Aggregate Indicators with and without Transmission to GDP, Entire Sample
(percent)

Indicator	Number of episodes	Average deviation from threshold	Maximum deviation from threshold
Present value of debt to GDP	4.0	14.4	20.7
Present value of debt to exports	0	0	0
Present value of debt to government revenues	7.8	15.7	14.8
Debt service to exports	0	0	0
Debt service to government revenues	8.3	20.3	17.6

Source: Authors.
Note: Numbers show the percentage in which the indicator calculated when there is transmission to GDP of the export shock exceeds the same indicator calculated when there is no transmission to GDP. The number in each cell is the maximum difference over all 48 possible combinations of export shocks and financial conditions.

Table 6.11 Risk Rating Criteria Used to Evaluate the Impact of Different Shocks on Countries' Risk Assessments

Level of risk of debt distress	Present value of debt to GDP	Present value of debt to exports	Present value of debt to revenues	Debt service to exports	Debt service to revenues
Number of episodes (or breaches) during the projection period					
Low	Threshold breached less than 5 times during projection period				
Moderate	Threshold breached 5–10 times during projection period				
High	Threshold breached more than 10 times during projection period				
Average deviation from threshold during the projection period[a]					
Low	≤ 5	≤ 25	≤ 25	≤ 2.5	≤ 2.5
Moderate	$5 \leq 10$	$25 \leq 50$	$25 \leq 50$	$2.5 \leq 5$	$2.5 \leq 5$
High	> 10	> 50	> 50	> 5	> 5

(continued next page)

Table 6.11 (continued)

Level of risk of debt distress	Present value of debt to GDP	Present value of debt to exports	Present value of debt to revenues	Debt service to exports	Debt service to revenues
Maximum distance from threshold during the projection period[b]					
Low	≤ 10	≤ 50	≤ 50	≤ 5	≤ 5
Moderate	10 ≤ 20	50 ≤ 100	50 ≤ 100	5 ≤ 10	5 ≤ 10
High	> 20	> 100	> 100	> 10	> 10

Source: Authors.

a. Step increases used correspond to a half- or one-step increase in the risk rating system under the World Bank–IMF DSF.

b. Step increases used are equal to or twice those used to assess the countries' risk ratings under the World Bank–IMF DSF.

burden indicators individually. For this reason, we use the more lenient criterion, indicated in table 6.11, rather than the actual World Bank– IMF DSA (for instance, in a standard DSA, a country is assessed as at low risk if all five indicators are well below the country-specific thresholds; see annex 6C).

The evidence reported in tables 6.12–6.14 shows that country risk assessments, as defined here, change significantly with respect to the baseline scenario, especially for long-lasting shocks and tighter financial conditions.[10] A drop in exports of 30 percent with recovery in eight years (X708x), a 10.25 interest rate, a five-year maturity, and no grace period (FC40) cause the number of countries rated at moderate risk of debt distress to increase to 10 (from 2 in the baseline) using the present value of debt to GDP ratio; to 13 (from 3 in the baseline) using the present value of debt to exports ratio; to 7 (from 2 in the baseline) using the present value of debt to revenue ratio; to 21 (from 0 in the baseline) using the debt service to exports ratio; and to 15 (from 1 in the baseline) using the debt service to revenues ratio.

The deterioration in the risk of debt distress assessments in table 6.12 appears less striking when one looks at the increase in the high risk of debt distress cases: for the same export shock and financial conditions, only the debt service to exports ratio deteriorates significantly, by up to five cases (up from one case under the baseline). This not very striking result occurs in part because the tighter financial conditions assume a shorter repayment period—that is, the number of "episodes," as defined here, increases less with tighter financial conditions.

Consequently, the change in risk ratings is much more striking in the case of deviations from thresholds, for both the average and the maximum (tables 6.13 and 6.14), where, with the exception of present value of debt

Table 6.12 Risk Ratings Based on Total Number of Episodes in Which Countries Exceed Their Thresholds under Different Export Shocks and Financial Conditions, Entire Sample
(number of countries)

Indicator	Present value debt to GDP			Present value debt to exports			Present value debt to revenue			Debt service to export			Debt service to revenue		
	Low risk	Medium risk	High risk	Low risk	Medium risk	High risk	Low risk	Medium risk	High risk	Low risk	Medium risk	High risk	Low risk	Medium risk	High risk
Baseline scenario	25	2	4	20	3	8	26	2	3	30	0	1	29	1	1
X708x															
FC10	16	3	12	11	6	14	21	4	6	30	0	1	29	1	1
FC20	13	5	13	8	7	16	19	3	9	23	3	5	24	2	5
FC30	14	6	11	8	11	12	20	5	6	14	8	9	17	9	5
FC40	16	10	5	9	13	9	21	7	3	5	21	5	13	15	3
X706x															
FC10	18	2	11	13	5	13	22	3	6	30	0	1	29	1	1
FC20	15	3	13	11	6	14	21	3	7	25	1	5	25	3	3
FC30	15	7	9	11	8	12	21	7	3	17	7	7	21	5	5
FC40	16	11	4	13	10	8	21	7	3	13	15	3	19	11	1

(continued next page)

Table 6.12 (continued)

Indicator	Present value debt to GDP			Present value debt to exports			Present value debt to revenue			Debt service to export			Debt service to revenue		
	Low risk	Medium risk	High risk	Low risk	Medium risk	High risk	Low risk	Medium risk	High risk	Low risk	Medium risk	High risk	Low risk	Medium risk	High risk
X808x															
FC10	19	2	10	13	6	12	23	2	6	30	0	1	29	1	1
FC20	16	3	12	12	5	14	21	4	6	26	3	2	26	4	1
FC30	16	6	9	11	10	10	21	6	4	20	6	5	22	4	5
FC40	17	10	4	14	9	8	21	7	3	14	14	3	20	10	1
X704x															
FC10	19	4	8	17	6	8	23	3	5	30	0	1	29	1	1
FC20	16	4	11	13	6	12	21	4	6	28	2	1	27	3	1
FC30	16	10	5	13	10	8	21	7	3	19	7	5	22	6	3
FC40	19	8	4	17	6	8	23	5	3	20	10	1	23	7	1
X806x															
FC10	20	3	8	18	5	8	23	4	4	30	0	1	29	1	1
FC20	17	3	11	13	6	12	22	3	6	28	2	1	29	1	1
FC30	18	6	7	15	8	8	22	6	3	23	5	3	23	5	3
FC40	19	8	4	16	7	8	22	6	3	18	12	1	23	7	1

X804x

	1	2	3	4	5	6	7	8	9	10	11	12	13	14	15
FC10	21	2	8	20	3	8	23	5	3	30	0	1	29	1	1
FC20	19	4	8	17	6	8	23	4	4	29	1	1	29	1	1
FC30	20	6	5	19	4	8	23	5	3	26	4	1	26	4	1
FC40	20	7	4	20	3	8	23	5	3	24	6	1	25	5	1

X702x

	1	2	3	4	5	6	7	8	9	10	11	12	13	14	15
FC10	21	4	6	20	3	8	23	5	3	30	0	1	28	1	2
FC20	20	3	8	20	3	8	23	5	3	30	0	1	27	1	3
FC30	19	8	4	20	3	8	23	5	3	27	3	1	23	5	3
FC40	20	7	4	20	3	8	24	4	3	27	3	1	24	5	2

X908x

	1	2	3	4	5	6	7	8	9	10	11	12	13	14	15
FC10	21	4	6	20	3	8	23	5	3	30	0	1	29	1	1
FC20	19	4	8	18	4	9	23	4	4	30	0	1	29	1	1
FC30	19	6	6	18	5	8	23	5	3	28	1	2	26	4	1
FC40	20	7	4	19	4	8	23	5	3	24	6	1	24	6	1

X906x

	1	2	3	4	5	6	7	8	9	10	11	12	13	14	15
FC10	21	4	6	20	3	8	24	4	3	30	0	1	29	1	1
FC20	21	3	7	20	3	8	23	5	3	30	0	1	29	1	1
FC30	21	5	5	20	3	8	23	5	3	28	2	1	27	3	1
FC40	21	6	4	20	3	8	24	4	3	27	3	1	26	4	1

(continued next page)

147

Table 6.12 (continued)

Indicator	Present value debt to GDP			Present value debt to exports			Present value debt to revenue			Debt service to export			Debt service to revenue		
	Low risk	Medium risk	High risk	Low risk	Medium risk	High risk	Low risk	Medium risk	High risk	Low risk	Medium risk	High risk	Low risk	Medium risk	High risk
X802x															
FC10	22	4	5	20	3	8	25	3	3	30	0	1	29	1	1
FC20	21	4	6	20	3	8	23	5	3	30	0	1	29	1	1
FC30	21	6	4	20	3	8	23	5	3	30	0	1	27	3	1
FC40	22	5	4	20	3	8	26	2	3	29	1	1	26	4	1
X904x															
FC10	22	4	5	20	3	8	26	2	3	30	0	1	29	1	1
FC20	21	4	6	20	3	8	23	5	3	30	0	1	29	1	1
FC30	21	6	4	20	3	8	24	4	3	30	0	1	27	3	1
FC40	21	6	4	20	3	8	25	3	3	29	1	1	27	3	1
X902x															
FC10	22	4	5	20	3	8	26	2	3	30	0	1	29	1	1
FC20	22	4	5	20	3	8	25	3	3	30	0	1	29	1	1
FC30	22	5	4	20	3	8	26	2	3	30	0	1	29	1	1
FC40	23	4	4	20	3	8	26	2	3	30	0	1	29	1	1

Source: Authors.

Note: Highlighting indicates the number of cases that are significantly larger than the number in the baseline (that is, cases in which the number of countries is at least twice that in the baseline for high risk of debt distress and cases in which the number of countries is more than twice that in the baseline for moderate [medium] risk of debt distress, using the definitions provided in table 6.11).

Table 6.13 Risk Ratings according to the Average Deviation by Which Countries Exceed Their Respective Thresholds across Different Export Shocks and Financial Conditions, Entire Sample (*number of countries*)

Indicator	Present value debt to GDP			Present value debt to exports			Present value debt to revenue			Debt service to export			Debt service to revenue		
	Low risk	Medium risk	High risk	Low risk	Medium risk	High risk	Low risk	Medium risk	High risk	Low risk	Medium risk	High risk	Low risk	Medium risk	High risk
Baseline scenario	23	5	3	21	3	7	23	5	3	28	2	1	27	1	3
X708x															
FC10	17	4	10	14	5	12	22	0	9	24	3	4	26	2	3
FC20	15	3	13	11	5	15	18	3	10	20	6	5	23	3	5
FC30	14	3	14	9	6	16	18	3	10	12	3	16	18	3	10
FC40	13	1	17	10	5	16	19	1	11	1	1	29	8	2	21
X706x															
FC10	17	3	11	17	2	12	22	0	9	26	0	5	26	1	4
FC20	14	6	11	13	6	12	20	2	9	25	2	4	25	2	4
FC30	14	5	12	11	6	14	20	1	10	15	4	12	21	0	10
FC40	14	3	14	12	4	15	20	1	10	1	3	27	10	3	18

(continued next page)

Table 6.13 (continued)

Indicator	Present value debt to GDP			Present value debt to exports			Present value debt to revenue			Debt service to export			Debt service to revenue		
	Low risk	Medium risk	High risk	Low risk	Medium risk	High risk	Low risk	Medium risk	High risk	Low risk	Medium risk	High risk	Low risk	Medium risk	High risk
X808x															
FC10	19	4	8	19	1	11	22	1	8	26	2	3	26	2	3
FC20	18	3	10	15	5	11	22	0	9	26	3	2	27	0	4
FC30	17	3	11	17	2	12	21	1	9	17	7	7	21	2	8
FC40	16	4	11	15	5	11	20	2	9	7	8	16	14	2	15
X704x															
FC10	20	2	9	17	3	11	22	1	8	26	0	5	26	1	4
FC20	17	4	10	16	3	12	22	0	9	26	2	3	27	0	4
FC30	15	4	12	15	3	13	20	2	9	19	8	4	22	2	7
FC40	15	4	12	14	4	13	20	1	10	7	6	18	14	2	15
X806x															
FC10	19	5	7	19	3	9	22	1	8	26	2	3	26	2	3
FC20	17	4	10	18	2	11	22	0	9	26	3	2	27	1	3
FC30	17	4	10	17	3	11	21	1	9	20	7	4	23	0	8
FC40	17	4	10	16	4	11	21	1	9	13	2	16	16	3	12

X804x

FC10	20	4	7	19	4	8	22	2	7	26	2	3	26	2	3
FC20	18	3	10	19	2	10	22	1	8	26	2	3	26	2	3
FC30	17	4	10	17	4	10	21	1	9	24	5	2	25	0	6
FC40	17	4	10	17	4	10	21	1	9	14	5	12	20	2	9

X702x

FC10	20	4	7	16	7	8	23	0	8	25	1	5	26	1	4
FC20	17	5	9	16	5	10	21	2	8	26	0	5	26	2	3
FC30	17	4	10	16	4	11	21	1	9	24	2	5	25	0	6
FC40	18	3	10	16	3	12	21	0	10	15	6	10	21	1	9

X908x

FC10	21	3	7	20	3	8	23	3	5	27	1	3	27	1	3
FC20	19	5	7	20	3	8	22	2	7	27	2	2	26	2	3
FC30	19	3	9	19	3	9	22	1	8	25	5	1	25	2	4
FC40	19	5	7	19	3	9	22	1	8	21	6	4	23	1	7

X906x

FC10	20	5	6	20	3	8	23	3	5	27	1	3	26	2	3
FC20	19	5	7	19	4	8	22	2	7	27	1	3	26	2	3
FC30	19	4	8	19	3	9	22	1	8	26	4	1	25	2	4
FC40	19	5	7	19	3	9	22	1	8	21	6	4	24	1	6

(continued next page)

Table 6.13 (continued)

Indicator	Present value debt to GDP			Present value debt to exports			Present value debt to revenue			Debt service to export			Debt service to revenue		
	Low risk	Medium risk	High risk	Low risk	Medium risk	High risk	Low risk	Medium risk	High risk	Low risk	Medium risk	High risk	Low risk	Medium risk	High risk
X802x															
FC10	20	5	6	19	4	8	23	2	6	26	2	3	26	2	3
FC20	20	4	7	18	5	8	22	1	8	26	2	3	26	2	3
FC30	19	4	8	18	5	8	21	2	8	25	3	3	25	2	4
FC40	19	3	9	17	5	9	21	2	8	24	3	4	24	0	7
X904x															
FC10	21	5	5	20	4	7	23	4	4	27	1	3	26	2	3
FC20	20	4	7	20	3	8	23	3	5	27	1	3	26	2	3
FC30	20	4	7	20	3	8	22	2	7	26	4	1	25	2	4
FC40	20	4	7	19	5	7	23	1	7	24	3	4	25	0	6
X902x															
FC10	23	5	3	20	4	7	23	5	3	27	1	3	27	1	3
FC20	20	6	5	20	4	7	23	2	6	27	1	3	27	1	3
FC30	20	6	5	20	4	7	23	3	5	27	1	3	26	1	4
FC40	20	6	5	20	4	7	23	2	6	26	3	2	25	1	5

Source: Authors.

Note: Highlighting indicates the number of cases that are significantly larger than the number in the baseline (that is, cases in which the number of countries is at least twice that in the baseline for high risk of debt distress and cases in which the number of countries is more than twice that in the baseline for moderate [medium] risk of debt distress, using the definitions provided in table 6.11).

Table 6.14 Risk Ratings Based on Maximum Breach by Which Countries Exceed Their Thresholds during Projection Period under Different Export Shocks and Financial Conditions, Entire Sample (number of countries)

Indicator	Present value debt to GDP			Present value debt to exports			Present value debt to revenue			Debt service to export			Debt service to revenue		
	Low risk	Medium risk	High risk	Low risk	Medium risk	High risk	Low risk	Medium risk	High risk	Low risk	Medium risk	High risk	Low risk	Medium risk	High risk
Baseline scenario	24	4	3	24	0	7	24	4	3	28	1	2	28	0	3
X708x															
FC10	19	3	9	18	3	10	22	1	8	26	2	3	26	2	3
FC20	14	6	11	11	8	12	18	3	10	23	4	4	24	2	5
FC30	14	4	13	11	7	13	18	3	10	14	4	13	19	2	10
FC40	14	5	12	11	6	14	20	1	10	0	2	29	9	2	20
X706x															
FC10	21	1	9	18	3	10	22	1	8	26	2	3	26	2	3
FC20	15	5	11	13	8	10	21	1	9	25	3	3	25	3	3
FC30	14	6	11	11	9	11	20	2	9	15	9	7	21	0	10
FC40	14	6	11	12	6	13	20	2	9	2	5	24	10	3	18

(continued next page)

Table 6.14 (continued)

Indicator	Present value debt to GDP			Present value debt to exports			Present value debt to revenue			Debt service to export			Debt service to revenue		
	Low risk	Medium risk	High risk	Low risk	Medium risk	High risk	Low risk	Medium risk	High risk	Low risk	Medium risk	High risk	Low risk	Medium risk	High risk
X808x															
FC10	21	2	8	18	5	8	22	3	6	28	0	3	26	2	3
FC20	19	2	10	19	2	10	22	1	8	27	1	3	26	2	3
FC30	18	3	10	17	4	10	22	0	9	18	8	5	21	2	8
FC40	17	4	10	17	4	10	22	0	9	9	6	16	16	1	14
X704x															
FC10	21	1	9	18	3	10	22	3	6	26	2	3	26	2	3
FC20	19	2	10	15	6	10	22	0	9	25	3	3	26	2	3
FC30	17	4	10	15	5	11	21	1	9	18	8	5	23	2	6
FC40	16	4	11	15	4	12	21	1	9	8	6	17	15	1	15
X806x															
FC10	21	2	8	19	5	7	22	3	6	28	0	3	26	2	3
FC20	20	2	9	19	2	10	22	1	8	28	0	3	26	2	3
FC30	19	2	10	18	3	10	22	1	8	22	5	4	23	2	6
FC40	20	1	10	17	4	10	22	1	8	15	1	15	16	4	11

X804x

FC10	21	3	7	19	5	7	23	3	5	28	0	3	27	1	3
FC20	21	1	9	19	3	9	22	3	6	28	0	3	26	2	3
FC30	21	0	10	18	3	10	22	3	6	26	2	3	25	1	5
FC40	21	0	10	18	3	10	22	2	7	16	8	7	20	2	9

X702x

FC10	21	2	8	18	3	10	23	2	6	26	2	3	27	1	3
FC20	21	0	10	16	5	10	22	3	6	26	2	3	26	2	3
FC30	19	2	10	16	4	11	21	3	7	24	4	3	25	1	5
FC40	19	2	10	16	3	12	21	2	8	16	8	7	21	2	8

X908x

FC10	21	6	4	20	4	7	23	5	3	28	0	3	26	2	3
FC20	21	4	6	20	4	7	22	4	5	28	0	3	26	2	3
FC30	21	3	7	21	3	7	22	3	6	26	2	3	25	2	4
FC40	21	2	8	21	3	7	22	3	6	21	6	4	23	1	7

X906x

FC10	21	6	4	20	4	7	23	5	3	28	0	3	27	1	3
FC20	21	4	6	20	4	7	22	5	4	28	0	3	26	2	3
FC30	21	4	6	21	3	7	22	4	5	28	0	3	25	2	4
FC40	21	3	7	21	3	7	23	2	6	24	4	3	24	1	6

(continued next page)

Table 6.14 (continued)

Indicator	Present value debt to GDP			Present value debt to exports			Present value debt to revenue			Debt service to export			Debt service to revenue		
	Low risk	Medium risk	High risk	Low risk	Medium risk	High risk	Low risk	Medium risk	High risk	Low risk	Medium risk	High risk	Low risk	Medium risk	High risk
X802x															
FC10	21	3	7	19	5	7	23	4	4	28	0	3	27	1	3
FC20	21	2	8	19	4	8	23	2	6	28	0	3	26	2	3
FC30	21	1	9	19	4	8	22	3	6	28	0	3	26	1	4
FC40	21	0	10	18	4	9	22	3	6	25	3	3	24	1	6
X904x															
FC10	21	6	4	20	4	7	23	5	3	28	0	3	27	1	3
FC20	21	5	5	20	4	7	23	4	4	28	0	3	26	2	3
FC30	21	4	6	21	3	7	23	3	5	28	0	3	26	1	4
FC40	21	4	6	21	3	7	23	2	6	27	1	3	25	1	5
X902x															
FC10	21	6	4	21	3	7	23	5	3	28	0	3	27	1	3
FC20	21	6	4	21	3	7	23	4	4	28	0	3	27	1	3
FC30	21	5	5	21	3	7	23	4	4	28	0	3	26	2	3
FC40	21	4	6	21	3	7	23	3	5	27	1	3	25	2	4

Source: Authors.

Note: Highlighting indicates the number of cases that are significantly larger than the number in the baseline (that is, cases in which the number of countries is at least twice that in the baseline for high risk of debt distress and cases in which the number of countries is more than twice that in the baseline for moderate [medium] risk of debt distress, using the definitions provided in table 6.11).

to exports, the majority of countries move from the low to the high risk category. In some cases, the deterioration persists even given the milder shocks and softer financing conditions.

Because of longer repayment periods, the increase in the number of cases of high risk of debt distress is larger using the number of "episodes" under less stringent financial conditions (see table 6.12). For instance, a shock in which exports fall 30 percent and the recovery period is eight years, the number of countries classified as at high risk of debt distress increases with respect to the baseline more significantly in the case of a 2.25 percent interest rate with a 10-year maturity and a 5-year grace period (FC20)—from 4 to 13, 8 to 16, 3 to 9, 1 to 5, and 1 to 5 using the five different debt burden indicators—than in the FC40 case.

Overall, the results from the simulations using ad hoc (but lenient) definitions for low, moderate, and high risk of debt distress highlight the importance of concessional financing for low-income countries, especially in a more severe (deep and protracted) crisis. Such financing may not be enough in cases in which the risk ratings deteriorate significantly even under the mildest negative financial conditions, however.

Concluding Remarks

In this chapter, we analyze the impacts of the global financial crisis on 31 IDA-only countries in Africa. In particular, we examine the impact on their (external) debt sustainability situation by looking at the possible effects of the crisis on the five debt burden indicators—the present value of debt over GDP, the present value of debt over exports, the present value of debt over government revenues, debt service over exports, and debt service over government revenues—used in the World Bank–IMF DSF. The analysis, conducted for 12 hypothetical shocks in exports, varying in depth and length, assumes that countries borrow under four sets of financial conditions to smooth out the effect of the crisis so that domestic absorption is not adversely affected. We project the five debt burden indicators for 2009–27 and analyze whether countries breach the country-specific thresholds established under the joint World Bank– IMF DSF. We focus on the duration of each breach and on the average and maximum breaches (distance from threshold) as an indicator of the probability of debt distress. The analysis is conducted indicator by indicator for the entire sample for the case in which the drop in exports causes a proportional slowdown in GDP.

As expected, debt burden indicators deteriorate significantly for all countries with the severity of the crisis, given the financial conditions under which a country finances (substitutes) its reduced export proceeds. A tightening of financial conditions leads to a significant deterioration in liquidity or debt service indicators; solvency or the present value of debt-based indicators deteriorate less because of the nonlinearities associated with present value calculations. More important, a tightening of financial conditions causes a significant increase in the probability of debt distress, assessed by distance from the threshold. The effect on the duration (or number of episodes during which a country's threshold is breached) is milder, because tougher financial conditions convey a shorter repayment period. The shorter repayment period may, however, imply that countries will not survive the crisis and will default on their coming due debt. Alternatively, the adjustment in fiscal expenditures and taxes needed to ensure continuity in debt service is significantly larger (albeit of shorter duration) under tighter financial conditions. This larger adjustment may imply significantly larger cuts in social expenditures and public investment or, if such cuts are deemed politically unfeasible, a sovereign default.

Although they overestimate the actual effect of the crisis on low-income countries,[11] the results from the simulations highlight the importance of concessional financing for low-income countries, especially under a severe (deep and protracted) crisis. Indeed, as shown in tables 6.12–6.14, under more stringent financial conditions and a protracted crisis, the number of countries at high risk of default increases significantly, reaching about half or more of the overall sample (from one or two cases under the baseline). Conditional financing may not be a sufficient remedy in cases in which risk ratings deteriorate significantly even under the mildest negative financial conditions if the crisis proves to be a protracted one. In these cases a fiscal adjustment may be unavoidable.

Annex 6A: Debt Burden Indicators for a Typical Low-Income Country

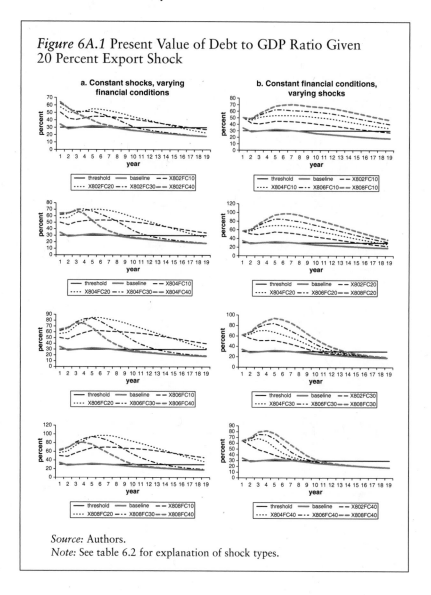

Figure 6A.1 Present Value of Debt to GDP Ratio Given 20 Percent Export Shock

Source: Authors.
Note: See table 6.2 for explanation of shock types.

Figure 6A.2 Present Value of Debt to Exports Ratio Given 20 Percent Export Shock

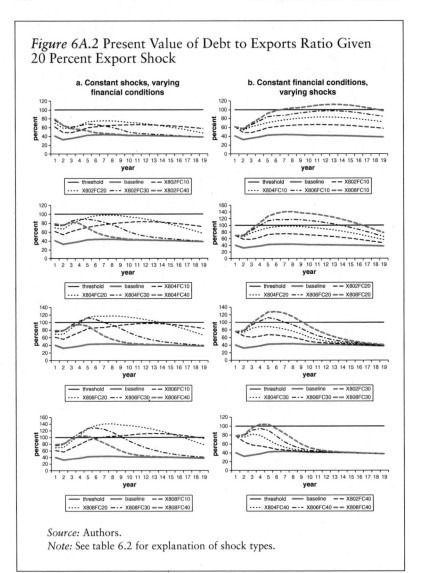

Source: Authors.
Note: See table 6.2 for explanation of shock types.

Figure 6A.3 Present Value of Debt to Revenues Ratio Given 20 Percent Export Shock

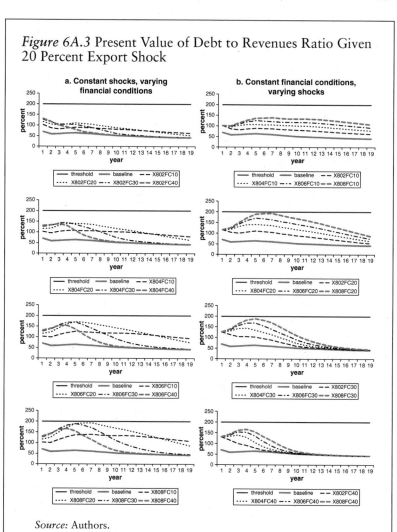

Source: Authors.
Note: See table 6.2 for explanation of shock types.

Figure 6A.4 Debt Service to Government Revenues Ratio
Given 20 Percent Export Shock

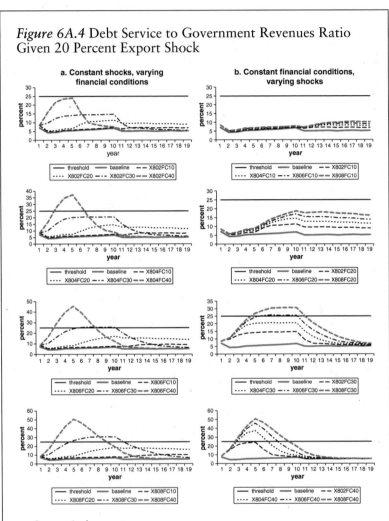

Source: Authors.
Note: See table 6.2 for explanation of shock types.

Figure 6A.5 Debt Service to Exports Ratio Given 20 Percent Export Shock

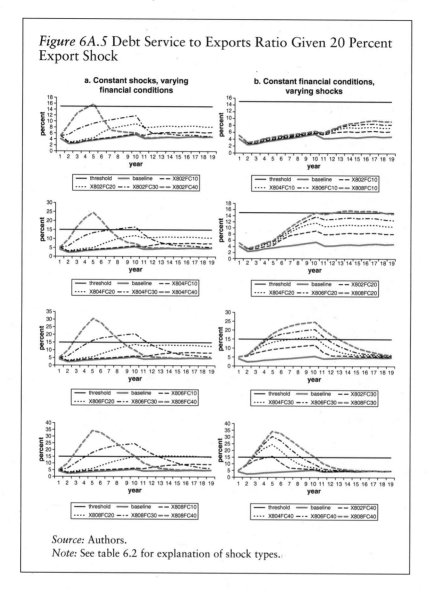

Source: Authors.
Note: See table 6.2 for explanation of shock types.

Annex 6B: Debt Burden Indicators for the Full Sample

Figure 6B.1 Number of Episodes above Threshold

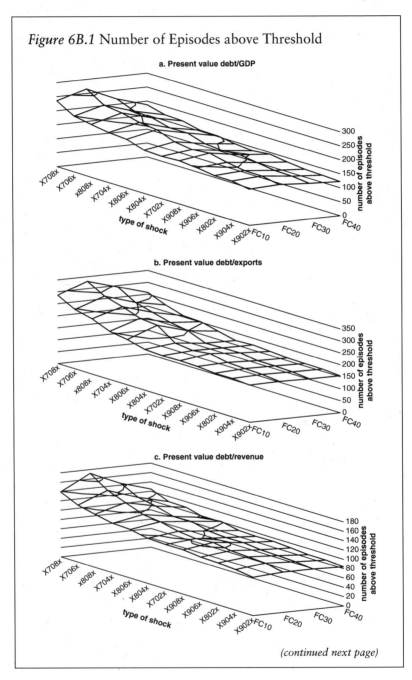

(continued next page)

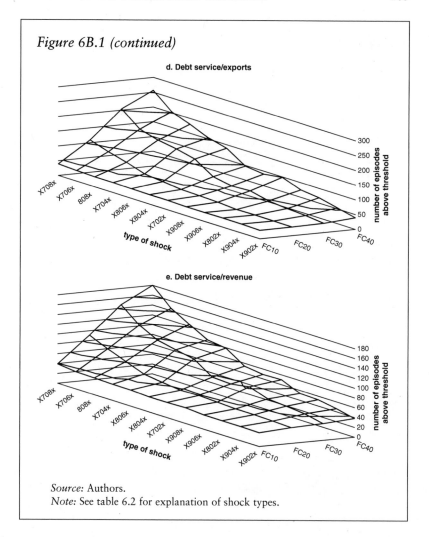

Figure 6B.1 (continued)

d. Debt service/exports

e. Debt service/revenue

Source: Authors.
Note: See table 6.2 for explanation of shock types.

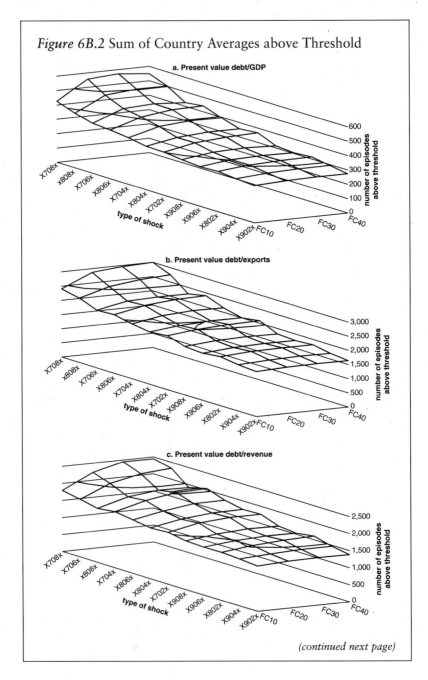

Figure 6B.2 Sum of Country Averages above Threshold

a. Present value debt/GDP

b. Present value debt/exports

c. Present value debt/revenue

(continued next page)

Figure 6B.2 (continued)

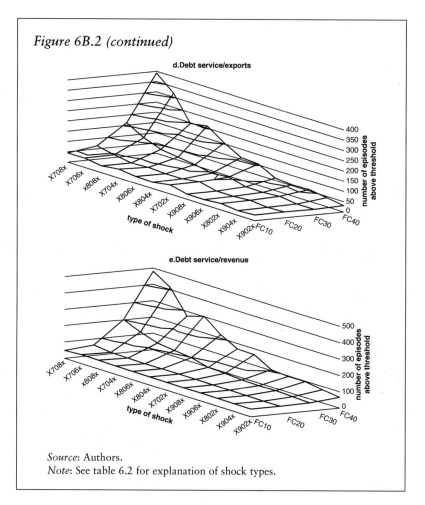

Source: Authors.
Note: See table 6.2 for explanation of shock types.

Figure 6B.3 Sum of Country Maximum above Threshold

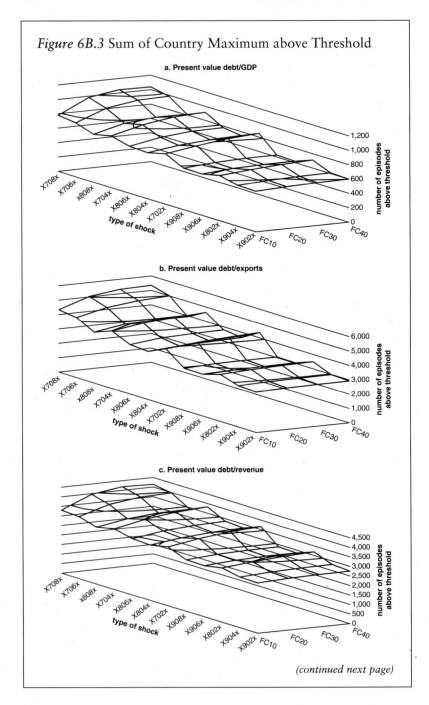

a. Present value debt/GDP

b. Present value debt/exports

c. Present value debt/revenue

(continued next page)

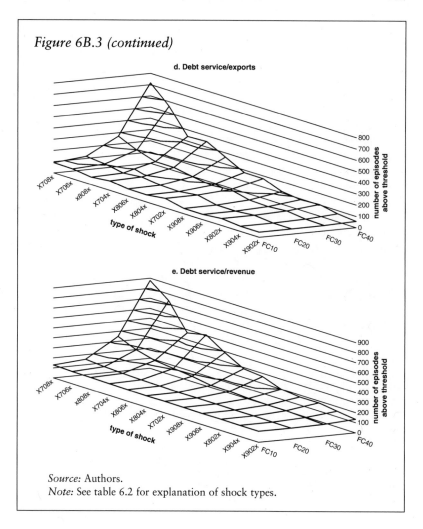

Figure 6B.3 (continued)

d. Debt service/exports

e. Debt service/revenue

Source: Authors.
Note: See table 6.2 for explanation of shock types.

Annex 6C: The Debt Sustainability Framework

The Debt Sustainability Framework (DSF) was adopted in 2005 by the World Bank and the IMF as the standard tool for analyzing debt-related vulnerabilities in low-income countries (see http://go.worldbank.org/A5VFXZCCW0). Its objective is to support these countries' efforts to meet their development goals without creating future debt problems. Under the DSF, the World Bank and the IMF annually perform Debt Sustainability Analyses (DSAs) assessing countries' risk of debt distress over a 20-year horizon. This forward-looking approach helps countries balance their need for funds with their current and prospective ability to repay. It also allows creditors to tailor their financing terms in anticipation of future debt distress situations.

DSAs conducted under the DSF focus on five debt burden indicators for public external debt: the present value of debt to GDP, the present value of debt to exports, the present value of debt to revenues, debt service to revenues, and debt service to exports. Each of these indicators has an indicative threshold in the framework that depends on a country's quality of policies and institutions, as measured by the three-year average of the Country Policy and Institutional Assessment (CPIA) index compiled annually by the World Bank (table 6C.1). The specific thresholds are as follows:

A rating of the risk of external debt distress is derived by reviewing the evolution of the debt burden indicators with respect to their indicative policy-dependent thresholds under a baseline scenario, alternative scenarios, and stress tests. There are four possible ratings:

Table 6C.1 External Public Debt Burden Thresholds under the Debt Sustainability Threshold

Policy	Net present value of debt as percentage of			Debt service as percentage of	
	Exports	GDP	Revenue	Exports	Revenue
Weak (CPIA index < 3.25)	100	30	200	15	25
Medium (CPIA index > 3.25 and < 3.75)	150	40	250	20	30
Strong (CPIA index ≥ 3.75)	200	50	300	25	35

Source: IMF/IDA 2009.
Note: CPIA index is measured as a three-year average.

- Low risk: All debt burden indicators are well below the relevant country-specific thresholds. Thresholds are not breached under any stress tests or alternative scenarios.
- Moderate risk: Although the baseline scenario does not indicate a breach of thresholds, alternative scenarios and stress tests result in a significant rise in debt service indicators over the projection period (nearing thresholds) or a breach of one or more thresholds.
- High risk: The baseline scenario indicates a protracted breach of debt burden thresholds, but the country does not currently face any payment difficulties. Alternative scenarios or stress tests show protracted threshold breaches.
- In debt distress: Current debt and debt service ratios are in significant or sustained breach of thresholds. Actual or impending debt-restructuring negotiations or the existence of arrears would generally suggest that a country is in debt distress.

The indicative policy-dependent thresholds in the DSF are set so that the probabilities of debt distress range between 18 and 22 percent for CPIA ratings of 3.25, 3.5, and 3.75 (the benchmarks for strong, medium, and weak performers, respectively). Therefore, a high risk rating (unlike an "in debt distress" rating) should not be interpreted as synonymous with an unsustainable debt situation.

Although the focus of DSAs is on public and publicly guaranteed external debt, they also include analysis of public debt sustainability. The DSF does not, however, include indicative thresholds for total public debt.

Notes

The authors are extremely grateful to Carlos A. Primo Braga for posing the question that led to this research. They are also grateful to Paulina Granados for her excellent and efficient assistance, without which this project could not have been possible, and to Mizuho Kida, Mona Prasad, Sona Varma, and an anonymous referee for their valuable comments.

1. Some countries experienced an increase in remittances as a result of the repatriation of capital from the host countries. This is a one-off phenomenon that reflects the closure of family businesses as a result of the recession in developed countries.

2. The 31 countries are Angola, Benin, Burkina Faso, Burundi, Cape Verde, Cameroon, Central African Republic, Chad, Comoros, the Democratic Republic of Congo, the Republic of Congo, Côte d'Ivoire, Eritrea, The Gambia, Ghana, Guinea, Guinea-Bissau, Kenya, Liberia, Madagascar, Mauritania, Mozambique, Niger, Rwanda, São Tomé and Principe, Senegal, Sudan, Tanzania, Togo, Uganda, and Zambia. For all but 11 of these countries, the latest DSA date is such that actual data end in 2007 (projected data start in 2008). For three of the remaining countries (the Democratic Republic of Congo, Guinea, and Zambia), the latest DSA date is such that projected data start in 2007. For the remaining eight countries (Angola,

Benin, Cameroon, the Central African Republic, Ghana, Guinea-Bissau, Kenya, and Senegal), actual data end in 2008 (projected data start in 2009).

3. The oil and food commodity prices boom that occurred before the financial crisis could arguably also bias the baseline in earlier DSAs. The sign of those biases will depend on each country's export composition.

4. This potential overestimation of the deterioration in countries' debt burden indicators refers exclusively to the effect on the numerator (the present value of debt or debt service) of the five debt burden indicators. The effect on the denominator, in particular total exports, works in the opposite direction.

5. These assumptions aim only at illustrating plausible scenarios for low-income countries; they are not based on a specific rationale. The extent to which these hypothetical scenarios resemble the actual situation in each country obviously depends on how integrated with the world economy each country is and how diversified its exports are.

6. We use partial equilibrium, which is the way alternative scenarios are modeled in DSA templates. A drop in exports does not automatically translate into lower GDP; GDP needs to be manually keyed into the macro framework. The mechanics of the sensitivity analysis built into the DSA template are presented at http://siteresources.worldbank.org/INTDEBTDEPT/Resources/DSAGUIDE_EXT200610.pdf.

7. In DSA templates, government revenues are projected as a proportion of GDP.

8. The 1:1 substitution of new debt for exports is not automatically linked to the effect of the crisis on GDP (that is, the transmission mechanism discussed earlier).

9. For each country, 48 scenarios (12 shocks varying in depth and duration times 4 financial conditions) need to be analyzed.

10. The tables highlight the number of cases that are significantly larger than the number in the baseline (that is, cases in which the number of countries is at least twice that in the baseline for high risk of debt distress and cases in which the number of countries is more than twice that in the baseline for moderate [medium] risk of debt distress, using the definitions provided in table 6.11).

11. For a preliminary assessment of the actual effects of the crisis on a group of low- and middle-income countries, see IMF (2010).

References

Claessens, S., M. A. Kose, and M. E. Terrones. 2008. "What Happens during Recessions, Crunches and Busts?" IMF Working Paper 08/274, International Monetary Fund, Washington, DC.

IMF (International Monetary Fund) 2010. "Preserving Debt Sustainability in Low-Income Countries in the Wake of the Global Crisis." SM/10/76. Washington, DC.

IMF (International Monetary Fund) and IDA (International Development Association). 2009. *A Review of Some Aspects of the Low-Income Country Debt Sustainability Framework.* August, Washington, DC.

Ratha, Dilip, Sanket Mohapatra, and Ani Silwal. 2009. "Migration and Development Brief 9." World Bank Migration and Remittances Team, Development Prospects Group, World Bank, Washington, DC.

7

Do Middle-Income Countries Still Have the Ability to Deal with the Global Financial Crisis?

Ralph Van Doorn, Vivek Suri, and Sudarshan Gooptu

A t the eve of the 2008 global financial crisis, most middle-income countries had been facing favorable market conditions and had improved their debt management capacity, reduced inflation, improved fiscal and current account balances, and accumulated foreign exchange reserves, in part because of sustained implementation of prudent macroeconomic policies between 2002 and 2007 and appropriate structural reforms. The crisis revealed differences across these countries. Many middle-income countries were better able to cope with the impact of the global crisis than they had been in the late 1990s to the early 2000s. Others were weaker, because of internal and external imbalances that emerged, and were thus hit harder, reducing their ability to respond in 2008 and 2009 and perhaps in the medium term if the global recovery is weak.

This chapter highlights these differences in a sample of 20 middle-income countries in order to stimulate debate about the way forward in dealing with the global financial crisis (table 7.1).[1] All 20 countries in the sample except Hungary are middle-income countries (Hungary, which graduated from middle-income status in 2008, was included because the impact of the global financial crisis and aftermath there warrants a similar type of analysis). The sample includes both manufactured goods and commodity exporters to ensure that the different initial conditions and

Table 7.1 Countries Included in the Sample, by Income Level

Income level	Countries
Lower middle	China, Arab Rep. of Egypt, India, Indonesia, Nigeria, the Philippines, Thailand, Ukraine
Upper middle	Argentina, Brazil, Chile, Colombia, Malaysia, Mexico, Peru, Poland, Russian Federation, South Africa, Turkey
High	Hungary

Source: Authors, based on the World Bank's July 2009 classification.
Note: Commodity exporters are defined here as countries in which dependence on a commodity sector manifested itself in a significant improvement in the fiscal balance between 1995–2001 and 2002–07. By this definition, Argentina, Brazil, Chile, Indonesia, Nigeria, and the Russian Federation are considered commodity exporters but Mexico is not. Hungary was classified as a middle-income country until mid-2008.

transmission channels of the commodity boom and bust cycle and the global financial crisis are captured.

The sample covers countries with very different population sizes and GDPs. At the same time, the countries share important similarities. Nearly all have tapped international capital markets, all have attracted large volumes of short-term external financing, and all are eligible for funding from the nonconcessional window of the World Bank (the International Bank for Reconstruction and Development) and other multilateral institutions. Most of the sample countries are linked to high-income countries through both trade and financial market channels. The global financial crisis thus affected them both directly, through capital flow reversals, exchange rate pressures, and increased borrowing spreads in international credit markets, and indirectly, through commodity prices, exports, portfolio and foreign direct investment (FDI) flows, and workers' remittances.[2]

The chapter is organized as follows. The first section describes the main global and country-specific developments from 2002 to 2007. The following section describes the direct impact of the global financial crisis on middle-income countries. The third section examines the initial fiscal response up to 2009. The fourth section assesses medium-term fiscal challenges and fiscal adjustment strategies under a number of scenarios. The last section provides some concluding remarks.

Global and Country-Specific Developments, 2002–07

Thanks to favorable international market conditions during 2002–07 and prudent domestic macroeconomic management, most countries in the sample were successful in reducing inflation, improving their fiscal and current account balances, and building up foreign exchange reserves. Some countries switched to inflation targeting; others implemented well-designed fiscal responsibility frameworks.[3]

Many countries were able to issue bonds in both foreign and domestic currency, thanks to record low spreads on their bond issuances over comparable U.S. Treasuries, as investors were looking for profitable opportunities. For some countries, this relatively loose financing environment led to a large buildup of public and private external debt, leading to internal and external imbalances and vulnerabilities down the road.

This period also witnessed commodity price hikes, which disproportionately benefited commodity-exporting countries. As food and fuel prices reached record highs between late 2007 and mid-2008, a significant gap in the external and fiscal positions of commodity exporters and other countries began to appear. Commodity-producing countries were therefore in a better position to weather the crisis when it struck in 2008.

These favorable market conditions and policy improvements contributed to the precrisis improvements in domestic indicators in most of these countries. The average rate of inflation came down in most countries, particularly in Argentina, the Russian Federation, Turkey, and Ukraine. In several countries, financial sector development increased residents' access to credit. The increase in credit as a share of GDP was especially large in Hungary and Ukraine. Many countries, including Chile, Nigeria, and Russia, increased their average fiscal and primary balances. Turkey improved its fiscal balance. This period also saw a decline in these countries' gross public indebtedness (as a share of GDP), partly because of rapid GDP growth (figure 7.1).[4]

In most of these countries, the current account deficits of 1995–2001 turned into surpluses in 2002–07. Total external debt relative to GDP decreased in most countries between 2002 and 2007 (figure 7.2). In Argentina, Indonesia, Nigeria, and the Philippines, external debt as a percentage of GDP fell the most relative to the 2002 level. In contrast, in Hungary, Poland, and Ukraine, external debt grew relative to 2002.[5]

In countries in which external debt decreased between 2002 and 2007, the decline mainly reflected rapid nominal GDP growth; exchange rate appreciation, which reduces the domestic currency value of external debt, played only a minor role.[6] In countries that saw large increases in external debt, the change primarily reflected increased borrowing, which allowed debt stocks to grow at a faster rate than nominal GDP.

Given the favorable developments many countries experienced during the precrisis period (2002–07), the macroeconomic space improved for many countries.[7] In order to compare countries in this regard, we computed an index of macroeconomic space for each country for each year (box 7.1).

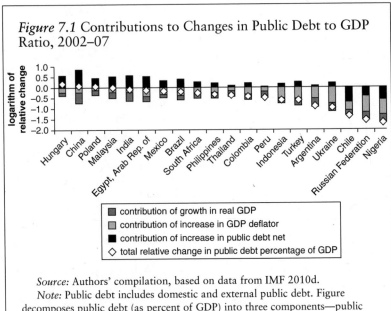

Figure 7.1 Contributions to Changes in Public Debt to GDP Ratio, 2002–07

Source: Authors' compilation, based on data from IMF 2010d.
Note: Public debt includes domestic and external public debt. Figure decomposes public debt (as percent of GDP) into three components—public debt in local currency, nominal GDP in constant prices, and the GDP deflator)—and shows the relative contribution of each in logarithmic terms. Public debt (percent of GDP) = Public debt (local currency)/[GDP (local currency, constant) × GDP deflator]. In relative changes in logarithm: Log [1+ percentage change in public debt (percent of GDP)] = Log [1+ percentage change in public debt (local currency)]—Log [1+ percentage change in GDP (local currency, constant)] – Log [1+ percentage change in GDP deflator].

The index of macroeconomic space indicates that the space of most countries in the sample increased between 2002 and 2007. China enjoyed the largest macroeconomic space in the sample, thanks to strong external subindicators and favorable fiscal and domestic subindicators. Nigeria's macroeconomic space largely reflected its favorable external subindicators, such as current account surpluses, high reserves, and low debt, which offset the rapid growth in credit to the private sector relative to GDP, which could eventually lead to higher inflationary pressure. Chile's macroeconomic space almost entirely reflected its prudent fiscal policy. Hungary had the least macroeconomic space, mainly because of its relatively weak external and fiscal subindicators. In Ukraine high inflation and weak external subindicators were more important, despite a fiscal subindicator that was actually more positive than a few higher-ranked countries.

Hungary and Ukraine are followed by Turkey and Argentina, both of which had mainly weak external subindicators (figure 7.3).

Direct Impact of the Global Financial Crisis

When the financial crisis became global, in September 2008, the immediate market reaction hit middle-income countries through multiple channels. Data for the quarter that followed showed that markets become more discriminating in their risk assessments, as demonstrated by spreads, exchange rates, and foreign exchange reserves. GDP growth also suffered in most of these countries, and their external debt burdens increased because of unfavorable exchange rate movements.

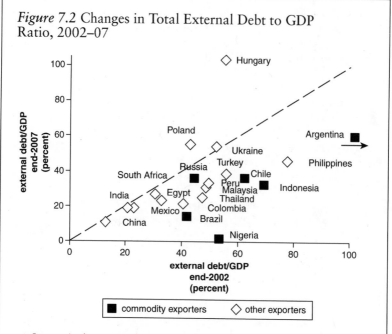

Figure 7.2 Changes in Total External Debt to GDP Ratio, 2002–07

Source: Authors' compilation, based on data from IMF 2010d.
Note: Figures are shown as percentages. Debt includes public and publicly guaranteed debt and private nonguaranteed debt. Points above the dashed line indicate that external debt was higher at the end of 2007 than at the end of 2002. In Argentina debt was reduced from 152 percent of GDP at the end of 2002 to 59 percent at the end of 2007.

Box 7.1 The Index of Macroeconomic Space

Our index of macroeconomic space summarizes the variables that have the greatest influence on a country's ability to implement a countercyclical fiscal policy or a fiscal stimulus program. In order for a country to be able to implement a countercyclical fiscal policy or a fiscal stimulus, it is neither necessary nor sufficient to have low fiscal deficits and low public debt. External and domestic conditions can support or constrain fiscal policy. For example, if a country has high inflation, a current account deficit, low reserves, high external debt, or rapid growth in credit to the private sector, a fiscal expansion might destabilize the economy. In contrast, even if a country has been running fiscal deficits and has a high level of public debt, it might still be able to run a fiscal expansion as long as markets are confident that the country's debt level will remain on a sustainable path and that macroeconomic stability will not be jeopardized. The nonfiscal components of the index represent some of the variables markets regularly monitor.

In countries with low public and external debt, large foreign exchange reserves, low inflation, moderate credit growth, and a positive or only moderately negative current account and fiscal balances, this fiscal expansion will probably have positive macroeconomic benefits (supporting growth while maintaining internal and external balances). Such countries are said to have macroeconomic space.

In a country with rapid credit growth to the private sector, the increase in domestic demand may accelerate inflation; rapid credit growth may also be a leading indicator for future calls on fiscal resources because of the building up of contingent liabilities in the financial sector. The increase in external demand will lead to deterioration in the balance of payments and may put the exchange rate under pressure. Under a fixed exchange rate, the country would lose foreign exchange reserves. Countries facing these conditions are said to have limited macroeconomic space.

In most countries there will be a mix of these positive and negative indicators. A country could have a fiscal surplus but still be constrained by high inflation, low foreign exchange reserves, or a current account deficit. A prudent country with low inflation and current account surpluses might be able to (temporarily) sustain higher fiscal deficits and enjoy confidence from the markets.

The index of macroeconomic space consists of the unweighted sum of the seven standardized variables displayed in the box table. These variables have been normalized with the sample mean and standard deviation for each year, so that the distribution of each variable across the sample in 2007 and 2009 is centered on zero with a unit standard deviation. (This

Box 7.1 *(continued)*

standardization prevents variables with typically high numerical values from dominating the index.) The exchange rate and the domestic interest rate are not included explicitly as variables in this index, in order to account for any endogeneity that may exist between these variables and the seven standardized variables in the index. This index of macroeconomic space thus tracks a country's ability to conduct countercyclical fiscal policy or even launch a fiscal stimulus program relative to the sample in any given year. The fiscal space in 2007, for instance, is normalized by the 2007 sample average and standard deviation, allowing countries to be ranked by their fiscal space at any point in time.

Table B1.1 Components of the Index of Macroeconomic Space

Sector	Subindicator	Negative impact on space if	Positive impact on space if
Domestic	Credit to private sector (percent of GDP, percent year-on-year change)	High	Low
	CPI inflation (percent change)	High	Low
External	Current account (percent of GDP)	Deficit	Surplus
	External debt (percent of GDP)	High	Low
	Log foreign exchange reserves to short-term debt ratio	Low	High
Fiscal	Fiscal balance (percent of GDP)	Deficit	Surplus
	Gross public debt (percent of GDP)	High	Low

Source: Authors.
Note: CPI = consumer price index.

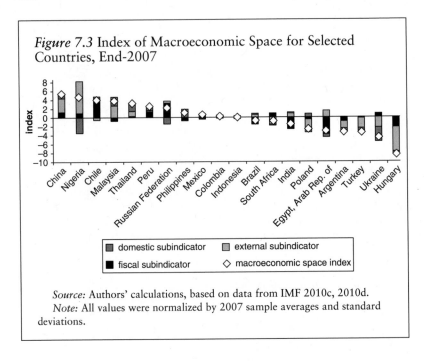

Figure 7.3 Index of Macroeconomic Space for Selected Countries, End-2007

domestic subindicator □ external subindicator
■ fiscal subindicator ◇ macroeconomic space index

Source: Authors' calculations, based on data from IMF 2010c, 2010d.
Note: All values were normalized by 2007 sample averages and standard deviations.

Spreads on sovereign bonds over comparable U.S. Treasuries shot up immediately across this sample of middle-income countries in September 2008, especially in Argentina, Hungary, Russia, and Ukraine (figure 7.4).[8] At the same time, with portfolio capital flows reversing, the balance of payments came under pressure in many countries. Some countries, such as Brazil, Chile, Colombia, the Philippines, and South Africa, immediately let their exchange rates adjust while preserving foreign exchange reserves. Other countries tried in vain to resist depreciation pressure while losing foreign exchange reserves.

As the initial wave of panic subsided, markets became more discerning and started to look at countries' fundamentals. Spreads started to decrease for most countries (they continued to widen in Argentina, Hungary, and Ukraine), although by March 2009 they had not yet returned to their precrisis levels. Meanwhile, exchange rates had become more stable, and some countries' foreign exchange reserves had increased again. A comparison of precrisis average peak-to-trough GDP growth (real year-on-year growth between third quarter 2008 and third quarter 2009) reveals that all countries in the sample were hit by a slowdown (figure 7.5). This was especially so for commodity exporters such as Chile and Russia as well as countries such as Hungary, Mexico, Turkey, and Ukraine. For developing countries as a whole, the economic downturn has been deeper and more broadly based than during previous recessions (World Bank 2010).

Initial Fiscal Response up to 2009

Faced with the impact of the global financial crisis, countries responded with a range of policy measures, including countercyclical fiscal policy, monetary policy, bank credit expansion, and international liquidity support facilities.[9] The cyclically adjusted primary balances between 2007 and 2009 deteriorated in all countries, except Hungary, where an IMF-supported fiscal consolidation program was quickly put in place after the crisis hit (figure 7.6) (IMF 2010b).[10]

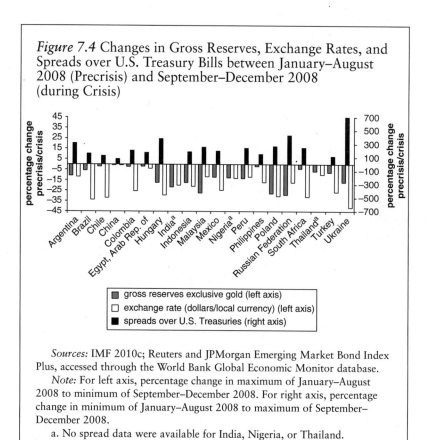

Figure 7.4 Changes in Gross Reserves, Exchange Rates, and Spreads over U.S. Treasury Bills between January–August 2008 (Precrisis) and September–December 2008 (during Crisis)

■ gross reserves exclusive gold (left axis)
□ exchange rate (dollars/local currency) (left axis)
■ spreads over U.S. Treasuries (right axis)

Sources: IMF 2010c; Reuters and JPMorgan Emerging Market Bond Index Plus, accessed through the World Bank Global Economic Monitor database.

Note: For left axis, percentage change in maximum of January–August 2008 to minimum of September–December 2008. For right axis, percentage change in minimum of January–August 2008 to maximum of September–December 2008.

a. No spread data were available for India, Nigeria, or Thailand.

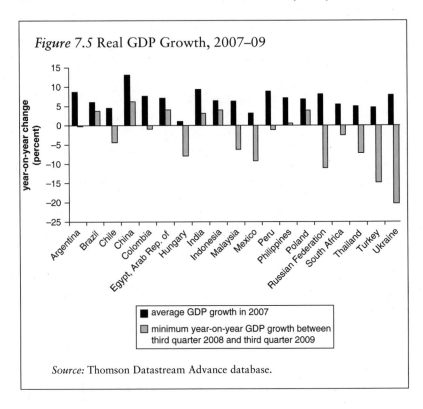

Figure 7.5 Real GDP Growth, 2007–09

Source: Thomson Datastream Advance database.

Countries with relatively large macroeconomic space at the end of 2007 typically increased their noninterest expenditure in 2008–09 the most, both as a share of GDP and in real terms.[11] Chile and Russia, which had healthy fiscal subindicators, showed the largest increase in noninterest expenditure as a share of GDP. China showed strong external subindicators but a large increase in real noninterest expenditure.[12] Although the increases in fiscal expenditure helped counteract the drop in other components of aggregate demand, in most cases they were unable to prevent a downturn. The new borrowing in response to the crisis, combined with the slowdown in growth and the depreciation of the exchange rate, reversed some of the earlier gains from a reduction of external and public debt (as a share of GDP) that these countries experienced in previous years. As a percentage of GDP, external debt increased in 11 countries in the sample between 2007 and 2009; between 2002 and 2007, it increased only in Hungary, Poland, and Ukraine.

The fiscal policy response in 2008 and 2009, and the external support packages put together for these countries, led to higher public (figure 7.7) and external debt in several countries. Some countries, such as Hungary, which had built up external debt relative to domestic debt, face increased

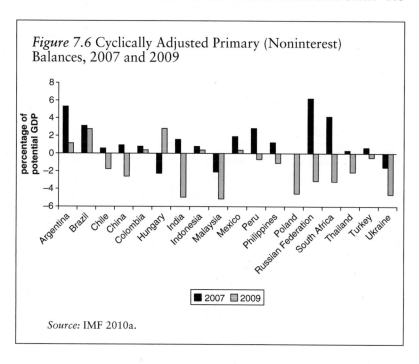

Figure 7.6 Cyclically Adjusted Primary (Noninterest) Balances, 2007 and 2009

Source: IMF 2010a.

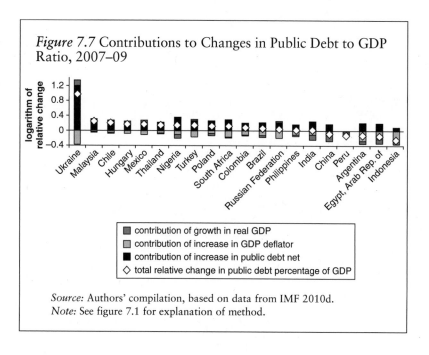

Figure 7.7 Contributions to Changes in Public Debt to GDP Ratio, 2007–09

Source: Authors' compilation, based on data from IMF 2010d.
Note: See figure 7.1 for explanation of method.

exchange rate risk. Others, such as Brazil, the Arab Republic of Egypt, and India, which had built up domestic debt relative to external debt, reduced their exchange rate risks. This evidence suggests that countries would do well to monitor the financial structure and composition of their debt portfolios.

Countries that had macroeconomic space at the onset of the crisis in late 2008 were able to rapidly respond by increasing their fiscal spending. The macroeconomic space at end-2007 and the change in the primary balance observed between 2007 and 2009 appear to be negatively correlated. However, at end-2009 most countries ended up with less macroeconomic space after the initial impact of the global financial crisis. The ranking of countries along the macroeconomic space index also changed, reflecting the relative space that had been "used up" as a result of the crisis (figure 7.8). Countries such as Argentina and Hungary improved their relative ranking but still had very narrow macroeconomic space.

By the end of 2009, Nigeria, Thailand, Chile, and China had the greatest room to respond to a more prolonged crisis. In Nigeria the large fiscal space reflected the country's strong external subindicator; in the other countries it reflected a more balanced mix of indicators.[13] Hungary and Ukraine had the least amount of fiscal space in the sample, reflecting both weak starting points and the strong negative impacts of the crisis.

Medium-Term Fiscal Challenges and Fiscal Adjustment Strategies under Various Scenarios

Given these elevated levels of debt after the initial crisis response, the attention of policy makers and capital market participants should shift to the medium term. The World Bank's *Global Economic Prospects 2010* concludes that the 2008 global crisis will have a lasting impact on financial markets, raising borrowing costs and lowering levels of credit and international capital flows. It projects that as countries adjust to tighter global financial conditions, growth of output in developing countries may be reduced by 0.2–0.7 percentage point a year until 2015–17. Given the depth of the recession and the weakness of the expected recovery, significant spare capacity, high unemployment, and weak inflationary pressures may emerge in both high-income and developing countries for some time (World Bank 2010).

What will happen to public debt if there is no adjustment to the primary balance in the medium term? What kind of fiscal adjustment will countries need to make to reduce or stabilize their public debt stocks? If the adjustment is too large to be politically credible, what will be the effect of a more gradual adjustment? This section addresses some of these questions by reporting on the results of illustrative scenarios:[14]

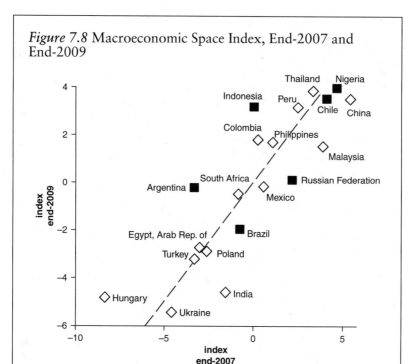

Figure 7.8 Macroeconomic Space Index, End-2007 and End-2009

Sources: Authors' calculations, based on data from IMF 2009a, 2010b, 2010c, 2010d; Credit Suisse 2010.

Note: Variables were normalized by the sample average and standard deviation in each year. Countries above the dashed line moved up in the ranking of macroeconomic space between 2007 and 2009.

- The baseline scenario fixes the primary balance at its historical value and takes the growth rate projections from the IMF's World Economic Outlook database (April 2010). This database assumes that after the crisis growth rates are permanently lower than before the crisis.
- Scenario 1 calculates the required primary balance if countries try to reach a debt target. These debt targets are to reduce debt to 40 percent of GDP by 2020 if the debt stock is above 40 percent of GDP at end-2009 or to permanently stabilize the debt to GDP ratio if the debt is below 40 percent of GDP at end-2009.[15] Comparing the required primary balances going forward with the country's historical values shows the extent to which a

country needs to adjust its primary balance to reach its desired debt target.

- Scenario 2 is similar to scenario 1, but it assumes that the crisis will last longer and that countries will need to continue to implement expansionary policies as they did in 2007–09, forcing them to accumulate additional debt. It then estimates the required primary balance if a country still aims to achieve the same debt target as under scenario 1, this time by 2020.
- Scenario 3 examines a more gradual approach to adjusting the primary balances in each country in order to reach the debt target (as specified in scenario 1). Such an approach may be necessary for some countries if the required fiscal adjustment under the first two scenarios is very large, politically infeasible, or both, or if such an adjustment might fuel further instability and perhaps a new downturn because of insufficient aggregate demand without a stimulus program.

The Baseline Scenario

Under the baseline scenario, in which the primary balance is set at the historical average, public debt in 2020 is expected to increase for a number of countries, in particular the countries with the highest public debt at end-2009 (Egypt, Hungary, and India). For Chile and Nigeria, public debt declines and becomes negative during the projection period. This indicates that both countries will accumulate fiscal assets (note that the simulation for these two countries used the average primary balance of 1996–2001; had the more favorable average primary balance of 2002–07 been used, public debt would have become even more negative in 2020).

Colombia, Peru, and Turkey, which are not among the major commodity exporters, had much higher average primary surpluses during 2002–07 than they did between 1996 and 2001. Although this increase may signal fiscal policy improvements, a key question will be whether these countries will be able to maintain such fiscal surpluses in a postcrisis world if commodity prices and global growth decline. For the baseline scenario for those countries, the historical primary fiscal balance is therefore assumed to be represented by their 1996–2001 average primary fiscal balance.

Scenario 1: 2020 Debt Target

Under scenario 1, countries set a specific public debt target for 2020. They may want to do so to account for the effect of the political cycle on debt, to commit future governments to maintain debt sustainability, or to benefit from the "announcement effect" with a view to assuring capital markets that their debt is sustainable and that the crisis response programs are indeed temporary. Under this scenario countries are assumed to adopt one of two debt targets: to reduce debt to 40 percent of GDP by 2020 if the end-2009 debt exceeds 40 percent of GDP or to stabilize debt at the end-2009 level if end-2009 debt is below 40 percent of GDP. Under this scenario Chile, China, Colombia, Indonesia, Malaysia, Nigeria, Peru, Russia, South Africa, and Ukraine will adopt the stabilization target. The remaining countries will adopt the debt reduction target.

Under the baseline growth projection, the primary fiscal balance required to achieve the target is lower than the historical primary balance for Chile, Indonesia, Mexico, Nigeria, Peru, the Philippines, South Africa, and Turkey. No unusual fiscal adjustment would thus be needed in those countries. China would have to achieve a higher primary balance than its historical balance, but given its low level of public debt at end-2009, its debt would still be below 40 percent of GDP if it continued to achieve its historical primary balance. Large adjustments of the primary balance would be needed in Argentina, Egypt, Hungary, India, and Poland.

Although a permanently lower GDP growth rate and higher world interest rates would increase the required adjustment, their effect on the required adjustment is smaller than the debt target itself.[16] However, these shocks would mean that countries like Mexico, Peru, the Philippines, and Turkey would have to adjust their primary fiscal balances to achieve the debt target (figure 7.9).

How would this fiscal adjustment take place? Countries could cut public spending, increase government revenue, or both. Much will depend on the pace of recovery of fiscal revenues in each country, which in turn will depend on GDP growth, international interest rates and exchange rates, pressure that ongoing higher social safety net expenditures are already putting on government budgets, and the political feasibility of cutting key recurrent spending items in the budget. The extent to which private sector consumption and investment demand respond to the fiscal and monetary stimulus efforts and the inventory cycle also introduce uncertainties. If the response is weaker than envisaged or efforts are prematurely halted, the recovery could stall (World Bank 2010).

Scenario 2: Prolonged Fiscal Expansion to 2012

Under scenario 2, the fiscal stimulus spending of 2008 and 2009 is continued for an additional two years, and countries are assumed to respond to it endogenously in the same way as they responded immediately after the crisis. After 2011, when this additional fiscal spending stops, countries are assumed to continue to aim toward the debt targets in 2020 under scenario 1, with the same baseline GDP growth and interest rate assumptions. Under

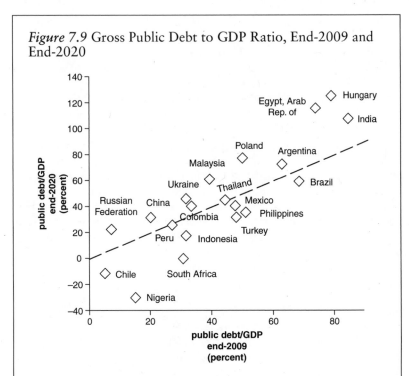

Figure 7.9 Gross Public Debt to GDP Ratio, End-2009 and End-2020

Source: Authors' calculations, based on IMF 2010d.
Note: Figures are shown as percentages. Negative numbers can be interpreted as fiscal assets. For points above the dashed line, public debt at end-2020 is higher than at end-2009.

scenario 2, if a country's public debt as a share of GDP increased in 2008 and 2009, it will continue to increase by the same share of GDP in 2010 and 2011. If public debt as a share of GDP decreased in 2008 and 2009, it will be kept constant as a share of GDP in 2010 and 2011 (this is the case for Argentina, Egypt, Indonesia, Peru, and Russia).

Given the additional debt accumulation in some countries and the lack of decline in debt levels in others, it will become more difficult for most countries to achieve their 2020 targets under this scenario. The debt target for Malaysia and Ukraine, where public debt was less than 40 percent of GDP at end-2009, would switch from public debt stabilization under scenario 1 to debt reduction under scenario 2. Mexico, the Philippines, and Turkey would need to adjust their primary balances further relative to their historical efforts (under scenario 1 no adjustment was needed) (figure 7.10).

Scenario 3: Gradual Fiscal Adjustment

In some countries, policy makers may deem the difference between the historical primary balance and the primary balance required to reach the debt target too large to be politically acceptable (or credible). Fears that further fiscal contraction in an already fragile macroeconomic and growth environment may fuel a new economic downturn could also postpone these efforts. Under scenario 3, countries are assumed to take a more gradual approach to adjusting their primary balances in order to reach the same target in 2020 as under scenario 1 (figure 7.11). Specifically, the annual fiscal adjustment is limited to 2 percentage points of GDP.

For most of the countries in the sample, the required adjustment in the primary balance under scenario 1 is less than 2 percent of GDP. These countries can adjust their primary balance entirely in 2010, putting debt on a downward trajectory or stabilizing it immediately. Where the required adjustment is larger than 2 percent of GDP, it would be made more gradually (five years in Hungary, four years in India and Egypt, and two years in Argentina and Poland). In Egypt, Hungary, and Poland (where the historical primary deficit is very large), debt would first increase during the adjustment, peaking in 2010 or 2011 before declining. For a number of years these countries will have to borrow heavily to finance their deficits. Debt and fiscal sustainability will therefore need to be carefully monitored. How much and at what terms these market-access countries will be able

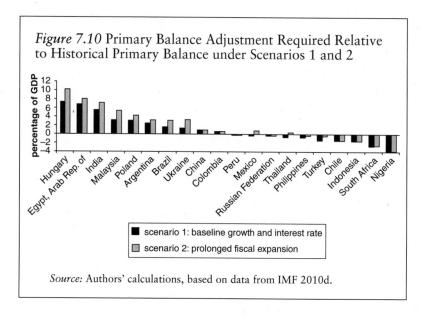

Figure 7.10 Primary Balance Adjustment Required Relative to Historical Primary Balance under Scenarios 1 and 2

Source: Authors' calculations, based on data from IMF 2010d.

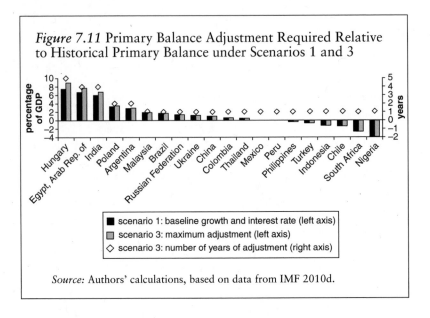

Figure 7.11 Primary Balance Adjustment Required Relative to Historical Primary Balance under Scenarios 1 and 3

■ scenario 1: baseline growth and interest rate (left axis)
□ scenario 3: maximum adjustment (left axis)
◇ scenario 3: number of years of adjustment (right axis)

Source: Authors' calculations, based on data from IMF 2010d.

to obtain financing will depend on the conditions of the financial markets for middle-income countries, the credibility of their adjustment strategy, and the effective communication of the strategy to market participants in a timely and credible manner.

Concluding Remarks

Our sample of 20 mostly middle-income countries entered the 2008 global financial crisis with different initial conditions. To show how these conditions affected their ability to implement countercyclical fiscal policy or a fiscal stimulus at any point in time, we create an "index of macroeconomic space." Favorable global conditions and policy improvements up to 2007 strengthened the macroeconomic space of a large number of middle-income countries, especially commodity exporters, by allowing them to accumulate foreign exchange reserves, reduce external and public debt, and achieve low inflation and low fiscal deficits. Other countries had already been weakened by high debt, high inflation, or persistent deficits by 2007. In large part, these initial conditions determined the extent of the countries' fiscal response to the global financial crisis. Since 2008 many countries have implemented expansionary fiscal policies that have used up their available macroeconomic space. Most countries have had to resort to increased borrowing by the public sector, both externally and domestically.

The most acute phase of the crisis may have passed, but if the fiscal interventions undertaken in the aftermath of the crisis are to continue, middle-income countries need to pay careful attention to the sustainability and composition of their debt levels (domestic and external). Debt levels will remain high and the recovery will be slow in high-income countries. For new borrowings from developing countries, world interest rates may rise and maturities shorten. Continuously monitoring and managing the interest rate, currency, and commodity price risks associated with their debt portfolios will be crucial. Middle-income countries also need to maintain credible debt management and financing strategies to support their fiscal spending and postcrisis fiscal adjustments.

Unless they embark on severe, unprecedented fiscal adjustments or are given more time to adjust than current projections seem to suggest, some countries will have limited room to maneuver. Although traditional external debt sustainability analyses will continue to be an important ingredient in the analytical toolkit, they need to be supplemented by a closer examination of public debt (domestic and external) and medium-term fiscal sustainability by the appropriate authorities on an ongoing basis. Attention should also be given to monitoring and managing the fiscal risks posed by the array of contingent liabilities incurred by some governments in the context of their responses to the global financial crisis. This will be necessary in order to minimize the risks of unforeseen calls on fiscal resources that may arise from such contingent liabilities from a source that may be "too big to fail."

Notes

The authors thank the anonymous reviewers for their insightful comments and suggestions on an earlier draft of this chapter as well as participants at the World Bank–AfDB Sovereign Debt and Financial Crisis conference in Tunis in March 2010 for their comments.

1. The World Bank classifies countries according to gross national income (GNI) per capita using the Atlas method. GNI per capita is $975 or less in low-income countries, $976–$3,855 in lower-middle-income countries, $3,856–$11,905 in upper-middle-income countries, and $11,906 in high-income countries (see http://go.worldbank.org/K2CKM78CC0).

2. Low-income countries have been typically hit only through indirect channels, such as commodity prices, exports, FDI flows, and remittances, as only a few have access to international capital markets. Given the larger share of income typically spent on food in low-income countries relative to middle-income countries, the food and fuel price boom that occurred just before the global financial crisis had a larger and broader impact on low-income countries than middle-income countries, weakening their position. Some countries have benefited from debt relief; they rely largely on long-term concessional funding and grants from multilateral and official bilateral creditors.

3. Between 1999 and 2006, 11 countries in the sample had moved to inflation targeting. They included Brazil, Chile, and Poland (1999); Colombia, South
Africa, and Thailand (2000); Hungary and Mexico (2001); Peru and the Philippines
(2002); Indonesia (2005); and Turkey (2006) (Rose 2006). Since 2000, 11 countries in the sample (Argentina, Brazil, Chile, Hungary, India, Indonesia, Mexico,
Nigeria, Pakistan, Peru, and Poland) have implemented fiscal rules, in the form of
debt limits, balanced budget rules, and expenditure and revenue rules (IMF 2009b).
These rules vary by level of government, enforcement, and the degree of flexibility
accorded by the center to subnational entities.

4. Most countries reduced their gross public debt. Argentina decreased its
debt from 170 percent of GDP in 2002 (as a result of the devaluation that year) to
70 percent of GDP in 2007, thanks to fast nominal growth; the stock of debt hardly
changed. In October 2005, Nigeria reached an agreement with Paris Club creditors
to cancel or repay almost all of the outstanding claims against it (IMF 2006).

5. Total debt in Hungary rose from 55 percent of GDP in 2002 to 103 percent
of GDP in 2007, but the figure includes a large increase in banking and intercom-
pany loans (IMF 2010b).

6. In the Arab Republic of Egypt and Mexico, exchange rate depreciation was
offset by rapid GDP growth. Nigeria benefited from a large reduction in external
debt in 2005.

7. The concept of macroeconomic space is similar to that of Heller (2005), who
defines fiscal space as the space for the government to implement a countercyclical
fiscal policy or even a fiscal stimulus program without jeopardizing the sustainability of its financial position or the stability of the economy.

8. Data are from the J.P. Morgan Emerging Markets Bond Index Global
(EMBI Global), which tracks total returns for U.S. dollar–denominated debt instruments issued by emerging market sovereign and quasi-sovereign entities.

9. In October 2008 the Federal Reserve arranged dollar liquidity swaps with
the central banks of Brazil and Mexico (http://www.federalreserve.gov/newsevents/
press/monetary/20081029b.htm). In April 2009 Colombia, Mexico, and Poland
requested flexible credit lines with the IMF. The Association of Southeast Asian
Nations (ASEAN) countries, together with China, Japan, and the Republic of
Korea, expanded the Chiang Mai Initiative's swap lines.

10. See appendix 1 of the IMF document for updated information on crisis-
related discretionary fiscal stimulus programs in the G-20 countries based on a
survey of IMF country desks.

11. The correlation between the overall macroeconomic index (fiscal, external,
and domestic subindicators) at end-2007 and the change in real noninterest expenditure between 2007 and 2009 is 46 percent. The correlation between the fiscal
subindicator alone and the change in real noninterest expenditure between 2007
and 2009 is much lower (20 percent), suggesting that nonfiscal variables play an
important role in determining macroeconomic space.

12. Only a small portion of China's fiscal stimulus package is visible in the budget data, as most is reflected in bank lending (Vincelette and others 2010): domestic
credit to the private sector surged, from 108 percent of GDP in 2008 to 134 percent
of GDP in 2009. The change—the largest increase and the highest level of private
credit in the sample—potentially reduces China's fiscal space to act down the road.

13. The indicators included a combination of fiscal and external indicators
for China, domestic and external indicators for Thailand, and fiscal and domestic
indicators for Chile.

14. All four simulations use projections from the IMF's World Economic Outlook database (April 2010). The nominal medium-term growth rate is the average
projected growth rate for 2010–14. The historical primary balance is the average primary balance for 2002–07. For commodity exporters the average primary balance

was very high, thanks to the commodity price boom; they may not be able to achieve these surpluses in the medium term. A similar argument applies to Colombia, Peru, and Turkey. Therefore, for these countries the (lower) average from 1996 to 2001 is used. The nominal interest rate growth rate differential $(r - g)$ is set at 1 percentage point for all countries. Using market data–based country-specific values for $(r - g)$ taken from Topalova and Nyberg (2010) does not make a significant difference.

15. The 40 percent of GDP target corresponds to the sample median of the 2004–07 average public debt level of middle-income countries (see IMF 2010a).

16. The lower growth rate case is three-quarters of the baseline growth rate, keeping the interest rate unchanged. The higher interest rate case is 2 percentage points higher than the baseline, leading to an interest rate–growth rate differential of 3 percentage points.

References

Credit Suisse. 2010. "Emerging Markets Quarterly, Q2 2010." Credit Suisse Emerging Markets Economics Global, March 10.

Heller, Peter. 2005. "Back to Basics. Fiscal Space: What It Is and How to Get It." *Finance & Development* 42 (2). http://www.imf.org/external/pubs/ft/fandd/2005/06/basics.htm.

IMF (International Monetary Fund). 2006. "Nigeria: First Review under the Policy Support Instrument - Staff Report." IMF Country Report 06/180, International Monetary Fund, Washington, DC.

———. 2009a. "Arab Republic of Egypt: 2008 Article IV Consultation Staff Report." IMF Country Report 09/25, International Monetary Fund, Washington, DC.

———. 2009b. "Fiscal Rules: Anchoring Expectations for Sustainable Public Finances." Fiscal Affairs Department, International Monetary Fund, Washington, DC.

———. 2010a. "Fiscal Monitor: Navigating the Fiscal Challenges Ahead." Fiscal Affairs Department, International Monetary Fund, Washington, DC.

———. 2010b. "Hungary: Fifth Review under the Stand-By Arrangement and Request for Modification of Performance Criterion." IMF Country Report 10/80, International Monetary Fund, Washington, DC.

———. 2010c. *International Financial Statistics*. Washington, DC: International Monetary Fund.

———. 2010d. *World Economic Outlook*. Washington, DC: International Monetary Fund.

Rose, Andrew. 2006. "A Stable International Monetary System Emerges: Inflation Targeting Is Bretton Woods, Reversed." NBER Working Paper 12711, National Bureau of Economic Research, Cambridge, MA.

Topalova, Petia, and Dan Nyberg. 2010. "What Level of Public Debt Could India Target?" IMF Working Paper 10/7, International Monetary Fund, Washington, DC.

Vincelette, Gallina, Alvaro Manoel, Ardo Hansson, and Louis Kuijs. 2010. "The Global Crisis and the Medium-Term Growth Prospects for China." World Bank Workshop on Crisis and Medium-Term Prospects for Growth, Washington, DC, December 17–18.

World Bank. 2010. *Global Economic Prospects*. Washington, DC: World Bank.

8

Small States, the Financial Crisis, and the Aftermath

Edgardo Favaro, Dörte Dömeland,
William O'Boyle, and Tihomir Stučka

Small states, defined as countries with populations of less than 2 million people, face unique economic and public management challenges.[1] The financial crisis has had a mixed impact on small states—severe in some countries, relatively mild in others. The crisis has also affected public debt trajectories, erasing recent gains in debt reduction in some countries and exacerbating already challenging debt situations.

Several findings emerge from our analysis of the effects of the crisis on small states:

- The crisis has had more profound effects on higher-income small states. In 2008 the median per capita GDP of countries whose GDP fell 10 percent was $13,574. Countries whose GDP fell at least 4 percentage points had a median per capita income of $2,814. Lower-income small states, which are further behind in their transformation to modern economies and more isolated from the global economy, have been less exposed to the global recession.
- The crisis has been more severe in countries that had large current account deficits as of end-2007.[2]
- In most cases, the origin of these current account deficits was a private sector savings–investment gap rather than a public sector gap.
- The bust was preceded in most countries by an economic boom fueled by foreign direct investment.
- The recession has been severe where a sudden stop in international capital flows was accompanied by disruption in the functioning of

the financial system, as it was in Iceland and the Eastern Caribbean Currency Union (ECCU).[3]

- The crisis resulted in a sharp increase in fiscal deficits across most small states, driven largely by a decline in tax revenue collection. This increase in fiscal deficits is particularly worrisome in countries with high public debt to GDP ratios.

- On average, the financial crisis reversed the decline in debt burden indicators that had been achieved throughout the early 2000s.

The chapter is organized as follows. The next section identifies the unique challenges small states face and provides an overview of the structural characteristics of their economies. The second section examines the impact of the global financial crisis on small states, looking at both the public savings–investment gap and debt burden indicators. The last section provides some concluding remarks.

Challenges Faced by Small States

Most small states are young, having achieved independence in the past four decades. Of the 47 small states listed in table 8.1, 43 (all but Bhutan, Iceland, Luxembourg, and San Marino) became independent after 1959 and 24 became independent after 1973.[4]

Political independence meant that national institutions suddenly had to provide services once provided by colonial institutions. It has also meant a gradual transformation from the production and export of a few agricultural commodities (in most cases, bananas and sugar) to production and export of services and, in a few cases, manufactured goods (Favaro 2008).

These changes have been costly and taken time. Small states that specialized in the production of sugar and bananas did not become suppliers of tourism or financial services overnight; displaced rural workers did not instantaneously develop the skills demanded by the expanding service sector. Also, even for the service industry there are costs for building infrastructure. Although necessary, the transformation has often been accompanied by experimentation and mistakes, expansion of government employment, sustained fiscal deficits, and in some countries, the buildup of a large public sector debt.

The shift into tourism and other services and away from agriculture has not reduced the exposure caused by the concentration of production and exports in a few products. As a result, shifts in external demand have a disproportionately large effect on the GDP of these states. Small market size also narrows the opportunities to diversify risk.

Despite disadvantages with respect to the possible exploitation of economies of scale and, in some cases, geographic isolation and exposure to natural disasters, small states had a median purchasing power parity

Table 8.1 Small States, by Region and Income Group

Region	Low income	Middle income	High income
East Asia and the Pacific	Solomon Islands	Fiji, Kiribati, Marshall Islands, Federated States of Micronesia, Palau, Samoa, Timor-Leste, Tonga, Vanuatu	Brunei Darussalam
Europe and Central Asia		Kosovo, Montenegro	Cyprus, Estonia, Iceland, Luxembourg, Malta, San Marino
Latin America and the Caribbean		Antigua and Barbuda, Belize, Dominica, Grenada, Guyana, St. Kitts and Nevis, St. Lucia, St. Vincent and the Grenadines, Suriname	The Bahamas, Barbados, Trinidad and Tobago
Middle East and North Africa		Djibouti	Bahrain, Qatar
South Asia		Bhutan, Maldives	
Sub-Saharan Africa	Comoros, The Gambia, Guinea-Bissau	Botswana, Cape Verde, Gabon, Mauritius, São Tomé and Principe, the Seychelles, Swaziland	Equatorial Guinea

Source: Authors, based on http://data.worldbank.org/about/country-classifications/country-and-lending-groups.
Note: Small states are defined here as World Bank member countries with populations of less than 2 million in 2008.

(PPP)–adjusted per capita income of \$5,597 in 2008. However, per capita income differed widely across small states, ranging from \$537 in Guinea-Bissau to \$36,902 in Iceland.[5]

The large differences in per capita income mainly reflect the extent to which each economy has been able to profit from the opportunities provided by the expansion of world trade, including through policies and regulations that facilitated their integration into world markets (Favaro 2008). Small states have actively relied on increasing external demand, opening themselves more than larger states to trade in goods and services (Alesina and Wacziarg 1998): at 110.1 percent, the median trade share (the ratio of exports plus imports to GDP) in small states in 2008 exceeded the 78.9 percent share in larger states. Small states are also more open to trade in factors of production: the median share of worker's remittances as a percentage of GDP was 2.3 percent in 2008, higher than the 1.7 percent average in larger states. The share of net foreign direct investment (FDI) flows in GDP was also much higher in small states (8.9 percent) than in larger states (3.6 percent).

The quality of policies, institutions, and regulatory frameworks has been instrumental in allowing several small states to successfully exploit international trade opportunities, natural resources and, in some cases, the export of manufactured goods; or to attract external savings to finance the transition from agriculture monoproduction to services. For instance, over the past three decades, Lesotho and Mauritius effectively used industrial policy and trade preferences to facilitate the development of their manufacturing industries and increase exports; Cape Verde and Maldives attracted FDI to develop their tourism sectors; and The Bahamas and Barbados developed international financial centers.

The Impact of the Global Financial Crisis on Small States

The volume of world trade in goods and services fell 11.3 percent in 2009 as a result of the slowdown in global economic activity caused by the crisis (IMF 2010c). Considering the relative openness of their economies, how did this decline affect key macroeconomic indicators in small states?

Real GDP Growth and Current Account Deficit

Table 8.2 presents the annual rate of growth of GDP from 2003 to 2009 and the change in the rate of growth between 2007, the peak of the expansion, and 2009.[6] With the exception of Comoros and Guinea-Bissau, the rate of growth fell in all small states from 2007 to 2009.[7] The fall was very pronounced (10 percentage points or more) in Bhutan, Botswana,

Table 8.2 GDP Growth in Selected Small States, 2003–09
(percent)

Country	2003	2004	2005	2006	2007	2008	2009	Change between 2007 and 2009
Bahamas, The	-0.9	-0.8	5.7	4.3	0.7	-1.7	-5.0	-5.7
Barbados	2.0	4.8	3.9	3.2	3.4	0.2	-5.3	-8.7
Belize	9.3	4.6	3.0	4.7	1.2	3.8	-1.1	-2.3
Bhutan	4.0	8.0	7.0	6.4	19.7	5.0	6.3	-13.4
Botswana	6.3	6.0	1.6	5.1	4.8	3.1	-6.0	-10.8
Cape Verde	4.7	4.3	6.5	10.8	7.8	7.8	5.9	-1.9
Comoros	2.5	-0.2	4.2	1.2	0.5	1.0	1.1	0.6
Eastern Caribbean Currency Union	—	3.9	5.6	6.3	5.2	1.8	-2.4	-7.6
Estonia	7.6	7.2	9.4	10.0	7.2	-3.6	-14.1	-21.3
Fiji	1.0	5.5	0.6	1.9	0.5	0.1	-2.5	-3.0
Gambia, The	6.9	7.0	5.1	6.5	6.3	6.1	4.6	-1.9
Guinea-Bissau	-3.5	3.1	5.0	2.2	0.3	3.5	3.0	2.7
Iceland	2.4	7.7	7.5	4.6	6.0	1.0	-6.5	-12.5
Kiribati	2.3	2.2	3.9	1.9	0.4	-1.1	-0.7	-1.1

(continued next page)

Table 8.2 (continued)

Country	2003	2004	2005	2006	2007	2008	2009	Change between 2007 and 2009
Lesotho	4.3	2.3	1.1	6.5	2.4	4.5	1.4	−1.0
Maldives	8.5	9.5	−4.6	18	7.2	6.3	−3.0	−10.2
Marshall Islands	3.4	5.6	1.7	1.3	2.0	1.5	0	−2
Mauritius	4.3	5.5	1.5	3.9	5.4	4.2	1.5	−3.9
Samoa	3.8	4.2	7.0	2.2	2.3	5.0	−4.9	−7.2
Seychelles	−5.9	−2.9	5.8	8.3	11.5	−0.9	−7.6	−19.1
Solomon Islands	6.5	4.9	5.4	6.9	10.7	7.3	−2.2	−12.9
Suriname	6.3	8.5	4.4	3.8	5.2	6.0	2.5	−2.7
Timor-Leste	0.1	4.2	6.2	−5.8	8.4	12.8	7.4	−1.0
Tonga	1.8	0	−0.2	−0.3	0.4	−0.5	−0.9	−1.3
Vanuatu	14.4	8.0	6.2	13.5	4.6	2.3	−3.5	−8.1

Source: IMF 2010b, IMF various years.
Note: — Not available.

Estonia, Iceland, Maldives, the Seychelles, and the Solomon Islands; large (4–10 percentage points) in The Bahamas, Barbados, the ECCU, Samoa, and Vanuatu; and moderate (less than 4 percentage points) in Belize, Cape Verde, Fiji, The Gambia, Kiribati, Lesotho, the Marshall Islands, Mauritius, Suriname, Timor-Leste, and Tonga. GDP fell in 20 of the countries included in table 8.2.

Table 8.3 presents the current account balance from 2003 to 2009 and the change in this balance between 2007 and 2009. With the exception of Bhutan, Botswana, Guinea-Bissau, Lesotho, Suriname, and Timor-Leste, all countries reported in the table had a current account deficit as of 2007; in 9 of these countries, the deficit exceeded 10 percent of GDP.[8]

Responses to the crisis were varied. Between 2007 and 2009, the current account balance improved (the deficit fell or the surplus increased) in half of the countries in the table and deteriorated (the deficit increased or the surplus fell) in the other half. Two groups of countries stand out: The Bahamas, Barbados, the ECCU countries, Iceland, Estonia, Maldives, and Samoa—all among the higher-income countries in the table—faced an abrupt decline in access to external savings (a sudden stop in capital inflows). Not surprisingly, these countries also experienced a sharp decline in the rate of growth of GDP. The second group of countries comprises the natural resource–based producers and exporters: Bhutan, Botswana, Suriname, and Timor-Leste. These countries suffered a sharp fall in exports as a result of the decline in world demand for commodities and a corresponding sharp fall in the rate of growth.

To explore more formally the relationship between the change in external conditions facing small states and changes in output, we regressed the change in the rate of growth of GDP (DG) against the balance in the current account as of 2007 (CA07) and a dummy variable for natural resource–based economies (table 8.4). The coefficient in both variables is negative and statistically significant: a 1 percentage point increase in the current account deficit as of 2007 is associated with an additional fall in the rate of growth of 0.25 percent. Countries that were more reliant on natural resource–based exports had larger declines in their GDP growth during the crisis.[9]

The Public Savings–Investment Gap

The current account balance is identical to the difference between savings and investment. The savings-investment gap is equal to the sum of these gaps in the public and private sectors. The information needed to disaggregate the two gaps is not available; for this reason, we measure the private sector balance as the difference between the current account balance and the overall public sector balance (table 8.5) (see annex).

Table 8.5 illustrates two important facts: as of 2007, some small states (Barbados, the ECCU, Kiribati, Maldives, the Seychelles, and Timor-Leste)

Table 8.3 Current Account Balances in Selected Small States, 2003–09
(percentage of GDP)

Country	2003	2004	2005	2006	2007	2008	2009	Change between 2007 and 2009
Bahamas, The	-5.2	-2.8	-9.6	-18.9	-17.5	-15.4	-11.4	6.1
Barbados	-6.3	-12.0	-13.1	-8.4	-5.4	-10.5	-5.1	0.3
Belize	-18.2	-14.7	-13.6	-2.1	-4.0	-10.1	-7.0	-3.0
Bhutan	-22.8	-17.6	-29.2	-4.3	12.2	-2.2	-9.6	-21.7
Botswana	5.7	3.5	15.2	17.26	15.4	4.9	-5.1	-20.5
Cape Verde	-11.2	-14.4	-3.4	-5.0	-8.7	-12.4	-19.4	-10.7
Comoros	-3.2	-4.6	-7.2	-6.1	-6.7	-11.6	-5.1	1.6
Eastern Caribbean Currency Union	-16.4	-22.4	-29.7	-34.8	-33.9	-24.2	-24.1	9.8
Estonia	-11.3	-11.3	-10.0	-16.9	-17.1	-9.4	4.6	22.4
Fiji	-6.4	-12.6	-9.9	-18.8	-13.6	-17.9	-9.6	4.0
Gambia, The	-4.9	-10.1	-18.5	-13.4	-12.3	-16.0	-14.3	-2.0

Guinea-Bissau	-3.3	4.6	-0.2	-5.5	5.8	2.8	1.6	-4.2
Iceland	-4.8	-9.8	-16.1	-25.6	-16.3	-15.8	3.8	20.1
Kiribati	-19.5	-11.1	-18.5	-2.9	-1.0	-0.6	-4.1	-3.1
Lesotho	-13.5	-6.1	-7.9	4.7	14.1	9.6	-1.5	-15.6
Maldives	-4.5	-15.8	-36.4	-33.0	-41.5	-51.4	-31.0	10.6
Marshall Islands	—	-3.8	-8.4	-10.3	-7.1	-12.2	-12.1	-5
Mauritius	1.7	-1.8	-5.2	-9.4	-5.6	-10.4	-8.2	-2.5
Samoa	-8.3	-8.4	-9.6	-11.1	-15.9	-6.2	-2.0	13.9
Seychelles	-0.2	-5.9	-19.7	-13.9	-20.8	-44.7	-23.1	-2.3
Solomon Islands	6.3	16.3	-7.0	-1.6	-8.2	-6.4	-21.2	-12.9
Suriname	-18.0	-10.3	-13.0	7.5	7.5	3.9	-2	-9.5
Timor-Leste	-15.4	20.7	78.4	165.2	296.1	404.8	191.0	-105.1
Tonga	0.7	0.4	-5.2	-8.2	-8.8	-11.6	-15.7	-6.9
Vanuatu	-5.7	-6.0	-8.4	-5.3	-6.9	-5.9	-2.2	4.7

Source: IMF 2010b, IMF various years.
Note: — Not available.

Table 8.4 Estimate of Change in Rate of Growth and Change in
Current Account Balance

Equation 1: Dependent variable: DG	Coefficient	Standard error	t-statistic	Probability
C	–3.25	1.68	–1.94	0.07
DNRB	–8.74	4.20	–2.08	0.05
CA07	0.26	0.10	2.49	0.02
R-squared	0.25			
Adjusted R-squared	0.18			

Source: Authors.
Note: DG = change in rate of growth; DNRB = dummy for nonresource-rich small states; CA07 = current account balance in 2007.

were running fiscal deficits of at least 4 percent of GDP, but most small states had small fiscal deficits or were running surpluses (as did Estonia, Iceland, Suriname, and Tonga). Second, there was a marked deterioration of the overall public sector balance in most small states between 2007 and 2009.

Table 8.6 estimates the private savings–investment gap, measured as the difference between the current account balance and the overall public sector balance. In 2007 the absolute size of the gap between private savings and investment was very large in most of the countries for which information is available. In fact, the private gap explains 70 percent or more of the current account balance in 14 of the 24 small states included in table 8.3 (including the six members of the ECCU). The change in the private savings–investment gap between 2007 and 2009 was very large; small states such as The Bahamas, members of the ECCU, Estonia, Iceland, Maldives, and Samoa underwent a drastic and large sudden stop in capital inflows. Not surprisingly, these states are among those that experienced steep declines in the rate of economic growth.

We can neither attribute which part of the private savings–investment gap corresponds to savings and which part to investment nor measure what part of the financing corresponds to new loans from the rest of the world and what part was financed through foreign direct investment. We do know, however, that private international capital flows were very important in the economic boom of 2005–07 and the economic bust of 2008–09. During these years, FDI was particularly high in The Bahamas, the ECCU, Estonia, Guyana, Iceland, São Tomé and Principe, and the Seychelles (table 8.7).[10]

Table 8.5 Overall Public Sector Balance in Selected Small States, 2003–09
(percentage of GDP)

Country	2003	2004	2005	2006	2007	2008	2009	Change between 2007 and 2009
Bahamas, The	—	—	—	−1.5	−2.5	−2	−4.7	−2.2
Barbados	−5.0	1.4	−6.9	−5.3	−8	−7.6	−8.4	−0.4
Belize	—	−6.4	−5.4	−2	−1.1	0.8	−1.0	0.1
Bhutan	—	—	−1.2	0.6	0.7	2.2	−3.3	−4.0
Cape Verde	−3.5	−4.0	−5.1	−5	−0.7	−1.2	−8.8	−8.1
Comoros	−0.3	−0.5	−1.7	−3.4	−2.3	−2.3	—	—
Eastern Caribbean Currency Union	—	−4.3	−4.4	−5.1	−4.4	−4.7	−6.8	−2.4
Estonia	2.3	1.6	1.6	3.3	2.9	−2.3	−3.0	−5.9
Fiji	—	—	—	−3	−1.6	−0.2	−2.9	−1.3
Gambia, The	—	—	—	−7.8	0.5	−2.2	−1.6	−2.1
Iceland	−1.6	−0.7	2.7	3.8	5.4	−0.5	−14.4	−19.8
Kiribati	—	−23.6	−15.3	−15.5	−16	−13.3	−12.2	3.8
Maldives	—	−1.8	−11.3	−7.2	−4.9	−13.8	−28.8	−23.9
Marshall Islands	—	−1.8	−4.7	1.9	0.4	−0.3	−0.3	−0.7
Mauritius	—	—	−5.3	−4.6	−4	−3.4	−4.5	−0.5
Samoa	—	0.3	−0.5	0.6	−1.8	−3.9	−7.1	−5.3
Seychelles	—	—	—	—	−8.7	−3.3	2.8	11.5
Solomon Islands	—	5.9	2.7	1.7	0.5	1.5	−0.4	−0.9
Suriname	—	—	−0.7	0.9	3	2	−1.8	−4.8
Timor-Leste	—	−9.3	−6.2	−6.2	−5.7	−4.6	−5.7	0
Tonga	0.3	2.1	−2.8	1.1	1.7	1.3	−3.9	−5.6

Source: IMF 2010, IMF various years.
Note: — Not available.

Table 8.6 Private Savings–Investment Gap in Selected Small
States, 2007 and 2009
(percentage of GDP)

Country	2007	2009	Change between 2007 and 2009
Bahamas, The	−15	−6.7	8.3
Barbados	2.6	3.3	0.7
Belize	−2.9	−6.0	−3.1
Bhutan	11.5	−6.3	−17.8
Cape Verde	−8.0	−10.6	−2.6
Eastern Caribbean Currency Union	−29.5	−17.3	12.2
Estonia	−20.0	7.6	27.6
Fiji	−12.0	−6.7	5.3
Gambia, The	−12.8	−12.7	0.1
Iceland	−21.7	18.2	39.9
Kiribati	15.0	8.1	−6.9
Maldives	−36.6	−2.2	34.4
Marshall Islands	−7.5	−11.8	−4.3
Mauritius	−1.6	−3.7	−2.1
Samoa	−14.1	5.1	19.1
Seychelles	−12.1	−25.9	−13.8
Solomon Islands	−8.7	−20.8	−12.1
Suriname	4.5	−0.2	−4.7
Tonga	−10.5	−11.8	−1.3

Source: IMF 2010b, IMF various years.

Debt Burden Indicators

A higher public debt to GDP ratio limits opportunities to offset the impact
of the global economic slowdown in the domestic market. So, what is the
public debt situation in small states? This section explores the public debt
situation in a sample of 46 countries. The sample updates the information
on central government debt of small states, provided in Panizza (2008),
using more recently available data from joint Bank-Fund Debt Sustainability Analyses and IMF Article IV Staff Reports. The data set includes
actual and projected data on small states' central government debt from
1990 to 2014.[11]

Table 8.7 Foreign Direct Investment in Selected Small States, 2003–09
(percentage of GDP)

Country	2003	2004	2005	2006	2007	2008	2009
Bahamas, The	3.5	4.8	9.4	11.3	10.9	—	—
Barbados	2.2	–0.4	2	3.3	3.9	5.2	1.2
Belize	–1.1	10.6	11.4	8.6	8.8	—	—
Bhutan	0.2	0.5	1.2	0.7	7.4	1.5	1.4
Botswana	5.0	4.0	2.7	4.4	–0.2	—	—
Cape Verde	4.9	7.3	1.7	10.2	9.0	12	6.6
Comoros	0.3	0.2	0.1	0.1	0.2	—	—
Eastern Caribbean Currency Union	—	13.6	17.3	26.3	27.7	22.6	16.3
Estonia	9.4	8.1	21.3	10.9	12.8	3.7	0.3
Fiji	1.6	6.9	5.4	11.8	8	8.8	8.4
Gambia, The	6.0	14.2	11.3	16.2	10.6	8.5	10
Guinea-Bissau	1.7	0.6	2.9	5.6	1.8	—	—
Guyana	3.5	3.8	9.7	11.2	14.1	—	—
Iceland	3.1	5.7	19.2	24.3	15.2	—	—
Lesotho	11.6	9.6	6.7	7.4	7.8	—	—
Maldives	2.0	1.9	1.3	1.5	1.4	1	0.7
Mauritius	1.2	0.2	0.7	1.6	5.0	4.1	3
Namibia	0.7	1.3	2.3	–0.4	1.9	—	—
Samoa	0.2	0.6	–0.7	4.6	0.5	—	—
São Tomé and Principe	3.5	3.3	13.8	30.1	24.4	—	—
Seychelles	8.3	5.4	9.7	15.1	27.3	38	25.1
Solomon Islands	–0.5	1.6	4.5	4.1	8.0	—	—
Suriname	–6.0	–2.5	1.6	–7.7	–10.2	—	—
Swaziland	–3.4	3.0	–1.8	4.5	1.3	—	—
Tonga	0	3.5	5.7	4.9	10.8	—	—
Vanuatu	6.4	6	3.6	10.5	6.7	—	—

Source: IMF 2010b, IMF various years.
Note: — Not available.

At the beginning of the decade, several small states experienced a sharp decline in total public debt and a change in the external/domestic composition (figure 8.1). After peaking at a mean of about 90 percent of GDP in 1994, total public debt declined to 60 percent of GDP just before the financial crisis.[12] The decline was driven entirely by the drop in external public debt; domestic debt continued increasing, stabilizing at roughly 25 percent of GDP before the financial crisis.

The reasons underlying the decline in the average debt to GDP ratio varied across countries and regions. Among low-income countries, implementation of the Heavily Indebted Poor Countries (HIPC) Initiative was an important source of debt relief (e.g., The Gambia). Debt restructuring in some countries (e.g., Solomon Islands) and more austere fiscal programs (e.g., Vanuatu) and economic growth in others (e.g., Cape Verde) underlay the downward trend in debt ratios. The decline in the external debt to GDP ratio largely determined the evolution of the public debt to GDP ratio; the average domestic debt to GDP remained constant throughout the decade. The average debt reversal is expected to be almost entirely undone by the recent crisis, as average public debt is projected to reach levels on the order of 70 to 80 percent of GDP. This time around, however, domestic debt is expected to play a more prominent role in the debt buildup.

Five small states (Comoros, The Gambia, Guinea-Bissau, Guyana, and São Tomé and Principe) benefited from debt relief under the HIPC Initiative. All but Comoros also received debt stock reductions under the Multilateral Debt Relief Initiative (MDRI), and MDRI-equivalent mechanisms. The debt to GDP ratio in countries that did not receive HIPC Initiative relief also fell (figure 8.2).

Figure 8.1 Actual and Projected Debt Stock Indicators in Small States, 1990–2014

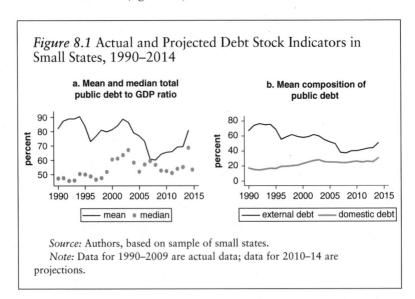

Source: Authors, based on sample of small states.
Note: Data for 1990–2009 are actual data; data for 2010–14 are projections.

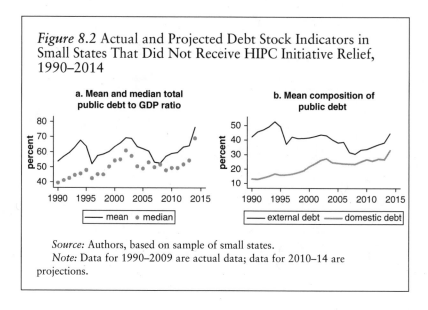

Figure 8.2 Actual and Projected Debt Stock Indicators in Small States That Did Not Receive HIPC Initiative Relief, 1990–2014

a. Mean and median total public debt to GDP ratio

b. Mean composition of public debt

Source: Authors, based on sample of small states.
Note: Data for 1990–2009 are actual data; data for 2010–14 are projections.

Of course, average ratios conceal significant differences across and within regions. In Sub-Saharan Africa, for example, once HIPCs are excluded from the sample, the decline in the average public debt to GDP ratio is less pronounced (figure 8.3). In some resource-rich small African states, such as Botswana, Equatorial Guinea, and Gabon, higher commodity prices led to sizable government revenues and a decline in government borrowing requirements. In Lesotho and Swaziland, a similar effect was ensured through revenue-sharing agreements, such as those established by the Southern African Customs Union (SACU). Other small middle-income states in Africa, such as Cape Verde and Mauritius, experienced steady output growth that resulted in downward public debt trajectories. The jump in public debt over the medium term is driven by two outliers, Guinea-Bissau and the Seychelles, whose debt is expected to rise above 200 percent of GDP by 2014. Without these outliers, the increase in public debt is projected to be much more benign, averaging roughly 60 percent of GDP by 2014.

In Latin America and the Caribbean, the average public debt to GDP ratio fell by some 20 percentage points during 2005–09. Even so, at 80 percent of GDP, it remained high (figure 8.4). There was also a wide range of experiences across countries: Belize and Dominica managed to put the public debt trajectory on a downward path from 2004 by running sizable primary surpluses. In contrast, Antigua and Barbuda, Grenada, and St. Kitts and Nevis followed an expansionary fiscal policy, which resulted in a sizable buildup of public debt. The onset of the crisis reversed the downward trend in debt to GDP ratios across all countries. By 2014 average public debt is expected to come close to 100 percent of GDP.

210 FAVARO, DÖMELAND, O'BOYLE, AND STUČKA

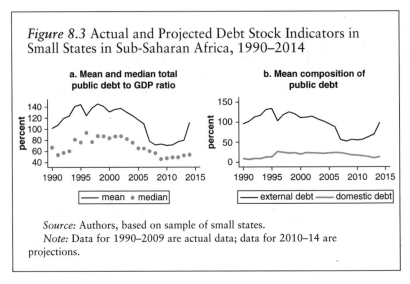

Figure 8.3 Actual and Projected Debt Stock Indicators in Small States in Sub-Saharan Africa, 1990–2014

Source: Authors, based on sample of small states.
Note: Data for 1990–2009 are actual data; data for 2010–14 are projections.

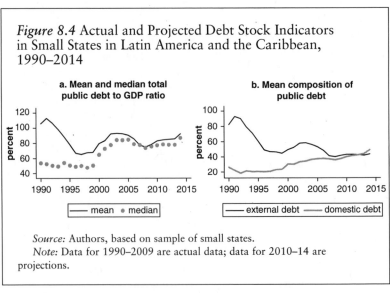

Figure 8.4 Actual and Projected Debt Stock Indicators in Small States in Latin America and the Caribbean, 1990–2014

Source: Authors, based on sample of small states.
Note: Data for 1990–2009 are actual data; data for 2010–14 are projections.

In Europe, small states' debt to GDP ratios averaged less than 40 percent of GDP before 2007 (figure 8.5). The sharp increase in the average public debt to GDP ratio was driven primarily by Iceland, with an expected debt level of more than 100 percent of GDP, and to a lesser degree Cyprus and Malta, with projected levels of close to 70 percent of GDP by 2014.[13]

Most small states in the South Pacific have had falling debt to GDP ratios, facilitated by debt forgiveness, exceptionally large external grants,

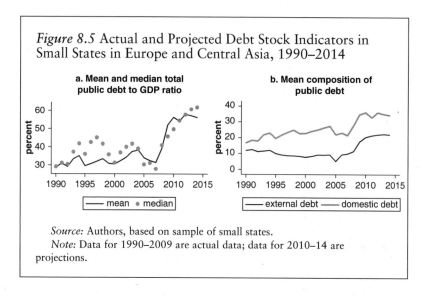

Figure 8.5 Actual and Projected Debt Stock Indicators in Small States in Europe and Central Asia, 1990–2014

Source: Authors, based on sample of small states.
Note: Data for 1990–2009 are actual data; data for 2010–14 are projections.

and, in some countries, large fiscal adjustments (figure 8.6). Sizable external grants to Kiribati (60 percent of GDP), the Marshall Islands (40 percent of GDP), and Palau (20 percent of GDP) explain the relatively benign public debt trajectory in the region. Sharp U-turns in fiscal policy can be found in the Federated States of Micronesia, Samoa, the Solomon Islands, and Vanuatu (Cas and Ota 2008). In the Solomon Islands, the debt trajectory improved in 2007 following the Honiara Club debt reduction and rescheduling agreement.[14]

Over the medium term, East Asian and Pacific islands do not appear to be much affected, on average, by the recent crisis, at least judging by the continuously declining public debt trajectory. The debt situation is, however, somewhat polarized: Kiribati, the Federated States of Micronesia, Palau, the Solomon Islands, and Vanuatu exhibit very small debt levels, the highest reaching roughly 20 percent of GDP compared to the Marshall Islands, Samoa, and Tonga with somewhat more elevated debt levels of between 40 and 60 percent of GDP. The latter debt levels, while elevated in regional terms, are still benign when compared to public debt levels in the Caribbean.

In South Asia, the debt stocks of Bhutan and Maldives increased substantially, albeit for different reasons (figure 8.7). Bhutan's debt buildup can largely be explained by external loans contracted for building hydropower plants. As this front-loaded debt accumulation is used for investment purposes to generate energy for which a buyer (India) has already been identified, the enhancement of foreign exchange–producing capacities leaves Bhutan with good debt prospects going forward. In contrast, in Maldives the debt buildup has been the result of severe fiscal

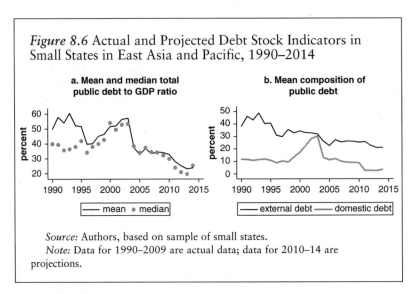

Figure 8.6 Actual and Projected Debt Stock Indicators in Small States in East Asia and Pacific, 1990–2014

a. Mean and median total public debt to GDP ratio

b. Mean composition of public debt

Source: Authors, based on sample of small states.
Note: Data for 1990–2009 are actual data; data for 2010–14 are projections.

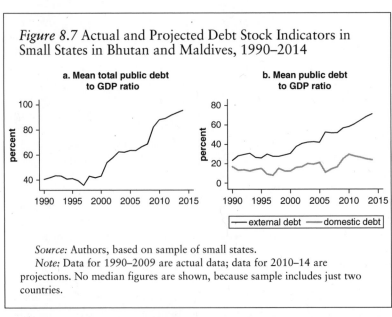

Figure 8.7 Actual and Projected Debt Stock Indicators in Small States in Bhutan and Maldives, 1990–2014

a. Mean total public debt to GDP ratio

b. Mean public debt to GDP ratio

Source: Authors, based on sample of small states.
Note: Data for 1990–2009 are actual data; data for 2010–14 are projections. No median figures are shown, because sample includes just two countries.

and external imbalances. After 2007, the global economic downturn had a significant negative impact on export and tourism receipts, depressing government revenues. As external financing was limited, domestic debt increased substantially before the onset of the financial crisis.

Over the medium term, public debt is expected to decline steadily to around 80 percent of GDP in the Maldives. Public debt in Bhutan

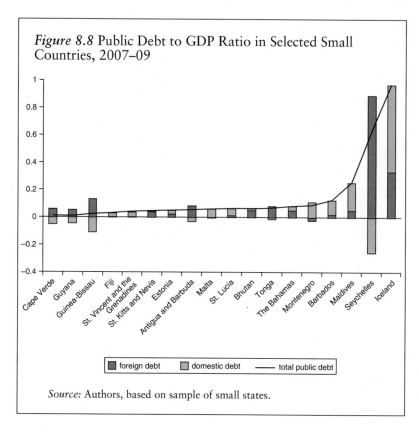

Figure 8.8 Public Debt to GDP Ratio in Selected Small Countries, 2007–09

Source: Authors, based on sample of small states.

is expected to peak at 110 percent of GDP in 2015; henceforth, the trajectory is projected to decline steeply as hydro facilities are put into operation.

Changes in debt to GDP ratios during the 2007–09 period ranged from minimal to explosive (Iceland and the Seychelles) (figure 8.8). The increase in debt in several countries in the Caribbean region is noteworthy in light of their initial (precrisis) debt to GDP ratios.

The financial crisis reversed the average reduction in debt burdens that had occurred in the early 2000s. Average public debt is now projected to reach roughly 70 percent of GDP by 2014–15, an average deterioration equivalent to 20 percent of GDP.

Concluding Remarks

Small states undergoing a deep recession in the wake of the global financial crisis have higher per capita income and are more closely integrated into the global economy than small countries experiencing milder downturns.

Does this mean that integration with the rest of the world has been the wrong development strategy for these countries? Such a conclusion would be misguided. A domestic-led growth strategy would have been a sure recipe for failure. At the same time, an export-led development strategy entails risks that should be closely monitored—risks that grow exponentially when the country is heavily indebted to the rest of the world.

The impact of the crisis has been greater among small states that had high levels of external exposure and among exporters of natural resource–based products. In the first group of countries, the crisis sharply reduced access to external savings (and in some case reversed its sign), causing a sharp drop in domestic demand and decline in GDP. In the second group of countries, the crisis operated through a decline in the demand for exports and the concomitant fall in the level of economic activity.

The importance of capital inflows in spurring an economic boom in several small states in 2004–07 and an economic bust between 2007 and 2009 cannot be overstated. The counterpart of these inflows was largely private sector decisions to increase consumption or investment rather than public sector deficits. Much remains to be learned about the management of these inflows. Importing capital by as much as 10 percent of GDP or more annually may accelerate closing the income gap with developed countries, but it also poses large adjustment risks when there are swift changes in international investors' perceptions.

These risks are by no means unique to small states. Even so, there is no escaping the fact that the cost of adjustment is much more pronounced for a small economy than for a larger one. In addition, these economies have little or no flexibility to reallocate resources away from tourism and into other goods and services; at the very least, the transformation requires a long time horizon and the acquisition of an entirely new set of skills. During such a transition, small states may be faced with sharp drops in consumption, declining foreign exchange reserves, and the accumulation of large public external debt.

Past imprudent fiscal management has resulted in high levels of public debt in several small states. The decline in debt to GDP ratios of the early 2000s has been wiped out, and several small states now have debt ratios that will adversely affect their capacity to provide basic public goods and encourage new investment and economic growth. Managing these higher levels of public debt in an uncertain economic environment will be a significant challenge for these small states going forward.

Despite clear challenges, a pessimistic view is by no means warranted. Small states are benefiting significantly from worldwide advances in information and communication technology as well as from deregulation of local markets. Although this technological change is benefiting all countries in the world, it is particularly important for small island economies, because it reduces the cost of communication with the rest of the world, opens the possibility of accessing education and health services available in high-income countries, and creates new business opportunities. Small states have only recently introduced regulatory reforms that may help them take advantage of these opportunities.

Annex 8A: Construction of the Data Set

The data used in tables 8.2–8.7 were compiled from Article IV Staff Reports of the IMF and the IMF's *World Economic Outlook* (WEO). The data used in figures 8.1–8.8 come from the Panizza (2008) database; they were enhanced with data from the Economic Policy and Debt Department of the World Bank. Details on data availability can be found in annex table 8A.2.

The WEO data set includes no data on savings and investment. To decompose the current account balance reported in tables 8.3, 8.5, and 8.6, we used the latest Article IV staff report available on the IMF's external Web site. This means that the information contained in these tables is not fully consistent with the information reported in table 8.2. The calculations in tables 8.3, 8.5, and 8.6 are consistent with the current account data reported in annex table 8A.1, which is based on IMF Article IV Staff Reports.

Although this inconsistency is unfortunate, the alternative of doing nothing until a more complete data set is available seemed worse than proceeding with inconsistent data sets. At the very least, the imperfect snapshot provided by this chapter will identify the data that international organizations and governments of small states need to collect.

Table 8A.1 Current Account Balances in Selected Small Countries, 2003–09

Country	2003	2004	2005	2006	2007	2008	2009	Change between 2007 and 2009
Bahamas, The	–8.6	–5.4	–11.7	–22.5	–20	14.4	–9.4	10.6
Barbados	–6.3	–12	–12.6	–8.4	–5.4	–10.5	–5.2	0.2
Belize	–18.7	–14.7	–13.6	–2.1	–4.1	11.2	–6.7	–2.6
Bhutan	—	—	–4.5	14.4	–2.1	–10.1	–7.4	–5.3

(continued next page)

Table 8A.1 (continued)

Country	2003	2004	2005	2006	2007	2008	2009	Change between 2007 and 2009
Botswana	5.6	3.1	15.2	17.6	19.8	—	—	—
Cape Verde	–11.4	–14	–4.0	–6.9	–13.6	–12.4	–19.4	–5.8
Comoros	–2.8	–3.3	–6.1	–6.7	–11.3	–8.0	–10.4	0.9
Eastern Caribbean Currency Union	–16.4	–22.4	–29.7	–34.8	–33.9	–24.2	–24.1	9.8
Estonia	–11.4	–11.8	–10.0	–16.8	–18.0	9.5	3.3	21.3
Fiji	–4.1	–13.6	–13.4	–22.6	–13.6	–17.9	–9.9	3.7
Gambia, The	0.9	–7.7	–9.4	–12.9	–8.2	–17.3	–19.3	–11.1
Guyana	–6.0	–2.5	–12.1	–19.8	–13.4	—	—	—
Iceland	–4.9	–10.0	–16.2	–25.5	–15.9	–10.7	–35.8	–19.9
Kiribati	—	–11.0	–20.2	–3.1	–1.3	–1.3	–3.5	–2.2
Lesotho	–13.5	–5.3	–7.4	4.4	12.7	—	—	—
Maldives	–4.5	–15.8	–36.2	–32.8	–40.1	–51.4	–29.6	10.5
Marshall Islands	—	–3.8	–8.4	–10.3	–7.1	–12.2	–12.1	–5
Mauritius	1.8	–1.8	–5.2	–9.4	–6.4	–11.3	–8.1	–1.7
Samoa	—	–6.8	–5.8	–10.6	–6.6	–2.1	–12.7	–6.1
Seychelles	–1.3	–8.6	–19.7	–13.8	–28.9	–44.7	–22.6	6.3
Solomon Islands	–12	–5	–21.8	–21.3	–12.4	–18.7	–11.1	1.3
Suriname	–12.5	–9.2	–8.1	5.2	7.6	3.9	–2	–9.6
Timor-Leste	—	21	78	165	296	405	191	–105
Tonga	–6.1	–7.6	–6.4	–6.5	–9.6	–21.3	–50.1	–40.5
Vanuatu	–7.9	–6.8	–9.2	–7.3	–6.8	—	—	—

Source: Authors, based on a sample of small states.
Note: — Not available.

Table 8A.2 Summary of Data Availability on Public Debt Levels in Small States

#	Country	Complete for 2000–10	Missing data	
			External	Domestic
1	Antigua and Barbuda	Yes	1990–99	1990–99
2	Bahamas, The	Yes		
3	Bahrain	No	2002–10	2008–10
4	Barbados	Yes		
5	Belize	Yes		
6	Bhutan	Yes		
7	Botswana	No	2000–04	2005–10
8	Brunei Darussalam	No	All	All
9	Cape Verde	Yes		
10	Comoros	Yes	1990–95	1990–95
11	Cyprus[a]	No	2009–10	2009–10
12	Djibouti	Yes	1990–99	1990–99
13	Dominica	Yes	1990–98	1990–98
14	Equatorial Guinea	Yes	1990–92	1990–92
15	Estonia	Yes	1990–94	1990–94, 2011–14
16	Fiji	Yes	2011–14	2011–14
17	Gabon	Yes	1990–97	1990–97
18	Gambia, The	Yes		
19	Grenada	Yes		
20	Guinea-Bissau	Yes		1990–99
21	Guyana	No	2010–14	2010–14
22	Iceland	Yes		
23	Kiribati	No	1990–2003	All
24	Luxembourg	No	1998–14	1998–14
25	Maldives	Yes		
26	Malta	Yes		
27	Marshall Islands	No	1990–2005	All
28	Mauritius	Yes	2013–14	2013–14

(continued next page)

Table 8A.2 (continued)

#	Country	Complete for 2000–10	Missing Data External	Missing Data Domestic
29	Micronesia, Federated States of	No	1990–2003, 2014	All
30	Montenegro	No	1990–2004	1990–2004
31	Palau	No	1990–2000, 2008–14	All
32	Qatar	No	1990–2001, 2009–10	1990–2001, 2009–10
33	Samoa	Yes		
34	San Marino	No	All	All
35	São Tomé and Principe	Yes		
36	Seychelles	No	1990–2004	1990–2004
37	Solomon Islands	Yes	1990–95	1990–95
38	St. Kitts and Nevis	Yes	1990–99	1990–99
39	St. Lucia	Yes		
40	St. Vincent and the Grenadines	Yes		
41	Suriname[a]	Yes	1990–98	1990–98
42	Swaziland	Yes	2014	2014
43	Timor–Leste	Yes		
44	Tonga	Yes	1990–94	1990–94
45	Trinidad and Tobago	Yes		2010–14
46	Vanuatu	Yes		

Source: Authors.

Note: Complete data are available for 31 of 46 countries. Data for Cyprus and Suriname are not broken down by external and domestic debt.

Notes

1. The population threshold is arbitrary. Population (rather than territory or GDP) is used as a scaling criterion for three reasons. First, population is highly correlated with a territory's size, so it highlights the limited resources of small states. Second, population is more homogeneous than territory, so it makes cross-country comparisons more meaningful. Third, using GDP as a scaling criterion would highlight constraints on exploiting economies of scale, but it would complicate

the selection of a threshold to differentiate between small and larger states (see Michaely and Papageorgiou 1998).

2. A similar result holds for larger states (IMF 2010a).

3. The ECCU includes Antigua and Barbuda, Dominica, Grenada, St. Kitts and Nevis, St. Lucia, and St. Vincent and the Grenadines.

4. Forty-eight small states are members of the World Bank.

5. The corresponding figure for larger states (defined as states with populations of more than 2 million) was $7,956 (World Bank 2010).

6. The economic indicators shown in tables 8.2–8.7 are not available for all small states. These tables are therefore based on a subset of small states.

7. The rationale for the selection of the period is that 2007 is the last year of the global expansion and 2009 is the last year for which data were available.

8. With the possible exception of Guinea-Bissau, these are natural resource–based producers and exporters.

9. Regression estimates inform about correlation rather than causality.

10. Overall, FDI inflows are preferred to more short-term financial inflows when it comes to managing the balance of payments.

11. The sample includes data on all small states listed in table 8.1, with the exception of Brunei Darussalam and Kosovo, for which insufficient data were available. The sample also includes data on Lesotho. Data up to 2007 consist of actual data; figures for 2008 are a combination of actual, estimated, and projected data; figures for 2009 consist of both estimated and projected data; data from 2010 onward are projections.

12. The same trend holds if the median rather than the mean is used for the period 2000–08.

13. Iceland suffered a financial crisis that involved the collapse of all three major banks and a major decline in real GDP.

14. The Honiara Club is a term denoting creditors consisting of the Australian Export Finance and Insurance Corporation, the European Commission, the European Investment Bank, the International Fund for Agricultural Development, the Kuwait Fund for Arab Economic Development, the OPEC Fund, the Export-Import Bank of the Republic of China, and the International Cooperation and Development Fund.

References

Alesina, Alberto, and Romain Wacziarg. 1998. "Openness, Country Size and the Government." *Journal of Public Economics* 69 (3): 305–21.

Cas, Stephanie Medina, and Rui Ota. 2008. "Big Government, High Debt, and Fiscal Adjustment in Small States." IMF Working Paper WP/08/39, International Monetary Fund, Washington, DC.

Favaro, Edgardo, ed. 2008. "Small States, Smart Solutions." World Bank, Poverty Reduction and Economic Policy and Debt Department, Washington, DC.

IMF (International Monetary Fund). 2010a. "How Did Emerging Markets Cope in the Crisis?" July 15, Washington, DC. www.imf.org/external/np/pp/eng/2010/061510.pdf.

———. 2010b. *World Economic Outlook*. June. Washington, DC: International Monetary Fund.

———. 2010c. *World Economic Outlook*. July. Washington, DC: International Monetary Fund.

————. Various years. *Article IV Consultations* (various countries). Washington, DC: International Monetary Fund.

Michaely, Michael, and Demetris Papageorgiou. 1998. "Small Economies Trade Liberalization, Trade Preferences, and Growth." *Iberoamericana: Nordic Journal of Latin American and Caribbean Studies* 28 (1–2): 121–59. Stockholm University, Institute for Latin American Studies.

Panizza, Ugo. 2008. "Domestic and External Public Debt in Developing Countries." Discussion Paper, United Nations Conference on Trade and Development (UNCTAD), Geneva.

World Bank. 2010. "World Development Index." April database. Washington, DC.

9

Europe's Crisis: Origins and Policy Challenges

Edgardo Favaro, Ying Li, Juan Pradelli, and Ralph Van Doorn

On May 9, 2010, a meeting of ministers of finance of European Union (EU) countries announced a €750 billion ($1 trillion) package to calm financial market uncertainty about the capacity of Greece and other countries to meet their outstanding debt obligations. The financial measures injected liquidity into the bond market and relieved some pressure, but they do not address underlying imbalances within the Euro Area and are unlikely to soothe concerns about the capacity of the public and private sectors to repay their debts (World Bank 2010).

This chapter places current financial events in the context of large and protracted current account imbalances within the Euro Area during the past decade and analyzes the likelihood of reversing these imbalances in light of adjustment experiences elsewhere. The chapter is organized as follows. The first section links the current debt situation to large and sustained current account imbalances and examines their origin. The second section examines how the political economy aspects of Europe's crisis are influenced by the buildup of cross-border private and public debts. The third section sheds light on the likelihood of success of deflation-based external adjustments by examining deflation experiences worldwide during the past four decades. The last section provides some concluding remarks.

Origins of the Crisis

Between 1999 and 2007, the Euro Area maintained a roughly balanced current account with respect to the rest of the world, but there were large and sustained imbalances within the area. Greece, Portugal, Spain, and to a lesser extent Ireland incurred substantial current account deficits; Germany, Luxembourg, and the Netherlands ran current account surpluses (figure 9.1).

Per capita GDP in the Euro Area grew 1.7 percent a year between 1999 and 2007, slightly above the 1.5 percent posted in 1992–98. Among the deficit countries, Ireland (4.5 percent), Greece (3.7 percent), and Spain (2.3 percent) were the economic champions of the decade. Portugal (1.1 percent) had weak growth performance, and Germany grew at just 1.5 percent a year.[1]

Marked differences in the sources of economic growth across countries are uncovered by decomposing the GDP growth rate by component of aggregate demand (see annex figure 9A.1). In Germany and Ireland, economic growth was led by exports; in Greece and Portugal, growth was led by a boom in private consumption; in Spain both private consumption and investment led growth.

Greece, Ireland, Portugal, and Spain financed their current account deficits through cross-border financial and capital movements. These movements were facilitated by the adoption of the common currency

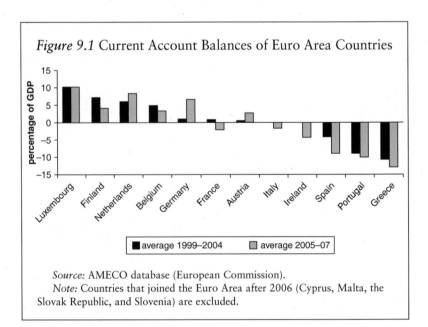

Figure 9.1 Current Account Balances of Euro Area Countries

Source: AMECO database (European Commission).
Note: Countries that joined the Euro Area after 2006 (Cyprus, Malta, the Slovak Republic, and Slovenia) are excluded.

in 1999 (which de facto eliminated currency risk) and the expansion of financial activities, most notably by French and German banks, as illustrated by the rising value of their claims on assets in deficit countries (Gros 2010) (figure 9.2).

The sources of the large and widening current account deficits varied across countries (figure 9.3). In Greece and Portugal, the external gap stemmed mainly from a low savings rate, which in turn reflected high public and private consumption rates. Between 1999 and 2007, Greece's current account deficit increased from 7.0 percent to 14.7 percent of GDP. The widening of the deficit was caused by a decline in the saving rate from 15.0 percent to 7.6 percent of GDP. This decline comprised

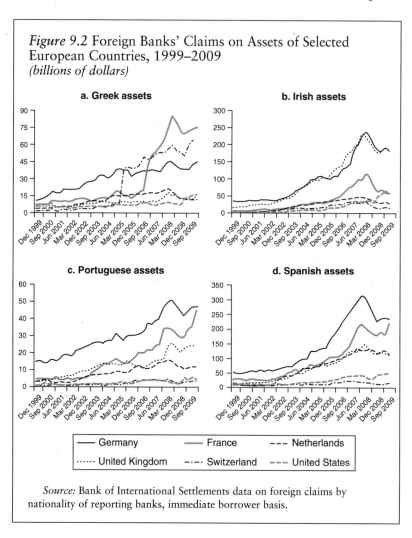

Figure 9.2 Foreign Banks' Claims on Assets of Selected European Countries, 1999–2009
(billions of dollars)

Source: Bank of International Settlements data on foreign claims by nationality of reporting banks, immediate borrower basis.

224 FAVARO, LI, PRADELLI, AND VAN DOORN

a 4.2 percentage point drop in the public savings rate and a 3.3 percentage point drop in the private savings rate. The investment rate remained fairly stable in 1999–2007 but fell by 4 percentage points of GDP between 2007 and 2009.

Portugal's current account deficit increased from 8.9 percent of GDP in 1999 to 9.8 percent in 2007. Over the same period, savings declined from 18.9 percent of GDP to 12.4 percent, and investments fell from

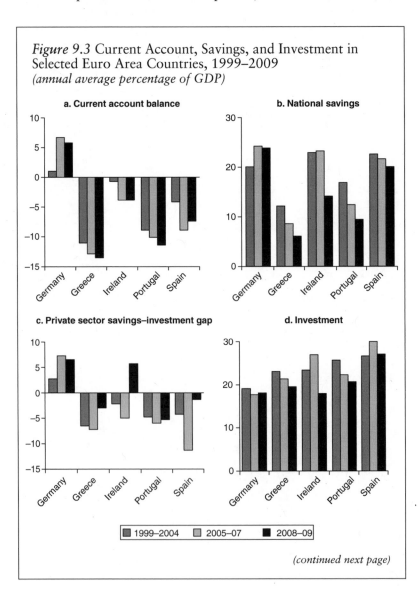

Figure 9.3 Current Account, Savings, and Investment in Selected Euro Area Countries, 1999–2009
(annual average percentage of GDP)

(continued next page)

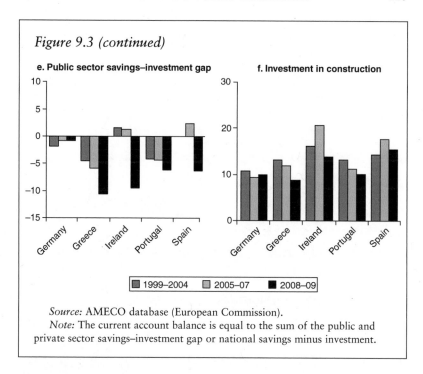

Figure 9.3 (continued)

e. Public sector savings–investment gap

f. Investment in construction

1999–2004   2005–07   2008–09

Source: AMECO database (European Commission).
Note: The current account balance is equal to the sum of the public and private sector savings–investment gap or national savings minus investment.

27.8 percent of GDP to 22.2 percent. Of the 6.5 percentage point decline in the savings rate, the public sector accounts for 1.4 percentage points.

In Ireland and Spain, an investment boom accounted for the current account deficits. Ireland's current account balance fell from a surplus of 0.3 percent of GDP in 1999 to a deficit of 4.3 percent in 2007. The deterioration in the external position was caused by a 2.4 percentage point increase in the investment rate and a 2.3 percentage point drop in the savings rate (which resulted from declining public savings and a stable private sector savings rate). Investment in construction rose from 14.7 percent of GDP in 1999 to 20.2 percent in 2007. During the crisis, the investment rate contracted 12 percentage points and the savings rate fell 10.2 percentage points (mainly as the result of a 12.1 percentage point decline in public savings).

Spain's current account deficit increased from 2.7 percent of GDP in 1999 to 10.0 percent in 2007. The widening of the deficit was caused by an increase in the investment rate, from 25.1 percent to 31.0 percent of GDP, the result of a 5.3 percentage point increase in construction. The increase in the investment rate indicates a high expected rate of return on investment. The savings rate remained constant between 1999 and 2007, but the composition of savings changed dramatically, with an increase in the public savings rate offsetting a decrease in the private savings rate.

Figure 9.4 Exports by Germany, 1998–2009

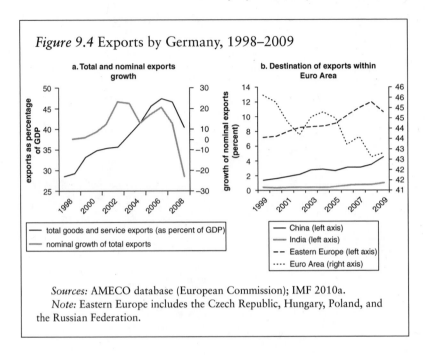

Sources: AMECO database (European Commission); IMF 2010a.
Note: Eastern Europe includes the Czech Republic, Hungary, Poland, and the Russian Federation.

External imbalances in the Euro Area also reflected different patterns in exports. The export share in GDP in Germany increased from 29.1 percent in 1999 to 47.5 percent in 2007 (figure 9.4, panel a). During the same period, the share of exports in GDP remained roughly constant in Greece and Spain, increased slightly in Portugal, and fell in Ireland. Germany's exports expanded not because of market share gains within the Euro Area but because of gains in China, India, and Eastern Europe (panel b). German exports increased even after the gradual appreciation of the euro observed since 2002, which reduced the external competitiveness of all Euro Area countries.

Differences in export performance are associated with huge disparities in the economic growth strategies and wage and labor policies pursued by European countries. Germany's growth strategy was export led; the strategies of Greece, Portugal, and Spain were based on expansion of domestic demand. Wage and labor policies supported growth strategies and eventually gave rise to wide differences in competitiveness. The dynamics of productivity growth and nominal wage inflation in Greece, Ireland, Portugal, and Spain with respect to Germany resulted in a steady increase in productivity-adjusted labor costs in those countries and flat labor costs in Germany (figure 9.5).

The counterpart of protracted current account deficits in Greece, Ireland, Portugal, and Spain was the accumulation of financial and equity claims

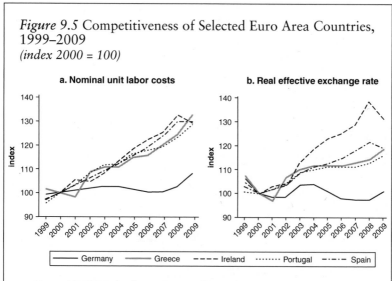

Figure 9.5 Competitiveness of Selected Euro Area Countries, 1999–2009
(index 2000 = 100)

a. Nominal unit labor costs   b. Real effective exchange rate

———— Germany   ———— Greece   – – – – Ireland   ········ Portugal   –··–··– Spain

Source: AMECO database (European Commission).
Note: Nominal unit labor costs are the ratio of compensation per employee to real GDP per person employed for the total economy. The real effective exchange rate is based on unit labor costs and reflects performance relative to 20 industrial countries.

by foreign investors (mainly residents in exporting/lending countries) on income generated domestically in the importing/borrowing countries. The consequence of capital inflows has been a fall in the net foreign asset position of Greece, Ireland, Portugal, and Spain and a sustained increase in the net factor income paid to foreigners (figure 9.6).[2] Greece and Portugal were net recipients of factor income in the late 1990s, but the buildup of external liabilities reversed income flows. By 2007 net payments abroad amounted to 3.6 percent of GDP in Greece and 2.3 percent in Portugal, representing one-quarter of the current account deficits in both countries. Net payments abroad in Spain rose from 1.0 percent of GDP in 1999 to 3.2 percent in 2007, representing one-quarter of the external deficit. Because of foreign direct investment and foreign firms operating in Ireland, net payments abroad have always been sizable, averaging 15 percent of GDP in 1999–2007 and thus absorbing most of the trade surplus.[3]

The global economic crisis put severe strain on government budgets and public debt, raising concerns about fiscal sustainability as well as external imbalances. The increase in fiscal deficits and the virtual explosion of public debt were immediate consequences of the crisis and the

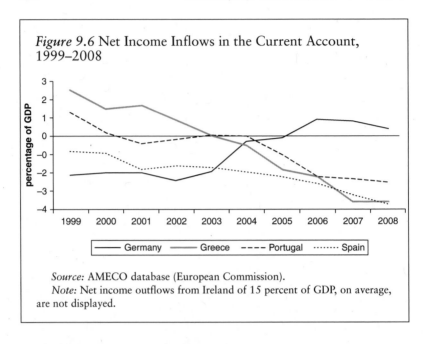

Figure 9.6 Net Income Inflows in the Current Account, 1999–2008

Source: AMECO database (European Commission).
Note: Net income outflows from Ireland of 15 percent of GDP, on average, are not displayed.

strong policy responses to cope with it (table 9.1). European governments resorted to automatic stabilizers and stimulus packages to partly offset the sudden contraction in private sector demand. The large increase in debt in Ireland was caused largely by the nationalization of its major banks.[4] Expansionary fiscal policies eventually limited the decline in output and employment but left government with debt burdens of an unprecedented magnitude (IMF 2010b).

The global economic crisis has made the Euro Area imbalances and structural constraints visible (European Commission 2010). The issue of fiscal sustainability, which had been discussed in relation to the prospective budgetary implications of aging populations, has quickly come to the fore, because debt stocks suddenly reached very high levels and the fiscal consolidation needed to reduce budget deficits is of such a scale that it risks jeopardizing the economic recovery. External sustainability has also been a concern, because importers/borrowers need to strengthen their capacity to export and substitute imports for exports in order to be able to service foreign private and public debts without major corrections in the current macroeconomic trends.

Questions about the capacity of the public and private sectors to service their debts remain. How will the borrower countries of the Euro Area repay the debts they have incurred? How can competitiveness be restored within the monetary union without abandoning the euro and resorting to currency devaluation?

Table 9.1 Debt Stock in Selected Euro Area Countries, 2008–09
(percentage of GDP)

Country/year	Debt stock	Change in debt stock		
		Primary deficit	*Automatic debt dynamics*	*Other debt-creating flows*
Germany				
2008	66.0	–2.7	0.9	2.7
2009	73.2	0.7	5.1	1.5
Greece				
2008	99.2	3.1	–0.5	0.9
2009	115.1	8.5	5.8	1.6
Ireland				
2008	43.9	5.9	2.5	10.6
2009	64.0	12.2	7.0	0.9
Portugal				
2008	66.3	–0.1	1.6	1.2
2009	76.8	6.6	3.9	0.1
Spain				
2008	39.7	2.5	0.4	0.7
2009	53.2	9.4	3.2	0.9

Source: AMECO database (European Commission).
Note: Automatic debt dynamics captures the effect of the interest rate–growth differential on the change in the debt to GDP ratio. Other debt-creating flows include privatization receipts, bank recapitalization, and recognition of implicit liabilities.

Policy Challenges Ahead

Recent developments have revealed two important aspects of Europe's crisis. The first is the political economy considerations constraining policy decisions at the EU level. The second is the assessment by the Euro Area countries and the International Monetary Fund (IMF) of the problems facing countries with large external and fiscal imbalances and the policy instruments available to address them.

The political economy aspects of Europe's crisis are influenced by the buildup of cross-border private and public debts that resulted from protracted external imbalances since 1999 and by the large fiscal imbalances that emerged during the 2008–09 crisis. Three stakeholders play an active role in shaping the policy responses to the financial turmoil: debt holders,

governments of Euro Area debtor countries, and governments of the stronger EU states (France and Germany). Debt holders harbor doubts about
European debtor countries' capacity to repay their debts and expect that
the stronger EU states and the IMF will provide funding to debtor countries that can be used to service debt. Debt holders, of course—especially
investors who bought bonds at higher prices before the crisis—would have
to absorb losses if solvency concerns eventually lead to debt restructuring.
Governments of Euro Area debtor countries expect some financial support
from the governments of the stronger EU states and the IMF so that they
can attenuate the contractionary and deflationary effects of prospective
fiscal adjustments. The governments of the stronger EU states (perhaps
along with the IMF) would have to provide financing to avoid contagion
to other countries and to ensure the viability of the Euro Area (France and
Germany are not only the largest economies in the Euro Area but also the
home of banks highly exposed to Euro Area debtor countries' liabilities).

In the diagnosis of Europe's crisis, there is consensus that Greece, Ireland, Portugal, and Spain must improve competitiveness and consolidate
public finances in order to reverse imbalances and restore external and
fiscal sustainability. The fiscal adjustment programs recently submitted
by several European countries suggest that expenditure-reducing policies
are perceived as appropriate for that purpose. It is also apparent from
the specifics of the EU/IMF rescue plan that the diagnosis is that debtor
countries face a liquidity problem not a solvency problem. Under the plan,
the Euro Area debtor governments are required to adjust budget deficits,
and they are offered a financial backstop if markets are reluctant to roll
over maturing debts over the next two or three years and seek to reduce
exposure to government debt (Roubini 2010). Furthermore, no proposals
have been advanced for restructuring public and private sector debts as
part of the required adjustment.

As restructuring existing debt is not among the policy options under
consideration, the reduction of debtor countries' foreign liabilities must
be achieved by generating current account surpluses (that is, increasing
exports, cutting imports, or both), so that the trade surplus exceeds net
factor payments. In the short and medium terms, Greece, Ireland, Portugal, and Spain could improve their competitiveness with respect to both
their Euro Area trading partners and the rest of the world through a depreciation of the real exchange rate that provides incentives to reallocate
resources from the production of nontradable goods to the production of
exportable goods. As all members of the Euro Area are strongly committed to maintaining the common currency, however, a correction of the real
exchange rate by nominal depreciation is excluded from the policy options
considered. To increase external competitiveness, these countries therefore
need to pursue cost deflation, especially in the tradable sector.

The EU/IMF rescue plan intends to cut aggregate demand and reduce
price and wage inflation of debtor countries, which is instrumental to

achieving cost deflation relative to their trading partners. As the European Central Bank monetary policy ensures that the Euro Area average inflation be fairly low, cost deflation would require adjusting countries to undergo price and wage deflation.[5]

The use of expenditure-reducing policies alone as a means to induce nominal deflation entails a number of risks. First, to the extent that it compresses firms' profit margins and reduces the incentive to produce, nominal deflation may slow economic recovery and even prolong the recession. Second, the fall in prices and wages may increase the real burden of government and private debts, exacerbating the problem of debt sustainability. Third, the trading partners of Euro Area debtor countries, which have themselves been affected by the crisis and are trying to consolidate their own fiscal deficits, may not be willing to accommodate an attempt by Greece, Ireland, Portugal, and Spain to promote economic recovery by expanding exports.

Recent Episodes of Deflationary Adjustment

What is the likelihood of success of an adjustment strategy based on containing demand and seeking nominal deflation? To shed light on this question, we examine episodes of deflationary adjustment in the past three decades and assess their success record.

Deflation is a low-probability event. Out of 4,632 annual observations of consumer price index (CPI) inflation from 183 countries over 1980–2008 (with some missing data), there are only 232 observations of deflation, just 5 percent of the total.

The severity of a deflation episode can be associated with the duration (measured by the number of consecutive years over which the CPI declines continuously) and intensity (measured by the cumulated decline in the CPI during those years) of the fall in prices. Most episodes of deflation are short-lived (one or two years); very few episodes are long-lived (three or more years of decline in the CPI) (figure 9.7).

Deflationary episodes are heterogeneous in terms of intensity, and there is no clear-cut relation between intensity and duration (figure 9.8). The 132 short-lived episodes led to an average accumulated CPI decline of 4.1 percent; the 17 long-lived episodes showed an average decline of 7.0 percent. The steepest declines in the CPI correspond to some short-lived deflations.[6] The median of cumulated CPI declines does increase with the episode duration, but the short-lived episodes exhibit high dispersion in terms of intensity.

The most important episodes of price deflation occurred in the CFA franc zone in the early 1990s, in some East Asian countries after the 1997 Asian crisis, in oil exporters in the 1990s and 2000s, and in Argentina in 1999–2001. In the cases of the CFA franc zone and East Asian countries,

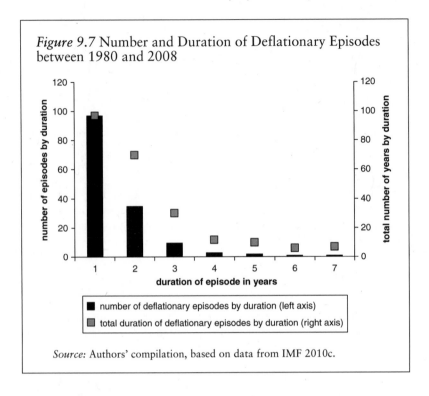

Figure 9.7 Number and Duration of Deflationary Episodes between 1980 and 2008

Source: Authors' compilation, based on data from IMF 2010c.

deflation was accompanied by an economic slowdown or recession; among oil exporters, the statistical relation between deflation and economic activity was less clear.[7]

The CFA franc zone is of interest because, as in the case of the Euro Area, it involves a multicountry central bank and fixed parities with respect to a large economy (France). Median inflation from 1986 to 1993 was 0.3 percent a year (figure 9.9), but several countries, including Chad, Cameroon, and the Republic of Congo, experienced deflation in 1992–93. GDP growth slowed during the deflation period, with median annual growth falling to 1.5 percent, down from 2.3 percent in 1987–91. The deflationary episode ended in 1994, with a balance of payments crisis, a banking crisis, and a large devaluation of the CFA franc with respect to the French franc. The devaluation of the currency eventually succeeded in boosting exports and output as well as stopping deflation: in 1995–99 median annual GDP growth was 4.6 percent and median inflation was 11.7 percent.

Deflationary episodes in Hong Kong SAR, China; Taiwan, China; and Singapore occurred in the aftermath of the 1997 Asian crisis. Following

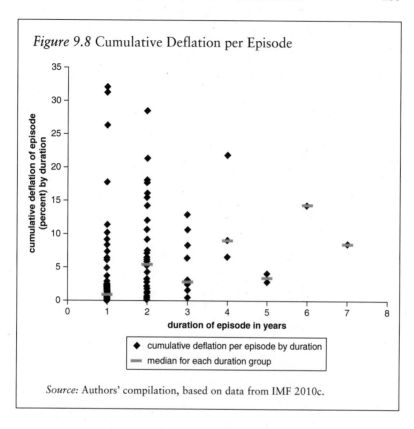

Figure 9.8 Cumulative Deflation per Episode

Source: Authors' compilation, based on data from IMF 2010c.

the large devaluations by Indonesia, the Republic of Korea, Malaysia, the Philippines, and Thailand, Hong Kong SAR, China, and China kept their exchange rate fixed with respect to the U.S. dollar, whereas Singapore and Taiwan, China, allowed for slight currency depreciation. As a consequence, these four economies lost competitiveness with respect to the other Asian economies and subsequently experienced a severe growth slowdown (table 9.2).

Argentina underwent three years of slight deflation before its collapse in 2001 (figure 9.10). During 10 years of fixed parity and real exchange rate appreciation, competitiveness problems gradually developed.[8] In a context of price deflation, GDP contracted 2.9 percent a year in 1999–2001, down from 4.1 percent average annual growth in 1994–98. Following a devaluation with respect to the U.S. dollar, output contracted 10.9 percent in 2002, but growth resumed thereafter, averaging 8.8 percent a year in 2003–07. Inflation accelerated to 26 percent in 2002 and averaged 9.4 percent in the following five years.

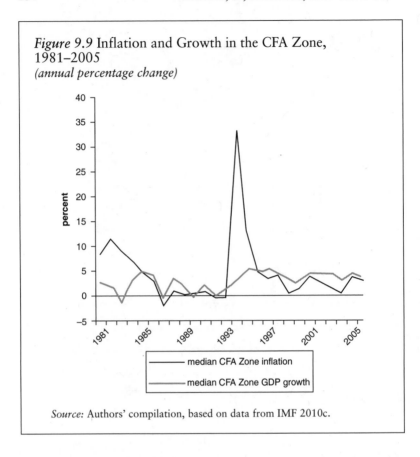

Figure 9.9 Inflation and Growth in the CFA Zone, 1981–2005
(annual percentage change)

Source: Authors' compilation, based on data from IMF 2010c.

Table 9.2 GDP Growth before and during Deflationary Episodes in Selected Asian Economies
(annual percentage change)

Economy	Annual GDP growth before deflationary episode	Annual GDP growth during deflation episode
China	11.5 (1993–97)	7.7 (1998–99)
Hong Kong SAR, China	4.7 (1993–97)	1.6 (1998–003)
Japan	4.0 (1981—90), 1.2 (1991–98)	1.3 (1999–005)
Singapore	9.5 (1993–97)	3.5 (1998–002)
Taiwan, China	5.2 (1996–2001)	2.4 (2001–03)

Source: Authors' compilation, based on data from IMF 2010c.

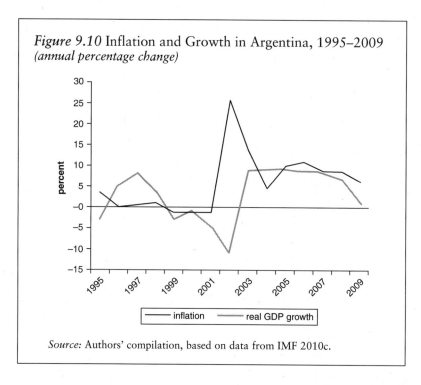

Figure 9.10 Inflation and Growth in Argentina, 1995–2009 *(annual percentage change)*

Source: Authors' compilation, based on data from IMF 2010c.

Two implications can be drawn from these episodes. First, there is a negative relation between nominal deflation and GDP growth, especially in countries with deteriorating competitiveness, such as the CFA franc bloc in the early 1990s, the East Asian countries that did not devalue in 1997, and Argentina in 1999–2001. At some point, these countries faced years of limited deflation and anemic growth, which hardly improved competitiveness and at best was instrumental in reducing external imbalances by contracting imports.

Second, as price and wage deflation did little to resolve competitiveness problems, the CFA franc zone and Argentina ultimately relied on currency devaluation to accelerate the external adjustment.[9] Changing the exchange rate parity immediately reduced the value of domestic costs in foreign currency, thus increasing the profitability of export and import-substitution sectors and adjusting real wages downward.

Concluding Remarks

The recent fiscal and refinancing difficulties in Greece—and to a lesser extent Ireland, Portugal, and Spain—originated from large and protracted current account deficits during the past decade. In Greece and Portugal, external deficits stemmed from a drop in the private savings rate and the expansion of the public sector; in Ireland and Portugal, they came from a boom in private investment. During the same period, Germany experienced large and protracted current account surpluses, originating largely from increasing private sector savings and declining private sector investment.

A thorough understanding of the cases of Ireland and Spain is important for the management of transition and capital inflows in middle-income countries. For both countries, the past decade can be interpreted as a period of convergence, as would be predicted by a simple Solow model for the Euro Area. Capital flowed to Ireland and Spain from the rest of the world, especially from the rest of the Euro Area, because the expected rate of return on investment was higher there than elsewhere and the risks were considered much reduced by the common currency. Commercial banks and other financial institutions lent funds to private firms to develop new investment projects (especially in residential construction). The transition as well as the crisis was led by the private sector. Because of the risk that the private sector may not be able to engineer a resolution of financial disputes by itself, governments have not left the adjustment to market forces. Governments must step in to coordinate the macroeconomic adjustment and mediate the allocation of losses among economic agents.

This interpretation of events has several implications for economic policy. First, high and protracted current account deficits may accelerate the closing of income gaps across countries, but they also create huge adjustment risks. The argument that a private sector–generated current account deficit should not be a concern for policy makers is incorrect. Second, international borrowing has embedded an external effect that probably depends on the size of private sector borrowing and is not taken into account by private parties when settling their operations. Financial and capital inflows should not escape from some form of regulation requiring parties to internalize such externalities. Third, once a problem of bad quality of lending flows or portfolio assets is identified, postponing the resolution of the problem, including the allocation of the corresponding losses, is a welfare-reducing strategy, because inertia clogs the functioning of the credit system and does not eliminate risks. The challenge is to apportion the existing losses and move forward.

In Greece, Ireland, Portugal, and Spain, productivity-adjusted labor costs rose steadily after 1999. Together with the appreciation of the euro after 2002, this trend hampered exports to the rest of the world and within the Euro Area. In contrast, Germany's productivity-adjusted labor costs remained constant over the decade, providing support to a steady increase in the export share in GDP. Bringing down production costs in the context of a fixed exchange rate is a major challenge, which most countries examined in this chapter did not meet. Germany was able to maintain a tight link between labor productivity and labor costs in the past decade. Greece, Ireland, Portugal, and Spain should do the same in the future.

Annex: Decomposition of Growth by Sources of Aggregate Demand in Selected Euro Area Countries

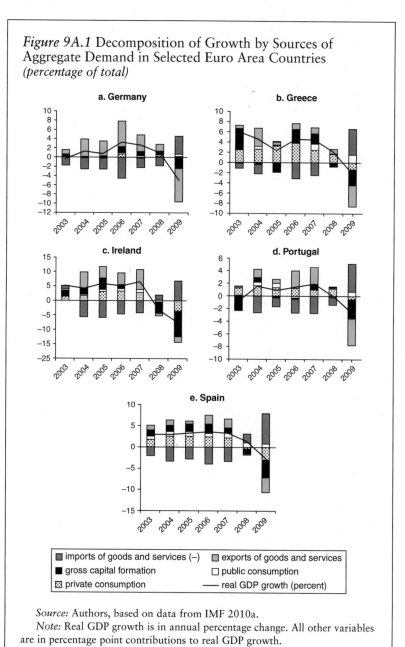

Figure 9A.1 Decomposition of Growth by Sources of Aggregate Demand in Selected Euro Area Countries *(percentage of total)*

Source: Authors, based on data from IMF 2010a.
Note: Real GDP growth is in annual percentage change. All other variables are in percentage point contributions to real GDP growth.

Notes

1. Germany is the largest economy in the Euro Area. Its GDP represents 26.9 percent of Euro Area GDP. Portugal (1.8 percent), Ireland (2.0 percent), and Greece (2.6 percent) are among the smallest countries (AMECO database [European Commission]).

2. From a notional level of 100, the net foreign asset position fell to 25 in Portugal, 33 in Greece, and 51 in Spain (AMECO database [European Commission]).

3. Germany offers a mirror image: net payments of 2.1 percent of GDP in 1999 turned into net receipts of 0.8 percent in 2007 (AMECO database [European Commission]).

4. In 2008–09 importing/borrowing countries underwent a dramatic adjustment in the private sector balance, driven largely by a collapse in private investment and consumption expenditure. As a proportion of GDP, private balances contracted 8.2 percentage points in Greece, 5.7 percentage points in Portugal, 17.2 percentage points in Spain, and 14.0 percentage points in Ireland. In Germany, by contrast, the private sector surplus remained stable, at about 7 percent of GDP, with just a slight decline in private expenditure (AMECO database [European Commission]).

5. Increasing competitiveness with respect to trading partners outside the Euro Area would probably boil down to running expansionary monetary policies aimed at euro depreciation. Such policies would be helpful for lenders/exporters if Euro Area countries stuck to an export-led recovery and growth strategy while reorienting exports to avoid reproducing external imbalances within the Euro Area. Such a strategy would nevertheless face an unfavorable global environment.

6. The largest cumulative deflations occurred in Samoa (32 percent in 1985), Cambodia (31 percent in 1987), Equatorial Guinea (29 percent in 1986–87), Lao PDR (26 percent in 1990), Libya (22 percent in 2000–03), and the Republic of Congo (21 percent in 1988–89). In Equatorial Guinea and the Republic of Congo, deflation coincided with a 20 percent appreciation of the CFA franc against the U.S. dollar. These large deflationary drops are unlikely to be relevant references for the Euro Area countries.

7. The characteristics of oil-exporting economies are hardly comparable with those of Euro Area countries and thus do not constitute relevant references. Oil-exporting countries suffered deflation episodes associated with falling oil prices in 1996–99 and 2000–02 (Bahrain in 1996–2002, Saudi Arabia in 1997–2001, and Oman in 2000–02). In these counties, deflation was not accompanied by a severe slowdown in GDP growth. In Bahrain, for instance, the five-year average annual GDP growth rate fell from 5.0 percent before the deflation episode to 4.5 percent a year during the episode. Both Oman and Saudi Arabia actually grew faster during the deflation than during the five years preceding it.

8. Competitiveness losses in export and import-substitution sectors often arise when a fixed exchange rate arrangement is adopted and relatively high domestic inflation materializes afterward or parity is fixed at a level that implies real misalignment (that is, real overvaluation). Some observers have argued that real overvaluation may have been the case in many European countries, which may have chosen wrong real parities when they adopted the euro, despite the cross-country inflation differentials observed afterward within the Euro Area.

9. In Argentina and the CFA franc zone countries, deflation was accompanied by bank runs, international credit rationing, and capital flight.

References

European Commission. 2010. "Public Finances in EMU:2010." Directorate General for Economic and Financial Affairs, European Economy, No. 4, Brussels.

Gros, Daniel. 2010. "Adjustment Difficulties in the GIPSY Club." CEPS Working Document 326, Centre for Economic Policy Studies, London.

IMF (International Monetary Fund). 2010a. *Direction of Trade Statistics.* Washington, DC: International Monetary Fund.

———. 2010b. "Navigating the Fiscal Challenges Ahead." *Fiscal Monitor* (May). Washington, DC: International Monetary Fund.

———. 2010c. *World Economic Outlook April 2010.* Washington, DC: International Monetary Fund.

Roubini, Nouriel. 2010. "Order from Chaos: A Restructuring Plan for Greece's Public Debt." *Financial Times,* June 28.

World Bank. 2009. *World Development Report.* Washington, DC: World Bank.

———. 2010. *Weekly Global Economic Brief* 49, May 13. Development Prospects Group, World Bank, Washington, DC.

Part III

Debt Restructuring Mechanisms: Lessons and Beyond

10

Avoiding Avoidable Debt Crises: Lessons from Recent Defaults

Yuefen Li, Rodrigo Olivares-Caminal, and Ugo Panizza

his chapter examines whether the recent experience with external
borrowing and sovereign default yields any lessons on the type of
policies that can be adopted to reduce the probability of debt crises.
The large-scale bailouts at the early stage of the crisis were unprecedented
and may have delayed the manifestation of the impact of the crisis on the
external debt of several developing countries. For this reason, we use four
case studies of recent default episodes, which highlight the importance of
external shocks, overborrowing, and the legal techniques used to restructure outstanding debt.

The chapter is organized as follows. The first section provides a flash
review of the legal and economic literature on sovereign debt and sovereign default. The second section looks at how the recent financial and
economic crisis affected the evolution of external debt in a sample of
56 developing and emerging economies. The evidence shows that debt
levels have increased but not exploded, possibly because the increased
risk aversion of international investors prevented some low-income
countries that may have wanted to borrow more from doing so. The
third section provides case study evidence on Belize, Ecuador, Grenada,
and the Seychelles. The last two sections discuss policy options for mitigating the probability of future debt crises and provide some concluding
remarks.

The Law and Economics of Sovereign Debt

Sovereign debt is different from private debt, because there is no structured approach for managing sovereign defaults or an effective procedure for enforcing sovereign debt contracts. Sovereign creditors have limited legal recourse for two main reasons. The first relates to the principle of sovereign immunity, which states that a sovereign cannot be sued in foreign courts without its consent unless it has submitted to jurisdiction or it falls within an exception (for example, commercial activity). The second has to do with the fact that even when creditors obtain a favorable ruling, sovereign debt contracts remain difficult to enforce, because creditors practically cannot attach assets located within the borders of the defaulting country. The legal literature on sovereign debt concurs that a sovereign state cannot be declared insolvent.

Given that contracts cannot be easily enforced, why do sovereigns repay? (Alternatively, why do lenders lend?) It must be that repaying is less costly than defaulting. Of course, we know what the cost of repaying is (the value of the loan), but what is the cost of default? A better understanding of the costs of defaults is a necessary condition for reforming the international financial architecture and devising policies that can jointly reduce the prevalence and the costs of sovereign default.

The economic literature on sovereign debt has focused on the reputational and trade costs of defaults. Economic models that focus on reputational costs assume that defaults lead to either higher borrowing costs or more limited access to international financial markets and, in the extreme case, to permanent exclusion from these markets (Eaton and Gersovitz 1981). Models that emphasize trade costs argue that defaulters will suffer a reduction in international trade, either as a consequence of direct trade sanctions (Bulow and Rogoff 1989; Díaz-Alejandro 1983) or because of lack of trade credit. Although there are several theoretical problems with these models (see Panizza, Sturzenegger, and Zettelmeyer 2009 for a survey of the literature), the real issue is that these assumptions do not seem to fit the real world. Reputational costs appear to be short-lived (Borensztein and Panizza 2009), and, although there is some evidence that defaults affect trade (Rose 2005), there is no evidence of formal trade sanctions (at least in recent times) or a strong causal nexus from default to trade through trade credit (Borensztein and Panizza 2009).[1]

A promising class of theoretical models moves the attention from the actions of nonresidents to the domestic effects of the default. These models assume that the government is contemporaneously interacting with several actors who are uncertain about whether they are dealing with a "good" or "bad" type of government. A default could reveal the "true" type of the government and modify the actions, not of the external creditors but of all actors who are still engaging with the government (Cole and

Kehoe 1998). One problem with this interpretation is that limited costs of default are observed, even when the focus is on the evolution of GDP growth (Benjamin and Wright 2008; Levy-Yeyati and Panizza forthcoming; Tomz and Wright 2007).

It is possible that only strategic defaults (that is, defaults that could easily have been avoided) carry a high cost. Defaults caused by true inability to pay are unavoidable. Therefore, they do not provide any signal on the type of government and do not carry a large cost (Grossman and Van Huyck 1988). Knowing the high cost of strategic default, countries will avoid them. To the contrary, they may even pay a large cost to postpone a necessary default in order to signal to all interested parties that the default was indeed unavoidable (Borensztein and Panizza 2009; Levy-Yeyati and Panizza forthcoming).

The legal literature has focused mainly on the restructuring aspects of sovereign debt. Broadly speaking, sovereign debt restructuring can be understood as the mechanism used by a sovereign state to prevent or resolve debt issues and achieve debt sustainability levels. Restructuring has two main aspects: procedural and substantial. The procedural aspect focuses on the way in which the restructuring should be performed (that is, its architecture); the substantial aspect is the actual restructuring of debt, which normally involves changing amortization schedules and writing off the debt principal (Olivares-Caminal 2010).

There is widespread agreement for a revamped sovereign debt-restructuring process for private claims. There is disagreement over what the actual process should be (Arora and Olivares-Caminal 2003): court-supervised workouts in a bankruptcy-type proceeding or a purely voluntary bond workout (Buchheit and Gulati 2002). Policy makers need to select the model that will provide orderly restructuring while safeguarding the rights of both creditors and the debtor.

The current debate is between the establishment of an international bankruptcy regime and the use of voluntary and contractual arrangements such as exchange offers, collective action clauses, and other devices. The International Monetary Fund (IMF) believes that the scope of some of the voluntary mechanisms used in the past has been greatly diminished, particularly as a result of the shift from syndicated bank loans to bonds in sovereign borrowing. This shift has led to a wider dispersion of creditors and debtors and a larger variety of debt contracts; it has been associated with the growing spread and integration of capital markets and innovations in sourcing foreign capital (UNCTAD 2001).

Debts documented in syndicated loans are relatively easy to restructure, because they are restructured within the framework of the London Club.[2] In the late 1990s (and in the wake of the 2001–02 Argentine crisis), most observers thought that bonded debt would have been much more difficult to restructure than syndicated loans. These worries were driven by the fact that bonds are held by different types of creditors encompassing different interests (the multilegitimacy problem). It was also thought that the restructuring of bonded debt would have been hampered by the presence of many outstanding series subject to different applicable laws (the applicable law is relevant when a sovereign is under distress because the debtor's alternatives depend on the applicable law).[3] It turned out that this was not the case. Even the Argentine debt exchange, with an acceptance rate of 76 percent in the first exchange offer, ended up being more successful than many expected.[4]

The method and techniques used for restructuring sovereign debt share several similarities with corporate debt restructuring. The most significant difference is that both parties in a corporate restructuring—debtor and creditor—know that upon failure of the debt-restructuring process there is a last resort (bankruptcy), which is not available in the case of a sovereign.

The Evolution of External Debt during the Crisis

The financial and economic crisis ignited by the collapse of the housing market in the United States may end up having severe repercussions on long-term debt sustainability in developing and emerging market countries (Li 2010). To capture the recent evolution of external debt in developing countries and transition economies, we draw on information from the World Bank's Quarterly External Debt Statistics (QEDS), which, at the time of writing, reported information on external debt through the third quarter of 2009.

Although this chapter focuses on sovereign debt and sovereign default, it discusses the evolution of public, publicly guaranteed, and total external debt (public and private). There are two reasons for covering total external debt. The first is that several crises have now completely discredited the Lawson-Robichek doctrine that only public external debt can lead to costly debt crises.[5] The current crisis is just one of many examples showing that private debt (especially that of banks) represents a large contingent liability for the public sector. This contingent liability becomes explicit as soon as the banking sector enters into crisis. The second reason for focusing on total external debt is that publicly available data do not distinguish between public and publicly guaranteed (PPG) debt and debt that is fully owed by private creditors.[6]

The average total external debt to GDP ratio in the 56 developing countries and transition economies covered by the QEDS increased by more than 8 percentage points between 2008 and 2009 (table 10.1).[7] The increase is in contrast with the trend over the previous four years, when external debt (both total and PPG) decreased by more than 20 percent.

The sample of countries covered by the QEDS is smaller than that normally used to describe the external debt of developing countries and transition economies.[8] Countries included in the QEDS have average levels

Table 10.1 Summary Statistics

Variable	Number of observations	Mean	Standard deviation	Minimum	Maximum
All countries with data through 2009					
Total external debt/GDP 2007 Q3	56	0.438	0.282	0.022	1.223
PPG external debt/GDP 2007 Q3	53	0.161	0.154	0.010	0.836
Total external debt/GDP 2009 Q3	56	0.520	0.399	0.023	1.859
PPG external debt/GDP 2009 Q3	53	0.192	0.146	0.019	0.643
Growth in external debt 2007–09	56	0.082	0.167	−0.194	0.746
Growth in PPG 2007–09	53	0.026	0.080	−0.194	0.276
Growth in external debt 2003–07	46	−0.221	0.318	−1.125	0.714
Growth in PPG 2003–07	46	−0.230	0.231	−1.087	0.045
Global Development Finance data for 2007					
Total external debt/GDP 2007 GDF	123	0.519	0.531	0.034	4.421
PPG external debt/GDP 2007 GDF	123	0.336	0.334	0.018	2.097
Countries in Europe and Central Asia with data through 2009					
Total external debt/GDP 2007 Q3	21	0.640	0.307	0.213	1.223
PPG external debt/GDP 2007 Q3	21	0.148	0.119	0.019	0.537
Total external debt/GDP 2009 Q3	21	0.875	0.432	0.347	1.859
PPG external debt/GDP 2009 Q3	21	0.225	0.148	0.021	0.564

(continued next page)

Table 10.1 (continued)

Variable	Number of observations	Mean	Standard deviation	Minimum	Maximum
Growth in external debt 2007–09	21	0.235	0.174	0.022	0.746
Growth in PPG 2007–09	21	0.077	0.090	-0.053	0.276
Growth in external debt 2003–07	15	-0.004	0.276	-0.439	0.714
Growth in PPG 2003–07	15	-0.134	0.096	-0.340	0.013
Low- and lower-middle-income countries with data through 2009					
Total external debt/GDP 2007 Q3	26	0.335	0.196	0.022	0.809
PPG external debt/GDP 2007 Q3	24	0.190	0.136	0.010	0.607
Total external debt/GDP 2009 Q3	26	0.372	0.242	0.023	0.899
PPG external debt/GDP 2009 Q3	24	0.217	0.134	0.019	0.560
Growth in external debt 2007–09	26	0.037	0.114	-0.105	0.380
Growth in PPG 2007–09	24	0.024	0.064	-0.085	0.187
Growth in external debt 2003–07	26	-0.340	0.279	-1.125	0.045
Growth in PPG 2003–07	26	-0.313	0.261	-1.087	-0.051

Source: Authors.
Note: PPG = public and publicly guaranteed (debt).

of debt that are markedly lower than those of the universe of developing countries and transition economies. As there may be substantial inertia in debt accumulation, the increase in debt in the full sample may be much larger than documented in table 10.1. Therefore, the results of this section should be taken with some caution.

The transition economies of Eastern Europe and Central Asia entered the crisis with higher levels of external debt than the cross-country average. They were severely hit by the global crisis, with average GDP growth falling from 10 percent in 2003–07 to zero in 2007–09 and the average external debt to GDP ratio skyrocketing from 42 percent to 88 percent.

In contrast, low- and lower-middle-income countries entered the crisis with a level of total external debt that was substantially lower than the cross-country average and a level of PPG external debt that was just above the cross-country average. During the crisis, they experienced, on average, a moderate increase in total and PPG external debt (although some countries in the group saw their debt increase by as much as 38 percent).

In 2005 all groups of countries included in the QEDS had similar levels of external debt (figure 10.1). While most countries were reducing their debt levels, the countries of the Europe and Central Asia region were rapidly accumulating debt liabilities. Countries in this region also entered the crisis with the lowest average level of PPG debt and started accumulating public debt at the end of 2008; by the end of 2009, they had levels of PPG that were comparable to those of low-income countries (figure 10.1). By the end of 2009, developing countries and transition economies included in the QEDS statistics had total external debt of almost $4 trillion. About 73 percent of this debt was owed by private creditors; the remaining 27 percent was public or PPG.

Case Study Analysis: Sovereign Defaults in the Second Half of the Past Decade

Examination of four recent default episodes, in Belize, Ecuador, Grenada, and the Seychelles, is instructive, given that it is probably too early to extract definitive lessons from the current crisis. Although the sample is small, it includes very different experiences and can thus suggest some lessons on the future of debt crises.

Belize

At the turn of the century, the government of Belize embarked on an ambitious debt-financed program aimed at rebuilding the infrastructure damaged by a wave of hurricanes and tropical storms that hit the country between 1998 and 2002. This massive reconstruction effort coincided with declining prices for some exports and led to a persistent trade deficit.

Figure 10.1 External Debt, Private External Debt, and Publicly Guaranteed External Debt as Share of GDP, 2005–09

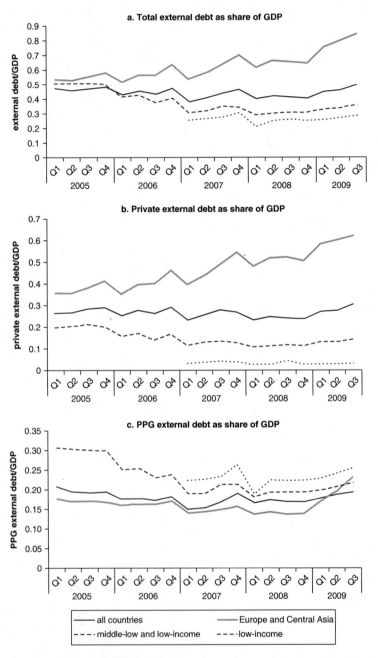

Source: Authors' calculations, based on data from the World Bank's Quarterly External Debt Statistics.

Exports of goods and services as a percentage of GDP declined steadily, from 68 percent in 1991 to 54 percent in 2003 while imports kept increasing. As a consequence, the current account deficit widened substantially, reaching 19 percent of GDP in 2003.

The fiscal situation kept deteriorating, with the public sector's external debt increasing from 46 percent of GDP in 1999 to 82 percent of GDP in 2006. The need to roll over such a large volume of debt led to a series of refinancing operations with higher and higher interest rates; by August 2006 Belize was spending more than 27 percent of its fiscal revenues servicing the interest on its debt. Meanwhile, the fiscal deficit was rising (the average fiscal deficit in 2004–05 exceeded 8 percent of GDP) and GDP growth contracting.

Belize's unsustainable situation led to the announcement of an "impending debt rearrangement" on August 2, 2006. The government decided to adopt a constructive approach. It started a process of intensive consultations with its creditors, which it described as very helpful in defining the terms. On December 6, 2006, a press release from the Minister of Finance announced the main financial terms of the exchange offer. Belize's sole and "unofficial" creditor committee endorsed the exchange offer through a press release dated December 22, 2006, stating that the members of the committee had unanimously decided to participate. The National Assembly approved the terms of the offer, which was executed between December 18, 2006 and January 26, 2007. Tenders representing 96.8 percent of the aggregate principal amount of the eligible claims were received. As a result of the use of a collective action clause (CAC) in a dollar-denominated bond issued in 2003, which was subject to New York law, the total amount covered by this financial restructuring represented 98.1 percent of the eligible claims.

Belize was the first sovereign in more than 70 years to use a CAC to amend the payment terms of a bond in a sovereign debt restructuring (Buchheit and Karpinski 2006). The fact that the 2003 bond included a CAC, which requires the written consent of holders of at least 85 percent of the bonds, greatly facilitated the exchange. Holders of 87.3 percent of the New York CAC bond accepted Belize's exchange offer, thereby consenting to the amendments, which included matching the terms of the "old" bonds with those of the "new" bonds. As a result of the exchange offer, Belize's bond ratings were upgraded.

Belize made two substantial contributions to the sovereign debt-restructuring toolkit. The first was the transparent approach. Belize posted all the information related to the debt rearrangement, including possible restructuring scenarios and a clear indication of the debt relief needed, on its Web site (Buchheit and Karpinski 2007).[9]

The second contribution was the invitation to creditors to form committees. The creation of the creditor committees differed from those formed in the 1980s and 1990s in certain aspects. Belize established criteria for the formation of creditor committees and their procedural rules, drawing on earlier experiences in forming these committees, incorporating those elements that enhanced dialogue and participation among creditors and avoiding those that obstructed negotiations. In the event, one bondholders' committee was formed, but it did not meet the requirements established by the government to be recognized as an official creditor committee.

Ecuador

Ecuador's default is probably the most interesting of those studied in this chapter. Because of previous debt-restructuring exercises and reserve accumulation as a result of high oil prices before its default, market participants did not perceive Ecuador as having an unsustainable debt situation. Ecuador decided to stop servicing a subset of its external bonds because the debt audit commission (Comisión para la Auditoría Integral del Crédito Público [CAIC]) mandated by a presidential decree in 2006 found the bonds to be illegitimate or illegal (see annex table 10A.2).[10] Following the recommendation of the CAIC, in November 2008 Ecuador suspended interest payment on the 2012 global bonds deemed illegitimate. After a 30-day grace period, it formally entered into default on December 15, 2008. At the moment of the default, Ecuador had three outstanding series of bonds: 12 percent dollar global bonds due 2012, dollar step-up global bonds due 2030, and dollar global bonds due 2015.

The 2012 and 2030 bonds were issued in 2000 to restructure the Brady bonds. The 2015 bonds were issued to purchase some of the 2012 bonds in accordance with the issuance terms of the mandatory prepayment arrangement included in its terms. Although the CAIC concluded that the 2012, 2015, and 2030 bonds and several other debt instruments were illegal or illegitimate, the government decided to default only on the 2012 and 2030 bonds.

On April 20, 2009, Ecuador launched a cash offer to repurchase the 2012 and 2030 bonds. The offer expired on May 15, 2009. The buyback transaction was structured as a modified Dutch auction with a minimum price of $0.30 per dollar of outstanding principal. Offers by bondholders were considered irrevocable. The buyback offer highlighted the risks of not participating in the invitation.

The final buyback price was $0.35 per dollar of outstanding principal, accepted by 91 percent of bondholders. Only 7.2 percent of the original $2.7 billion issued under the 2030 bonds and 18.7 percent of the $510 million of the 2012 bonds remained outstanding in the market.

The Ecuadoran default is a landmark case because it is the first default in modern history in which ability to pay played almost no role.[11] It remains to be seen whether Ecuador will pay a long-term reputational cost for its action or its actions will have an effect on the market for the sovereign debt of other emerging market countries.

Ecuador's default on the 2012 and 2030 bonds and its buyback transactions may lead to some changes in sovereign debt instruments. New sovereign debt issuances will include strict contractual provisions increasing the standard of trustee responsibility in postdefault scenarios and tightening regulations regarding a borrower's ability to repurchase its defaulted debt (Buchheit and Gulati 2009).

Ecuador allegedly engaged in an aggressive secondary repurchase through intermediaries when the price for the defaulted 2012 and 2030 bonds hit rock bottom but before an official moratorium was announced or a default actually occurred (Miller 2009; Porzecanski forthcoming). The 2012 and 2030 Ecuadoran bonds included a debt purchase provision (a mandatory prepayment arrangement). This contractual arrangement required the retirement of an aggregate outstanding amount for each type of bond by a specified percentage each year starting after 6 years for the 2012 bonds and 11 years for the 2030 bonds, through purchases in the secondary market, debt-equity swaps, or any other means.[12]

This contractual provision included in the Ecuadoran bonds clearly denotes that the purchase in the secondary market of a debtor's own debt is not only legal but also desirable, because it can reduce the amount of outstanding debt to make it more manageable. However, Ecuador's repurchase took place after certain events that could have affected the trading price of the debt instruments, including announcements of the delay in interest payments and videos showing the finance minister privately discussing debt instruments with other individuals (Economist 2007). This behavior revealed a systemic failure affecting "market integrity," as Ecuador could have disclosed information that affects the market while deciding whether to default.[13] Therefore, even if the ties between the secondary actors and the Ecuadoran government were to be proven, the actual default made it very difficult to demonstrate an undesirable behavior, as the default occurred, mooting possible allegations of deliberate market manipulation.[14]

Grenada

Grenada, a small island economy, entered 2004 with a large current account deficit (almost 13 percent of GDP) and substantial external debt. Both the debt and the deficit had been shrinking in comparison with previous years, and the country appeared to be on the path to achieving external sustainability. The situation changed after Hurricane Ivan hit, in September 2004, causing economic damage that exceeded 200 percent of Grenada's GDP. The hurricane rendered inoperable about 70 percent of hotel rooms and damaged 70 percent of the producing acreage of nutmeg plantations, the country's main sources of income.[15] As a result, unemployment rose sharply and the current account deficit almost tripled.

In July 2005 Grenada was hit by Hurricane Emily, which had an economic cost of 12 percent of GDP.

Grenada could not respond to these large external shocks and current account deficits by devaluing its currency, because its currency is pegged to the U.S. dollar. As a result, output contracted by almost 6 percent in 2004. Output recovered in 2005 but contracted by 2.4 percent in 2006 and 2007, when the current account deficit surpassed 40 percent of GDP.

Grenada stopped servicing its external debt in the fall of 2004; it made an exchange offer to holders of eligible commercial debt in September 2005. More than 85 percent of the holders of the eligible debt (bondholders and holders of other types of commercial debts) accepted the offer. About 15 percent of creditors neither exchanged their debt instruments nor reached a later agreement. This put Grenada in a deadlock situation, because it did not want to repudiate its debts but did not have the means to satisfy the requests of the holdout creditors. Grenada addressed this issue by adopting language similar to that used in the Commonwealth of Dominica's 2004 exchange offer.[16] Grenada did not commit any additional funds to service the nontendered instruments, but it allowed for the possibility of servicing these debts once additional resources became available. No actual promises were made, but the debt was not repudiated.

The treatment of holdout creditors provided by Grenada—that is, neither repudiating nor repaying the debt but waiting until there is a clearer picture—can be dubbed the Caribbean Approach (Buchheit and Karpinski 2006). The name is appropriate not only because the approach was used by Grenada following Dominica's restructuring experience but also because the term was coined by the Caribbean-born U.S. Secretary of the Treasury, Alexander Hamilton, in a U.S. exchange offer in 1790. Although the sovereign is not providing an actual solution, it is not providing a legal ground for claims based on the repudiation of the debts of debtholders who decide not to participate in the exchange offer.

The other relevant feature of the Grenadian exchange offer is the structuring of individual enforcement rights under the trust indenture, which was subject to New York law. There is a substantial difference between English trust deeds and U.S. trust indentures regarding the extent of the trustee's enforcement powers.[17]

The Seychelles

The Seychelles is a small island country that depends heavily on imported commodities and tourism revenues (tourism represents about 70 percent of total foreign exchange earnings). The period 2006–07 was characterized by rapid growth as well as mounting structural imbalances. Although an overvalued currency was causing unsustainable current account deficits on the order of 32 percent of GDP, the central bank was reluctant to depreciate the currency because of concerns over the fiscal costs of negative balance sheet effects. Although at 3.7 percent of GDP the fiscal deficit was not very high, large current account deficits led to a rapid accumulation of external debt (mostly to commercial creditors), which more than doubled over the period 2005–07.

The hike in commodity prices in 2007–08 and the collapse in tourism revenues that followed the global crisis amplified the effects of these structural imbalances. On July 31, 2008, the Seychelles notified bondholders of its intention to default on privately placed bonds worth €54.8 million ($78 million) maturing in 2011. The government stated that the reason for missing the payment was the presence of "irregularities in the issuance-approval process and a lack of transparency in the note documentation" (Bloomberg 2008).

In October 2008, when its international reserves were basically depleted, the government announced that it would not be able to make a coupon payment on a $230 million eurobond and would approach creditors to seek an agreement on a comprehensive debt restructuring.[18] The exchange offer was launched in December 2009 and completed in mid-January 2010, with 89 percent of the aggregate amount of the eligible claims settled.

The default process was accompanied by an IMF program aimed at supporting public debt restructuring and restoring external sustainability. In November 2008 the Seychelles agreed to a comprehensive reform program in exchange for a two-year IMF Stand-By Arrangement of SDR 17.6 million (about $26.6 million). The main elements of the program consisted of a more flexible exchange rate policy and tighter fiscal and monetary policies.

In mid-April 2009, Paris Club creditors granted exceptional debt treatment to the Seychelles under the Paris Club's Evian approach, reducing the initial debt stock of $163 million by 45 percent in nominal terms in two phases and agreeing to reschedule the remaining amount over 18 years, including a five-year grace period. They also agreed to defer part of the payments due in the coming years.

The Debt Sustainability Assessment conducted by the IMF in July 2009 found that the Seychelles' public debt remained unsustainable. The finding probably reflected the country's substantial obligations with commercial creditors, which may have been resolved with the bond exchange of January 2010. On February 1, 2010, after the successful bond exchange, Fitch gave the Seychelles Issuer Default Ratings (IDRs) ratings of B– on its long-term foreign currency debt and B with positive outlooks on its local currency debt.

The restructuring carried out by the Seychelles included a partial guarantee on interest payments from the African Development Bank, a novel element aimed at sweetening the terms and reaching agreement. The guarantee was executed as a side agreement, but its text was included in the prospectus. The guarantee states that if the Seychelles fails to make payments of interest under the new bonds, the African Development Bank will be responsible for an aggregate maximum guarantee in the amount of $10 million. The guarantee is a senior, unsubordinated, unconditional, and unsecured obligation by the African Development Bank. The amounts payable do not include principal, costs, fees, expenses, or other amounts or any payment of interest that in aggregate exceeds $10 million.

What Is Missing? New Policies and New Institutions

The discussion in the previous sections highlights three basic causes of debt crises: overborrowing by the public and private sectors; large external shocks, caused either by natural disasters or sudden drops in external demand; and the presence of contentious debt contracts. Policies at the national and international levels aimed at reducing the probability of a debt crisis should focus on these three problems.

Avoiding Overborrowing

Favorable external and domestic conditions often lead to a climate of global optimism. Investors and policy makers start thinking that rapid debt accumulation is justified by the fact that rapid growth will allow emerging market countries to sustain higher and higher levels of debt. The story usually ends in tragedy, with default episodes clustered at the end of periods of rapid credit expansion (Borensztein and Panizza 2009).

This pattern suggests that the first step toward achieving debt sustainability is to borrow for the right reason and not to borrow too much during "good times." Debt should be used to finance projects that generate returns that are higher than the interest rate charged on the loan (such projects may include certain types of social expenditure, such as education, which have a positive impact on economic development), and foreign currency borrowing should be limited to projects that either directly or indirectly generate the foreign currency necessary to service the debt (UNCTAD 2008).[19]

Policies aimed at limiting overborrowing need to recognize that politics often lies at the center of borrowing decisions. Politicians tend to overborrow in the run-up to elections in order to stimulate the economy and maximize the probability of reelection. Moreover, politicians with a limited time horizon may incur debt in order to avoid difficult fiscal adjustments and put the onus on their successors. Public sector overborrowing can be limited by increasing the transparency of the budgetary process and the reliability of fiscal and debt statistics and by maintaining a well-functioning system of automatic fiscal stabilizers.

The situation of low-income countries is more complicated than that of middle-income emerging market countries, because many low-income countries have limited ability to sustain debt but need external resources in order to build their productive capacity and finance social expenditures. The ideal solution would be to increase aid flows to these countries. However, for any given aid envelope, difficult decisions need to be made on the optimal degree of concessionality. In the extreme, such decisions boil down to whether donors should give only grants or blend grant and loans. Under the current approach, donors start by conducting forward-looking debt sustainability analyses, using the outcome to determine the mix between grants and loans. As grants are subject to a volume discount with respect to loans, the outcome of the debt sustainability exercise also determines the size of the total transfer.[20] Although this approach makes sense from a theoretical point of view, it suffers from serious implementation problems. The most important of these problems is that estimating long-term debt sustainability requires forecasting GDP growth for the next 20–30 years. Such predictions often end up being completely useless.[21]

Private debt can also lead to public debt crises, as a result of contingent liabilities or because the government may need to step in to sustain aggregate demand if private demand collapses. In fact, there are conditions under which private external debt may generate more vulnerabilities than public sector external debt (UNCTAD 2010). Excessive private sector borrowing can be limited by prudential regulation of banks and other financial intermediaries. Because the use and abuse of complex derivative instruments limit the ability of regulators to monitor the external exposure of the private sector, there are instances in which the introduction of controls on capital inflows is the only effective way to limit private sector overborrowing.

Moving to Contingent Debt Contracts

Debt crises and defaults are often triggered by unexpected external shocks. Such shocks can take the form of natural disasters, abrupt drops in external demand, or a sudden tightening of external financial conditions.

How can countries maintain debt sustainability in the aftermath of external shocks? One possible approach is self-insurance, which consists of not accumulating net external debt (countries may still have a gross external debt, which is then matched by the accumulation of international reserves). This is exactly what many emerging market countries have been doing since the Asian and Russian crises of the late 1990s. Not all countries can afford to self-insure. Moreover, self-insurance appears to be suboptimal, because resources are tied up in international reserves invested in low-return assets such as U.S. government bonds.

An alternative is to buy insurance from third parties. Countries can either buy standard insurance contracts or issue contingent debt instruments (that is, debt contracts in which the repayment depends on the realization of a given event). Such instruments exist, but they tend to be underutilized because of adverse selection and political economy problems.[22]

Adverse selection relates to the fact that only countries that think they face a significant risk have an incentive to buy insurance, reducing the number of countries in the insurance pool and increasing the cost of insurance. Moreover, the decision to buy insurance may lead to an increase in the premium, because insurers may interpret a country's decision to buy insurance as a signal that policy makers in the country have privileged information on the probability that the insured risk will indeed materialize.

Political economy obstacles are even more important. Self-interested policy makers with short time horizons have limited incentives to engage in contingent debt contracts, which imply a cost that must be paid up front and a benefit that may accrue only years later.[23] Even altruistic politicians may face difficulties using contingent debt instruments, because if the risk does not realize, they can be accused of having wasted the country's money. Mexico, for example, paid $1.5 billion in the summer of 2008 to insure all of its oil exports against the possibility of a sudden drop in the price of oil. In 2009, when oil prices fell, the Mexican minister of finance, Agustin Carstens, was universally applauded for having purchased these contracts, which delivered an $8 billion windfall exactly when the country needed the money the most. However, one could imagine the reaction of the Mexican public if the price of oil had not decreased. In the best of cases, Carstens would have been criticized for having wasted a large amount of public money. In the worst case, he would have been accused of outright corruption. Yet the decision to insure would have been the right one even if prices had increased (with high oil prices, Mexico would not have needed the extra money as much as it needed it at a time of deep crisis). The source of the political economy problem is that any optimal contract would involve a payout by the country in some state of the world.[24]

A universal mandate forcing all countries to issue contingent debt instruments would solve both adverse selection and political economy problems. Although it would be impossible to impose contingent debt contracts on unwilling sovereign borrowers and private lenders, the official sector could promote the use of these types of contracts by using only contingent loans.

Dealing with Defaults

Even with better domestic and international policies and institutions, defaults are still bound to happen. The international financial architecture still lacks a mechanism for resolving such defaults swiftly and limiting their costs.

Until the early 1990s, most international debt of developing countries was owed to official creditors (multilaterals or bilateral) or to banks.

This meant that debt renegotiations involved a relatively small number of parties. After Brady swaps transformed defaulted syndicated bank loans into Brady bonds, policy makers started worrying that the presence of a large number of dispersed and heterogeneous creditors would lead to long and costly debt renegotiations. These concerns motivated several proposals aimed at reducing collective action problems. The United Nations Conference on Trade and Development (UNCTAD) was the first international organization to call for an orderly workout procedure for external debt of developing countries drawing on national bankruptcy laws, notably Chapters 9 and 11 of U.S. bankruptcy law (UNCTAD 1986). In 2001 the IMF proposed the creation of a sovereign debt-restructuring mechanism (SDRM). The establishment of such a mechanism was eventually rejected. The market response was the use of contractual features: exit consent or exit amendments and the use CACs.[25]

Some authors argue that the failure to establish a mechanism aimed at a speedier and more efficient resolution of default episodes is a good thing for the international debt market. Their rationale is that the costs of default sustain the existence of the international debt market and that any policy aimed at reducing these costs will shrink international lending, make it more expensive, or both (Dooley 2000; Shleifer 2003; for an alternative view, see chapter 12 of this volume). However, the possibility that countries may suboptimally try to delay unavoidable defaults puts an interesting spin on the discussion of the desirability of international policies aimed at mitigating the costs of default. If it is indeed true that a country's attempt to defend its reputation creates a deadweight loss, the creation of an agency with the ability to certify the causes of a default episode could potentially protect the reputation of "good" countries without forcing them to go through a painful postponing exercise. Such certification would represent a Pareto improvement, because it could potentially reduce the costs of defaults while increasing recovery values on defaulted debt and thus increasing access and reducing the overall costs of borrowing (see Levy-Yeyati and Panizza forthcoming and chapter 14 in this volume).

Principles for Promoting Responsible Sovereign Lending and Borrowing

Proposals for establishing a crisis resolution mechanism date back to 1971, when the Group of 77 adopted the "Declaration and Principles of the Action Programme of Lima."[26] The program called for orderly debt workouts that would explicitly take into account the development implications of a heavy debt-servicing burden and stressed the need to create a new international mechanism for dealing with debt problems in developing countries. [27] The fact that almost four decades after this proposal there has been no substantive progress toward establishing such a mechanism highlights the difficulty in building international consensus on this issue.

In the absence of such a mechanism, a set of universally agreed on principles for responsible sovereign lending and borrowing could promote adherence to a code of conduct and discourage reckless sovereign lending or borrowing. It could also lead to the establishment of criteria to assess whether the contracting of sovereign debt is performed responsibly, both ex ante and, in some cases, ex post. The parties would then not only have a common reference point in the case of a dispute, they would also be encouraged to follow generally accepted principles that enhance responsible practices.

The past few years have witnessed heated debate over what constitutes legitimate and responsible sovereign lending and borrowing. Nongovernmental organizations and some sovereigns have put question marks on the legitimacy of contracting parties, lending purposes, environmental and social consequences, and a range of other factors. Building on the momentum, UNCTAD initiated a project aiming at drawing up a set of guidelines and principles.

Fiduciary duties of national governments could be the cornerstone of such a set of principles. Both lending and borrowing governments should be guided by the best interests of their current and future citizens when drawing up debt contracts.

Producing realistic debt sustainability analyses for borrowers is in the joint interest of both borrowers and lenders. The process for contracting and meeting sovereign debt obligations must be transparent ex ante and politically accountable, particularly when borrowing may have implications for revenue streams that affect future generations. The legal dimension should be in agreement with the national and international law regulating sovereign lending and borrowing and take into consideration such basic elements as respect for the sovereignty and obligations of the parties involved. Proper approval and disclosure should be followed diligently. The social dimension could embody such elements as human rights, protection of the environment, and respect for internally accepted minimum standards on social issues, labor, and environmental protection. In addition, consideration should be given to issues related to debt renegotiation, comparable treatment, and the interests of low-income countries, to name just a few.

Concluding Remarks

This chapter surveys how the global economic crisis is affecting debt sustainability in developing and emerging market countries by examining four case studies. It shows that the root causes of the defaults in three of these countries (Belize, Grenada, and the Seychelles) were similar. All of them involved small and poorly diversified economies that had limited ability to respond to the large external shocks to which their economies were exposed.[28] In all three cases, policy action was constrained by the presence of a fixed exchange rate regime which led to a real appreciation and large external imbalances. In Belize and Grenada, these external imbalances were amplified by excessive public sector borrowing. In Grenada and the Seychelles, defaults were triggered by a large external shock (Hurricane Ivan in Grenada, the global economic crisis in the Seychelles). In contrast, in Belize the default was a more direct outcome of excessive public spending (although expenditure growth was triggered by previous natural disasters). These findings suggest that emerging market and developing countries remain underinsured against external shocks. Promoting the use of contingent debt mechanisms would improve debt sustainability in these countries.

Belize, Grenada, and the Seychelles also seemed equally interested in protecting their reputations. All three countries adopted similar, creditor-friendly approaches to restructuring their debt. In addition to cooperating with creditors, the three countries asked for advice and financial help from the international community.

Belize, Grenada, and the Seychelles are three cases of sovereign debt crises with some preventable elements. If policies to avoid overborrowing and encourage responsible sovereign debt practices had been in place— jointly, through an international move toward contingent debt contracts to minimize the impact of external shocks—the outcome in these countries could have been less severe.

The issue of the legitimacy of the defaulted debt was at the center of the Ecuadoran default. Ecuador defaulted on two bonds because the debt audit commission created by President Rafael Correa found that part of Ecuador's external debt was illegitimate or illegal. The key question is whether Ecuador will suffer a long-lasting reputational cost from its decision to default on its bonds. Although the literature suggests that reputational cost tends to be short-lived, the case of Ecuador may end up being different, because markets may perceive its actions as strategic. It is also possible that the short memory of market participants will prevail and that Ecuador will end up paying a very limited cost for its recent default. A more interesting question is whether Ecuador's landmark decision will have an impact on the workings of the international sovereign debt market. If it does, market participants may anticipate these actions and reprice the sovereign risk of certain emerging market borrowers. The result could be a dry-up of credit similar to the one that followed the 1998 Russian crisis (Kogan and Levy-Yeyati 2008).

Annex

Table 10A.1 Debt Ratios of Selected Low- and
Lower-Middle-Income Countries, 2007 and 2009

	Total PPG debt/GDP		*Total external debt/GDP*	
Country	*2007Q3*	*2009Q3*	*2007Q3*	*2009Q3*
Albania	0.166	0.250	0.240	0.347
Argentina	0.261	0.220	0.465	0.412
Armenia	0.144	0.331	0.261	0.541
Bahamas, The	0.044	0.065	0.044	0.065
Belarus	0.019	0.145	0.213	0.394
Bolivia	0.160	0.166	0.397	0.348
Brazil	0.050	0.047	0.178	0.190
Bulgaria	0.114	0.112	0.936	1.228
Cameroon	0.113	0.115	0.113	0.115
Chile	0.023	0.026	0.327	0.458
Colombia	0.112	0.122	0.209	0.224
Costa Rica	0.060	0.057	0.292	0.286
Croatia	0.158	0.105	0.759	1.022
Czech Republic	0.078	0.099	0.387	0.434
Dominica	0.649	—	0.649	0.555
Ecuador	0.220	0.135	0.386	0.281
Egypt, Arab Rep. of	0.163	0.140	0.245	0.172
El Salvador	0.249	0.254	0.482	0.460
Estonia	0.026	0.059	1.076	1.419
Ethiopia	0.123	0.144	0.123	0.144
Georgia	0.179	0.327	0.470	0.765
Honduras	0.159	0.167	0.239	0.227
Hungary	0.348	0.564	1.113	1.859
India	0.047	0.053	0.175	0.196
Indonesia	0.188	0.188	0.326	0.326
Israel	0.195	0.140	0.530	0.407
Kazakhstan	0.023	0.021	0.899	1.037
Korea, Rep. of	0.034	0.081	0.326	0.497

Table 10A.1 (continued)

Country	Total PPG debt/GDP		Total external debt/GDP	
	2007Q3	2009Q3	2007Q3	2009Q3
Kyrgyz Republic	0.537	0.539	0.809	0.831
Latvia	0.048	0.273	1.223	1.777
Lebanon	0.836	0.643	0.836	0.643
Lithuania	0.112	0.180	0.668	0.948
Macedonia, FYR	0.185	0.223	0.478	0.618
Madagascar	0.230	0.264	0.241	0.266
Malaysia	0.033	0.019	0.324	0.372
Mexico	0.057	0.080	0.183	0.214
Moldova	0.209	0.210	0.705	0.805
Nicaragua	0.607	0.560	0.675	0.630
Nigeria	0.022	0.023	0.022	0.023
Pakistan	0.267	—	0.282	0.266
Paraguay	0.169	0.286	0.253	0.286
Peru	0.201	0.156	0.288	0.270
Poland	0.181	0.209	0.491	0.650
Russian Federation	0.041	0.035	0.338	0.381
Rwanda	0.152	0.138	0.178	0.145
Slovak Republic	0.125	0.401	0.529	0.780
Slovenia	0.201	0.289	0.971	1.189
South Africa	0.066	0.075	0.254	0.274
Thailand	0.010	0.019	0.248	0.249
Tunisia	0.310	0.300	0.574	0.548
Turkey	0.133	0.154	0.363	0.460
Uganda	0.130	0.161	0.130	0.161
Ukraine	0.080	0.209	0.518	0.899
Uruguay	0.420	0.356	0.449	0.389
Yemen, Rep. of	0.266	0.232	0.266	0.232

Source: World Bank's Quarterly External Debt Statistics.

Table 10A.2 Summary of Findings of CAIC Audit Report

Finding	Observation
Increase in interest rates by U.S. Federal Reserve in late 1970s constitutes illegal practice.	Ecuador does not have jurisdiction to determine the legality of the monetary policy of the U.S. Federal Reserve.
Conversion of accrued interests in arrears in Past Due Interest (PDI) Brady Bonds and Interest Equalization (IE) Brady Bonds resulted in anatocism (interest on interest) and is therefore illegal.	Conversion of accrued interest in arrears into Brady bonds implied a novation of the original obligation, giving rise to a new debt instrument with its own terms and conditions. Inclusion of an interest rate in bonds is a common and legal practice.
Submission to foreign court jurisdiction is contrary to Ecuadoran law.	Submission to foreign court jurisdiction is common practice in international sovereign debt transactions. Usually, a specific exception is obtained for that purpose, as acknowledged in the CAIC report.
Waiver of sovereign immunity is contrary to Ecuadoran law.	Waiver of sovereign immunity is common practice in international sovereign debt markets. In the United Kingdom and the United States, activities in which the action is based on a commercial activity are considered as exceptions to the general state immunity from jurisdiction.

Maintaining a relationship with multilateral organizations is contrary to Ecuadoran law.	The illegal practice is to agree in a written contract that Ecuador will maintain a formal relationship with multilateral organizations (that is, to continue being a member of organizations such as the IMF and the World Bank).
The lack of registration of certain bonds with the U.S. Securities and Exchange Commission is against the law.	According to U.S. securities law, bonds can be sold to qualified institutional buyers by means of a private placement of unregistered securities outside the United States. Doing so requires substantially less disclosure and lower costs. After a seasoning period, the securities can target U.S. private investors.
The choice of foreign governing law is illegal under Ecuadoran law.	The choice of a foreign governing law in international sovereign bond issuances is a common practice that is usually resolved by a specific norm authorizing it as an exception to the general rule. For example, the Ecuador Noteholder Circular dated April 20, 2009, to submit in a modified Dutch auction to sell bonds for cash states that the choice of a foreign law in the area of public debt affects national sovereignty. However, the circular itself is subject to English law, which accounts for a similar situation.

Source: Authors, based on CAIC 2008.

Notes

The authors thank Carlos A. Primo Braga for inviting them to write this chapter; Gallina A. Vincelette, Mark L. J. Wright, and an anonymous referee for helpful comments and suggestions; and Mackie Bahrami for help with the data.

1. Not everyone would agree with this summary of the empirical evidence. Tomz (2007), for instance, claims that reputational concerns are very important and describes some historical cases in which default did affect reputation. Kohlscheen and O'Connell (2006) show some cases in which trade credits fell after defaults but do not present a formal test or try to establish causality.

2. The London Club is an informal group of commercial banks that join together to negotiate their claims against a sovereign debtor.

3. During the 2001–02 Argentine debt crisis, 152 series of bonds were governed by eight different laws. Transactions are ruled by the law chosen by the parties; in the case of a bond issuance it is the issuer who decides which will be the applicable law (Olivares-Caminal 2005). It was estimated that at the moment of the default, Argentina had more than 700,000 creditors around the globe.

4. An incipient theoretical literature examines why bond debt restructuring ended up being easier than expected (Bai and Zhang 2008; Bi, Chamon, and Zettelmeyer 2008).

5. Lawson-Robichek takes its name from Nigel Lawson and Walter Robichek. In a 1988 speech on the current account deficit of the United Kingdom, then Chancellor of the Exchequer Nigel Lawson stated that the position of his country was strong because the current account deficit was driven by private sector and not public sector borrowing. Walter Robichek, Director of the Western Hemisphere Department of the IMF in the 1980s, held similar beliefs on the difference between current account deficits driven by private and public debt.

6. In fact, as ballooning domestic debt is often at the root of external debt crises (Reinhart and Rogoff 2009), we should have been even more ambitious and focused on both domestic and external debt. We focused on external debt only because of the paucity of data on total (external and domestic) public debt.

7. The QEDS includes 60 developing countries and transition economies; it has data updated to the third quarter of 2009 for only 56 of these countries (see annex table 10A.1). The QEDS collects data from two reporting systems, the Special Data Dissemination Standard (SDDS) and the General Data Dissemination Standard (GDDS). Some countries use both reporting systems. The GDDS follows guidelines similar to those in the World Bank's *Global Development Finance*; it includes figures for total external, total public, and total PPG long-term external debt. Countries that report their date through SDDS include disaggregate figures for the debt of the general government, the monetary authorities, banks, other sectors, and foreign investors. For these countries we computed PPG debt by summing the debt of the general government and the monetary authorities. We recognize that in doing so, we underestimate total PPG debt, as some bank and other sector debt could be guaranteed by the public sector.

8. The World Bank's *Global Development Finance* contains data on more than 120 countries, but they are updated only to 2008.

9. The information posted included its own drafted document or those provided by the IMF or its financial advisers. These drafts covered the country's economic position, financial projections, and debt servicing capacity, as well as issues related to the financial position of the country and its future prospects.

10. The objective of the CAIC is to audit the processes by which public debt has been incurred to determine its legitimacy, legality, transparency, quality, efficacy, and efficiency, considering legal and financial aspects; economical, social, gender,

and environmental impacts; and the impacts on nationalities and people. The audit covered agreements, contracts, and other forms of public financing between 1976 and 2006.

11. In the Ecuadoran Noteholder Circular dated April 20, 2009, it was stated that as of December 31, 2008, the total internal and external debt represented 26.1 percent of GDP, which was easily manageable. A 2008 financial report stated that "it is still difficult to argue that Ecuador's debt faces a sustainability problem … the current situation is triggered by a lack of willingness to pay (rather than a lack of ability to pay)" (Deutsche Bank 2008, p. 1).

12. According to an IMF publication, "This feature is intended to give bond-holders some assurance that the aggregate amount of the new bonds would be reduced to a manageable size before their maturity dates while giving Ecuador flexibility to manage its debt profile" (IMF 2001, p. 33). If Ecuador failed to meet the reduction target, a mandatory partial redemption of the relevant bond would be triggered, an amount equal to the shortfall.

13. As Porzecanski (forthcoming) argues, there are clear links between the drop in Ecuadoran central bank reserves and the purchase of debt in the secondary market during the default period. It is also alleged that the vehicle used was Banco del Pacifico, acting through a broker.

14. Ecuador allegedly managed to acquire about half of the total outstanding debt in each series in the secondary market, which could have distorted the readings from the outcome of the buyback exercise.

15. Nutmeg trees require five to eight years to grow to maturity. Recovery of the sector will therefore take time.

16. Under the section entitled "Treatment of Eligible Claims Not Tendered," the Commonwealth of Dominica's offer stated that "if any Eligible Claims are not tendered in connection with this Offer, the Government intends to pay those nontendered Eligible Claims as and when resources to do so become available to the Government. The Government does not intend, however, to pay any amount in respect of a nontendered Eligible Claim if, at the time such payment is due, a payment default then exists under any Short Bond, Intermediate Bond or Long Bond." For clarification purposes, the new bonds issued by Dominica as a result of the exchange offer were dubbed "short bonds" (10 years), "intermediate bonds" (20 years), and "long bonds" (30 years) (see Commonwealth of Dominica Offer to Exchange Eligible Claims for XCD 3.5 percent bonds due 2014, 2024, and 2034, dated April 6, 2004).

17. Under English trust deeds, enforcement power is vested on the trustee, who has the right to receive the payment (in trust) and therefore the right to enforce any payment. If the trustee declines the enforcement of the debt instrument, bondholders recover their enforcement rights. In contrast, U.S. trust indentures are constrained by §316(b) of the Trust Indenture Act (TIA) of 1939. Section 316(b) protects the bondholders' rights to collect principal and interest when due and to sue if necessary without the consent of other bondholders in a collective enforcement action. Thus, under English trust deeds, only the trustee can enforce bondholders' rights (unless there is a decline); under U.S. trust indentures, the bondholders' right to sue cannot be impaired by a qualified number of creditors. Although the TIA does not apply to sovereign bonds issued in the United States, no sovereign state dared include a restriction on the enforcement rights contrary to §316(b) of the TIA. Grenada was the first sovereign to include English deed–style enforcement right limitations on a bond governed by New York law (Buchheit and Karpinski 2006).

18. Standard & Poor's downgraded the eurobond (9.125 percent due 2011) to D (default) and assigned a recovery rating of 4, indicating its expectation of an average recovery of 30–50 percent on defaulted debt.

19. Because money is fungible, the statement that foreign currency borrowing should be limited to projects that either directly or indirectly generate the foreign currency necessary to service the debt need not be applied literally. However, whenever a country borrows abroad, it needs to make sure that its economy can generate the external resources necessary to service the debt.

20. The International Development Association (IDA) uses the World Bank–IMF Debt Sustainability Framework to divide countries into three groups: red light, yellow light, and green light. Countries in the first group are considered to be at high risk of debt distress and thus receive only grants. Countries in the second group are considered to have an intermediate risk of debt distress and receive large transfers, half in grants and half in concessional loans. Countries in the third group are considered to have a low risk of debt distress and receive even larger transfers, all as concessional loans.

21. Estimates of long-run growth are usually formulated by projecting trend growth, controlling for country characteristics. The problem with this methodology is that the correlation of growth rates across decades is very low (0.1–0.3) and country characteristics tend to be stable (Easterly and others 1993). There is also the issue that in developing countries it is almost impossible to separate the business cycle from the trend growth (Aguiar and Gopinath 2007).

22. Another problem relates to the fact that there is a substantial fixed cost involved in creating new debt instruments, which individual agents have limited incentives to pay. Moreover, these debt instruments tend to be complex, and not all debt management offices have the ability to evaluate the costs and benefits related to issuing and managing them. (UNCTAD is providing support to debt management offices interested in developing sounder risk management techniques and moving toward issuing contingent debt instruments.) Moral hazard does not seem to be a problem, because it seems unlikely that policy makers would voluntarily reduce the growth prospects of their country or amplify the effects of a natural disaster in order to limit debt repayments.

23. Contingent contracts need to be issued during good times and therefore will carry an up-front cost.

24. Australia, for example, had to abandon its successful foreign exchange strategy after the Treasury made large losses in one quarter. (The authors thank Mark L. J. Wright for suggesting this example.)

25. Exit consent is the technique by which holders of bonds in default who decide to accept an exchange offer grant their consent to amend certain terms of the bonds being exchanged. The exchange offer is thus conditioned to a minimum threshold of creditors' acceptance, and the amendments to the terms are performed once the required majority has been obtained. By means of these amendments, the defaulted bonds subject to the exchange offer become less attractive (in legal and financial terms), forcing a larger number of bondholders to accept the exchange offer. If holdout bondholders do not accept the exchange offer, they will be holding an impaired bond that no longer features some of the original contractual enhancements. Where they are included in the prospectuses of the bonds, CACs require the interaction of the bondholders. There are four types of CACs: collective representation clauses, majority action clauses, sharing clauses, and acceleration clauses. Majority action clauses have been strongly pursued by the official sector and many academics; they were effectively incorporated in bond issuances. Majority action clauses enable the amendment of any of the terms and conditions of the bonds, including the payment terms, if the required majority therein established is obtained. In most countries the required threshold to amend the terms of the bonds containing majority action clauses has been 75 percent of the aggregate principal amount of the outstanding bonds. Belize is the only country that has required 85 percent.

26. The Group of 77 was established on June 15, 1964, by the "Joint Declaration of the Seventy-Seven Countries," issued at the end of the first session of UNCTAD in Geneva. It was formed to articulate and promote the collective economic interests of its members, strengthen their joint negotiating capacity on all major international economic issues in the United Nations system, and promote South-South cooperation for development. The membership of the G-77 has expanded to 130 member countries, but the original name has been retained because of its historical significance.

27. According to a November 12, 1971, announcement by UNCTAD, "The criteria and procedures of rescheduling ... should be reviewed and revised so as to ensure that the rescheduling of debts does not interfere with the orderly process of development planning in debtor countries and should be systematically designed to prevent both disruption of long-term development plans and need for repeated rescheduling. A special body should be created within the machinery of UNCTAD to find practical solutions to the debt-servicing problems of developing countries."

28. Grenada and the Seychelles have populations of less than 100,000 each and GDPs of less than $700 million. Belize has about 300,000 inhabitants and a GDP of $1.4 billion.

References

Aguiar, Mark, and Gita Gopinath. 2007. "Emerging Market Business Cycles: The Cycle Is the Trend." *Journal of Political Economy* 115 (1): 69–102.

Arora, Alinna, and Rodrigo Olivares-Caminal. 2003. "Rethinking the Sovereign Debt Restructuring Approach." *Law and Business Review of the Americas* 9 (4): 101–41.

Bai, Yan, and Jing Zhang. 2008. "Sovereign Debt Renegotiation and Secondary Market." Paper presented at the Conference of the Society for Economics Dynamics, Boston, July 10–12.

Benjamin, David, and Mark L. J. Wright. 2008. "Recovery before Redemption: A Theory of Delays in Sovereign Debt Renegotiations." Department of Economics University of California at Los Angeles.

Bi, Ran, Marcos Chamon, and Jeromin Zettelmeyer. 2008. "The Problem That Wasn't: Collective Action Problems in Sovereign Debt Exchanges." International Monetary Fund, Washington, DC.

Bloomberg. 2008. "Cutler, Seychelles to Hold Talks with IMF Following Default on Notes." September 5.

Borensztein, Eduardo, and Ugo Panizza. 2009. "The Costs of Default." *IMF Staff Papers* 56 (4): 683–741.

Buchheit, Lee, and Mitu Gulati. 2002. "Sovereign Bonds and the Collective Will." *Emory Law Journal.* 51: 1317–64.

———. 2009. "The Coroner's Inquest." *International Financial Law Review* 29 (9): 22–25.

Buchheit, Lee, and Elizabeth Karpinski. 2006. "Grenada's Innovations." *Journal of International Banking Law and Regulation* 4: 227.

———. 2007. "Belize's Innovations." *International Banking and Finance Law* 22: 278.

Bulow, Jeremy, and Kenneth Rogoff. 1989. "A Constant Recontracting Model of Sovereign Debt." *Journal of Political Economy* 97 (1): 155–78.

CAIC (Comisión para la Auditoría Integral del Crédito Público). 2008. "Final Report of the Integral Auditing of the Ecuadorian Debt Audit." Quito http://www .auditoriadeuda.org.ec/index.php?option=com_content&view=article&id=89.

Cole, Harold L., and Patrick J. Kehoe. 1998. "Models of Sovereign Debt: Partial versus General Reputations." *International Economic Review* 39 (1): 55–70.

Deutsche Bank. 2008. "Ecuador: On the Likelihood of Debt Restructuring." EM Special Publication, November 17, Global Markets Research, New York.

Díaz-Alejandro, Carlos F. 1983. "Stories of the 1930s for the 1980s." In *Financial Policies and the World Capital Market: The Problem of Latin American Countries*, ed. Pedro Aspe Armella, Rudiger Dornbusch, and Maurice Obstfeld. Chicago: University of Chicago Press.

Dooley, Michael. 2000. "International Financial Architecture and Strategic Default: Can Financial Crises Be Less Painful?" *Carnegie-Rochester Conference Series on Public Policy* 53 (1): 361–77.

Easterly, William, Michael Kremer, Lant Pritchett, and Lawrence Summers. 1993. "Good Policy or Good Luck? Country Growth Performance and Temporary Shocks." *Journal of Monetary Economics* 32 (3): 459–83.

Eaton, Jonathan, and Mark Gersovitz. 1981. "Debt with Potential Repudiation: Theoretical and Empirical Analysis." *Review of Economic Studies* 48 (2): 289–309.

Economist. 2007. "Caught on Camera: A Setback for Rafael Correa." July 26.

Grossman, Herschel, and John Van Huyck. 1988. "Sovereign Debt as a Contingent Claim: Excusable Default, Repudiation, and Reputation." *American Economic Review* 78 (5): 1088–97.

IMF (International Monetary Fund). 2001. "Involving the Private Sector in the Resolution of Financial Crisis: Restructuring International Sovereign Bonds." Policy Development and Review and Legal Departments, Washington, DC.

Kogan, Joe, and Eduardo Levy-Yeyati. 2008. *Global EM Strategy: Contagion from Ecuador. Repricing the Cost of Default*. London: Barclays Capital, Global Emerging Markets Strategy, November 21.

Kohlscheen, Emanuel, and Stephen A. O'Connell. 2006. *A Sovereign Debt Model with Trade Credit and Reserves."* Department of Economics, University of Warwick, United Kingdom.

Levy-Yeyati, Eduardo, and Ugo Panizza. Forthcoming. "The Elusive Costs of Sovereign Default." *Journal of Development Economics*.

Li, Yuefen. 2010. "Collateral Damage from the Global Financial Crisis: Could Developing Countries Land in Another Round of Debt Crises?" In *Responding to the Challenges Posed by the Global Economic Crisis to Debt and Development Finance*, 55–77. Geneva: United Nations Conference on Trade and Development.

Miller, Ben. 2009. "Ecuador Restructuring: Inside Job." *Latin Finance* July 1.

Olivares-Caminal, Rodrigo. 2005. "The Use of Corporate Debt Restructuring Techniques in the Context of Sovereign Debt." *International Corporate Rescue* 2 (5): 262–69.

———. 2010. *Legal Aspects of Sovereign Debt Restructuring*. London: Sweet & Maxwell.

Panizza, Ugo, Federico Sturzenegger, and Jeromin Zettelmeyer. 2009. "The Economics and Law of Sovereign Debt and Default." *Journal of Economic Literature* 47 (3): 651–98.

Porzecanski, Arturo. Forthcoming. "When Bad Things Happen to Good Sovereign Debt Contracts: The Case of Ecuador." *Duke Law and Contemporary Problems.*

Reinhart, Carmen, and Kenneth Rogoff. 2009. *This Time Is Different: Eight Centuries of Financial Folly.* Princeton, NJ: Princeton University Press.

Rose, Andrew K. 2005. "One Reason Countries Pay Their Debts: Renegotiation and International Trade." *Journal of Development Economics* 77 (1): 189–206.

Shleifer, Andrei. 2003. "Will the Sovereign Debt Market Survive?" *American Economic Review* 93 (2): 85–90.

Tomz, Michael. 2007. *Reputation and International Cooperation: Sovereign Debt across Three Centuries.* Princeton, NJ: Princeton University Press.

Tomz, Michael, and Mark L. J. Wright. 2007. "Do Countries Default in 'Bad Times'?" *Journal of the European Economic Association* 5 (2–3): 352–60.

UNCTAD (United Nations Conference on Trade and Development). 1986. *Trade and Development Report 1986.* Geneva: UNCTAD.

———. 2001. *Trade and Development Report 2001.* Geneva: UNCTAD.

———. 2008. *Trade and Development Report 2008.* Geneva: UNCTAD.

———. 2010. *Responding to the Challenges Posed by the Global Economic Crisis to Debt and Development Finance.* New York and Geneva: UNCTAD.

11

Managing Subnational Credit and Default Risks

Lili Liu and Michael Waibel

S tate and local government debt and guarantees for quasi-public agencies debt have been growing in importance in developing countries. In Brazil subnational debt accounts for about 30 percent of total public sector net debt.[1] The debt of Indian states represents about 27 percent of India's GDP.[2] Subnational debt financing has been historically important in the United States, with outstanding subnational debt at $2.36 trillion at the end of 2009.[3]

The increasing share of subnational debt in consolidated public debt is not limited to federal countries. In China urban investment companies have been borrowing from financial institutions to finance large-scale infrastructure investments (Liu 2008). In France subnational governments account for more than 70 percent of public investment.

The increasing importance of subnational debt reflects, among other factors, the increasing decentralization of spending responsibilities, taxation power, and borrowing capacity to subnational governments. The unprecedented scale of urbanization in developing countries requires large-scale infrastructure investment financing to absorb massive influxes of people from rural areas. Subnational borrowing finances infrastructure more equitably across multigenerational users of infrastructure services, as the maturity of debt service paid for by the beneficiaries can match the economic life of the assets the debt is financing. In practice, however, subnational governments often also borrow for current expenditures.

With subnational borrowing come the risks of subnational insolvency.[4] Systemic subnational insolvency may impede the growth of subnational capital markets, curtail fiscal space for infrastructure investments, and threaten financial stability and core public services, which may create pressures on the central government to provide financial assistance to ensure the continuing provision of essential public services. More autonomy for subnational governments increases the need for strong regulation for fiscal responsibility. During the 1990s subnational debt crises occurred in countries such as Argentina, Brazil, Mexico, and the Russian Federation, which have led to reforms to strengthen regulatory frameworks for subnational borrowing and insolvency.

The global financial crisis has had a profound impact on subnational finance across countries (Canuto and Liu 2010a). Subnational finances deteriorated across a broad range of countries at all income levels, although the degree of impact varied. Rating agencies viewed the impact of the economic downturn on the credit qualities of subnational governments as significant because of declines in the tax base, expenditure pressures or rigidities, and growing and more expensive debt (Fitch 2009; Moody's 2010; Standard & Poor's 2010).

The fragility of the global recovery and the growth of public debt have increased the importance of prudently managing subnational default risks. Beyond the current crisis, the structural trends of decentralization and urbanization are expected to continue with force, requiring prudent management of subnational default risks.

This chapter draws lessons from previous episodes of subnational financial distress and their interaction with sovereign defaults. It pays particular attention to the legal and institutional principles underpinning the debt-restructuring and fiscal adjustment process in subnational insolvency proceedings. Looking across countries, regulatory frameworks for subnational insolvency share central features, although the historical context and entry points for reform explain important variations. An important objective of the regulatory framework is to address soft budget constraints and the problem of overgrazing of the common resources by subnational governments. Fiscal rules for subnational governments or ex ante regulation attempt to limit the risk of subnational defaults; ex post regulation predictably allocates default risk while providing breathing space for orderly debt restructuring and fiscal adjustment, as well as the continued delivery of essential public services. However, ex ante and ex post regulatory systems alone cannot ensure the sustainability of subnational debt. The development of intergovernmental fiscal systems and financial markets, which falls outside the scope of this chapter, is equally important.

The chapter is structured as follows. The next section presents the motivation and rationale for regulating subnational debt financing. This motivation is country specific and shapes the design of the regulation. The second section summarizes regulatory frameworks, focusing on fiscal rules for subnational governments with respect to debt issuing, specifying the purpose, types, amount, and procedures of debt financing. The third section explores key issues in designing insolvency mechanisms, encapsulated in the trade-off between protecting creditor's contractual rights and maintaining minimum public services. The last section presents concluding remarks and draws policy lessons.

Rationale for Regulating Subnational Debt Financing

In response to the subnational fiscal stress and debt crises of the 1990s, countries such as Brazil, India, Mexico, and the Russian Federation have developed regulatory frameworks for subnational debt financing. Some newly decentralizing countries, such as Peru, developed frameworks for subnational debt while initiating decentralization, based on lessons learned from other countries on the fiscal risks associated with decentralization. Developed countries such as France and the United States have had their own experiences of subnational insolvency, which led to the establishment of systems to regulate the risks.

Subnational Debt Crises

Although expenditure-revenue imbalances may cause the development of subnational fiscal stress, the regulatory framework for debt financing profoundly affects the fiscal sustainability of subnational governments, because accumulation of fiscal deficits is feasible only when they have been financed. Such financing can take multiple forms, including direct borrowing and running arrears.

Unregulated subnational borrowing grew rapidly in countries such as Hungary and Russia in the 1990s, contributing to subnational fiscal stress. Borrowing by subnational governments was also facilitated by decentralization, which granted substantial autonomy in debt financing to subnational governments but failed to impose hard budget constraints.

Unregulated borrowing is particularly risky in an uncertain macroeconomic environment, as illustrated by the subnational debt crises in Russia, where at least 57 of 89 regional governments defaulted on debt payments between 1998 and 2001. Unfettered market access by subnational borrowers, especially in newly minted, speculative, and unregulated security markets, can outpace the development of sound revenue streams and a regulatory framework. In particular, foreign borrowing in an uncertain macroeconomic environment with the risk of currency speculation can be costly (Alam, Titov, and Petersen 2004). Because of the effect of macroeconomic policies, including interest rates and exchange rates, on subnational fiscal profiles, the rating of the sovereign typically binds the ratings of its subnational entities.[5]

The fiscal deficit itself may not be a problem if borrowing finances capital investment and economic growth.[6] However, subnational governments borrowed heavily to finance substantial operating deficits in countries such as Hungary, India, and Russia in the 1990s, leading to unsustainable debt paths. In India much of the growth in states' fiscal deficits in the late 1990s was driven by borrowing to finance revenue deficits.[7] At the height of the crisis, more than 70 percent of new borrowing was used to refinance existing debt in some states.[8]

Certain debt profiles of subnational governments can have inherent rollover risks, which are exacerbated by macroeconomic and financial shocks. Before the macroeconomic crisis in Mexico in the mid-1990s and in Russia in the late 1990s, subnational governments in these countries had risky debt profiles—short maturities, high debt-service ratios, and variable interest rates. The macroeconomic crisis exposed the vulnerability of subnational governments to these fiscal positions and triggered widespread subnational debt crises.[9]

Implicit or contingent liabilities have been a major source of fiscal deterioration in various developing countries. In the late 1990s, guarantees by Indian states to support market borrowing of loss-making public sector undertakings, a contingent liability, grew rapidly. Early episodes of subnational debt development in the 1840s in the United States show how contingent liabilities contributed to states' debt crises (Wallis 2004). Important sources of implicit or contingent liabilities include off-budget entities wholly or largely owned by subnational governments, subnational civil servant pension liabilities under a pay-as-you-go system, nonperforming assets of financial institutions owned by subnational governments, and debt financing through arrears under the cash accounting system. (For a summary of hidden and contingent liabilities in several developing countries, see Liu and Waibel 2006.)

Soft Budget Constraints

Subnational debt-financing behavior is strongly influenced by the design of the intergovernmental fiscal system, the quality of the public financial management system, and the structure of financial markets. Market participants may tolerate the unsustainable fiscal policy of a subnational government if history backs their perception that the central government implicitly guarantees the debt service of the subnational government (Ianchovichina, Liu, and Nagarajan 2007). A gap-filling grant transfer system, for example, induces subnational governments to run fiscal deficits by reducing incentives to raise revenue and increasing incentives to spend. Lack of own-source revenues for subnational governments in many countries undermines the ability of subnational governments to engage in fiscal correction, a core element of any debt-restructuring proceeding. Furthermore, a competitive capital market prices risks and returns of subnational lending, helping screen and discipline subnational borrowing. This market discipline could be undermined by the dominance of lending to subnational governments by public banks. Abolishing central government's explicit guarantees for subnational debt is not sufficient for nurturing the development of capital markets, as a range of factors, including implicit guarantees, affect demand and supply in the municipal finance market.

Soft budget constraints, a key aspect of fiscal incentives, allow subnational governments to live beyond their means, negating competitive incentives and fostering corruption and rent-seeking (see Weingast 2007 for a summary of the literature within the context of second-generation fiscal federalism). Unconditional bailouts of financially troubled subnational entities by the national government create moral hazard and the implication of a sovereign guarantee, which encourage fiscal irresponsibility and imprudent lending. In the United States, the no-bailout principle was established during the first subnational defaults in the 1840s (English 1996; Wallis 2004). In Hungary, one motivation for establishing a regulatory framework for subnational bankruptcy was to reduce moral hazard, impose a hard budget constraint on municipalities, shrink contingent liabilities of the central government, and change the perception among lenders that there was an implied sovereign guarantee (Jókay, Szepesi, and Szmetana 2004). After repeatedly bailing out subnational governments, Brazil adopted a stricter approach, demanding subnational fiscal adjustment in return for fiscal relief (box 11.1).

Box 11.1 Subnational Debt Crisis and Reforms in Brazil

Brazil substantially strengthened its ex ante regulations in response to repeated waves of subnational debt crises. Statutory controls on subnational borrowing have always existed in Brazil—controls on new borrowing and the total stock of debt, expressed as percentages of revenue—but subnational governments had been creative in evading them. The regulations were strengthened in the late 1990s, leading to the unifying framework in 2000. The federal government bailed out subnational debtors in earlier crises, but resolution of the third debt crisis in 1997 was conditioned on states undertaking difficult fiscal and structural reforms. Unconditional bailouts were avoided in 1997 in order to resolve moral hazard. The strengthened ex ante borrowing regulations were embedded in the debt-restructuring agreements between 25 states and the federal government in 1997, sanctioned by legislation. The 2000 Fiscal Responsibility Law consolidated various pieces of legislation into one unifying framework.

Sources: Dillinger 2002; Webb 2004.

Khemani (2002) tests the predictions implied by the common pool game in federations, where subnational governments are more likely to run higher deficits, because they do not internalize the macroeconomic effects of fiscal profligacy. She finds that in 15 major states in India over 1972–95, states have substantially higher spending and deficits (higher by about 10 percent of the sample average) when their government belonged to the same party as that governing at the center and that intergovernmental grants tend to have a (counterintuitive) negative effect on spending and deficits. These findings underscore the importance of political institutions in determining the consolidated government deficit relative to specific rules of intergovernmental transfers. A substantial reform undertaken by Indian states in the early to mid-2000s was the enactment of fiscal responsibility legislation.

Legal and regulatory frameworks for subnational debt financing serve as a commitment device to allow such governments to access the financial market within a common framework. An individual subnational government may adopt unsustainable fiscal policies for a variety of reasons. Inherent incentives exist for it to free ride, as it bears only part of the cost and reaps all of the benefits of unsustainable fiscal policies. Realizing these benefits depends on good fiscal behavior by most of the other subnational governments. Collectively, therefore, governments benefit from a system of rules that discourage defection and free riding. This commitment device controls and coordinates subnational governments in various localities and across time to commit future governments to a common borrowing framework (Webb 2004).

Developing Regulatory Frameworks

The motivations for developing regulatory frameworks differ significantly across countries, reflecting a country's political, economic, legal, and historical context and triggering events. These differences affect the entry point for reform, the framework's design, and its relation to subnational borrowing legislation. In particular, the frameworks for subnational debt financing and restructuring define the roles of different branches and tiers of government; a country's political and economic history plays a key role in shaping the design.

Chapter 9 of the Bankruptcy Code of the United States (1937), for example, was conceived with the narrow objective of resolving the holdout problem, against the background of a mature intergovernmental fiscal system and a market-oriented financial system.[10] Although the U.S. system offers a valuable reference, it cannot be copied without care. The Municipal Finance Management Act of South Africa (2003) was intended to address a number of challenges, including the development of a diversified and competitive subnational credit market (South Africa National Treasury 2001). The Hungarian Law on Municipal Debt Adjustment (1996) sought to impose a hard budget constraint on subnational governments, establish a transparent rule-based debt-restructuring procedure without ad hoc political interventions, and rebut the presumption of any implied sovereign guarantee.

Subnational default risk can be managed through two channels: fiscal rules for subnational governments with respect to debt financing (that is, ex ante regulation of borrowing and monitoring of the subnational fiscal position) and ex post debt restructuring in the event that subnational governments become insolvent. Regulatory frameworks in many countries are still evolving, and the pace of putting together a full range of regulatory elements varies.

Ex ante fiscal rules and ex post insolvency mechanisms complement one another. Insolvency mechanisms increase the pain of circumventing ex ante fiscal rules for lenders and subnational borrowers, thereby enhancing the effectiveness of preventive rules. Without insolvency mechanisms, ex ante regulations could lead to excessive administrative control and game playing between the central and subnational governments.[11] Overreliance on ex ante regulations could limit the role of markets in monitoring subnational borrowing and debt, however. In Canada and the United States, markets play a vital role in the surveillance of subnational borrowing. Although it takes time to develop market systems, developing countries can gradually foster the role of the market in the design of regulatory frameworks.[12]

Fiscal Rules for Subnational Debt Financing: Ex Ante Regulation

Fiscal rules for subnational debt financing deal with debt-issuing procedures. They specify the purpose, type, amount, procedures, and monitoring of debt financing. Regulatory frameworks for subnational debt financing have been strengthened in various countries (table 11.1).

Liu and Waibel (2008) identify several common elements in ex ante borrowing regulation across several countries. First, borrowing is allowed only for long-term public capital investments. Some European countries, such as Germany and the United Kingdom, have enacted fiscal rules requiring a balanced budget net of public investment (the "golden rule").[13] This rule recognizes that only such borrowing is beneficial (and may be in the interest of future generations). A number of middle-income countries, including Brazil, Colombia, India, Peru, Russia, and South Africa, have recently adopted the golden rule (see Liu and Waibel 2008 for details).

Second, the frameworks set limits on key fiscal variables, such as the fiscal deficit, the primary deficit, debt service ratios, and ceilings on guarantees issued. In India the 12th Finance Commission mandated fiscal responsibility legislation for all states, with the revenue deficit to be eliminated and the fiscal deficit reduced to 3 percent of gross state domestic

Table 11.1 Fiscal Rules for Subnational Debt Financing, by Selected Country

Country	Rule
Brazil	Fiscal Responsibility Law (2000)
Colombia	Law 358 (1997), Law 617 (2000), Fiscal Transparency and Responsibility Law (2003)
France	Various borrowing regulations and balanced budget rules
India	States Fiscal Responsibility and Budget Management Acts, following the recommendations of the 12th Finance Commission
Peru	Fiscal Responsibility and Transparency Law (2003), General Debt Law (2005)
Poland	Public Finance Law (2005)
South Africa	Municipal Finance Management Act (2003)
Turkey	Various regulations since 2000
United States	States' regulation

Sources: Liu and Waibel 2008; ongoing research by the authors.

product (GSDP) by fiscal 2009.[14] Colombia established a traffic-light system to regulate subnational borrowing (Law 358 in 1997 and the Fiscal Transparency and Responsibility Law in 2003). Subnational governments rated in the red-light zone are prohibited from borrowing; those in the green-light zone are permitted to borrow. The red-light zone is reached when the interest to operational savings ratio is greater than 40 percent and the debt stock to current revenues ratio is greater than 80 percent. In Brazil the debt-restructuring agreements between the federal government and the states established a comprehensive list of fiscal targets, including the debt to revenue ratio, primary balance, personnel spending, and a list of state-owned enterprises or banks to be privatized or concessioned. In the United States, states set borrowing limits for themselves and, with a few exceptions, for their local governments.

Third, several legal frameworks, such as those in Brazil, Colombia, and Peru, include procedural requirements that subnational governments establish a medium-term fiscal framework and a transparent budgetary process. This requirement is intended to ensure that fiscal accounts move within a sustainable debt path and that fiscal adjustment takes a medium-term approach to better respond to shocks and differing trajectories for key macroeconomic variables that affect subnational finance. The transparent budgetary process facilitates debates by executive and legislative branches on spending priorities, funding sources, and required fiscal adjustments.

Fiscal transparency is increasingly becoming an integrated part of fiscal frameworks. Transparency includes having an independent audit of subnational financial accounts, making periodic public disclosures of key fiscal data, exposing hidden liabilities, and moving off-budget liabilities on budget. In Brazil, for example, Article 48 of the Fiscal Responsibility Law (2000) enshrines fiscal transparency as a key component of the new framework. Proposals, laws, and accounts are to be widely distributed, including through the use of electronic media (all reports are made available on the Web site of the Ministry of the Treasury). Article 54 requires that all levels of government publish quarterly fiscal management reports that contain the major fiscal variables and indicate compliance with fiscal targets. Pursuant to Article 57, the report is to be certified by the audit courts.

Fiscal rules for subnational debt financing can be supported by regulations on lenders. To improve fiscal transparency, Mexico introduced a credit-rating system for subnational governments. Although subnational participation is voluntary, the requirements of the capital-risk weighting of bank loans introduced in 2000 and of loss provisions introduced in 2004 aim at imposing subnational fiscal discipline through the market pricing of subnational credit. In Colombia the Fiscal Transparency and Responsibility Law (2003) tightened the regulations on the supply side. Lending to subnationals by financial institutions and territorial development institutions must meet the conditions and limits of various regulations, such as Laws 617 and 817. If it does not, the credit contract is invalid and borrowed funds must be restituted promptly without interest or any other charges.

Control and monitoring mechanisms can substantially reduce the risk of insolvency. Two contrasting examples are presented below: France, a unitary country, and the state of Ohio in the United States, a federal country, where local governments are political subdivisions of the states.

Notwithstanding considerable fiscal autonomy of subnational governments, the central state in France exercises strong supervision and monitoring of subnational governments' financial accounts through three institutions: the prefect, the *chambres régionales des comptes* (regional chambers of accounts [CRC]), and public accountants. In the case of a budget deficit, late approval, or nonbudgeted mandatory expenses (such as debt service), the prefect (as well as any interested person) can refer the case to the CRC. If the subnational government does not follow the recommendations made by the CRC, the prefect can adopt the budget. The CRC also exercises financial supervision.

The key element of internal control in France is the separation of decision making (handled by the president of the local government council, who contracts expenditure) from actual payment (handled by the public accountant, who is part of the central government). This separation means that there are two sets of departmental accounts, which must tally. Public accountants themselves are subject to audit and control by the central government.

The Fiscal Watch Program in Ohio, implemented by the Office of Auditor of State, acts as an early warning system to prevent local governments, including counties, municipalities, school districts, and state universities and colleges, from slipping into fiscal distress.[15] A local government that is approaching a state of fiscal emergency, as defined by specific financial indicators, is placed under the fiscal watch program.

A local government under the program takes fiscal corrective actions. The fiscal watch remains in effect until the auditor determines that the conditions are no longer present and cancels the watch or until the auditor determines that the local government be placed under the fiscal emergency program under the predefined fiscal indicators. A commission will be formed for a local government under the fiscal emergency program, to assist in preparing and implementing a long-term financial recovery plan accepted by both the local government and the commission. The Auditor of State's Office serves as financial supervisor to the commission and provides technical support and advice. It also examines the system of governmental accounting and reporting and identifies improvements that need to be made in a report.

The commission stops its activity under two conditions. The first is the elimination of the fiscal emergency conditions that prompted the initial declaration and the adoption by the local government of the necessary improvements in its accounting and reporting system. The second is the achievement by the local government of the objectives set forth by the financial recovery plan and the preparation of a five-year financial forecast that meets the evaluation criteria of the Auditor of State. If the fiscal emergency is terminated before these conditions are met, the Auditor of State is required to monitor the progress of the government to ensure full implementation of an effective accounting system and the elimination of the emergency conditions.

Regulatory Frameworks for Subnational Debt Financing: Insolvency Mechanisms

Ex post regulation deals with insolvent subnational governments.[16] Notwithstanding fiscal rules for ex ante control, defaults can occur as a result of a subnational's own fiscal mismanagement or as a result of macroeconomic or exogenous shocks. A well-designed insolvency mechanism serves multiple objectives: it enforces hard budget constraints on subnational governments, maintains essential services while restructuring debt, and restores the financial health of the subnational government so that it may reenter the financial market.

The need for a collective framework for resolving debt claims is driven by conflicts between creditors and the debtor and among creditors. Individual creditors may have different interests and security provisions for the debt owed to them; they may demand preferential treatment and threaten to derail debt restructurings voluntarily negotiated between a majority of creditors and the subnational debtor—the so-called holdout problem (McConnell and Picker 1993). Individual ad hoc negotiations are costly, impracticable, and harmful to the interests of a majority of creditors. The holdout problem is less serious if debts are concentrated in a few banks. A collective framework for insolvency restructuring takes on more importance as subnational bond markets, with thousands of creditors, are more developed.

Clear creditor remedies allow collective enforcement and facilitate efficient debt adjustment. Creditors' remedies in contract laws, rather than bankruptcy mechanisms, are effective at enforcing discrete unpaid obligations. However, individual lawsuits or negotiations become ineffective if there is a general inability to pay. This holdout problem causes uncertainty and prolongs the debt-restructuring process. Resolving the holdout problem was the primary motivation behind the United States' enactment of Chapter 9 (McConnell and Picker 1993).

Key design considerations arise concerning insolvency procedures—namely, the fundamental differences between public and private insolvency, the choices between judicial or administrative approaches, and the operation of the insolvency procedure itself. Each of these design considerations is examined below.

Public versus Private Bankruptcy

The public nature of the services provided by governments is the source of the fundamental difference between public insolvency and the bankruptcy of a private corporation. As a matter of public policy, public services essential for the public health, welfare, and safety must be maintained. This factor leads to the basic tension between protecting creditors' rights and maintaining essential public services. Creditors have narrower remedies available for dealing with defaulting subnationals than they do for dealing with defaulting corporations, which leads to greater moral hazard (strategic defaults). When a private corporation goes bankrupt, all assets of the corporation are potentially subject to attachment. By contrast, the ability of creditors to attach assets of subnational governments is greatly restrained in many countries. In the case of subnational insolvency, the insolvency mechanism generally involves reorganization rather than the liquidation of assets. Additionally, subnational governments typically have some taxation power.

The debt discharge protects the subnational entity and its population from long-term harm caused by sharp reductions in public service delivery.

Thus, the insolvency system needs to balance incentives for the subnational entity to grow out of bankruptcy and the need to repay creditors. Crucial issues in designing such legislation are determining the balance between the legitimate contractual interests of private creditors and the delivery of essential public services, and providing subnational governments with the flexibility to grow out of their financial constraints.

The public nature of the debtor may justify limitations on creditors' contractual remedies—a justification that does not apply to private debtors. Creditors will insist that all valid debts be honored and repaid. Ex ante the subnational entity may pledge assets for financial resources; ex post it will argue that many assets cannot be used for the satisfaction of creditors because they serve a public purpose. The tension between creditor rights and a subnational debtor's inability to pay is here to stay. This tension is at its peak when a debt discharge is needed.

In principle, the answer of an insolvency framework to these competing interests is an equitable sharing of misery, a limitation on the subnational government's ability to provide nonessential services, and a limitation on creditors' remedies, including the discharge of debt. A subnational bankruptcy framework also provides guidance on the priority of settling competing creditor claims. Clear rules ease the distributional struggle between the need to maintain essential minimum services and the need to honor creditors' contractual rights. This distribution also matters ex ante, as it shapes the expectations and behavior of the borrower and lenders in the next cycle of borrowing.

Judicial versus Administrative Approaches

There are two main approaches to subnational insolvency: judicial and administrative. Various hybrids also exist. Judicial procedures place courts in the driver's seat. Courts make key decisions to guide the restructuring process, including when and how a municipal insolvency is triggered, a priority structure for allocating credits among competing claims, and a determination of which services will be maintained. Because the debt discharge is highly complex, the judicial approach has the advantage of neutralizing political pressures during the restructuring. However, because mandates for budgetary matters lie with the executive and legislature in many countries, the courts' ability to influence fiscal adjustment of subnational entities is limited.

Administrative interventions, by contrast, usually allow a higher level of government to intervene in the entity concerned, temporarily taking direct political responsibility for many aspects of financial management. Such interventions may also create a belief among lenders that the central government will intervene, thereby creating moral hazard.

The choice of approach varies across countries, depending on the history, political and economic structure, and motivation for establishing an insolvency mechanism. In Hungary the desire to neutralize political pressure for bailing out insolvent subnational governments favored the judicial approach. South Africa's legal framework for municipal bankruptcy is a hybrid of the two approaches, blending administrative intervention with the role of courts in determining debt restructuring and discharge. After having bailed out insolvent subnational entities in the earlier debt crises, Brazil's federal government chose an administrative approach in dealing with the third debt crisis, imposing a fiscal and debt adjustment package that was based on reform conditions.

The United States has both judicial and administrative approaches. In response to widespread municipal defaults during the Great Depression, in 1937 the U.S. Congress adopted the municipal insolvency law known as Chapter 9 of the U.S. Bankruptcy Code.[17] Chapter 9 is a debt-restructuring mechanism for political subdivisions and agencies of U.S. states. It provides the procedural machinery through which a debt-restructuring plan acceptable to a majority of creditors can become binding on a dissenting minority.

Many states have adopted their own frameworks for dealing with municipal financial distress, for two reasons. First, municipalities are political subdivisions of the states. Second, state consent is a precondition for municipalities to file for Chapter 9 in federal court. Moreover, federal courts may not exercise jurisdiction over policy choices and budget priorities of the debtor. No uniform approach exists across states.[18] New York City's bankruptcy in 1975 and Ohio's early warning fiscal monitoring system of the municipalities are two prominent examples of direct state intervention in resolving financial distress.

Insolvency Procedures

An effective insolvency procedure contains three main elements: definition of the insolvency trigger for the procedure, fiscal adjustment by the debtor to bring spending in line with revenues and borrowing in line with the capacity to service debt, and negotiations between debtor and creditors to restructure debt obligations. Specific legal definitions serve as procedural triggers for initiating insolvency proceedings. Hungary (Law on Municipal Debt Adjustment 1996) and the United States (Chapter 9) define *insolvency* as inability to pay; South Africa uses one set of triggers for serious financial problems and another for persistent material breach of financial commitments (Municipal Financial Management Act 2003). In all three countries, the bankruptcy code empowers the bankruptcy court to dismiss petitions not filed in good faith. Because bankruptcy procedures have the power to discharge debt, a subnational entity may file purely for the purpose of evading debt obligations. An initial determination must be made as to whether the situation reflects a genuine inability to pay or merely unwillingness to pay. The U.S. bankruptcy code erects obstacles to municipal filing beyond those faced by private debtors, thereby discouraging strategic municipal bankruptcy filings.

Which parties may commence an insolvency proceeding differs across countries. In the United States, only the municipality can file for bankruptcy, conditional on being insolvent, having worked out or attempted to work out a plan to deal with its debts, and having been authorized by the state to file for bankruptcy. The more stringent requirement for filing under Chapter 9, as compared with Chapter 11, partly reflects the constraints imposed by the 10th Amendment to the U.S. Constitution, under which a creditor cannot bring a municipality into a federal court against its will. Like Chapter 9, Schwarcz's (2002) model law for subnational insolvency allows only municipalities to file for bankruptcy. In South Africa any creditor can trigger the insolvency procedure (Chapter 13, Section 151(a), 2003 Municipal Financial Management Act). In Hungary a creditor can petition the court if a municipality is in arrears for more than 60 days (Law on Municipal Debt Adjustment [Law XXV 1996]).

Fiscal adjustment and consolidation are preconditions for financial workouts. Often a subnational government's own fiscal mismanagement is the root cause of insolvency. Even when subnational insolvency is triggered by macroeconomic shocks, fiscal adjustment is inherent to any insolvency procedures, requiring the difficult political choices of cutting expenditure, raising revenues, or both.

Ianchovichina, Liu, and Nagarajan (2007) present a framework for analyzing subnational fiscal adjustment. Real interest rates, economic growth of the subnational economy, and the subnational government's primary balance determine subnational debt sustainability. They argue, however, that subnational fiscal adjustment qualitatively differs from national fiscal adjustment. Unable to issue their own currency, subnational governments cannot use seigniorage finance. They cannot freely adjust their primary balance because of the constraints on the taxation and expenditure system within the intergovernmental fiscal system.

Debt restructuring lies at the heart of any bankruptcy framework. In administrative interventions, the higher level of government often restructures the subnational's debt obligations into longer-term debt instruments. In the case of New York City, the Municipal Assistance Corporation was set up to issue longer-term state bonds to repay maturing short-term obligations of the city, conditioned on the city making fiscal and financial management reforms (Bailey 1984). The 1997 debt agreements between the Brazilian federal government and 25 of its 26 states, which focused on ex ante regulations, may also be viewed as an ex post intervention, because the agreements were imposed on a case-by-case basis as a condition of debt restructuring.

Debt discharge is a major departure from the principle that contracts ought to be fulfilled.[19] A mature judicial mechanism is well placed to ensure that discharges are fair and equitable. In South Africa, for example, the municipality needs to go to the court for a discharge. Administrative procedures tend to lack the power to discharge debt.

The adjustment of debt obligations is a major intervention in contract rights. Insolvency law attempts to balance creditor rights, the inability of a subnational entity to pay, and the continued need of the subnational governments to provide essential public services. It formalizes the relationship between creditors and the subnational debtor in financial distress. Insolvency law preserves the legal order by superseding contractual violations with a new legal act.[20] A procedure for subnational insolvency recognizes that resolving financial distress through mechanisms guided by law is preferable to muddling through repeated, costly, and often unsuccessful negotiations.

One basic question with respect to debt restructuring is who holds the cramdown power when the sides fail to reach an agreement.[21] Under Chapter 9 of the U.S. Bankruptcy Code, municipal debtors propose the debt adjustment plan, which may modify the terms of existing debt instruments. Such adjustment plans may be adopted over the objection of hold-out creditors. Chapter 9 incorporates basic Chapter 11 requirements: at least one impaired class of claims approves the plan, and secured creditors must receive at least the value of the secured property. Unsecured creditors thus often lose out (for case histories, see Kupetz 1995; McConnell and Picker 1993).

Unlike private entities, subnationals have no stockholders. Their officials need not pay off unsecured creditors to remain in control. Unsecured creditors are protected by §943 (b) (7) of Chapter 9, which requires the court to decide that the plan is in the "best interests of creditors and is feasible." The court ensures that bondholders effectively receive what they would have received outside of bankruptcy.[22]

In Hungary the Debt Committee, which is independent of the local government, is charged with preparing a reorganization plan and debt settlement proposal.[23] A debt settlement is reached if at least half of the creditors whose claims account for at least two-thirds of the total undisputed claims agree to the proposal. Creditors within the same group must be treated equally.[24] The law also stipulates the priority of asset distribution. If disagreements arise on distribution, the court makes the final decision, which cannot be appealed.[25]

South Africa's legislation stipulates that debt discharge and settlement of claims must be approved by the court. Under the Municipal Finance Management Act, claims are settled in the following order: secured creditors, provided that the security was given in good faith and at least six months before mandatory intervention by the provinces; preferences provided by the 1936 Bankruptcy Act; and nonpreferential claims.[26]

A clear priority structure for settling competing claims expedites the resolution of debt restructuring. Priorities also ease the pain of sharing the reduced assets for distribution, because losses suffered by creditor groups may be predicted in advance. Hence, these priorities are more likely to be accepted. Moreover, the structure can keep the absolute size of losses in check, as the costs of protracted negotiations and litigation are high and often take priority over other claims. Priorities are a policy choice with a variety of trade-offs. If the lending community perceives that financial distress is resolved largely on its back, desirable future lending could suffer. The priorities backstop voluntary restructuring negotiations, because creditors know their position in the hierarchy of payment in the insolvency procedure. The shadow of priorities shapes the bargaining power of creditors and debtors even outside bankruptcy.

Distributing the pool of available assets in bankruptcy is not only about efficiency and equal treatment. Which policy is most appropriate will depend on the distributional preferences of the society concerned and the effect of a chosen priority structure on the capital market and its impact on new financing during a liquidity crunch. It is also important to allow sufficient flexibility within a general priority framework.

Concluding Remarks

As a result of decentralization around the world, subnational debt accounts for an increasing share of countries' public debt. Rapid urbanization and demand for large-scale urban infrastructure will continue to put pressure on the public finance system to finance sustainable investments. In many countries decentralization has devolved responsibility for most infrastructure investments to subnational governments. Managing subnational debt financing and its sustainability is critical to a sustainable public finance system and sovereign financial health.

As Canuto and Liu (2010a) note, the financial crisis has had a significant impact on the financial accounts of many subnational governments, as a result of slower economic growth, uncertainty over the cost of financing, and pressure on primary balances. Beyond the current crisis, the structural trends of decentralization and urbanization and the need to finance urban infrastructure are likely to continue.

Subnational governments in various major developing countries entered the current global financial crisis with stronger fiscal positions than they previously had, as a result of their reforms in the fiscal rules and regulatory frameworks.[27] However, the uncertainty of the global public debt market, the potential risks of the rising cost of capital, the fragility of global recovery, and currency uncertainties and associated refinancing are continuing to put pressure on subnational finance (Canuto and Liu 2010b).

There are also risks of increasing contingent liabilities. Shifting borrowing off-budget may become a convenient way of circumventing fiscal rules. Subnational governments may turn to alternative forms of infrastructure investing, including public-private partnerships, special purpose vehicles, and off-budget financing. Such financing, if not properly regulated, can increase government's contingent liabilities.

A range of middle-income countries, and low-income countries in transition to market access, are also contemplating expanding subnational borrowing and debt financing. Before they do so, their first priority should be to establish clear fiscal rules that specify the type and purpose of borrowing, identify the procedural steps for contracting debt, indicate any limitations on borrowing, and control and account for off-budget liabilities.

Ex post insolvency mechanisms are also essential to the sustainability of subnational debt financing. Even if rarely invoked, they shape expectations about defaults and encourage stakeholders to resolve subnational financial distress efficiently. Notwithstanding the fiscal problems of a particular subnational government, an effective insolvency system helps maintain access of other subnational governments to the public finance markets. Clear and predictable rules on priority of repayment ease the struggle and allow faster resolution of financial distress. Effective insolvency and creditor rights systems allow better management of financial risks.[28]

The management of subnational default risks is intertwined with broader macroeconomic and institutional reforms. Macroeconomic stability and sovereign strength cap the financial ratings of subnational governments, thereby affecting the availability and cost of funds for subnational governments. Moreover, the intergovernmental fiscal system underpins the fundamentals of the subnational fiscal path. Without increased fiscal autonomy and greater own-source revenues, subnational governments will rarely be in a position to borrow sustainably on their own. Managing default risks does not mean minimizing subnational governments' access to debt financing. On the contrary, developing a competitive and diversified subnational credit market is critical to intermediating national savings and infrastructure financing. An effective management of subnational default risks thus goes in tandem with broader development of capital markets.

Notes

The authors thank Brian Pinto, Gallina A. Vincelette, Michael De Angelis, Norbert Gaillard, Juan Pedro Schmidt, Raju Singh, and Xiaowei Tian for their comments, which have been incorporated.

1. The term *subnational* refers here to all tiers of government and public entities below the federal or central government, including states, counties, cities, towns, public utility companies, and other special-purpose public entities that have the capacity to incur debt. In Brazil net debt is the difference between gross debt and assets. Data are as of December 2009 (www.bcb.gov.br/?FISCPOLICY).

2. Figures are as of December 2009 (www.rbi.org.in). Debt would be higher if debt on the balance sheets of companies such as power and water, which are wholly or largely owned by the states, were included.

3. See www.federalreserve.gov.

4. In a legal sense, *subnational insolvency* refers to the inability to pay debts as they fall due. Definitions of *insolvency* vary across countries, however. In addition to default (failure to pay according to the terms of the debt instrument), insolvency is characterized by a genuine, and not merely a temporary, shortfall of resources to service debt (see Liu and Waibel 2009).

5. For a discussion of how sovereign ratings affect subsovereign ratings, see Gaillard (2009). For a discussion of how international rating agencies rate subnational creditworthiness, see Liu and Tan (2009).

6. This statement assumes that economic growth translates into increased capacity to service debt, which may not happen if a subnational government is unable to exploit its growing tax base. In this case borrowing can still provoke a fiscal crisis, even when the proceeds have been put to good use. The statement also assumes the general government debt is compatible with market financing capacity without crowding out private demands.

7. The revenue deficit is the amount of current expenditure (such as wages, pension outlays, subsidies, transfers, and operation and maintenance) net of total revenues.

8. Ianchovichina, Liu, and Nagarajan (2007) analyze key factors influencing subnational fiscal sustainability.

9. Between 1998 and 2001, at least 57 of 89 regional governments in Russia defaulted (Alam, Titov, and Petersen 2004). In 2001, six years after the peso crisis, 60 percent of subnational governments in Mexico still struggled financially (Schwarcz 2002). One interesting difference between Mexico and Russia is that subnational governments were allowed to borrow overseas in Russia, whereas such borrowing was prohibited in Mexico. Subnational governments in Mexico were not insulated from foreign exchange risks, however, which were transmitted through inflation and interest rates.

10. The holdout problem occurs when individual creditors who have different interests and security provisions for the debt owed to them demand preferential treatment and threaten to derail debt restructurings voluntarily negotiated between a majority of creditors and the subnational debtor (see McConnell and Picker 1993).

11. The focus in this chapter is on demand-side regulation. On the supply side, various elements of the financial system, including competition and prudential regulations, come into play.

12. A clear objective of South Africa's restructuring of its legal framework for municipal finance and management systems in the postapartheid period was to nurture a competitive private municipal credit market in which private investors play a dominant role (South Africa National Treasury 2001).

13. Short-term borrowing for working capital is still allowed, but provisions should be built in to prevent governments from rollover borrowing as a way of long-term borrowing for operating deficits.

14. The fiscal targets were relaxed in response to the 2008–09 global financial crisis (www.rbi.org.in).

15. See http://www.auditor.state.oh.us.

16. The boundary between ex ante regulation and ex post insolvency is not clear cut. Fiscal responsibility regulation, for example, may incorporate elements of ex post consequences. Webb (2004) includes transfer intercepts and lender control mechanisms as part of ex post consequences. The focus here is on insolvency proceedings.

17. The Bankruptcy Act of 1938 (Chandler Act), 50 Stat. 654 (1937), amending the 1898 U.S. Bankruptcy Act, was the first piece of legislation in the world governing municipal bankruptcy.

18. Some states give blanket consent to municipalities to file in federal court, some states attach important conditions, and some states grant permission on a case-by-case basis (see Laughlin 2005).

19. The Contracts Clause of the U.S. Constitution (Article I. 10.1) puts the principle of *pacta sunt servanda* (agreements must be kept) into constitutional form.

20. The U.S. experience suggests that in the absence of a bankruptcy framework, public entities in financial distress will use every possible technicality to challenge the validity of their outstanding obligations. Widespread challenges in a default wave during the 19th century led to the development of the bond counsel opinion, which certifies that the obligation is legal, valid, and enforceable.

21. Cramdown involves court confirmation of bankruptcy plans despite the opposition of certain creditors. Under section 1129(b) of Chapter 11 of the U.S. Bankruptcy Code, courts may confirm a plan if it was accepted by at least one impaired class, does not discriminate unfairly, and is fair and equitable.

22. The best interest test ensures that unsecured creditors are treated as well inside bankruptcy as outside of it. Creditors may nevertheless receive less than 100 percent of their claims. Unsecured creditors of municipalities are protected from the moral hazard problem of opportunistic bankruptcy filings not by the cramdown limit but by the best interests of the creditors standard (see McConnell and Picker 1993).

23. The Law on Municipal Debt Adjustment, Law XXV, 1996, Chapter II, § 9 (3) stipulates a financial trustee's independence.

24. Law on Municipal Debt Adjustment, Law XXV, 1996, Chapter III, § 23.

25. Law on Municipal Debt Adjustment, Law XXV, 1996, Chapter IV, § 31, assets are distributed to creditors in the following order: regular personnel benefits, including severance pay; securitized debt; dues to the central government; social insurance debts, public contributions, and taxes; other claims; and interest and fees on debt obligations continued during the bankruptcy proceeding.

26. South Africa, Municipal Finance and Management Act, 2003, Chapter 13, Section 155 (4).

27. In Brazil, subnational governments' net debt as a percent of GDP fell from 18 percent in 2003 to 14 percent in 2007. In India, the fiscal deficit of states declined from 4.0 percent of GDP, on average, in 2000–05 to 1.5 percent in 2007–08, and states achieved positive operating balances. In Colombia gross debt by subnational governments as a share of GDP declined from 3.6 percent in 2001 to 1.4 percent in 2008. Subnational governments in both China and Russia had positive fiscal balances in 2007.

28. The World Bank (2005) addresses creditor rights and insolvency standards in the context of corporate bankruptcy. Key principles apply to the subnational context, bearing in mind the differences between public and private bankruptcy.

References

Alam, Asad, Stepan Titov, and John Petersen. 2004. "Russian Federation." In *Subnational Capital Markets in Developing Countries: From Theory to Practice*, ed. Mila Freire and John Petersen, 571–92. Washington, DC: World Bank.

Bailey, Robert W. 1984. *The Crisis Regime: The MAC, the EFCB, and the Political Impact of the New York Financial Crisis.* Albany: State University of New York Press.

Canuto, Otaviano, and Lili Liu. 2010a. "Subnational Debt Financing and the Global Financial Crisis." Premise Note. World Bank, Poverty Reduction and Economic Management Network, Washington, DC.

————. 2010b. "Subnational Debt Finance: Make it Sustainable." In *The Day after Tomorrow: A Handbook on the Future of Economic Policy in the Developing World*, ed. Otaviano Canuto and Marcelo Giugale. Washington, DC: World Bank.

Dillinger, William. 2002. *Brazil: Issues in Fiscal Federalism*. Report 22523–BR. World Bank, Latin America and the Caribbean Region, Brazil Country Management Unit, PREM Sector Management Unit, Washington, DC.

English, William B. 1996. "Understanding the Costs of Sovereign Default: American State Debts in the 1840s." *American Economic Review* 86 (1): 259–75.

FitchRatings. 2009. *European Local and Regional Government Outlook 2010*. December 16. New York.

Gaillard, Norbert. 2009. "The Determinants of Moody's Sub-Sovereign Ratings." *International Research Journal of Finance and Economics* 31: 194–209.

Ianchovichina, Elena, Lili Liu, and Mohan Nagarajan. 2007. "Subnational Fiscal Sustainability Analysis: What Can We Learn from Tamil Nadu?" *Economic and Political Weekly* 42 (52): 111–19.

Jókay, Charles, Gábor Szepesi, and György Szmetana. 2004. "Municipal Bankruptcy Framework and Debt Management Experiences, 1990–2000." In *Intergovernmental Finances in Hungary: A Decade of Experience*, ed. Mihály, Kopányi, Deborah L. Wetzel, and Samir El Daher. Washington, DC: World Bank.

Khemani, Studi. 2002. "Federal Politics and Budget Deficits: Evidence from the States of India." World Bank Policy Research Working Paper 2915, Washington, DC.

Kupetz, David S. 1995. "Municipal Debt Adjustment under the Bankruptcy Code." *Urban Lawyer* 27 (3): 531–605.

Laughlin, Alexander M. 2005. *Municipal Insolvencies: A Primer on the Treatment of Municipalities under Chapter 9 of the U.S. Bankruptcy Code*. Washington, DC: Wiley Rein & Fielding. http://www.wileyrein.com/publication.cfm?publication_id=11309.

Liu, Lili. 2008. "Creating a Regulatory Framework for Managing Subnational Borrowing." In *Public Finance in China: Reform and Growth for a Harmonious Society*, ed. Jiwei Lou and Shuilin Wang, 171–90. Washington, DC: World Bank.

Liu, Lili, and Kim Song Tan. 2009. "Subnational Credit Ratings: A Comparative Review." World Bank Policy Research Working Paper 5013, Washington, DC.

Liu, Lili, and Michael Waibel. 2006. "Subnational Borrowing Notes on Middle-Income Countries." Economic Policy and Debt Department, World Bank, Washington, DC.

————. 2008. "Subnational Borrowing, Insolvency and Regulations." In *Macro Federalism and Local Finance*, ed. Anwar Shah. Washington, DC: World Bank.

————. 2009. "Subnational Insolvency and Governance: Cross-Country Experiences and Lessons." In *Does Decentralization Enhance Service Delivery and Poverty Reduction?* ed. Ehtisham Ahmad and Giorgio Brosio. Cheltenham, United Kingdom: Edward Elgar.

McConnell, Michael, and Randal Picker. 1993. "When Cities Go Broke: A Conceptual Introduction to Municipal Bankruptcy." *University of Chicago Law Review* 60 (2): 425–35.

Moody's Investors Service. 2010. *Sub-Sovereign Outlook 2010*. January. New York.

Schwarcz, Steven L. 2002. "Global Decentralization and the Subnational Debt Problem." *Duke Law Journal* 51 (4): 1179–250.

South Africa National Treasury. 2001. *Intergovernmental Fiscal Review*. Pretoria.

Standard & Poor's. 2010. *The Outlook for Europe's Local and Regional Governments*. February 4. New York.

Wallis, John Joseph. 2004. "Constitutions, Corporations and Corruption: American States and Constitutional Changes, 1842–1852." NBER Working Paper 10451, National Bureau of Economic Research, Cambridge, MA.

Webb, Stephen B. 2004. "Fiscal Responsibility Laws for Subnational Discipline: The Latin American Experiences." Policy Research Working Paper 3309, World Bank, Washington, DC.

Weingast, Barry R. 2007. "Second-Generation Fiscal Federalism: Implications for Development." Department of Economics, Stanford University, Palo Alto, CA.

World Bank. 2005. *Creditor Rights and Insolvency Standard*. Washington, DC: World Bank.

12

Restructuring Sovereign Debts with Private Sector Creditors: Theory and Practice

Mark L. J. Wright

Sovereign debt is time consuming and costly to restructure. Throughout history, defaults on debt owed to private sector creditors, such as commercial banks and bondholders, have taken almost a decade, on average, to conclude. Recent research has also found that private creditors lose, on average, 40 percent of the value of their claim, and debtor countries exit default as or more highly indebted than when they entered default.

Motivated by these facts, this chapter reviews the empirical evidence on the outcomes of sovereign debt–restructuring negotiations with private sector creditors with a view to uncovering the mechanisms at work and deriving policy implications. It finds large differences in sovereign debt–restructuring outcomes across debtor countries. Debts owed by low-income countries to foreign private sector creditors, such as banks and bondholders, have been the most time consuming to restructure, taking 75 percent more time than the debts of upper-middle-income defaulting countries. Delays are particularly long in Sub-Saharan Africa. Private creditor losses from default ("haircuts") have also been greatest on loans to low-income countries, with losses averaging more than 50 percent compared with less than 30 percent for upper-middle-income countries.

Most strikingly, and despite the larger creditor losses, low-income countries receive little debt relief from private creditors, as measured by comparing countries' debt to GDP ratios upon completing the restructuring process with their debt to GDP ratios at the beginning of the default episode. In fact, the average defaulting country exits default with the ratio of debt owed to private creditors to GDP as high, or higher, than when it entered default. This phenomenon is particularly pronounced for low-income countries, whose debt to GDP ratios rose by more than 50 percent, and Sub-Saharan African countries, whose indebtedness ratios more than doubled.

The chapter is organized as follows. The next section reviews recent empirical work on default and debt restructuring and presents new results on the variation in debt-restructuring outcomes across countries at different levels of development and in different regions. The following section reviews the recent theoretical literature on the process of restructuring sovereign debts to private creditors, with a view to identifying the underlying causes of these outcomes. It finds that a number of explanations are capable of explaining the lengthy delays in completing debt-restructuring operations, some of which also explain the size of observed haircuts. Few, however, have much to say about the causes of the substantial rise in indebtedness. The last section provides some concluding remarks.

Sovereign Debt Restructuring in Practice

This section reviews evidence on the outcomes of sovereign debt restructuring with private sector creditors in practice. After describing data sources, the evidence on delays in restructuring, creditor haircuts, and changes in indebtedness are presented in turn.

Data

Attention is restricted to defaults on sovereign debts owed to private sector creditors, such as commercial banks and bond holders, because such defaults seem most difficult to resolve in practice, as measured by the duration of the default.[1] One limitation of this restriction is that the interaction between the debt relief obtained from official creditors and relief obtained from private creditors cannot be studied. This interaction is frequently important, as in the case of debt relief under the Heavily Indebted Poor Countries (HIPC) Initiative. Eligible countries receive HIPC Initiative debt relief from participating official and private creditors. The total cost of committed debt relief under the HIPC Initiative was $58.5 billion in net present value terms ($72 billion in nominal terms) at the end of 2009. Private sector creditors provided about 6 percent of total HIPC relief.[2] Under the Multilateral Debt Relief Initiative (MDRI), eligible countries also receive relief from the World Bank, the International Monetary Fund (IMF), the African Development Bank, and the Inter-American Development Bank. MDRI relief amounted to $26.6 billion in net present value terms ($45 billion in nominal terms) at the end of 2009.

Sovereign debt includes debt owed either directly by a country's national government or indirectly by virtue of a government guarantee. The most comprehensive and widely used source of data on the dates of defaults on sovereign debt owed to private sector creditors, as well as the dates of settlements of these defaults, is published by Standard & Poor's (S&P) (Beers and Chambers 2006). S&P defines a default on a debt contract to have occurred if a payment is not made within any grace period specified in the contract or if debts are rescheduled on terms less favorable than those specified in the original contract. S&P defines the end of a default as occurring when a settlement occurs, typically in the form of an exchange of new debt for old debt, and when it judges that "no further near-term resolution of creditors claims is likely" (Beers and Chambers 2006, p. 22). Countries often default, restructure their debts with a new debt issue, and then default again the same or the following year. S&P treats such events as part of the same default episode.

Data on private creditor losses are drawn from Benjamin and Wright (2009), who use a method based on earlier estimates by Cline (1995). In order to obtain the largest sample possible, and to ensure consistency of treatment across default episodes, they base their measures on the World Bank's estimates of debt stock reduction, interest and principal forgiven, and debt buybacks, as published in *Global Development Finance (GDF)* (2009). The World Bank's estimates of the reduction in the face value of the debt are combined with estimates of the forgiveness of arrears on interest and principal. As the World Bank data do not distinguish between forgiveness of debts by private creditors and forgiveness by official creditors, the total amount of forgiveness is scaled by estimates of the total amount of debt renegotiated and the proportion of debt owed to private creditors, using data from both the *GDF* and the Institute of International Finance (2001). This process is only approximate; it is possible that errors remain.

The resulting series on private creditor haircuts covers 90 defaults and renegotiations by 73 separate countries that were completed after *GDF* data on debt forgiveness first became available, in 1989, and that ended before 2004. The data on default dates and haircuts are combined with data on various indicators of economic activity taken from the World Bank's *World Development Indicators* (2009) and *GDF* (2009) data on the stock of long-term sovereign debt outstanding and owed to private creditors. Short-term debt is excluded because data disaggregated by type of creditor are not available.

It is important to note that the sample may not be entirely representative. The data on haircuts, for example, were constructed from the World Bank data on debt forgiveness, which were not available for all episodes. Moreover, not all defaults began and ended within the period 1989–2004, for which these data are available. This means that the sample is both left and right censored. However, it appears that the sample contains the vast majority of all defaults on private sector debts during this period. Tomz and

Wright (2007) report that there were 121 defaults in the years after 1970 and 110 since 1980, implying that the data set used here, with its 90 defaults, covers three-quarters of the defaults that occurred. The sample does not include debt-restructuring operations that were conducted solely with official creditors under the auspices of the Paris Club or under the HIPC Initiative. Morais and Wright (2008) report 297 reschedulings of debt to official creditors and 130 of debt to private creditors in the postwar period.

Findings

This subsection presents the empirical findings. It begins by examining the observed delays in restructuring before turning to creditor haircuts and changes in indebtedness.

Delays in Restructuring. Looking across all countries in our sample of sovereign defaults on debts owed to private sector creditors, delays in restructuring averaged 7.4 years.[3] The distribution is highly skewed, with the median default taking about six years to be resolved. These figures are slightly lower than the average duration of default recorded in a census of defaults over the past two centuries by Pitchford and Wright (2007), who report an average delay of 8.8 years; they are slightly higher than their 6.5-year estimate of delays for defaults ending after 1976. There are three instances of defaults being contiguous in time, in the sense that S&P dates a default by a country as ending in the same year or the year before another default begins. These cases seem inconsistent with the practice by S&P of merging contiguous default events. Treating these defaults as a single default episode raises the estimated delays only slightly, however, to an average of 7.6 years.

There is considerable variation in delays across groups of countries. The average low-income country experienced delays of more than nine years, while the average upper-middle-income country was able to restructure its debts in just over five and a half years (figure 12.1).[4] Delays were longer in Sub-Saharan Africa (8.5 years) than in Latin America and the Caribbean (7.5 years) or Europe and Central Asia (4.5 years) (figure 12.2). Because the number of defaults in some regions was small, one must be careful about making generalizations, however.

Haircuts. Using the same sample of debt-restructuring episodes used in this chapter, Benjamin and Wright (2009) find that haircuts, weighted by the level of outstanding debt, averaged 38 percent. The median haircut was slightly higher, at 42 percent. There was considerable variation in the size of haircuts across countries, with some groups of private creditors not losing at all from a restructuring and others losing as much as 90 percent of the value of their claim.

There is a tendency for haircuts to decline as the income level of a country increases (see figure 12.1). Haircuts were largest in low-income

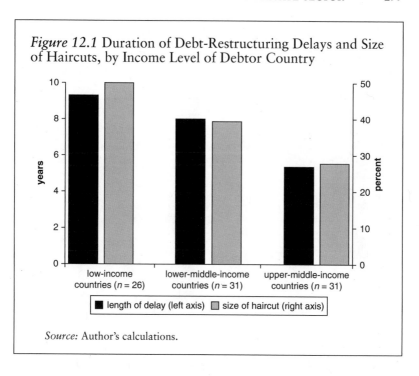

Figure 12.1 Duration of Debt-Restructuring Delays and Size of Haircuts, by Income Level of Debtor Country

Source: Author's calculations.

countries, where they exceeded 50 percent, on average, and lowest in upper-middle-income countries, at about 38 percent. Lower-middle-income countries were at the sample mean of 39 percent. The data also confirm the strong correlation between delays in restructuring and haircuts found in Benjamin and Wright (2009): longer defaults were associated with larger haircuts.

Somewhat less dispersion appears when the data are disaggregated by region. The largest haircuts were in Sub-Saharan Africa, where they averaged almost 50 percent; in the small sample of East Asian and Pacific defaults, haircuts were 38 percent (see figure 12.2). The average haircut across the Europe and Central Asian, Latin American and the Caribbean, and Middle East and North African regions was about 30 percent.

Indebtedness and Debt Relief. A restructuring that imposes a large haircut on private sector creditors need not result in a substantial reduction of the debt burden facing a country, at least when the debt burden is defined as the ratio of debt to GDP, as Benjamin and Wright (2009) note. Even if a country's debt is written down, if its GDP falls by more, the debt to GDP ratio will rise. Somewhat less obviously, calculations of haircuts will reflect the time cost of waiting for the settlement, which will not be reflected in the debt to GDP ratio of the country. Finally, as the data are measured

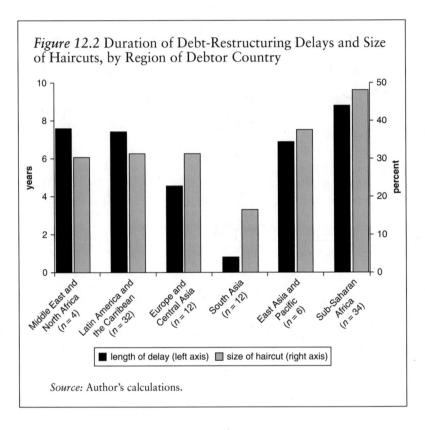

Figure 12.2 Duration of Debt-Restructuring Delays and Size of Haircuts, by Region of Debtor Country

length of delay (left axis)   size of haircut (right axis)

Source: Author's calculations.

annually, a country that issues new debt in the same year as the settlement will show a rise in indebtedness unrelated to the settlement terms received by creditors.[5]

Using the same sample used in this chapter, Benjamin and Wright (2009) show that although haircuts by private creditors averaged about 40 percent, the median country exited default with as much as, if not a little more than, debt owed to private creditors relative to the size of its economy when it entered default. This does not imply that the average country received no debt relief (a country may benefit from a delay in repayment). It does suggest that debt restructuring does not always successfully reduce a country's long-term debt burden.

The results indicate that although debt to private creditors by the lowest-income countries took the longest to restructure, these private creditors also received the largest haircuts. Did these countries also receive the largest reductions in their debt burden? The data show a marked tendency for both lower- and lower-middle-income countries to exit default more highly indebted than when they entered default (figures 12.3 and 12.4). Among both groups of countries, the increase is substantial: debt to GDP ratios rose almost 60 percent in lower-income countries and 70 percent in lower-middle-income countries. Upper middle-income countries fared better, but even among them, debt to GDP ratios fell by less than 10 percent.

Indebtedness levels fell almost 10 percent in South Asia and 5 percent in the Middle East and North Africa; in every other region, indebtedness levels rose. The increases were especially large in Sub-Saharan Africa, where debt restructuring left countries almost twice as indebted to private sector creditors as before they entered default.

To promote a deeper perspective on these findings, this chapter examines next the evolution of indebtedness to private creditors for three Sub-Saharan African countries, chosen to illustrate key features of the data. Nigeria defaulted twice in the past 40 years. Total debt owed to private creditors increased from about 10 percent of gross national income (GNI) in 1982 at the start of Nigeria's default to more than 30 percent by the end of the default in 1992 (figure 12.5). This increase was driven almost entirely by the increase in the "other private creditor" category, with commercial bank debt having been extinguished by the end of the default and replaced with a smaller issuance of new sovereign bonds. The focus on

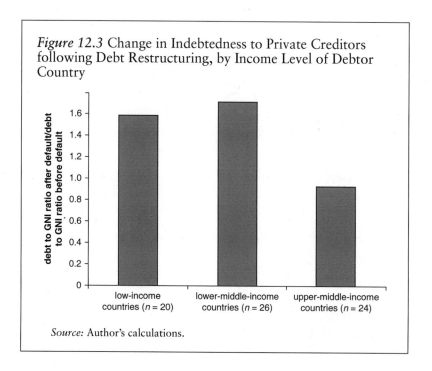

Figure 12.3 Change in Indebtedness to Private Creditors following Debt Restructuring, by Income Level of Debtor Country

Source: Author's calculations.

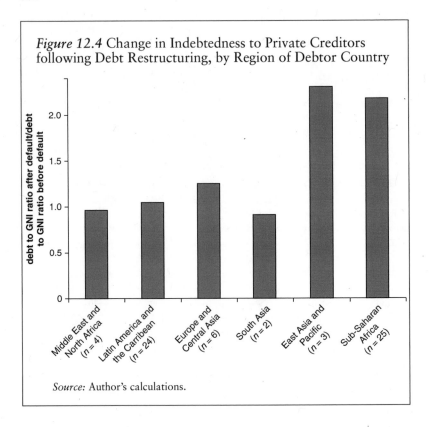

Figure 12.4 Change in Indebtedness to Private Creditors following Debt Restructuring, by Region of Debtor Country

Source: Author's calculations.

debt owed to private creditors drastically understates the growth in total indebtedness, which rose from almost 15 percent of GNI in 1982 to more than 100 percent of GNI in 1992, once official debts are included. By contrast, the 2002 default was associated with small declines in all types of indebtedness.

In the Seychelles, a substantial increase in lending from other private creditors also outweighs a slight reduction in commercial bank indebtedness, resulting in an overall increase in indebtedness to private creditors (figure 12.6). The picture is magnified once official debts are included.

In both Nigeria and the Seychelles, the focus on private sector creditors tended to understate the rise in indebtedness following a settlement. In other cases, in which indebtedness to private sector creditors falls, a rise in official debts results in a different qualitative picture. Sierra Leone was in default in 1986–1995 and 1997–98. By the end of the first default, debt owed to private creditors had fallen from more than 50 percent of GNI to roughly 10 percent (figure 12.7). However, the decline was more than off-set by a rise in official debt that pushed total indebtedness from 70 percent

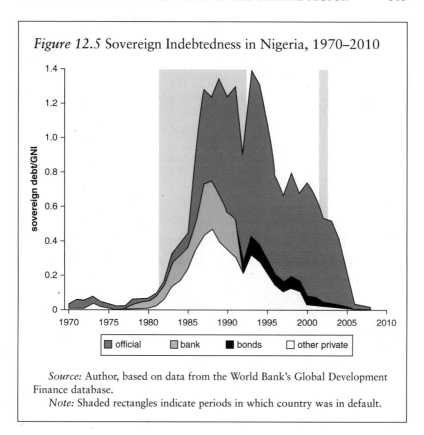

Figure 12.5 Sovereign Indebtedness in Nigeria, 1970–2010

Source: Author, based on data from the World Bank's Global Development Finance database.

Note: Shaded rectangles indicate periods in which country was in default.

to more than 100 percent of GNI. During the second default, by contrast, both private and official indebtedness rose, presumably because official creditors lend to low-income countries in arrears to private creditors. As such lending is much less likely in the case of middle-income countries, it may exacerbate the relative changes in indebtedness.

Theories of and Policy Lessons for Sovereign Debt Restructuring

What explains the pattern of default, settlements, creditor losses, and debt relief identified above? Are these patterns likely to persist into the future? If so, can domestic policy makers, creditor country governments, or supranational institutions do anything to implement more desirable debt-restructuring outcomes in the future?

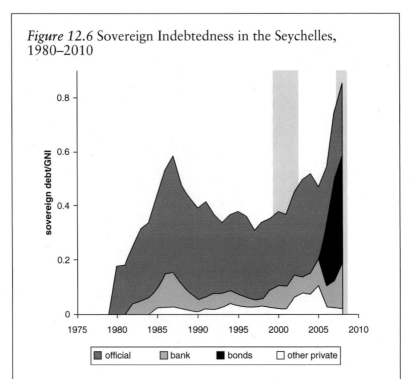

Figure 12.6 Sovereign Indebtedness in the Seychelles, 1980–2010

Source: Author, based on data from the World Bank's Global Development Finance database.

Note: Shaded rectangles indicate periods in which country was in default.

This section reviews alternative theoretical explanations for the patterns of debt restructurings in an attempt to answer some of these questions. It begins by examining theoretical explanations for debt-restructuring outcomes, taking as given the fact that the debtor country has already defaulted. Creditors are modeled as maximizing profits; hence, the theories speak to the process of restructuring debts owed to private creditors as opposed to official debt restructuring, where considerations of equity often come into play.

Much of the early literature on bargaining over sovereign debt and debt restructuring abstracted from the possibility of delays in bargaining or found that no delays occurred in equilibrium. One of the most important early dynamic bargaining models of sovereign debt is by Bulow and Rogoff (1989), who model repeated bargaining between the debtor and a single creditor to study the constant recontracting of sovereign debt over time

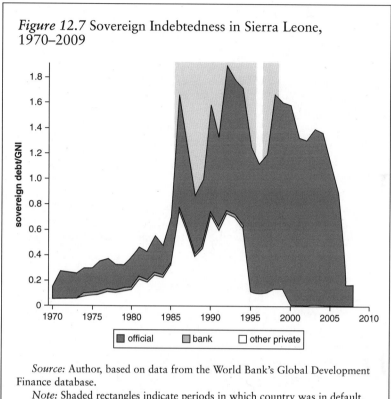

Figure 12.7 Sovereign Indebtedness in Sierra Leone, 1970–2009

Source: Author, based on data from the World Bank's Global Development Finance database.
Note: Shaded rectangles indicate periods in which country was in default.

in which the new contract is implemented immediately. Fernández-Arias (1991) incorporates a richer specification of the debtor economy without changing this fundamental result. Fernández and Rosenthal (1988, 1989) also model bargaining over time with feedbacks to the domestic economy, but they do not focus on cases in which negotiations span multiple periods. Aggarwal (1996) presents a suite of models, which he uses to interpret the history of sovereign default without emphasizing delay. By contrast, the focus here is on models that produce a delay in equilibrium.

Throughout, this chapter discusses those policy interventions that are likely to be most desirable. In doing so, it is important to bear in mind that there may exist a conflict between actions that reduce the costs of default today and actions designed to ensure more favorable access to credit in the future. In particular, once a country has defaulted, it is tempting to undertake actions that reduce the cost of default to that country. However, international credit markets may perceive such actions as creating an incentive for that country, as well as other countries, to default in the future, raising the interest rates charged on sovereign borrowing. This is a classic time inconsistency problem: a country that wishes to issue debt will want to commit to measures that make the cost of default high in order to secure lower interest rates today, but it will want to undo these measures in the event that a default actually occurs. Below, a number of reforms a country can commit to in whole or in part are examined with a view to determining their possible effects on both the cost of default ex post and the welfare of debtor countries ex ante (see Dooley 2000 for a discussion).

Many of the explanations for the debt-restructuring outcomes documented above, in particular explanations for the substantial delays in concluding debt-restructuring operations, focus on the difficulties faced by creditors in coordinating to make mutually beneficial agreements with the debtor. Three such explanations are reviewed before turning to explanations that focus on the institutional environment within the defaulting country and the information and enforcement possibilities that govern sovereign borrowing in the first place.

Restructuring Negotiations with Uncoordinated Creditors

Debt is often owed to a large number of private sector creditors. In the case of the bank loans that were restructured following the 1980s debt crisis, many countries had to negotiate with dozens of banks; in the case of bond issues, it is not uncommon for bond holders to number in the thousands. Negotiating a debt restructuring is therefore difficult both mechanically (it is costly to catalogue and communicate with a dispersed group of creditors) and because of a number of collective action problems associated with debt restructuring, three of which are discussed here.

The first collective action problem, which was highlighted during the 1980s debt crisis, concerns the public good nature of debt relief. If any one bank agrees to offer debt relief by reducing its claims on a country, the value of all other banks' claims may increase. There is a classic free-rider problem, in which some banks do not offer debt relief in the hope that they can free ride on the debt relief offered by other banks.

A variety of informal mechanisms arose to deal with this problem among private creditors, albeit imperfectly. Bank advisory committees were set up in which representatives of the major bank creditors were responsible for, among other things, convincing smaller banks to participate in the restructuring process. A number of different methods were used. Devlin (1989) argues that larger banks used their contact with these smaller banks in other markets as an inducement to participate. Milivojević (1985) suggests that such incentives work through the "network of influence" that large banks have on small banks, which includes threats to exclude free riders from future syndicates, terminate correspondent banking facilities, and cut interbank lines. In addition, in some cases debtors appear to have discriminated against free-riding banks during a restructuring (Cline 1995; more generally, see the discussion in Lipson 1981, 1985). Sachs (1983) and Krugman (1985) present theoretical models of bank collusion to prevent free riding.

A version of this argument applies to the interaction between the debt relief offered by official creditors and that offered by private creditors. If a country owes substantial debt to official creditors, as many low-income countries do, private creditors have an incentive to delay settlement in order to free ride on debt relief provided by the official sector. In response to this concern, official debt-restructuring agreements typically contain some form of "comparability of treatment" clause designed to limit such free riding by private creditors. The application of these clauses is limited, however, by the difficulty of defining comparable treatment for private claims, which are very different from official claims (issues of coordination between private and official creditors are discussed below).

The second collective action problem concerns the role of litigious creditors engaging in holdout, which has become more important over the past few decades with the development of innovative legal strategies for encouraging repayment. Although it has been possible to bring suit against a country in default in most major creditor jurisdictions since the early 1970s, when the doctrine of sovereign immunity was weakened by, among other things, the passage of the Foreign Sovereign Immunities Act of 1976 in the United States and similar legislation in other countries, the attachment of assets remains difficult. The main difficulty lies in the fact that debtor countries typically hold few assets in creditor country jurisdictions. One asset lying within the jurisdiction of creditor countries that may be attached is the funds associated with new loans and the servicing of those loans. Some private creditors have had success pursuing court action where the disbursal of these funds has been halted by injunction. In the highly publicized case of Elliott Associates v. Peru, funds that were to have been used to pay interest on newly rescheduled debt under the Brady plan were frozen, with the result that Peru was forced to settle with Elliott Associates in full in order to avoid default on the Brady bonds (see Alfaro 2006).

The result of this and other successful legal actions against sovereigns has led to a substantial increase in such legal action, with at least 54 court cases filed by commercial creditors against highly indebted poor countries over the past decade (World Bank and IMF 2010). The fact that such holdout creditors earn very high returns (see Singh 2003) has increased the incentives to hold out from the regular restructuring process.

To see why this is the case, consider a country that has defaulted on debts that are larger than its capacity to repay. As a result, creditors as a whole must accept some reduction in the value of their claims. However, because any one creditor acting alone has the ability to hold up repayment of new debt issues using legal tactics, new creditors will be reluctant to lend to a country until every last creditor has settled. Thus, individual creditors have an incentive to delay agreeing to any restructuring proposal involving a reduction in the value of their claim in the hope that other creditors will agree first and allow the holdouts to extract full repayment later on. Pitchford and Wright (2007, 2009) have constructed models of this phenomenon that show that such incentives are strong enough to explain the substantial delays in restructuring that are observed in practice.

A number of policy proposals have been advanced to deal with this problem. Early proposals included the reintroduction of bondholder councils (Eichengreen and Portes 1989, 1995; Eichengreen 2002) and the introduction of a supranational bankruptcy court (Krueger 2001, 2002a, 2002b). Most notable has been the introduction of collective action clauses into bond contracts that allow a supermajority of bondholders to impose common restructuring terms on minority holdouts (see Taylor 2002). Collective action clauses have now become standard in bonds issued under New York law. Pitchford and Wright (2007) examine the likely effect of such clauses within the context of their calibrated model. They find that such clauses will likely reduce, although not eliminate, delays in restructuring. They also show that although collective action clauses will increase the incentive for debtor countries to default, the cost of borrowing by these countries will likely not increase, because the increased default risk is offset by larger and more timely settlement payments.

A third collective action problem—the potential for free riding on negotiation costs—is at the heart of why Pitchford and Wright (2009) find that collective action clauses are likely to reduce but not eliminate delay. When collective action clauses are used to impose common settlement terms on bond holders, they reduce the latitude of discriminatory settlements being used to compensate those bond holders who take the lead in negotiations and by consequence bear the brunt of these costs. Pitchford and Wright (2009) provide evidence that these costs are very large (more than 3 percent of the value of a restructuring in some complicated cases) and often hard to verify and thus difficult to compensate directly through reimbursement of expenses. Collective action clauses may thus remove the ability of bondholders to hold out for full repayment but exacerbate the incentive for bondholders to free ride on negotiation costs.

A number of policy options are available to debtor and creditor governments and to supranational institutions to deal with collective action problems. From the perspective of debtor governments, the results of Pitchford and Wright (2007) suggest that by issuing debt that is easier to restructure, sovereigns may actually reduce the cost of their borrowing. Policy innovations aimed at easing restructuring may be extended beyond the introduction of collective action clauses—which are now widespread—to include arbitration procedures and perhaps even the most favored creditor clauses discussed, but not fully implemented, in the restructuring of Argentina's debt in 2004.[6] From the perspective of creditor country governments, there are now international agreements designed to ensure that creditors do not sell their own claims on defaulted countries to litigating creditors, a practice that occurred in Paris Club and European Union countries in 2007 and 2008 (World Bank and IMF 2010). For supranationals, the Debt Reduction Facility (DRF) of the World Bank's International Development Association (IDA) can be used to buy back debt from private creditors at a steep discount.[7] In at least one case, it has been used to buy back the claims of litigating creditors, a procedure that could be expanded. However, it is important that these funds be used to settle with all litigating creditors and to extract concessions from these creditors, in order to avoid problems like those associated with the 1988 Bolivian buyback (see Bulow and Rogoff 1988 for a discussion).

To what extent can any of these theories explain the patterns in debt-restructuring outcomes across countries described above? It is not implausible to think that some of these collective action problems are most severe for low-income countries. For example, the costs of bargaining with low-income countries may be higher than those associated with middle-income countries because of imperfect public debt management systems and records of debt holdings. In addition, if low-income countries suffer from a more severe debt overhang problem than higher-income countries, concessions by fewer creditors (in particular official creditors) will substantially increase the value of outstanding private debts, magnifying the free-rider problem of private creditors. Middle-income countries tend to have a larger number of debts and a larger proportion issued as bonds, which are often widely held. Whether these conjectures have merit and are quantitatively significant in explaining outcomes is a topic for future research.

Restructuring Negotiations with an Uncoordinated Debtor

The above explanations assume that the debtor country can be regarded as a single decision maker—that is, that agents within the country coordinate perfectly. In practice, some of the delay in restructuring may reflect conflicting agendas within the debtor country. In particular, if the costs of a restructuring cannot be shared equally by all groups within a country, there may be delay as different groups hold out for a smaller share of the costs. It is precisely this intuition that underlies Alesina and Drazen's (1991) model of delays in the adoption of a stabilization policy. Their idea is most easily presented by an example.

Consider a country in default that is made up of two provinces. As long as a restructuring deal is not reached, government spending is reduced, and both provinces lose, as a result of higher taxes and reductions in investments in infrastructure. A debt restructuring requires that the country further reduce spending, increase taxation, or both, in order to generate a fiscal surplus with which to repay creditors. For simplicity, suppose that the fiscal surplus can be generated only by reducing transfers to one or both of the provinces and that there is no way to force an equal reduction on both provinces. In such a world, the residents and representatives of both provinces have an incentive to incur short-term costs with the aim of forcing the other province to accept the greater reduction in provincial transfers. In particular, each province has an incentive to delay agreeing to a restructuring in the hope that the other province concedes first and accepts the larger share of the reduction in transfers.

Competition between different groups in a society as to who should bear the greater cost of reform is common. If this phenomenon is more severe in low-income countries, it might explain the heterogeneity in outcomes documented above. In theory, the solution to such a situation is adoption of an institutional structure that allows for the equitable imposition of the costs of reform on all competing parties. In practice, doing so may be difficult: in the example discussed above, the size of transfers to the provinces may be constrained in the constitution of the country and therefore be difficult or impossible to change without the agreement of both provinces. In such a case, there may be a role for creditor country governments and supranational institutions to encourage domestic stakeholders to engage in reform discussions and to reward cooperation with the transfer of new funds (a bailout) or greater debt forgiveness.

Delays with Coordinated Debtors and Creditors

Delays can occur in debt restructurings for many other reasons. The need to compile and consolidate a list of the outstanding claims affected by the default may cause delays (this is often true in cases in which the debts of private sector agents within the debtor country are assumed by the government during a default, as was the case in República Bolivariana de Venezuela in the mid-1980s, as described in Holley 1987). Alternatively, both debtors and creditors might agree to delay restructuring debts if the cost of doing so is expected to fall in the future, perhaps because the effects of an adverse shock are expected to dissipate (see, for example, Bi 2008; Dhillon and others 2006; Merlo and Wilson 1995). This section examines two other explanations for delays in bargaining that abstract from collective action problems, emphasizing aspects of the information and enforcement environment surrounding sovereign borrowing.

One of the most popular approaches to explaining delays in bargaining across a wide variety of situations is to assume that there is an asymmetry of information between the parties to bargaining. In the case of negotiations to restructure sovereign debts, a debtor country likely has more precise information about the political and economic costs it would face by agreeing to a settlement than does the creditor. For its part, the creditor is likely to have more information about the state of its balance sheet and the set of alternative investment opportunities it faces. In such a world, neither party knows the value the other party places on agreeing to a settlement.[8]

A number of formulations of bargaining in the presence of so-called "two-sided asymmetric information" have been presented. Cramton (1984) studies a two-sided asymmetric information version of Admati and Perry's (1987) bargaining environment in which the time between offers is chosen endogenously by the bargaining parties. In such a world, delay—which is implemented by making nonserious offers that are rejected—serves to reveal information about the value each player places on a settlement, with each party becoming more pessimistic about the other party's valuation as time goes on. Delay is informative, because the more the player values agreement, the more costly is delay. When offers are eventually made in such a world, the valuations of both creditor and debtor are revealed. Delay is socially inefficient, which begs the question of whether there may be other, less costly means of revealing a player's type. In a related context, Horner and Sahuguet (forthcoming) show that the ability to signal one's type by committing resources (other than through the time cost of delay) acts to essentially eliminate delay. One implication for policy makers is that they should investigate mechanisms that allow for faster, less socially costly means of revealing information.

An alternative explanation for delays in debt restructuring is based on the limited enforceability of contracts. In particular, if agreement to a restructuring produces benefits for the country both at the time of settlement and in the future, possibly as the result of better capital market access, creditors will bargain over a share of these future benefits. If agents are patient, these future gains are likely to far exceed current gains; the only way for the debtor to share these gains with the creditor will be to issue debt. However, such debt may not be very valuable if the creditor perceives that the debtor will likely default on it. Thus, it may be optimal to wait until future default risk is low before agreeing to a debt restructuring.

Benjamin and Wright (2009) formalize this intuition, showing that this mechanism is further strengthened by the fact that reaccess to international credit markets is more valuable to the country when future default risk is low (because the country can borrow on better terms), giving the parties another reason to delay. Thus, sovereign debt–restructuring outcomes are driven by the determinants of future default risk, including the evolution of the sovereign's economy, the evolving political trade-offs within the economy, and the evolving institutions governing debt restructuring that affect the relative bargaining powers of the parties. Benjamin and Wright place particular emphasis on the development of official lending into private arrears as reducing creditor bargaining power and prolonging the 1980s debt crisis.

They show that a calibrated version of their model can explain the fact that the level of indebtedness to private creditors typically does not decline following a settlement. They are unable to explain the large increases in indebtedness to private creditors observed following debt-restructuring operations involving the lowest-income countries, including those in Sub-Saharan Africa. Their model is capable of explaining the longer delays and larger haircuts for the private creditors of low-income nations if there is more persistence in output fluctuations or debtor bargaining power among such countries. This seems plausible, to the extent that greater official lending to low-income countries implies a larger role for official lending into arrears in influencing private creditor bargaining power.

What are the implications for policy makers? Benjamin and Wright (2009) emphasize the role of bailouts as both a cause of and solution to these delays. They show that bailouts in which supranational governments transfer resources to a country conditional on reaching a settlement can reduce delays in bargaining, albeit at the cost of making it more tempting to default, which reduces country welfare overall. They argue that uncertainty over both the likelihood and the size of a future bailout can increase delays, underlining the importance of having a transparent and timely process for providing these funds.

Enhanced coordination between the official and private sectors aimed at preserving the bargaining position of private creditors could also be effective. One possibility would be for the World Bank, the IMF, and creditor country governments to tie their own debt relief to the requirement that the sovereign bargain with private creditors in good faith.[9] In return, private creditors might be expected to commit to accepting a standardized haircut and to lending appropriately in the first place (by, for example, observing the Equator Principles on project financing and lending only to countries with low risk of debt distress).

Concluding Remarks

Restructuring sovereign debt is very time consuming. It is also ineffective at preserving the value of private creditors' claims or reducing the level of indebtedness to private creditors of defaulting countries. This chapter presents evidence that these problems are particularly severe among the low-income countries of Sub-Saharan Africa, where delays are longest, private creditor haircuts are largest, and indebtedness to private creditors rises most following debt restructuring.

Theoretical research has uncovered numerous explanations for why negotiations to structure debts might be inefficient and time consuming, several of which appear capable of explaining the size of private creditor losses. Much less work has been devoted to understanding the causes of the dramatic rises in indebtedness to private creditors experienced by low-income countries following a default. This is surely a priority for future research.

Notes

The author thanks, without implicating, Stephanie Huynh for outstanding research assistance, Dörte Dömeland, Brian Pinto, Federico Gil Sander, Gallina A. Vincelette, two anonymous referees, numerous conference participants, and, especially, Mike Tomz, for comments.

1. With regard to the restructuring of debts owed to official creditors, one typically observes only the date at which an agreement is reached with the country, not the date when negotiations began. Anecdotal evidence suggests that such deals are usually concluded quickly, however.

2. Most multilateral financial institutions and Paris Club bilateral creditors have provided debt relief under the HIPC Initiative. Delivery of HIPC Initiative relief from private creditors is a key challenge to the implementation of the initiative. For more information, see World Bank and IMF (2010).

3. Three instances of defaults are contiguous in time. This finding seems inconsistent with S&P's practice of merging contiguous default events. Treating these defaults as a single default episode increases the average delay only slightly, to 7.6 years.

4. Data on the high-income subgroup were dropped because the group contained only two defaults.

5. Broader measures of debt, including official debt, may also increase as the debtor substitutes different forms of finance.

6. In principle, most favored creditor (MFC) clauses would allow creditors participating in an initial exchange offer to exchange their new claims under the terms of any subsequent exchange offer or settlement. The final draft of Argentina's MFC clause removed the ability of such creditors to participate in future "settlements." See Gelpern (2005) for a discussion.

7. The boards of the International Bank for Reconstruction and Development (IBRD) and IDA established the World Bank's Debt Reduction Facility for IDA-Only Countries (DRF) in 1989. The DRF helps extinguish commercial debts through buybacks at a deep discount. Its objective is to help reforming highly indebted poor countries reduce their commercial external debt as part of a comprehensive debt resolution program. As of September 2010, the DRF had supported 25 buybacks in 22 countries, extinguishing about $10.2 billion of external commercial debt.

8. For more on the effect of asymmetric information and reputation on the development of sovereign debt markets, see Tomz (2007).

9. I thank Frederico Gil Sander for these suggestions.

References

Admati, Anat R., and Motty Perry. 1987. "Strategic Delay in Bargaining." *Review of Economic Studies* 54 (3): 345–64.

Aggarwal, Vinod K. 1996. *Debt Games.* Cambridge: Cambridge University Press.

Alesina, Alberto, and Allan Drazen. 1991. "Why Are Stabilizations Delayed?" *American Economic Review* 81 (5): 1170–88.

Alfaro, Laura. 2006. "Creditor Activism in Sovereign Debt: 'Vulture' Tactics or Market Backbone." Harvard Business School Case 9–706–057, Boston, MA.

Beers, David T., and John Chambers. 2006. "Default Study: Sovereign Defaults at 26-Year Low, to Show Little Change in 2007." Standard & Poor's Ratings Direct, New York.

Benjamin, David, and Mark L. J. Wright. 2009. "Recovery before Redemption: A Theory of Delays in Sovereign Debt Renegotiations." Department of Economics, University of California at Los Angeles.

Bi, Ran. 2008. "'Beneficial' Delays in Debt Restructuring Negotiations." IMF Working Paper 08/38, International Monetary Fund, Washington, DC.

Bulow, Jeremy, and Kenneth S. Rogoff. 1988. "The Buyback Boondoggle." *Brookings Papers on Economic Activity* 2: 675–98.

———. 1989. "A Constant Recontracting Model of Sovereign Debt." *Journal of Political Economy* 97 (1): 155–78.

Cline, William R. 1995. *International Debt Reexamined*. Institute for International Economics, Washington, DC.

Cramton, Peter C. 1984. "Bargaining with Incomplete Information: An Infinite-Horizon Model with Two-Sided Uncertainty." *Review of Economic Studies* 51 (4): 579–93.

Devlin, Robert. 1989. *Debt and Crisis in Latin America: The Supply Side of the Story*. Princeton. NJ: Princeton University Press.

Dhillon, Amrita, Javier García-Fronti, Sayantan Ghosal, and Marcus Miller. 2006. "Debt Restructuring and Economic Recovery: Analysing the Argentine Swap." *World Economy* 29 (4): 377–98.

Dooley, Michael P. 2000. "International Financial Architecture and Strategic Default: Can Financial Crises Be Less Painful?" *Carnegie-Rochester Conference Series on Public Policy* 53 (1): 361–77.

Eichengreen, Barry. 2002. *Financial Crises and What to Do about Them*. Oxford: Oxford University Press.

Eichengreen, Barry, and Richard Portes. 1989. "After the Deluge: Default, Negotiation and Readjustment during the Interwar Years." In *The International Debt Crisis in Historical Perspective*, ed. Barry Eichengreen and Peter Lindert, 12–47. Cambridge, MA: MIT Press.

———. 1995. *Crisis? What Crisis? Orderly Workouts for Sovereign Debtors*. Centre for Economic Policy Research, London.

Fernández, Raquel, and Robert W. Rosenthal. 1988. "Sovereign-Debt Renegotiations: A Strategic Analysis." NBER Working Paper 2597, National Bureau of Economic Research, Cambridge, MA.

———. 1989. "Sovereign Debt Renegotiations Revisited." NBER Working Paper 2981, National Bureau of Economic Research, Cambridge, MA.

Fernández-Arias, Eduardo. 1991. "A Dynamic Bargaining Model of Sovereign Debt." World Bank Policy Research Working Paper 778, Washington, DC.

Gelpern, Anna. 2005. "After Argentina." *Institute for International Economics Policy Brief* 05 (02).

Holley, H. A. 1987. *Developing Country Debt: The Role of the Commercial Banks*. Royal Institute of International Affairs, London.

Horner, Johannes, and Nicolas Sahuguet. Forthcoming. "A War of Attrition with Endogenous Effort Levels." *Economic Theory*. http://www.springerlink.com/content/95n777213q310778/.

Institute of International Finance. 2001. *Survey of Debt Restructuring by Private Creditors*. Washington, DC.

Krueger, Anne O. 2001. "A New Approach to Sovereign Debt Restructuring." Address to Indian Council for Research on International Economic Relations,

Delhi, December 20. http://www.imf.org/external/np/speeches/2001/112601 .htm.

————. 2002a. *A New Approach to Sovereign Debt Restructuring.* International Monetary Fund, Washington, DC.

————. 2002b. "Sovereign Debt Restructuring Mechanism: One Year Later." Address to European Commission, Brussels, December 10. http://www.imf.org/ external/np/speeches/2002/121002.htm.

Krugman, Paul. 1985. "International Debt Strategies in an Uncertain World." In *International Debt and the Developing Countries,* ed. G. Smith and J. Cuddington, 79–100. Washington, DC: World Bank.

Lipson, Charles. 1981. "The International Organization of Third World Debt." *International Organization* 35 (4): 603–31.

————. 1985. "Bankers' Dilemmas: Private Cooperation in Rescheduling Sovereign Debts." *World Politics* 38 (1): 200–25.

Merlo, Antonio, and Charles Wilson. 1995. "A Stochastic Model of Sequential Bargaining with Complete Information." *Econometrica* 63 (2): 371–99.

Milivojević, Marko. 1985. *The Debt Rescheduling Process.* New York: St. Martin's Press.

Morais, Bernardo, and Mark L. J. Wright. 2008. "International Financial Crisis Facts." Working Paper, Department of Economics, University of California at Los Angeles.

Pitchford, Rohan, and Mark L. J. Wright. 2007. "Restructuring the Sovereign Debt Restructuring Mechanism." Department of Economics Working Paper, University of California at Los Angeles.

————. 2009. "Holdout Creditors in Sovereign Debt Restructuring: A Theory of Negotiation in a Weak Contractual Environment." Department of Economics Working Paper, University of California at Los Angeles.

Sachs, Jeffrey. 1983. "Theoretical Issues in International Borrowing." NBER Working Paper 1189, National Bureau of Economic Research, Cambridge, MA.

Singh, Manmohan. 2003. "Recovery Rates from Distressed Debt: Empirical Evidence from Chapter 11 Filings, International Litigation, and Recent Sovereign Debt Restructurings." IMF Working Paper 03/161, International Monetary Fund, Washington, DC. http://www.imf.org/external/pubs/cat/longres .cfm?sk=16487.0.

Taylor, John B. 2002. "Sovereign Debt Restructuring: A U.S. Perspective." Remarks at the conference "Sovereign Debt Workouts: Hopes and Hazards?" Institute for International Economics, Washington, DC. http://www.ustreas.gov/press/ releases/po2056.htm.

Tomz, Michael. 2007. *Sovereign Debt and International Cooperation: Reputational Reasons for Lending and Repayment.* Princeton, NJ: Princeton University Press.

Tomz, Michael, and Mark L. J. Wright. 2007. "Do Countries Default in 'Bad Times'?" *Journal of the European Economic Association* 5 (2–3): 352–60.

World Bank. 2009a. *Global Development Finance: Charting a Global Recovery.* Washington, DC: World Bank.

————. 2009b. *World Development Indicators.* Washington, DC: World Bank.

World Bank and IMF (International Monetary Fund). 2010. *Heavily Indebted Poor Countries (HIPC) Initiative and Multilateral Debt Relief Initiative (MDRI): Status of Implementation.* www.worldbank.org/debt.

13

A Standing Arbitral Tribunal as a Procedural Solution for Sovereign Debt Restructurings

Christoph G. Paulus

There is no generally applicable process for resolving sovereigns' financial or economic problems; sovereign debt restructuring is currently handled on an ad hoc basis. The approach lacks transparency, predictability, and efficiency—all critical elements in restructuring debt and for the rule of law in general. As the recent example of Greece and other European countries suggests, the problem affects all countries, not just developing countries.

This chapter examines past sovereign debt restructuring and develops a feasible and desirable approach to restructuring through the establishment of a standing arbitral tribunal (modeled after, for example, the Iran–U.S. claims tribunal). The chapter is organized as follows. The first section describes and rates the techniques applied to date and identifies their deficiencies. The second section proposes the establishment of a tribunal and addresses the nine most important problems related to its creation. The last section provides some concluding remarks.

Deficiencies of the Current System

For many years, the Paris and London Clubs handled the restructuring of sovereign debt when crises occurred. In recent years, the need for their involvement has declined, as the capital markets have emerged as the leading source of credit.

The call for a code of conduct—as voiced, for instance, by the former governor of the Banque de France Jean-Claude Trichet—is commendable. Such a code, which stresses the importance of creditor behavior, would provide an additional tool for developing fair solutions to sovereign debt resolutions (see Couillault and Weber 2003; IIF 2004).[1] However, as a "soft law," a code of conduct is nonenforceable; there is almost no sanction—at least no legal one—against a violation of this self-imposed obligation. For this reason, the approach lacks predictability.

Many versions of the concept of "odious debt" exist; it remains doubtful that any of them is legally binding (Bohoslawsky 2009; Michalowski and Bohoslawsky 2009; Paulus 2008). Insofar as the discussion of odious debt emphasizes creditors' co-responsibility, it is likely, however, that legally binding standards will evolve (Buchheit and Gulati 2010), but it is hard to imagine that any such co-responsibility will ever be applicable to ordinary bond holders who invest in sovereigns through the capital market. This approach may be of some help in the future, but because it will not govern most creditors, it will not be an all-encompassing solution.

Collective action clauses have also been viewed as an effective mechanism for handling debt restructurings (see Galvis and Saad 2004; Gugiatti and Richards 2004; Hopt 2009; Schier 2007; Szodruch 2008). Their main advantage is that they address the problem of holdout profiteers by allowing majority decisions to be binding on all creditors. Such clauses exert discipline on creditors by preventing the strategic waiting or action that is possible when unanimity is required (see Paulus 2002).

The problem with collective action clauses is that they are binding only within a single bond issuance. If there are two or more bond issuances, it is difficult to achieve intercreditor equity (see Buchheit and Pam 2004; IMF 2005; Szodruch 2008). This deficiency must not be underestimated, as intercreditor equity is perceived as essential to fairness.[2]

Another reason why collective action clauses do not solve the problem of sovereign debt restructuring is that they are applicable only to bond holders and not to more traditional lenders, such as foreign states or banks. If traditional claims form the bulk of a sovereign's debts, the collective action clause approach is likely to have little effect.

Taking all these pros and cons into consideration, the most appropriate solution to the sovereign debt–restructuring problem appears to be to learn from the private law model governing commercial and individual insolvency and introduce a full-fledged proceeding. The huge advantage of this approach is that it has the potential to guarantee both transparency and predictability and can lead to an all-encompassing solution through its obligatory inclusion of all (or at least most) creditors. To be sure, the design of such a proceeding needs to balance the interests involved; simply copying the insolvency statute of a jurisdiction will certainly not suffice.

Initial steps along this path have been made (see Buckley 2009; Hagan 2005; Mayer 2005; Paulus 2003b; Schier 2007). Because of political considerations, however, they are—at least at this point—highly unlikely to develop into a full-fledged type of insolvency proceeding for sovereigns (Setser 2008).

A Procedural Solution: The Sovereign Debt Tribunal

Given this state of affairs, it appears prudent to give up the ambitious goal of establishing a full-fledged bankruptcy system.³ A better approach seems to be to go the longer and probably somewhat thornier route of starting with a modest first step (Paulus 2009).

Establishment of the Sovereign Debt Tribunal

Court-like institutions already exist. The Iran–U.S. tribunal is the most prominent example (Gibson and Drahozal 2006).⁴ The tribunal established for the restructuring of Iraq's Saddam-era debts, which has been quite successful so far, is another example (Deeb 2007). A sovereign debt tribunal based along the lines of these tribunals could provide the legal structures that are indispensable to establishing smooth procedures for sovereign debt restructuring.

As to where this tribunal would be located, how it would be constituted, and how it would function, various scenarios are imaginable. Relevant stakeholders could identify an institution with credibility and a strong reputation that is not an actual or potential creditor to sovereigns. The procedures might include time-bound mediation as a precursor to arbitration or as a complement to ongoing restructuring negotiations. The creation of a sovereign debt tribunal would also build confidence for ultimately embracing broader reform objectives.

Creation of a sovereign debt tribunal is likely to be confronted with reservations, concerns, and obstacles.⁵ As there is no enforcement mechanism, such a tribunal could be created based only on consensus among relevant stakeholders that the problems of a defaulting sovereign are better solved with a sovereign debt tribunal than without one.

Creating an international arbitral tribunal has several advantages:

- It is based on consensus among key stakeholders.
- It handles disputes between creditors and the sovereign debtor in a neutral forum, thereby toning down some of the emotions that affect such disputes.
- It brings cohesion and structure to what is often a disorganized group of anxious stakeholders who initiate individual strategies (usually in different places) to secure the most profitable outcome for themselves.

- Unlike collective action clauses, it covers both creditors and the sovereign debtor.
- It could create confidence on the part of sovereigns and creditors that a pool of expert arbitrators possess the experience and knowledge needed to resolve the complex issues of sovereign defaults.

The proposal described here differs from similar proposals put forward by nongovernmental organizations (NGOs) that have long advocated resolution of sovereign debt restructurings through arbitration. When such NGOs discuss arbitration, they are generally referring to an ad hoc arbitration process like that used in certain types of commercial disputes. In this kind of arbitration, each party typically appoints one arbitrator. The two arbitrators then select a third arbitrator.

Although a number of well-established and well-respected international arbitration institutions, such as the International Chamber of Commerce in Paris, are used in the commercial arbitration context, the pool of potential arbitrators maintained by such institutions is so large that there is a danger of anonymity. This problem could erode coherence, prevent the pool of arbitrators from steadily gaining expertise, and result in inconsistent rulings across panels.

In contrast, the proposal suggested here envisages a model based on the Iran–U.S. Claims Tribunal, which comprises a small number of high-profile panelists. The arbitrators would have the opportunity to become acquainted with one another and discuss issues of common concern, thereby allowing them to develop a common thread of reasoning in addressing similar cases.

The advantages of a sovereign debt tribunal are manifold. By its design and structure, such a body would necessarily develop expertise. Cases would be adjudicated by a small, highly qualified pool of international judges rather than judges from New York, London, or wherever parties agreed to have their forum. In contrast to traditional collective action clauses, a sovereign debt tribunal would establish clear procedural rules, thereby enhancing transparency and legitimacy. A self-imposed constraint on procedural issues would allow for sufficient flexibility in regard to substantive matters, which are often viewed (particularly by nonlegal professions) as more important than procedural issues.

Creation and Composition of an Arbitral Tribunal

In order to enjoy the benefits of institutional backing and international reputation, the tribunal should be established under the auspices of a highly reputed institution that does not lend to sovereigns. This restriction rules out the International Monetary Fund (IMF) and the World Bank Group (Waibel 2007).

Although the International Centre for Settlement of Investment Disputes (ICSID) is a well-established and functioning arbitration center, it could not serve as an sovereign debt tribunal for at least two reasons. First, ICSID belongs to the World Bank Group, a source of perceived bias. Second, although many sovereign debts are investment related, many others are not. The highly complex issue of a sovereign in default must not be stripped of all its complexities, including political, economic, legal, and social implications, and reduced to a mere investment problem.

An international institution that appears appropriate is the United Nations. Alternatively, a country such as the Netherlands or Norway could host the tribunal (the Netherlands is currently exploring the possibilities for such an undertaking). The advantage of housing the institution outside a multilateral institution is that it could be created more quickly than it could under UN auspices, given the United Nation's many stakeholders.

Some commentators (Reinisch 2003; Stiglitz 2003) have proposed another alternative, namely, establishing a global bankruptcy court associated with, say, the International Court of Justice. As appealing as this idea may appear at first blush, even if a special sovereign bankruptcy chamber were completely separated from the judiciary of the International Court of Justice, it could suffer some of the same acceptance, recognition, and enforcement problems the International Court of Justice has experienced.

Whatever institution creates the tribunal, various questions regarding its functioning and operation need to be addressed. These questions regard the selection process for the pool of arbitrators, the establishment of a permanent secretariat, the creation of a Web site, the payment of arbitrators, and related issues.

The selection of arbitrators could be handled in the way the IMF proposed in its attempt to set up its Sovereign Debt-Restructuring Mechanism (SDRM) (Paulus 2003a). A public figure with international stature—such as the secretary-general of the United Nations, for instance—would select 20–30 arbitrators (or, in the interest of even greater neutrality, 10 arbitrators, who would select the 20–30 arbitrators). The selection would reflect a diversity of national and professional backgrounds. The arbitrators would elect one of their members as president of the tribunal.

The selection of arbitrators in this manner has the potential advantage of fostering trust—no small consideration given the importance of perception in sovereign debt restructuring. The president's task would be to draft the procedural rules for the tribunal, which would be enacted only after all or a majority of arbitrators gave their consent and the public figure responsible for selecting the arbitrators had been informed of the proposed rules. The president of the tribunal would also appoint arbitrators to specific cases. The president would be the only full-time arbitrator; all others would work when called upon by the tribunal's president.

The details of the panels might depend on the needs of each case. Some cases, for example, might require only a single arbitrator, whereas others might require as many as three arbitrators. Depending on the scope of the tribunal's tasks, the applicable substantive law might need to be determined.

A necessary feature of any arbitration tribunal is that it have no intrinsic authority to initiate or decide cases on its own. Any such authority will be dependent on the contractual agreement to arbitration by all relevant parties; such agreement to arbitration is the critical underpinning of any international arbitration process. The requirement for prior agreement stands even if the circumstances are as uniquely pressing as they were in the cases of the Iran–U.S. Claims Tribunal and the debt rescheduling of Iraq after 2003.

In both of these cases, the tribunals were created after the onset of the crisis. One cannot assume that such an ex post result can be achieved in every case, however. In most cases, it is unlikely that all stakeholders will consent to a sovereign's offer for arbitration once a debt crisis has begun. The introduction of an arbitral tribunal will thus usually depend on a precrisis consensus among the parties, making it critical to include an arbitration clause in all issuances of sovereign bonds and other instruments used to issue sovereign debt.[6]

Given this dependence on contractual agreement between the parties, a downside of the proposal is obvious: parties that do not enter such a contractual agreement with the sovereign are not subject to the tribunal's jurisdiction. Such debts will have to be dealt with in the traditional manner. The proposal thus deals only with contractual obligations on debt instruments such as bond issuances. It is hoped that once such a tribunal is established, it will become generally acceptable and create spillover effects on the legal treatment of other state obligations.

Jurisdiction and Competence of the Tribunal

The tasks and duties of a debt-restructuring tribunal can be manifold, depending on the configuration of the debt-restructuring mechanism itself. The type of mechanism used depends on how far one wants to extend the influence of the arbitral tribunal. The scope of its tasks should be carefully delineated in the relevant bond issuance clause or other relevant debt instrument providing for arbitration.

In accordance with what is considered here to be a pragmatic and modest approach, the arbitral tribunal should, at a minimum, be empowered to address matters related to the verification of creditor claims, as well as voting issues related to the approval of the restructuring plan and similar matters. Beyond that, the extent to which the tribunal is empowered to address specific issues should be left to the discretion of the parties. The period during which the tribunal functions must also be determined. One option is to disband it after the proceeding is closed. Another is to allow it to function until all case-related disputes, even those that emerge after the course of the proceeding, are resolved.

As a practical matter, the bond-issuing sovereign may draft the arbitration clause and propose it to the investor community, which then decides whether to accept it. Depending on the details of the clause proposed, it could create a buying incentive or disincentive for investors. It is conceivable that, with the passage of time and the development of experience in this area, certain practices may gain acceptance in the market, with the result that certain standard arbitration clauses may emerge in sovereign bond issuances.

One of the major issues to be addressed is which disputes the tribunal should be competent to decide. Should the tribunal be restricted to deciding narrow, technical legal issues? Should it be limited to deciding on the legal validity of each individual creditor claim or permitted to determine the legal validity of the sovereign's proposal for debt restructuring? Other issues that could possibly be handled by the international tribunal (subject to prior contractual agreement by the parties) include the following:

- What constitutes sustainable debt for the sovereign in question (the IMF could be permitted to make submissions on this matter, even though it is not a party to the arbitration, possibly subject to certain confidentiality restrictions, given the sensitivity of the information)
- Whether the economic assumptions underpinning a restructuring plan are reasonable[7]
- Satisfaction of the commencement criteria for invoking the arbitration mechanism (for instance, the excusability of the default)
- Whether the parties have engaged in good faith negotiations
- The feasibility and reasonableness of any proposed restructuring plan
- Whether the debt in question constitutes a lodgable debt; if so, whether it constitutes an "odious debt"; and what, if any, implications follow from that determination.[8]

Who Is to Be Bound by the Tribunal's Decisions: Intercreditor Equity

An agreement could include a rule setting forth the degree to which a decision of the tribunal would be binding on other creditors. If the tribunal is empowered in its decisions to take into account issues of intercreditor equity, its decisions could be binding only on issuances that have their own arbitration clauses. The tribunal could then weigh, for instance, the different maturities, the risk level (rating) of each issuance, the promised interest rates, and all other relevant details.

The binding effect would extend only to creditors that agreed to subject themselves to arbitration when they signed the contract purchasing the sovereign's bonds or extending credit to the sovereign in some other manner (such as through bank loans). Creditors that did not sign a contract containing an arbitration clause would not be bound by the tribunal's decisions. Therefore, arbitration (as distinct from collective action clauses) can address the issue of nonconsenting creditors in a debt restructuring only to the extent that such creditors agreed to an arbitration provision in the underlying debt instruments.

This somewhat sobering legal conclusion does not exclude mechanisms designed to make quasi-voluntary participation in the sovereign debt tribunal process more attractive. One way to incentivize participation would be to bind the public sector, the banking sector, or both—for instance, upon the condition that a certain threshold portion of the private sector be bound.

Decisions by the sovereign debt tribunal would probably not constitute binding precedents, as a tribunal is not a common law court. However, depending on its authority—which, in turn, depends on its convincing and unbiased reasoning—its decisions (like those of existing arbitration tribunals) would form part of an evolving body of public law on sovereign debt restructuring that ultimately could lead to a well-established body of law on its own.

Triggers for Invoking the Arbitral Mechanism

The announcement of a default—as defined in the issuance contract—would trigger the use of the arbitration tribunal. Depending on how the parties draft the language of the arbitration clause, a default could commence even before such an announcement, when insolvency appeared imminent. The parties to a sovereign debt issuance should determine whether the tribunal's competence should include determination of whether the prerequisites of such a default trigger have materialized.

The agreement should also specify which side—only the sovereign or both the sovereign and creditors—shall be allowed to invoke the arbitration mechanism. Although from a disciplining perspective, it would appear to be preferable to bestow such a right on both sides, sovereigns may not be willing to allow creditors to subject them to such proceedings. Thus, for political reasons, pulling the trigger might be left to the sovereign debtor alone or to the sovereign debtor and creditors acting in unison.

Governing Law and Applicable Insolvency Rules and Principles

Which laws should govern the proceedings of the sovereign debt tribunal? If it is the law of a particular jurisdiction, should issues of public international law be included, in toto or partially? How should intercreditor equity be achieved in cases in which some bond holders will be judged under English law, whereas others will be judged under the laws of New York State or Germany?

Given the complexity and intricacy of these questions, it may be worth considering giving the institution that creates the arbitral tribunal (for instance, the United Nations) an option available for all bond issuances that the tribunal would (if agreed to by the parties to the relevant debt instrument) apply something like general insolvency rules and principles. For the sake of gaining the necessary global acceptance, these general rules and principles would not simply be the law of a particular jurisdiction but rather something along the lines of the "law merchant."

Such rules and principles might be found in the general principles of insolvency law established by leading international institutions (for example, the principles specified in the relevant texts of the World Bank 2005, the United Nations Commission on International Trade Law [UNCITRAL 2004], the IMF, and other international institutions). The insolvency rules that these international institutions have developed apply to commercial enterprises, however, rather than sovereigns. Some adaptation would presumably be required if the sovereign debt tribunal were to look to these principles for guidance.

After it has gained some experience, the tribunal could establish substantive rules regarding the treatment of sovereign debt restructurings. Creation of such rules would obviate the need to draft contractual clauses, as borrowers and debtors could simply add a reference indicating whether all, some, or none of these rules apply.

Representation of Creditors in the Arbitral Proceeding

For the sake of transparency, creditor participation is important. It is clearly not practical, however, for all sovereign creditors to participate in an arbitral proceeding. Creditors thus have to develop and specify a mechanism for creditor representation (see Buchheit 2009; Group of Ten 2002). For example, bondholders in a sovereign debt issuance could specify in one of the underlying debt instruments (the bond indenture, the trust indenture, another document) who would represent the creditors in the arbitral proceeding.[9]

If the bond-issuing sovereign wants a creditors' committee to represent creditors, the clauses have to address a variety of issues. How would the committee be selected and constituted? Would it consult with the larger body of creditors, or would it be the indenture trustee acting on behalf of and taking instructions from the bondholders in a prescribed manner? These issues need to be confronted head on before the issuance of the sovereign bonds. If they are not, the arbitration process may become unwieldy and unworkable.

Mediation as Precursor to Arbitration

As a complement to the proposal for a sovereign debt–restructuring tribunal presented here, it may be worth having the parties to a sovereign debt issuance consider whether they wish to require mediation, which by its nature is nonbinding on the parties, as a precursor to a binding arbitration procedure.[10] The parties could specify in their arbitration clause whether mediation is a necessary step to be exhausted before they are permitted to resort to arbitration. Even if mediation is not specified as a formal prerequisite to arbitration, the parties could still resort to mediation if they think it might help resolve disputes or otherwise advance the restructuring process. To inhibit procedural abuse (and to discipline stakeholders), it is probably necessary to impose time restrictions within which mediation would have to be initiated and completed.

The possibility of mediating disputes could provide parties with a less adversarial forum for resolving their disputes before they turn to a higher stakes and potentially more protracted and adversarial arbitration process. Whether or not mediation is a formal prerequisite to binding arbitration, it can be seen as a tool to bridge the differences between the parties on any outstanding negotiating issues, assisting them in any ongoing efforts to reach a restructuring agreement. In this light, mediation can be viewed as a useful mechanism for helping the parties reach the necessary thresholds of creditor support set forth in any applicable collective action clauses.

Financing and Support for an Arbitral Tribunal

The basic financing and support for the arbitral tribunal should come from the sponsoring organization (for instance, the United Nations or the country hosting the tribunal). This financing would need to cover the salary of the tribunal president, office space, and a small secretariat to handle general administrative matters, including keeping tribunal members abreast of current developments in sovereign debt restructurings and defaults and coordinating the roster of designated arbitrators. The parties to an actual arbitration proceeding would be solely responsible for defraying the costs of the arbitration, including the fees and expenses of the arbitrators, which can be significant.

Concluding Remarks

The proposal outlined here is merely the initial formulation of an idea. The idea may deserve serious consideration in order to address a problem that may grow more acute with the growing gaps between rich and poorer countries. As the United Nations (2004, p. 2) notes in its report *A More Secure World: Our Shared Responsibility*, "combating poverty will not only save millions of lives but also strengthen the State's capacity to combat terrorism, organized crime and proliferation. Development makes everyone more secure." Moreover, as globalization is increasing the complexity and the number of relevant actors in the world of sovereign finance, the need to develop a predictable and reliable procedure for resolving the problems of sovereigns in default is likely to become more pressing, requiring the attention of policy makers and stakeholders.

Successful use of the sovereign debt tribunal proposed here could build confidence for embracing broader objectives in the area of sovereign debt reform. Positive experiences—particularly a series of positive experiences—could increase the willingness of stakeholders in sovereign debt restructurings to consider other more fundamental reforms to the sovereign debt–restructuring process.

Notes

1. See also the Equator Principles (www.equator-principles.com).
2. Paulus (forthcoming) draws conclusions from the so-called Ultimatum Game in order to explain the prominence of any bankruptcy system.
3. This section is based on an unpublished paper written by the author and Steven T. Kargman.
4. For full information on the tribunal, see www.iusct.org.
5. In the spring of 2010, the German government came up with a proposal to enact a kind of insolvency law for overindebted states within the Euro Area. In this context, the establishment of an insolvency court was briefly considered. Ultimately, attempts to enact such a law were put off until some later time.
6. As these clauses will not be retroactive, problems are likely to arise for some time when debt obligations without such clauses exist alongside those with such clauses.
7. A sovereign may have overlooked obvious possibilities of reducing costs—by cutting the 13th salary for state employees, for instance, an important cost saver when this group is large.
8. To the degree that the issues listed include economic analysis, the pool of arbitrators must include some with expertise in economics.
9. There is a somewhat parallel mechanism in the determination of a trustee of an indenture.
10. Doing so would to a certain degree follow the example of ICSID's conciliation mechanism.

References

Bohoslawsky, Juan Pablo. 2009. *Créditos abusivos*. Buenos Aires, Argentina.

Buchheit, Lee C. 2009. "The Use of Creditor Committees in Sovereign Debt Workouts." *Business Law International* 10 (3).

Buchheit, Lee C., and G. Mitu Gulati. 2010. "Responsible Sovereign Lending." http://ssrn.com/abstract=1584624.

Buchheit, Lee C., and Jeremiah S. Pam. 2004. "The Pari Passu Clause in Sovereign Debt Instruments." *Emory Law Journal* 51 (869).

Buckley, Ross. 2009. "The Bankruptcy of Nations: An Idea Whose Time Has Come." *International Lawyer* 43 (1196): 1189–1216.

Couillault, Bertrand, and Pierre-Francois Weber. 2003. "Toward a Voluntary Code of Good Conduct for Sovereign Debt Restructuring." Banque de France, *Financial Stability Review,* June, Paris.

Deeb, Hadi Nicholas. 2007. "Project 688: The Restructuring of Iraq's Saddam-Era Debt." *Cleary Gottlieb Restructuring Newsletter* Winter: 3–10.

Galvis, Sergio J., and Angel L. Saad. 2004. "Collective Action Clauses: Recent Progress and Challenges Ahead." *Georgetown Journal of International Law* 35 (713). http://www.allbusiness.com/legal/3589138-1.html.

Gibson, Christopher S., and Christopher R. Drahozal. 2006. "Iran–United States Claims Tribunal Precedent in Investor-State Arbitration." *Journal of International Arbitration* 23 (521).

Group of Ten. 2002. *Report of the G-10 Working Group on Contractual Clauses.* www.bis.org/publ/gten08.pdf.

Gugiatti, Mark, and Anthony Richards. 2004. "The Use of Collective Action Clauses in New York Law Bonds of Sovereign Borrowers." *Georgetown Journal of International Law* 35 (815).

Hagan, Sean. 2005. "Designing a Legal Framework to Rescue Sovereign Debt." *Georgetown Journal of International Law* 36 (299).

Hopt, 2009. "Neues Schuldverschreibungsrecht–Bemerkungen und Anregungen aus Theorie und Praxis." In *Festschrift Eberhard Schwark,* ed. Stefan Grundmann, Christian Kirchner, Thomas Raiser, Hans-Peter Schwintowski, Martin Weber, Christine Windbichler. Munich: C. H. Beck.

IIF (Institute for International Finance). 2004. *Principles for Stable Capital Flows and Fair Debt Restructuring in Emerging Markets.* November. Washington, DC.

IMF (International Monetary Fund). 2005. *IMF Progress Report on Crisis Resolution.* www.imf.org/external/np/pp/eng/2005/092105.pdf.

Mayer, Christian. 2005. "Wie nähert man sich einem internationalen Insolvenzverfahren für Staaten?" *Zeitschrift für das gesamte Insolvenzrecht* 9 (454).

Michalowski, Sabine, and Juan Pablo Bohoslawsky. 2009. "Ius Cogens, Transitional Justice and Other Trends of the Debate on Odious Debts: A Response to the World Bank Discussion Paper on Odious Debts." *Columbia Journal of Transnational Law* 48 (1): 61–120.

Paulus, Christoph G. 2002. "Some Thoughts on an Insolvency Procedure for Countries." *American Journal of Comparative Law* 50 (3): 531–39.

———. 2003a. "Die Rolle des Richters in einem künftigen SDRM." In *Insolvenzrecht im Wandel der Zeit: Festschrift für Hans-Peter Kirchhof,* ed. Walter Gerhardt, Hans Haarmeyer, and Gerhard Kreft.

———. 2003b. "A Statutory Proceeding for Restructuring Debts of Sovereign States." *Recht der Internationalen Wirtschaft* 40: 401.

———. 2008. "The Evolution of the 'Concept of Odious Debts.'" *Zeitschrift für ausländisches öffentliches Recht und Völkerrecht* 68 (2): 391–430.

———. 2009. "Rechtliche Handhaben zur Bewältigung der Überschuldung von Staaten." *Recht der Internationalen Wirtschaft* 46: 11.

————. Forthcoming. "Ist das Insolvenzrecht wirklich eine Schlüsselmaterie für die Wirtschafts- und Finanzstabilität eines Landes? Der Versuch einer Antwort." In *Festschrift für Klaus Hubert Görg,* ed. Michael Dahl and Hans-Gerd Jauch.

————. Die Weltbank und das Insolvenzrecht.

Reinisch, August. 2003. "Ein Insolvenzrecht für Staaten?" *Wirtschaftspolitische Blätter* 50: 285.

Schier, Holger. 2007. *Toward a Reorganisation System for Sovereign Debt.* Leiden: Martinus Nijhoff Publishers.

Setser, Brad. 2008. "The Political Economy of the SDRM." Initiative for Policy Dialogue Task Force on Sovereign Debt, Columbia University. http://www.cfr .org/content/publications/attachments/Setser_IPD_Debt_SDRM.pdf.

Stiglitz, Joseph. 2003. "Odious Rulers, Odious Debts." *Atlantic Monthly,* November. www.odiousdebts.org/odiousdebts/index.cfm?DSP=content&ContentID=8577.

Szodruch, Alexander. 2008. "Staateninsolvenz und private Gläubiger–Rechtsprobleme des Private Sector Involvement bei staatlichen Finanzkrisen im 21." *Jahrhundert.*

UNCITRAL (United Nations Commission on International Trade Law). 2004. *Legislative Guide on Insolvency Law.* Vienna. www.uncitral.org/uncitral/en/ uncitral_texts/insolvency/2004Guide.html.

United Nations. 2004. *A More Secure World: Our Shared Responsibility.* New York: United Nations. http://www.un.org/secureworld/.

Waibel, Michael W. 2007. "Opening Pandora's Box: Sovereign Bonds in International Arbitration." *American Journal of International Law* 101 (4): 711–59.

World Bank. 2005. *Principles for Effective Insolvency and Creditor Rights Systems,* rev. ver. Washington, DC: World Bank.

14

International Lending of Last Resort and Sovereign Debt Restructuring

Eduardo Fernández-Arias

F inancial crisis—that is, the interruption of normal access to financing—
is a serious and growing threat to economic development in developing countries that are financially integrated with the rest of the world.
The crisis experience of the past two decades and the unrelenting pace of
financial globalization in the developing world point to an increasing need
for an international lender of last resort (ILLR) prepared to act when no
other lender is capable or willing to lend in sufficient volume to deal effectively with financial crises.

Progress in establishing an effective ILLR has been slow and unsatis-
factory for the most part. It is time to take advantage of the momentum
created by the empowerment of the International Monetary Fund (IMF) to
address the global crisis and the new multilateral impetus associated with
it. The proposal in this chapter supports and builds on recent initiatives
by the IMF concerning precautionary facilities. In particular, it brings debt
restructuring under the ILLR umbrella.

Crisis experiences since the Brady debt restructuring in several countries show that modern international finance is volatile and crisis prone.
The financial crises of emerging countries are becoming important sources
of lessons for an ever-wider set of countries with access to borrowing from
commercial sources. The recent global recession and attendant public debt
expansion have dangerously weakened solvency in a number of countries,
advanced and emerging alike. Jamaica's debt restructuring in 2010 may be
the first in a new wave after the dust of the global crisis settles.[1]

Although progress has been made in response to the recent crisis (IDB 2010), multilateral safety nets for financial crises remain full of holes.[2] Despite proposals to reform the international financial architecture to address liquidity crises and financial contagion in the new financial order that have been advanced for more than a decade, liquidity facilities remain inadequate.[3] Furthermore, no multilateral framework exists to deal with sovereign debt restructuring. In the past decade, restructurings have found their way—sometimes amicably, sometimes acrimoniously but always unpredictably and in ways that enrich imaginative lawyers (Panizza, Sturzenegger, and Zettelmeyer 2009).

This chapter discusses the intrinsic limitations on current ILLR facilities growing to become a generic solution to the problem of financial crises in emerging markets. It proposes instead an integrated system of specialized ILLR facilities that builds on existing institutional machinery and creates tiers to accommodate countries with different capacities. Such a system makes use of existing multilateral instruments to provide a transition path from liquidity to adjustment to debt restructuring depending on the circumstances as financial crises evolve and morph. The multilateral ILLR system proposed in this chapter would allow the international financial architecture to deal with country financial crises in a robust and consistent way despite the typical confusion as to whether liquidity, adjustment, or debt restructuring is necessary or sufficient to resolve the crisis.

The chapter is organized as follows. The first section characterizes the construct of ILLR, taking the traditional doctrine of lending of last resort in the domestic arena as a starting point. Based on the review of the limitations of this model in the international arena, the second section proposes a feasible ILLR framework that integrates liquidity provision with potential adjustment and debt restructuring. The third section goes one step further, exploring how legal reform to establish an international bankruptcy institution for sovereign creditors would substantially improve ILLR capacity to manage financial crises involving adjustment and debt restructuring. The fourth section discusses the supporting role of multilateral development banks in an ILLR system. The last section provides some concluding remarks.

Modeling ILLR after the Traditional Doctrine of Lending of Last Resort

It is natural to try to model ILLR on the basis of the traditional doctrine of lending of last resort (LLR) in the domestic context, which deals with both the prevention and the mitigation of financial crises of domestic institutions.[4] In this section, we characterize the traditional doctrine and then discuss the limitations of such a model in the international context (see Fernández-Arias 2010 for a more detailed analysis).

The traditional doctrine makes a critical distinction between liquidity and solvency crises. In the case of a liquidity crisis—that is, a financial crisis faced by solvent borrowers—there is a coordination problem: the provision of normal lending would result in a perfectly satisfactory outcome for all, but panicked or constrained lenders massively withdrawing financing create real adjustment costs and ultimately insolvency, thus self-validating the withdrawal. This kind of crisis is avoidable. By contrast, in the case of a solvency crisis—that is, a financial crisis suffered by an insolvent borrower—the mere disposition to lend or provision of liquidity by LLR will not restore normalcy and avoid the crisis. In this case, there is a single crisis equilibrium in which the LLR can help only by mitigating the adjustment costs of insolvency and adjudicating losses in an efficient, sustainable way.

Traditional Lending of Last Resort

To obtain the desired effects in liquidity crises, speed, certainty, and power are critical to bridge the financial gap and remove the unwarranted lack of investor confidence. Bagehot (1873) and subsequent researchers have proposed a number of principles for LLR for liquidity crises, which can be summarized as follows:

- Lend against any marketable collateral valued at its value in normal times.
- Lend in large amounts (on demand) at terms steeper than market terms in normal times.
- Establish the above principles ex ante and apply them automatically.

Because liquidity crises are characterized by the existence of multiple equilibriums (the good equilibrium is attainable by avoiding self-fulfilling expectations of lack of creditworthiness), the principles of LLR are calibrated to prices in normal times (that is, the good equilibrium). Penalty terms are applied to ensure that the capital of LLR is not used beyond the period of financial distress.

In solvency crises, bankruptcy proceedings incorporate the principles of applicable LLR, which can be summarized as follows:

- Provide or arrange emergency financing as a senior lender on an interim basis (in lieu of lending freely against collateral at penalty terms) to avoid the costly interruption of operations.
- Temporarily suspend rights of stakeholders to coordinate crisis management and debt restructuring while the insolvent institution is reorganized or liquidated.
- Establish the above principles ex ante and apply them automatically.

A practical difficulty in applying these principles is determining whether the crisis is a liquidity or a solvency crisis. The condition of illiquidity merits a temporary diagnosis, to be reversed if the provision of liquidity does not produce the expected normalization results. In addition to the risk of LLR financial losses, the natural tendency of beneficiaries to avoid restructuring and bet on resurrection suggests the need to err on the side of caution.

A less obvious cost of the difficulty of diagnosing the type of crisis is moral hazard. Moral hazard is not an issue in the case of lending into liquidity crises; it becomes relevant if a solvency crisis is misdiagnosed as a liquidity crisis (Fernández-Arias 1996). Moral hazard would also justify erring on the side of adjustment rather than financing.

Applying the Traditional Doctrine to the International Context

In cross-border LLR to sovereigns or ILLR, the consolidated public sector (including the central bank) replaces the domestic institution as the beneficiary of LLR.[5] The key difference between domestic LLR and ILLR is that ILLR is subject to sovereign risk. Sovereigns are not bound by laws enforceable in foreign courts. Because multilateral creditors are "preferred," however, the risk for a multilateral ILLR is smaller than for other creditors. Another difference connected to sovereignty is that a multilateral ILLR ought to take into account international linkages that may create important repercussions outside the beneficiary country and hold the key to solving financial distress in other countries. ILLR interventions in a specific country may be justified because of their international spillovers; LLR interventions are based only on the national interest.

In a liquidity crisis, the above principles could be applied by and large mutatis mutandis. Although in common practice sovereign collateral is not posted, the issue is immaterial as long as ILLR is applied in the presence of adequate financial safeguards ("sufficient implicit collateral"), because the provision of collateral serves the purpose only of ensuring that the LLR will not suffer financial losses at the expense of the beneficiary.

In a solvency crisis, the very concept of solvency needs to be redefined. Sovereign insolvency should be interpreted not as the ability to pay in a financial sense but as willingness to pay in an economic sense. Furthermore, the concept of bankruptcy reorganization needs to be redefined more specifically as the economic adjustment and policy reform needed to regain solvency, which may or may not include the debt restructuring typical in corporate bankruptcies. These differences are arguably not fundamental, in that the question of how to deal with a solvency crisis in an efficient way—which in the sovereign case means appropriate adjustment and debt restructuring—remains.

The traditional principles of ILLR are fundamentally inapplicable for a different reason: in the sovereign context, there is no equivalent to a bankruptcy code or a court to ensure enforcement of ILLR determinations limiting the property rights of stakeholders. In the absence of a bankruptcy-like institution, existing lenders have the right to flee, which opens the possibility that ILLR financing is siphoned off (a lender's bail-out). Furthermore, for the ILLR, it is difficult to catalyze new lending in the absence of granting seniority protection, which compromises the financial soundness of the rescue effort.[6] Finally, the ILLR cannot play a crisis management role; the same "equity holders and management" need to be retained.

The prudential regulation used in the traditional doctrine to limit moral hazard is also infeasible in the sovereign context because of unenforceability. Lending conditionality appears as a natural substitute (Cordella and Levy Yeyati 2005). The ILLR cannot mandate but can only add to what stakeholders agree to do unilaterally (for example, adjustment and reform) or under bilateral agreement (for example, market debt restructuring); its only power is to condition financial support on certain actions of stakeholders, such as policy conditionality (for example, with respect to a country's adjustment). The role of ILLR is constrained to the selective use of carrots and sticks concerning its own financing depending on the country's behavior.

Another key dimension in need of adaptation from the traditional doctrine of LLR to the international context is private sector involvement. The inability of granting senior status protection to fresh lending is a fundamental impediment to restoring the confidence of the private sector. ILLR could catalyze private sector lending in a financial crisis within the existing legal framework by using sufficiently powerful multilateral guarantees, but such a remedy would be prohibitively risky and costly. ILLR could encourage countries to contract insurance or insurance-like credit lines, perhaps triggering contingent credit lines when ILLR acts, but doing so would require the country's willingness to pay a substantial up-front premium (see Fernández-Arias 2007).

Impeding capital outflows may be a more effective way of securing additional financing. The Bretton Woods system conceived the use of capital controls to deal with capital flows precisely to ensure that capital mobility would not provoke financial crises (Fischer 1999). Insurance-like controls on capital outflows triggered by certain agreed-upon events in financial markets, such as a generalized "sudden stop" certified by the ILLR, could also be stipulated contractually and be part of the set of tools used to bail in private creditors in implicit financial crises. Of course, being market friendly, it would also entail an insurance premium cost.[7]

In all cases, ILLR needs to be expeditious. The need for speed is explicit in the case of preventing a liquidity crisis from developing into a solvency crisis. Speed is also critical in the case of adjustment and restructuring to prevent the economy from stalling for lack of an adequate arrangement among stakeholders.

Four unequivocally desirable characteristics of a feasible ILLR are similar to those inspiring the traditional doctrine:[8]

- *Power*—sizable support that is sufficient to meet short-term financial obligations and prevent a collapse (of either demand or supply) in a liquidity crisis or inefficient adjustment in a solvency crisis
- *Speed*—timely, immediate disbursements to prevent crises rather than cure their consequences or, if already under way, mitigate and resolve them at minimum cost
- *Certainty*—automatic (nondiscretionary) financial assistance according to prearranged mechanisms and conditions with an adequate repayment period to match extraordinary financial needs (uncertainty undermines confidence that the ILLR will do its job and fosters crises)
- *Focus*—low or no commitment fee, to incentivize the preventive use of the facility, and substantial charges on delivery without prepayment impediments, to disincentivize the use of facilities outside a financial crisis.

Four distinctive characteristics of a feasible ILLR must be borne in mind:

- *Financial safeguards.* In the absence of actual collateral or legal senior creditor status, ILLR financial safety needs a satisfactory country risk assessment.
- *Catalytic action.* In the absence of an international liquidity issuer and a bankruptcy framework to grant seniority to fresh money, a powerful ILLR function may need (prearranged) financial collaboration with official lenders and private sector to configure a coherent and sufficiently large interim financial crisis package.
- *Prudential conditionality.* In the absence of legally binding prudential regulation, the ILLR needs to resort to satisfactory prior compliance with prudential conditionality.
- *Adjustment (and debt-restructuring) conditionality.* In the absence of an enforceable bankruptcy system to reorganize stakeholders' claims in an efficient manner, the ILLR needs assurances from countries and lenders that solvency-related conditionality will be fulfilled.

An Integrated System of International Lenders of Last Resort

In contrast to domestic legal provisions, sovereign conditionality cannot be enforced. The system therefore needs to define what to do if a conditionality is not met or will likely not be met to an acceptable standard. To the extent that the fulfillment of certain prerequisites is critical for success-fully addressing a financial crisis, the ILLR needs to define standards for country eligibility.

The need for prudential and adjustment conditionality may involve both ex ante conditions of eligibility and ex post conditions of approval that deserve closer examination. Conditionality on economic adjustment, policy reform, and debt restructuring would stipulate the needed conditions to resolve a solvency crisis. Because ex post conditionality implies negotiating conditions of approval that collide with the principles of speed and certainty, it should be used only when the required adjustment or debt restructuring would otherwise be expected to be ignored or delayed and the solvency crisis left to drag on. Prudential conditionality is of little effect when applied ex post, after the horse has left the barn. Conditionality is better applied ex ante in lieu of missing regulation and bankruptcy codes. Therefore, ILLR would ideally define standards for eligibility precondi-tions to the maximum extent possible.

Ex ante country eligibility—on the basis of preset conditions of country economic health, as measured by the soundness of fundamentals, the qual-ity of the policies in place, and the degree of commitment to sustain them, including conditions pertaining to multilateral financial safety—covers both prudential conditions and conditions related to economic adjustment or restructuring. A policy framework aimed at promoting stability and quality adjustment could include the following features:

- Frameworks for financial system stability based on international standards
- Prudent macroeconomic liquidity policies, such as low short-term debt[9]
- Prudent fiscal policies, such as fiscal rules consistent with fiscal and public debt sustainability
- Sound monetary, fiscal, and exchange rate policy regimes to respond efficiently to shocks
- Constructive relations with official and private lenders and investors.

Given the element of sovereign country choice in ILLR, setting condi-tions, either ex ante or ex post, is far from equivalent to setting legally enforceable regulation or bankruptcy frameworks. The most favorable case is one in which the country's fundamentals and policy framework comply with desired prudential standards and are so strong that the coun-try can be presumed to be willing and able to react appropriately to adverse shocks autonomously. In this case, the ILLR could dispense with unde-sirable ex post conditionality. This situation is arguably the case of the recently established flexible credit line (FCL), which is based entirely on ex ante conditions of eligibility. The FCL is a substantial improvement over its predecessors and in many ways an approximation to the principles of a feasible ILLR outlined above. However, it is available to only the strongest countries. If eligibility conditions are sufficiently strict, a large number of countries would choose to remain outside the system rather than reform to meet the standard, something that is not consistent with a satisfactory ILLR system.

For all the benefits brought by providing incentives to countries to improve their fundamentals and policy frameworks to a high standard in exchange for ILLR qualification, there is the cost of denying ILLR to countries achieving lower standards. Because a fully powerful ILLR needs to be highly selective in terms of target countries, it would leave most countries unprotected; however, an ILLR protecting most countries would offer unnecessarily low protection to well-deserving countries. A menu of facilities catering to countries' capacities is thus needed to provide the best protection overall.

At the same time, ILLR features depend on the type of shock. At one extreme—the case of a global liquidity crisis—a widely available ILLR (subject to basic financial safeguards and possibly conditioned on internationally friendly policies) could greatly benefit most countries, even if their policy frameworks are substandard, at least if they do not require substantial adjustment to the shock, as is typically the case. In this case, the costs of exclusion are substantial. At the other extreme—the case of a financial crisis in an individual country, possibly prompted by concerns about its fundamentals and possibly requiring adjustment—stringent standards for eligibility may be needed to ensure that the resources are used effectively to solve the underlying problems. In this case, higher standards are needed.

The upshot is that a feasible ILLR, designed to address any type of shock generating a financial need, must be based on generic eligibility preconditions and minimal structure. The FCL is a perfect example. For a global liquidity shock, such as the generalized "sudden stop" to emerging markets after the Russian crisis, FCL standards or the eligibility conditions cited above would be too stringent. The recent global financial crisis came close to that situation. In fact, the economic downturn in developing countries was strongly associated with the liquidity profile of the countries' liabilities (Blanchard, Faruquee, and Das 2010). For most countries, standards weaker than those required for an FCL would have been enough for successful ILLR. At the same time, for a few countries, the global recession that followed the crisis affected them so severely that they are now in need of substantial adjustment and perhaps debt restructuring, which may require ex post conditionality.

In summary, eligibility conditions and operational characteristics of ILLR ought to be contingent on the type of shock or financial crisis in order to avoid inappropriate or excessive conditionality. A noncontingent ILLR is bound to lead to rigid, excessive conditionality in the case of widespread liquidity shocks of the kind seen repeatedly in the new global financial economy. A fully front-loaded ILLR is bound to be very selective and require excessively strong eligibility, leaving out countries that a weaker ILLR with more ex post conditionality may help.[10] What is needed is an integral system of specialized facilities that reflect the type of contingency prompting the financial crisis and allow for a transition path as country circumstances change, so that the system provides appropriate treatment to countries at all times. Such a system may look complex, but a simpler system is bound to be ineffective, in terms of protection power, country coverage, or both.

Fernández-Arias, Powell, and Rebucci (2009) group economies requiring ILLR into three categories:

- Economies with only liquidity problems, where little or no adjustment is needed
- Economies in which adjustment and reform are needed to regain solvency but debt restructuring is not expected
- Economies that require both adjustment and debt restructuring to regain solvency.

In what follows, I describe the specialized facilities envisioned for these three types of situations.[11] I propose an integrated system of specialized ILLRs or pillars, each designed to address a type of financial crisis or contingency and structured in tiers to accommodate countries' conditions and capacities. Upper tiers, with more stringent eligibility requirements, entail stronger automatic support and weaker ex post conditionality.[12] When one or more of the contingencies is triggered, each country would have access to the ILLR facilities in its tier. Certification of the right contingency entails a judgment that may be impaired by political economy reasons if it is not based on objective indicators. To the extent possible, objective indicators would therefore serve as presumptive evidence of the contingency triggers, barring explicit countervailing justification.

Liquidity Facility

One important contingency that merits special treatment is widespread liquidity turmoil or a generalized sudden stop, which could be certified by the ILLR on the basis of indexes such as the overall Emerging Markets Bond Index. This liquidity facility, which would be activated by a systemic liquidity crunch, as measured by these indexes, would liberally provide financing on an emergency basis. A basic tier, with minimal eligibility requirements, would cover all countries in good standing (that is, countries that are involved in IMF Article IV consultations and not in arrears), granting them automatic access to certain quotas (at steep rates to discourage unnecessary use of scarce funds except for the emergency at hand). A higher tier, with additional eligibility requirements related to solid fundamentals and policy framework (and low multilateral credit risk), would screen out countries at risk of developing solvency problems (Fernández-Arias and Hausmann 2002). Countries in this tier would have access to larger amounts of financing up front. Countries able to pledge marketable international collateral (for example, sovereign wealth fund assets) could receive additional liquidity. The establishment of this liquidity facility would reduce an individual country's incentives to accumulate excessive international reserves as self-insurance, a practice that is financially costly and systemically destabilizing.[13]

International financial safety nets fail to protect against a generalized liquidity crisis: facilities are mostly geared toward the possible need for adjustment in individual countries rather than the liberal provision of financing in the event of a systemic liquidity crunch. The recent global recession gave rise to the FCL, which provides unconditional financing to a handful of countries but is not specifically designed to address liquidity crises. The main novelty of the proposed liquidity facility lies in its ability to provide widespread automatic financial support triggered by objective indicators of a systemic liquidity crisis.

It is difficult to ascertain whether a financial crisis can be solved solely by providing liquidity; although it may be worthwhile trying this non-invasive recourse, the liquidity facility ought to consider the possibility that it may fail to solve the crisis and that solvency strengthening may be required. Weak fiscal sustainability indicators would inform such a presumption. If liquidity is not the solution, adjustment will be needed.

Adjustment Facility

I start with the case in which debt sustainability indicators suggest that adjustment and reform will be sufficient to ensure solvency, so that no debt restructuring is expected. Disregarding the need for debt restructuring requires a minimum standard of fundamentals and policy framework compatible with the level of indebtedness. At one extreme, the adjustment facility could include a top tier in the spirit of the FCL, designed for any adverse shock and granting ample financial support only on the basis of strong precondition requirements, with no ex post conditionality. A lower tier could be available to all countries exceeding some satisfactory standard of fundamentals and policy framework as an eligibility requirement. This tier would feature more limited automatic support up front and complementary ex post conditionality concerning economic adjustment and policy reform (always under the expectation that debt restructuring will not be needed). More than one lower tier could be created, with the level of the automatic up-front support dependent on the strictness of the eligibility requirements. This tiered approach has the advantage of providing breathing space to most countries not qualifying for the top tier to receive automatic support up front and then seamlessly arrange a traditional stabilization program with ex post conditionality.

Adjustment facilities have made considerable progress in increasing access to a first unconditional tranche for preselected eligible countries.

The debate over how to formalize precautionary contingent lines to supplement the FCL appears to point in this direction of combining up-front financial support with ex post conditionality. This proposal supports this trend and highlights the importance of a tiered structure for such facilities.

The system may also consider specific contingencies that would trigger additional lending on top of the previous facilities. For example, a supplementary facility may be associated with contingencies in which the predominant shock is exogenous to the country in question (for example, a collapse in terms of trade). This facility could give access to additional up-front drawing rights, to distinguish it from the case in which the financial crisis is triggered by internal events more likely associated with an inadequate policy framework. Such a facility would recognize that under this contingency, ex post conditionality is probably less necessary for the country to adequately adjust to the shock. The new element this proposal brings to this point is that facilities need to be designed not only for countries' capacities but also for the type of shock leading to financial need. Of course, facilities specialized in specific contingencies like this could also be organized in tiers.

Whether debt restructuring is needed to regain solvency is difficult to ascertain, but it usually becomes clearer as information on adjustment performance comes in and the market reacts to the country's developments. If the market expects debt restructuring, it is paramount to move quickly, before the financial situation unravels. In practice, debt restructuring usually takes too long to be implemented. A multilateral facility is therefore needed to help countries with unsuccessful adjustment programs to transition to debt restructuring.

Debt-Restructuring Facility

A debt-restructuring facility is needed. Debt restructuring and "bankruptcy protection" may be triggered by countries asking for protection from the ILLR against lenders and other claimants (and at the same time relinquishing access to the other facilities). Often, however, countries incur costly delays in restructuring their debt. Weak debt sustainability indicators and a negative review of the prospects of sensible adjustment and reform to avoid debt restructuring under the previous facilities would also prompt a switch to this facility.[14]

Eligibility for this facility ought to be as wide as possible, leaving out only countries unable to work under multilateral ILLR rules (for example, countries severed from Article IV consultations). Under this facility, the ILLR would establish whether debt restructuring is needed and manage interim financing, adjustment, and debt restructuring using the power of conditionality. The certification that debt restructuring is justified and under way would amount to a declaration of "excusable default" (Grossman and Van

Huyck 1988), which would reduce the reputational cost of nonpayment or emergency controls on capital outflows or even eliminate these costs if these actions are part of ILLR conditionality.

The novelty of this facility is that it brings debt restructuring under the ILLR umbrella and deals with it by financing a justified debt workout rather than pretending that adjustment is always a feasible solution to regain solvency and leaving it to the market to sort out insolvency if it is not. This proposal calls for a reconsideration of the debate that led to the abandonment of the Sovereign Debt Restructuring Mechanisms (SDRMs) announced by the IMF in 2001, this time in the context of an ILLR certifying and financing a justified debt workout.

Implementing the ILLR System

A practical system of ILLRs needs to confront a number of practical implementation problems. One class of problems has to do with political pressures on the ILLR to be more flexible with certain countries with political clout. In this regard, elements of automaticity and objectivity— rules rather than room for discretion—are helpful (Obstfeld 2009). A particularly difficult problem of this nature is how to disqualify a country that ceases to comply with eligibility criteria (for example, an FCL country after a negative semiannual review). Although the signaling value of such determination is unavoidable, the gradual removal of privileges (for example, through lower caps, steeper charges, or both) may help the transition. The tiered approach proposed could also help solve the problem of exit or disqualification by providing a smoother transition to a lower tier.

Another problem that has plagued this kind of facility is the stigma of joining a program designed to provide emergency financing. Fear of signaling weakness by doing so led to the total failure of the Contingent Credit Line (CCL) and subsequent predecessors of the FCL, all of which could otherwise have prevented crises, to attract clients. Although the FCL is by design accessible to a select group, which helps reduce the stigma problem, and has attracted three countries (Colombia, Mexico, and Poland), countries with the strongest policy frameworks have not joined, and it is not clear that the stigma issue has been overcome. Currently, countries are confidentially invited to make an informal application whose result would be communicated privately, so that there is no loss of reputation attached to being rejected (unless there is a leak at some point in the process). However, unless the strongest countries decide to apply, this system allows the stigma problem to persist. A system announcing the criteria used for eligibility would inspire more confidence and probably be an improvement, but it would not change the fact that the strongest countries would still presumably not participate. An alternative, transparent system would be to officially produce and disclose a list of eligible countries—that is, prequalify countries unilaterally—making sure that the strongest countries are included. By proactively producing the list of eligible countries in each tier based on set criteria, this alternative would reduce or eliminate the stigma problem. Such a system would also, however, publicly identify countries unqualified for each tier, suggesting that, although superior to the current system, it would not be unanimously acclaimed.

A key reason why countries have historically not relied on these facilities is mistrust that when funds are needed, there could be a last-minute impediment to disbursement approval, a last-minute push to extract (perhaps extraneous) conditionality. Preset eligibility for automatic up-front support for every ILLR tier would eliminate much of this worry for eligible countries (essentially for all countries if prequalification for eligibility were proactive). Nevertheless, uncertainty about ex post conditionality would persist. The new top-tier FCL, based exclusively on ex ante conditionality and no additional activation clause, solves this problem for the handful of countries eligible for it. However, even countries eligible for a FCL may mistrust the criteria that would be used for recertification every six months and be concerned about losing their qualification. Despite added flexibility in the setting and verification of conditionality, ineligible countries still face most of the same uncertainties of the past. Trust can be built by increasing transparency and incorporating trusted institutions into the process (a possible role for multilateral development banks and other multilateral institutions).

Radical Reform to ILLR: International Bankruptcy Framework and Sovereign Debt Restructuring

The absence of stipulated and enforceable laws akin to those governing bankruptcy proceedings significantly limits the ILLR when solvency and debt overhang considerations are dominant. As in the case of a domestic institution going through bankruptcy, efficiency calls for appropriate adjustment and debt restructuring, but the ILLR cannot rely on the traditional legal instruments to produce these results. Country conditionality may steer crisis resolution in the optimal direction, but it does not guarantee the kind of resolution that would be feasible with bankruptcy-like legal power, as strong conditionality may fail to be fulfilled and weak conditionality is bound to have limited effect. Control over the behavior of private creditors appears even less powerful. The impediments to effective private sector involvement in ILLR are critical, because the sheer size of private sector capital flows makes them fundamental to containing liquidity crises and managing solvency crises.

Because of sovereignty, it would be naive to propose the creation and empowerment of an international bankruptcy court similar to its domestic counterpart. Even if sovereigns attempted to cede ex ante some sovereignty prerogatives by accord in order to bring ILLR country conditionality closer to a legal framework, the commitment to such submission would be unenforceable. However, international legal reform to empower ILLR with respect to international lenders along the lines of a bankruptcy framework appears feasible, either by treaty or contractually, and may bring substantial improvements.[15] Law may not bind governments, but it may bind private creditors.

The absence of an international bankruptcy system creates two critical limitations with respect to financing adjustment in an insolvency situation. First, lenders and other stakeholders with conflicting interests cannot be forced to collaborate. Beyond coordination, the ILLR cannot supersede the rights of creditors to free ride and cash in; it cannot force them to wait until a viable debt-restructuring arrangement is designed and agreed to under efficient rules (a standstill on debt payments). Coordination among lenders is necessary but not sufficient for efficient restructuring.

Second, it is difficult to obtain new lending during the reorganiza-tion process, because there is no court able to grant seniority priority to interim financing, making it almost impossible to attract fresh private sec-tor financing to accompany ILLR (a point emphasized by Bolton and Skeel 2005). In the absence of legal power, ILLR is limited to indirect means of influencing private lenders, such as tying its financial support to their collective behavior and hoping that they are able to coordinate a rational response, as in lending into arrears. Without any mechanism for catalyzing private sector participation, ILLR may thwart the entire effort.

In this context, the SDRM proposal represented a moderate attempt to institute certain rules to facilitate creditors' collective action for debt restructuring in order to overcome these limitations without impinging on creditor rights (as in the imposition of a stay on payments and litigation or the imposition of junior status on old debt). It fell short of effectively addressing both limitations.[16]

As it stands now, countries can control financial flows in an insolvency situation only by using blunt and conflictive instruments, such as arrears and hastily arranged debt restructuring. True, the fear that impediments to collective action of post-Brady securitized debt holders would make sovereign debt-restructuring negotiations collapse and arrears permanent did not materialize, and debt exchanges were completed. Even in the best of circumstances, however, debt restructuring agreed upon on the basis of an offer that (some qualified majority of) lenders "cannot refuse" is a breach of contract, with nasty consequences for the future even in the absence of holdouts. Like arrears, the imposition of controls on capital outflows on the part of countries may be a way out in certain circumstances, but it may also carry enormous costs for the future if such controls poison the well of financial integration. ILLR can help diffuse the reputational cost of arrears by lending into arrears if a country is making a good faith effort at restructuring. It can also help by activating its lending and declaring the occurrence of certain financial contingencies that merit impediments on capital outflows, thus providing cover to countries exercising controls in those circumstances ("excusable" capital controls). However, all of these methods rely on individual countries' unilaterally breaching their obligations and living with the legal and reputational consequences.

The cleanest and safest way to achieve control over financial flows in a crisis situation while avoiding arrears or forced debt restructuring and capital outflow controls would be to endow the ILLR with legal powers to grant a standstill on international payments when a country's ability to service its debt is insufficient, based on rules similar to those governing standstill orders in a domestic bankruptcy court. In this way, the ILLR would provide a standard for "excusable" default. At the same time, countries not meeting the standard and unilaterally defaulting would be exposed as opportunistic in the judgment of the ILLR, increasing the reputation cost of frivolous default. Discriminating between justified and unjustified defaults and debt-restructuring terms, so that low default costs apply only to ILLR–certified debt restructuring based on technical criteria, is fundamental to ensure that the ex post efficiency gains of an orderly workout managed by ILLR do not translate into incentives to default opportunistically (Sturzenegger and Zettelmeyer 2007).[17]

The ability to legally impose a standstill on payments and capital outflows provides the flexibility needed to restructure while keeping sovereign risk under control, because a multilateral ILLR is an honest broker not suffering from the sovereign's willingness-to-pay problem (Fernández-Arias and Hausmann 2002). Granting this authority would empower the ILLR in three ways. First, it would enable the ILLR to disburse funds automatically, without concern that its lending could translate into increased capital outflows and little real effects. Second, it would help coordinate lenders and investors and buy time for an appropriate debt restructuring under equitable conditions for all involved. Third, by conditioning the lifting of the standstill on an appropriate debt-restructuring agreement, it would give the ILLR an effective instrument with which to ensure that adjustment and restructuring will be successful. This point is worth elaboration, because it is one of the main benefits of this radical legal reform.

As in domestic bankruptcy, stakeholders need to agree on an overall proposal for adjustment and debt restructuring. The interest of the ILLR is to promote a reorganization that combines country adjustment (including policy reform) and debt restructuring in a way that serves the best interests of the country. There are many ways in which such a combination may be faulty. Inadequate coordination by creditors may lead to chaos. Short-sighted governments may favor excessive debt reduction, hurting the country's prospects for future financing. Alternatively, debt restructuring may be negotiated too late, because governments do not want to face its political costs, preferring instead to "gamble for resurrection," which results in inefficient adjustment (Sturzenegger and Zettelmeyer 2007). Countries with unsound governments may engage in overadjustment followed by excessive debt reduction.

Even if creditors coordinate perfectly and governments maximize national welfare, debt reduction bilaterally agreed on by lenders and borrowers may be too shallow and fail to remove adverse debt overhang effects.[18] This is a distinct possibility if ILLR financing is perceived to depend on a country's postrestructuring financial needs, the typical case of a deep-pocketed third party taking advantage in a bilateral negotiation. The ability to maintain the standstill on payments until a satisfactory package on adjustment and debt restructuring is found and lenders agree, as well as the ability to remove such standstill if the country does not engage in adjustment and debt negotiations in a constructive manner, would provide powerful leverage to the ILLR on both adjustment and debt restructuring.

The other key element of legal reform is the ability of the ILLR to grant seniority to fresh interim lending. The alternatives to voluntary new financing reviewed earlier rely on substitutes of legal priority that are costly or difficult to obtain. If these substitutes are based on official guarantees, they are a contingent liability of ILLR and therefore costly. If they are based on insurance contracts or insurance-like provisions in debt contracts, they are difficult to implement and typically seen as too costly by short-sighted governments for traditional insurance aversion reasons. More generally, new lenders may be unable to provide fresh money because of legal interference by existing lenders in arrears. Legal seniority would resolve this issue by implicitly creating a built-in insurance mechanism. The country would implicitly pay for this (mandatory) insurance through higher spreads caused by the expected dilution costs of regular debt in the event of a financial crisis, thus aligning the allocation of costs and benefits of the risk covered.

By creating the conditions for fresh voluntary market financing, this legal power would act as a strong catalyst, reducing the financial resources needed by the ILLR. In the extreme, the ILLR would be able to concentrate on its management role rather than financing. In the absence of legal power to grant seniority status to fresh money, it is likely that new money will always have to come from official sources and require political agreement to sustain sizable funds.

The Role of Multilateral Development Banks in Supporting the ILLR

Official ILLRs include both multilateral and bilateral institutions. Unlike private sector lenders, which need to be granted substantial enhancements or somehow coaxed into lending into a financial crisis, multilateral development banks are natural components of an ILLR system, because they are guided by development goals that make them more willing to lend in riskier environments if social returns are high. At times of difficulty, or crisis, the risk of losses is high—but so is the corresponding social return of containing them. In parallel, given their preferred creditor status, multilateral development banks have a superior enforcement capacity to recover their capital at risk, which makes them more able to withstand risk. Both differences between multilateral development banks and private lenders become dominant in high-risk situations, such as severe downturns or financial crises.

These differences explain why private lending is procyclical and lending by multilateral development banks is countercyclical. The historical record and econometric analysis document that countercyclical lending by multilateral development banks replaces retrenching by private creditors (Fernández-Arias and Powell 2006; Levy Yeyati 2010). In the typical developing country, the share of multilateral development bank disbursements relative to private disbursements increases significantly during growth downturns and decreases in upturns.[19] More to the point, in the typical developing country, the level of multilateral development bank disbursements is inversely related to the rate of economic growth.

Although the institution at the center of ILLR functions is the IMF, coordination with other ILLRs is important for success. The question is whether the active countercyclical role of multilateral development banks during downturns and financial crises would remain under the ILLR system proposed above. The answer is probably yes, on several counts:

- ILLR applies only in extreme financial situations. Multilateral development banks modulate specific development projects and policy reform to the economic circumstances of countries, including by helping devise effective countercyclical fiscal policies where there is fiscal space that can accelerate economic recovery or by limiting the size of contractions while ensuring development value.
- Under a number of scenarios, multilateral development banks may be called on to be a partner of the ILLR. Because multilateral development banks are willing to lend in a financial crisis and to do so long term, under normal operations they are implicitly partners of ILLRs. The IMF may fail to serve as the ILLR because it is not permitted to disburse sufficient resources to a particular country. Under such circumstances, countries could benefit from multilateral development banks as explicit partners. It is also possible that for small countries, the IMF may find it more practical to delegate ILLR functions to multilateral development banks, subject to its supervision (Fernández-Arias, Powell, and Rebucci 2009). The ILLR will also miss opportunities because of country ineligibility, stigma, or mistrust; in these cases, partnering with multilateral development banks may be necessary to reach a constructive result. In particular, multilateral development bank participation may help build trust in ILLR adjustment and debt-restructuring views in solvency crises in particular countries.

- ILLR is critical for providing countries with a larger financial envelope to shape crisis policies; multilateral development banks are called upon in times of difficulty to participate in the actual reassignment of public sector activities within the available envelope. They contribute through project- and policy-based loans (including the reformulation of the loan portfolio). They support the development integrity of key aspects of the overall public expenditure framework, which may collapse under fiscal adjustment pressure; help design and protect social programs to contain the effects of recessions on the poor and future generations; and safeguard investment projects and policy reforms that may be victims of disorderly adjustment. Given the high volatility of economic activity in developing countries, which contributes to poor economic performance, these responsibilities are crucial for economic development. They cannot be addressed by an ILLR concerned only with macroeconomic balances. Participation of multilateral development banks would reduce the need for ILLR adjustment conditionality.
- Times of crisis may create opportunities to pursue growth-enhancing reforms, including development-oriented structural reforms through policy-based loans, that would otherwise not be undertaken. The IMF is in charge of monitoring the budget envelope in the short run; multilateral development banks focus on reforms that generate better frameworks for fiscal policy. Multilateral development banks can design fiscal institutions that not only serve the purpose of fiscal adjustment under ILLR but also ensure fiscal sustainability going forward. Their participation would improve ILLR conditionality.

In all cases of extraordinary financing of this sort, the IMF and multilateral development banks need to act in concert to ensure that the ILLR function is performed efficiently, in the context of an overall lending program. It is especially important that multilateral development banks refrain from lending more leniently than the IMF under contingencies covered by its ILLR facilities, because such competition would undermine the ILLR system. (Of course, this is equivalent to saying that the ILLR system is undermined if the IMF is harsher than multilateral development banks deem appropriate.) In the last analysis, an ILLR system needs to be agreed upon and coordinated by all multilaterals. For example, once an ILLR system is agreed upon, countries asking multilateral development banks for extraordinary financing may be required to ask for eligibility to ILLR facilities (if they do not already qualify for them), so that the ILLR assessment can be taken into account in determining the terms and conditions of such financing. This coordinated procedure would also strengthen membership in the ILLR system and secure prequalification, which is key for the success of a crisis prevention and mitigation tool in which speed and certainty are critical.

In a tiered ILLR system like the one proposed, the ILLR assessment is highly informative for a multilateral development bank willing to retain appropriate flexibility. For example, there should be a strong expectation that a country eligible for the top tier (for example, a country with an ongoing FCL arrangement with the IMF) could freely access extraordinary financing. In contrast, a country that would not qualify even for the lowest tier would be expected to be denied such financing. Without prejudging the overall conclusion on the part of the multilateral development bank, there would be a substantial burden of proof to overturn such presumptions on the basis of macrofinancial indicators and other relevant dimensions of the macroeconomic and structural policy framework as well as market-based indicators of country creditworthiness. For all other less clear-cut cases, ILLR status would be less decisive in forming the judgment of the multi-lateral development bank. The IMF's shorter-run focus and the market's exclusive concern with commercial credit risk mean that both may ignore longer-run sustainability and development issues that multilateral development banks take into account.

Concluding Remarks

As financial globalization deepens and spreads, there is a growing need for a system of ILLR to deal with financial crises in vulnerable countries. Multilateral progress to address liquidity and solvency crises has been inconsistent, with no meaningful distinction between the two; in particular, there is still no framework for sovereign debt restructuring. The proposals suggested in this chapter support and build on recent initiatives at the IMF to expand the facilities created in 2009 to address the global crisis on a permanent basis.

This chapter follows the strategy of adapting traditional domestic institutions of lending of last resort and bankruptcy resolution so that multilateral institutions can engineer a feasible ILLR. It proposes an integrated system of specialized ILLR facilities to address problems of liquidity, adjustment, and debt restructuring as situations evolve and the nature of the crisis morphs. Each facility is structured in tiers, defined by prequalification standards, to cater to countries' capacity. In all cases, facilities provide sufficient automatic support up front so that they can seamlessly arrange a country program, if needed, subject to minimum ex post conditionality.

Eligibility to facilities depends on both the strength of a country's fundamentals and the nature of the financial crisis (liquidity/solvency, systemic/country specific). For example, a facility designed to cover systemic liquidity crises would deliver substantial up-front lending to almost all countries in need, subject to monitoring to detect individual cases requiring transition to facilities addressing solvency crises. By contrast, idiosyncratic financial crises traceable to weak fundamentals would be addressed by an adjustment facility, which, except for its most select tier, would tie part of the financial support to some ex post conditionality.

The chapter also proposes legal reform to subject creditors to standstills and seniority dilution, as in domestic bankruptcy, thus empowering the ILLR to facilitate orderly workouts when debt restructuring is necessary to restore solvency. This reform would make efficient financial reorganization, including the attraction of (senior) new private lending, possible, thereby minimizing ILLR financial involvement. In this way, old debt would be diluted in the case of overindebtedness, and ex ante incentives of countries and creditors would become aligned. The debt-restructuring facility would be called by countries in need of "bankruptcy" protection or by the ILLR if other facilities proved insufficient to deal with financial crises in particular countries. The ILLR would set standards on "excusable defaults" and apply its financial muscle to help countries adjust and regain solvency, thus reducing the costs of justified restructuring while exposing frivolous defaults.

The IMF is at the center of the ILLR system, but multilateral development banks have a number of supporting roles to play in the system. All institutions involved in the system must act in concert to mutually reinforce country eligibility for emergency facilities.

Notes

The author is thankful for insightful discussions with Alessandro Rebucci and comments by Anna Gelpern, three anonymous referees, and participants at the two Sovereign Debt and Financial Crisis conferences, one held in Tunis in March 2010 and the other held in Washington, D.C., in June 2010.

1. Greece's collapse, which occurred after this chapter was written, provides another warning.

2. For an analysis of the failed attempts at establishing safety nets for financial crises in the past and the shortcomings that persist, see Fernández-Arias (2010).

3. See, for example, Fernández-Arias, Gavin, and Hausmann (2000) and other chapters in IDB (2000), based on the Washington Conference on World Financial Stability held in the wake of the Russian crisis.

4. Fernández-Arias, Gavin, and Hausmann (2000) and Fernández-Arias and Hausmann (2002) also model international financial architecture after the classical principles of LLR to domestic banks (liquidity crises) and domestic bankruptcy institutions (solvency crises), subject to sovereignty constraints. This section draws heavily on both papers.

5. There are intermediate cases not addressed here. There is the issue of the proper role of the central bank in using its reserves to bankroll the fiscal accounts in a financial crisis; I sidestep this issue and purposely consolidate the entire public sector facing a financial crisis requiring support from abroad. In a globalized economy, the power of the traditional domestic LLR becomes more limited because

of currency mismatch between lending power and financial needs as well as the global repercussions of domestic lending. The internationalization of firms may also lead to cross-border LLR to private institutions.

6. Some assurance to private sector lenders would also be desirable in the case of liquidity crises.

7. Insurance-like mechanisms need to be arranged ex ante and may very well be part of multilateral conditionality. This chapter focuses on ex post mechanisms with which to respond following the onset of financial crises.

8. For an early proposal along these same lines after the liquidity crises in emerging countries of the 1990s made it clear that ILLR needed to break with the past, see Fernández-Arias, Gavin, and Hausmann (2000).

9. A policy framework could also include adequate insurance-like arrangements.

10. Excessive conditionality may also result from an ILLR designed to use the countries' need in times of crisis to extract (ex ante or ex post) extraneous conditionalities not actually needed to ensure the effectiveness of a particular ILLR operation. Such an action may lead to unnecessary crises in countries not willing to further "optimize" their policy frameworks. Experience shows that official views on optimal policies are not infallible, which calls for caution and parsimoniousness in designing pertinent, let alone extraneous, conditionality.

11. Just as a presumed liquidity crisis may develop into or turn out to be a solvency crisis requiring other facilities, the expectation that debt restructuring is not needed may require revision and a change of facility.

12. I prepared a first draft of this proposal in 2009 (IDB 2010). After the note was written, it was brought to my attention that an IMF Staff Position Paper (IMF 2009) also envisioned a variety of scenarios and country eligibility requirements for ILLR that are broadly compatible with my own (albeit not integrated with a debt-restructuring function).

13. This point is moot in countries in which the driver of reserves accumulation is export promotion rather than risk management.

14. Arrears (which would disqualify countries for the other facilities) would also be an indication that this facility is needed, with the same caveat applied to customary policies of lending into arrears of good faith negotiation with private creditors.

15. The precedent of the UN Security Council protecting Iraq's oil assets against foreign creditors, valid in the jurisdictions of all country members, offers a model of how existing institutions may help shape this legal reform.

16. The proposal did envisage a standstill on payments (the "hotchpot" rule). Even this moderate proposal was shelved, however, in favor of a contractual approach to the problem to include collective action clauses in new bond issues, which are now the standard.

17. If default costs were reduced indiscriminately, incentives to default would increase (Dooley 2000).

18. In the absence of risk-sharing features such as GDP-linked coupons, the negotiated debt reduction is likely to be too limited to enable lenders to potentially extract higher payments later on.

19. This pattern suggests that the growing financial integration of most countries will lead to an increasing need for countercyclical support.

References

Bagehot, W. 1873. *Lombard Street: A Description of the Money Market*. London: H. S. King.

Blanchard, O., H. Faruqee, and M. Das. 2010. "The Initial Impact of the Crisis on Emerging Market Countries." *Brookings Papers on Economic Activity*, forthcoming.

Bolton, P., and D. Skeel. 2005. "Redesigning the International Lender of Last Resort." *Chicago Journal of International Law* 6 (1): 177–202.

Cordella, T., and E. Levy Yeyati. 2005. "A (New) Country Insurance Facility." IMF Working Paper 05/23, International Monetary Fund, Washington, DC.

Dooley, M. 2000. "International Financial Architecture and Strategic Default: Can Output Losses Following International Financial Crises Be Avoided?" NBER Working Paper 7531, National Bureau of Economic Research, Cambridge, MA.

Fernández-Arias, E. 1996. "Balance-of-Payments Rescue Packages: Can They Work?" Working Paper 33, Inter-American Development Bank, Research Department, Washington, DC.

———. 2007. "Riesgos de integración financiera internacional en países en desarrollo: desafíos y oportunidades." *Revista del Fondo Latinoamericano de Reservas* 3 (Junio): 49–58.

———. 2010. "International Safety Nets for Financial Crises." Working Paper 192, Inter-American Development Bank, Research Department, Washington, DC.

Fernández-Arias, E., M. Gavin, and R. Hausmann. 2000. "Preventing Crisis and Contagion: The Role of International Financial Institutions." In *Wanted: World Financial Stability*, ed. E. Fernández-Arias and R. Hausmann. Baltimore, MD: Johns Hopkins University Press.

Fernández-Arias, E., and R. Hausmann. 2002. "The Redesign of the International Financial Architecture from a Latin American Perspective: Who Pays the Bill?" In *Debating the Global Financial Architecture*, ed. L. Elliott Armijo. Albany: State University of New York Press.

Fernández-Arias, E., and A. Powell. 2006. "Multilateral and Private Sector Sovereign Lending: What Makes MDBs Different?" Inter-American Development Bank, Research Department, Washington, DC.

Fernández-Arias, E., A. Powell, and A. Rebucci. 2009. "The Multilateral Response to the Global Crisis: Rationale, Modalities, and Feasibility." Working Paper 683, Inter-American Development Bank, Research Department, Washington, DC.

Fischer, S. 1999. "On the Need for an International Lender of Last Resort." Paper presented at the joint luncheon of the American Economic Association and the American Finance Association, New York, January 3.

Grossman, H., and J. Van Huyck. 1988. "Sovereign Debt as a Contingent Claim: Excusable Default, Repudiation and Reputation." *American Economic Review* 78 (5): 1088–97.

IDB (Inter-American Development Bank). 2000. *Wanted: World Financial Stability*, ed. E. Fernández-Arias and R. Hausmann. Baltimore, MD: Johns Hopkins University Press for the Inter-American Development Bank.

———. 2010. *The Aftermath of the Crisis: Policy Lessons and Challenges Ahead for Latin America and the Caribbean*, coordinated by A. Izquierdo and E. Talvi. Washington, DC.

IMF (International Monetary Fund). 2009. *The Debate on the International Monetary System*. IMF Staff Position Paper SPN/09/26, Washington, DC.

Jeanne O., D. J. Ostry, and J. Zettlelmeyer. 2008. "A Theory of International Crisis Lending and IMF Conditionality." IMF Working Paper 08/236, International Monetary Fund, Washington, DC.

Levy-Yeyati, E. 2006. "Optimal Debt? On the Insurance Value of International Debt Flows to Developing Countries." *Open Economies Review* 20 (4): 489–507.

Obstfeld, M. 2009. "Lenders of Last Resort in a Globalized World." *Monetary and Economic Studies* 27(1): 35–52.

Panizza, U., F. Sturzenegger, and J. Zettelmeyer. 2009. "The Economics and Law of Sovereign Debt and Default." *Journal of Economic Literature* 47 (3): 651–98.

Sturzenegger, F., and J. Zettelmeyer. 2007. *Debt Defaults and Lessons from a Decade of Crises.* Cambridge, MA: MIT Press.

Part IV

Managing Public Debt in Crises: How Experiences Differ

15

Managing Public Debt and Its Financial Stability Implications

Udaibir S. Das, Michael G. Papaioannou,
Guilherme Pedras, Jay Surti, and Faisal Ahmed

Sovereign debt has traditionally received much attention as a crucial component of a country's macroeconomic and financial policy framework. Indeed, past crises have been triggered by debt crises. The recently heightened attention on sovereign risk from policy makers and financial markets stems from the realization that how debt is managed considerably influences the soundness and solvency of the overall public sector balance sheet. Debt management is also perceived as an important factor that underpins the credibility and reputation of a sovereign, and conditions the stability of debt capital markets and the financial institutions that hold public debt. The sharp increase in debt levels in developed countries and the recent contagion fears in Euro Area countries through the banking systems have reinforced this perception.

This chapter explores the relationship between the level and management of public debt and financial stability, and explains the channels through which the two are interlinked. It suggests that the broader implications of a debt management strategy should be carefully analyzed by debt managers and policy makers in terms of their impact on the government's balance sheet, macroeconomic developments, and the financial system.

An extensive body of literature examines how the stage of financial market development affects the structure of public debt in a country and how fiscal policy and the resulting level of debt affect macroeconomic stability. However, to the best of our knowledge, researchers have not comprehensively analyzed how debt and debt management contribute to financial stability.[1] Moreover, only recently have some studies explicitly acknowledged the role of the proper management of domestic public debt in promoting macroeconomic-financial stability. Reinhart and Rogoff (2009) point out that cases of default and restructuring of domestic public debt are far more common than those of external public debt, implying that more attention should be devoted to the domestic debt episodes.

Allen and others (2002) propose a framework for exploring the debt portfolio management and macroeonomic-financial stability nexus by examining the implications of alternative combinations of cross-sectoral balance sheets within the economy. An analytical model explains a financial crisis in emerging markets as a function of the balance sheet vulnerabilities of different sectors of the economy to exogenous shocks and the way in which such sector-specific vulnerabilities spill over to other sectors. Rosenberg and others (2005) explore the role of (private and public sector) debt-related vulnerabilities in emerging markets' financial crises.

The lack of adequate data remains a serious constraint on this type of analysis. Jeanne and Guscina (2006) use a database on government debt covering 19 emerging market countries since 1980. They present stylized facts on debt structures and show that there are significant differences in structures across countries from different regions of the world. Using the same data set, Guscina (2008) shows that a country's debt structure often reflects its recent past macroeconomic background, which materially affects its financial stability.

Although the models developed in these papers allow for analysis in both closed- and open-economy settings, the models have been applied primarily to open-economy settings, which allow researchers to get a better handle on the dynamics of the development of capital account crises. Clearly, however, unsustainable domestic debt levels caused by factors such as expansionary fiscal policy, under fixed-exchange rates or exchange-rate bond arrangements, can also lead to currency crises, with large, discrete devaluations and substantial macroeconomic dislocation. Where ineffective capital controls are in place, financial stability can be compromised by the depletion of foreign exchange reserves (Krugman 1979). Although the story is once again one of debt levels, it highlights the constraints imposed on public debt management by macroeconomic policy and the policy regime. Public debt management represents optimization in the cost-risk space within the constraints set by macroeconomic policy; in the long run, even the best public debt managers cannot substitute for unsound policy making.

At a strategic level, debt management plays a vital role in securing the economic benefits of a sound policy framework in several ways. First, improvements in the debt structure can be an essential complement to fiscal consolidation in ensuring a robust recovery in a postcrisis environment. Second, such improvements, when implemented opportunistically (that is, during a cyclical upswing), can strengthen the effectiveness of countercyclical macroeconomic policy going forward, at a relatively low cost. Measures include the substitution of debt denominated in domestic currency for foreign currency or foreign currency–linked debt; an extension of the maturity profile of the debt portfolio at a reasonable cost; the assignment of maturity brackets that avoid a bunching of refinancing need; and a widening of the investor base through, for example, attracting foreign investors into the domestic debt market.

The task is operationally complex and requires debt managers to make difficult trade-offs. The goal of avoiding the bunching of maturities, for example, may have to be evaluated against the goal of establishing an issuance volume substantial enough to ensure adequate liquidity in the security.[2]

A complex strategic issue for debt managers that has important implications for macroeconomic-financial stability is the decision to broaden the investor base by attracting foreign investors. Some recent studies focus on the role of foreign investors in reducing the cost of sovereign debt issuance. Peiris (2010), for example, estimates the impact of the entry of foreign investors on the volatility and level of emerging markets' government bond yields, concluding that the significant presence of foreign investors could reduce borrowing cost. It is important for governments to bear in mind the cost-risk trade-off of attracting foreign investors as a strategy for broadening the investor base.

In an ideal world, debt managers would be able to issue the low-cost paper demanded by foreign investors through a liability structure in which their exit is negatively—or weakly—correlated with macroeonomic risk factors or exit triggers for other investors.[3] If this is not possible, the low issuance cost may come at a heavy price in terms of riskiness of the debt sold to foreign investors. Although in some cases foreign lenders have contributed to the demand for longer-term instruments, in others they may prefer points on the yield curve that carry substantial refinancing risk for the sovereign; in the case of domestic debt, they may want to index the bonds to the exchange rate or the rate of inflation. Depending on the country and the point in the business cycle, this could be very risky. Carry-trade investors can be drawn in at relatively low rates conditional on maintenance of an open capital account, but resulting debt maturities are typically short and positions often rapidly unwound if macroeconomic conditions deteriorate. Thus, the volume and nature of foreign investors' presence in the domestic debt market need to be carefully assessed in raising and managing public debt.

In addition to strategic improvements through a long-term plan of action, debt managers play an important role in stabilizing markets through tactical decisions. Active liability management through tactical market intervention can serve the goal of stabilizing markets by sending an unambiguous signal regarding the debt manager's intent and ability to secure the value of its obligations to investors. Moreover, debt managers' mature perspective on the impact of alternative debt restructuring strategies on market expectations is valuable in promoting financial stability. Kumhof and Tanner (2005) observe that debt managers are more reticent than the academic literature in proposing debt default or debt restructuring, given the potential damage these events can inflict on the financial sector.

The chapter is organized as follows. The next section defines financial stability. The following section outlines, in general conceptual terms, the contribution of public debt and debt management to financial development and financial stability. The third section follows up with an in-depth discussion of recent country experiences that illustrate the channels through which sound debt management practices can bolster financial stability by complementing improvements to the macroeconomic policy framework. This section also outlines the relevance of these factors and channels for countries at different stages of economic and financial development. The fourth section briefly describes commonly used risk mitigation policies. The last section offers some concluding remarks.

Defining Financial Stability

Financial stability can be broadly considered as stability of financial markets, reflected in a low level of volatility of a number of economic and financial indicators, including prices, the money supply, credit to the private sector, the exchange rate, equity prices, bond spreads, interest rates, and cross-currency swap rates, among others. A traditional and intuitive notion of financial stability can focus on a single dimension (price) and a single characteristic (low volatility) at relevant frequencies. Some examples include the nominal exchange rate of the domestic currency, stock indexes, bond yields, oil and commodity futures, and valuation of derivatives contracts (for example, credit default swap or asset swap spreads).

Dislocations are not always accompanied, or generated, by volatility in the price domain, however. They also stem from imbalances in the quantity domain (that is, in demand and supply imbalances). A broader definition would thus encompass the magnitude and volatility of bid-ask spreads quoted by market makers and of trading volume and turnover in key markets.

Houben, Kakes, and Schinasi (2004) suggest three main roles of finance in modern economies that could help develop a broader definition of financial stability. They include the promotion of an efficient allocation of real economic resources across activities and time, the facilitation of the transformation of maturities to meet lenders' and borrowers' needs, and the appropriate pricing and management of financial risks.

Schinasi (2004) makes three observations that can be used in defining financial stability:

• Financial stability is a broad concept, encompassing different aspects of finance (infrastructure, institutions, and markets).
• Financial stability implies that resources and risks are allocated and priced efficiently and that the system of payment functions smoothly.
• Financial stability relates not only to the absence of financial crises but also to the inherent ability of the financial system to avoid, contain, and deal with imbalances that could pose a threat to the system or to economic processes.

One criterion in evaluating financial stability would be whether the system allows a smooth flow of funds, so that savings can be efficiently channeled into investments. This criterion presupposes the existence of financial intermediaries that are able to efficiently manage portfolio risk. Given the centrality of government finances in most countries, it presupposes that, all other things equal, financial intermediaries are willing and able to hold government bonds that carry low default and extension risks and are liquid. Government securities are endowed with the characteristics necessary for them to constitute a benchmark relative to which the risk features of other (financial) assets in the economy can be measured. Governments, particularly debt managers, play a crucial role in securing low risk and high liquidity for sovereign bonds.

A definition that can thus be used here is "a financial system is in a range of stability whenever it is capable of facilitating (rather than impeding) the performance of an economy and of dissipating financial imbalances that arise endogenously or as a result of significant adverse and unanticipated events" (Schinasi 2004, p. 8). This definition, although flexible, may not allow for a specific quantitative measurement. The concept of financial stability needs to address possible impacts (positive and negative) of exogenous and endogenous shocks on the structure of the financial system and even to the economy in a concrete sense.

Public Debt, Debt Management, and Financial Stability

The state of government finances, financial stability, and real sector performance and prospects are codependent. This linkage becomes painfully apparent during recessions triggered by a financial crisis. It is especially apparent for banks, which typically (need to) hold an adequate quantity of government paper. They do so for several reasons: to conserve on equity capital funding cost, as the risk weight on this investment is typically nil; to meet the regulatory and internal risk limits on liquidity buffers; and to meet regulatory constraints concerning asset classes eligible for investment of regulatory capital instruments.

Reflection suggests that the linkage between government finances and financial stability is symmetric through the cycle. In an upswing, the quality of financial institutions' exposure to the government is high, as public bonds carry low default, extension, and liquidity risk. Moreover, the ease of issuance facilitates establishment of government securities as a benchmark for efficient pricing of private sector credit, often at a low spread during a boom. During a downswing, especially in the case of a recession triggered by a financial sector dislocation, maintenance of the asset quality of the government's liabilities, although far more elusive, is much more critical in containing adverse developments in the real and financial sectors.

For banks this is so because the quality of exposure to the private sector sinks rapidly, as measured in terms of either credit or liquidity risk. Government finances that are not in good order to begin with can greatly exacerbate the downturn and prolong the recovery. Recent cases of major macroeconomic-financial crises include a number of examples in which the public debt structure was in a weak starting position (for example, the debt stock was high, the time to maturity of a significant proportion of the outstanding volume of public sector debt was very short, or too much government debt was either floating rate or foreign currency–denominated or linked).

A weak debt structure greatly inhibits the sovereign's ability to conduct effective countercyclical macroeconomic-financial policy. Market participants typically reassess the risk of public liabilities with potentially rapid and substantial ratings downgrades, which limit borrowing capacity because of the narrowing of the investor base and the increase in issuance cost. It also exacerbates pressure on financial institutions' balance sheets, incomes, and capital reserves, particularly where marking to market of government securities in financial institutions' portfolios implies reductions in income and through an increase in the risk weight—for banks using advanced Internal Ratings Based (IRB) methodologies under Basel-II—a reduction in capital. Finally, from an investor's perspective, market pessimism can narrow the investor base for the sovereign's issues, which may translate into reduced liquidity of public debt.

The need for state-sponsored systemic bank resolution and restructuring in a recession hampers the government's ability to smoothly and credibly carry out such operations, substantially increasing the real and fiscal costs of the crisis. Rising costs, in turn, exert a negative impact on government finances, potentially generating a vicious cycle. Some of this dynamic appears to be on display in the recent crisis episodes, where the sharper real sector and labor market impact and relatively poor starting positions of the public debt portfolio in some countries fed off each other.

The debt to GDP ratio decreased in many emerging market countries over the past decade (figure 15.1). The opposite pattern can be observed for most developed market economies, highlighting the increasing importance of public debt for this group of countries.[4]

In general, the presence of a well-functioning government debt market helps build and develop efficient financial markets. Financial market

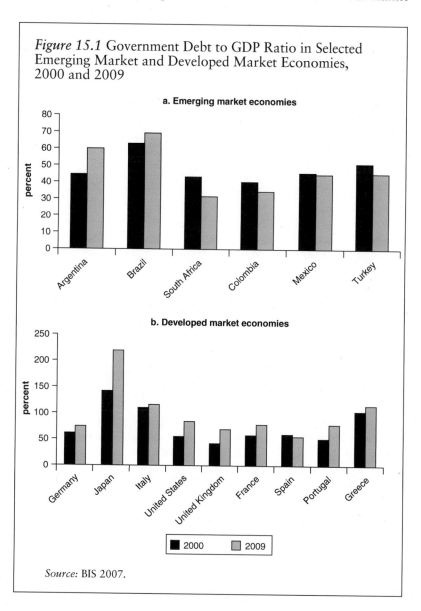

Figure 15.1 Government Debt to GDP Ratio in Selected Emerging Market and Developed Market Economies, 2000 and 2009

Source: BIS 2007.

development is essential for ensuring stable economic growth. A sound financial market allows a country's savings to be channeled into investments in a more effective way. More efficient financial markets also allow for longer-term loans for individuals and companies. Such loans help boost investment in a more stable way, allowing the financial system to promote an efficient allocation of capital and transformation of maturities. Given their size and lower risk relative to other domestic issuers, public debt issues are the appropriate instrument with which to facilitate this process. The instruments should be designed to contribute to the development of deep and liquid government bond markets upon which private sector funding in the economy can be benchmarked.

Actions taken and policies implemented by debt managers can promote financial market development and financial stability. Their role has gained elevated status in the context of managing the effects of the recent crisis, during which debt levels in many countries rose significantly in a relatively short period of time. Increases in debt levels have heightened the pressure on markets to meet the higher funding needs of governments, which risks driving up yields and generating a suboptimal composition of debt structures (because, for example, of the temptation to sell a debt stock with a shorter maturity profile).

Debt management strategy is an essential complement to sound macroeconomic policies, an appropriate political environment, and the judicious choice of policy regime in achieving financial stability. It can be used at favorable points in the cycle to reduce risk at low cost. For example, fiscal consolidation in a postcrisis phase is often an essential policy ingredient in ensuring a robust recovery. Its beneficial impact can be bolstered through the gradual extension of the maturity profile of public debt, changing the debt mix in favor of nominal bonds issued in domestic currency.

How Debt Management Affects Financial Stability: Some Recent Experiences

This section discusses the implications of the level and composition of debt on financial stability. Analytically, financial stability can be viewed as a function of the level of the debt stock, the debt profile, the investor base, the stage of development of the capital market, and institutional factors. In what follows, we analyze the manner in which each of these factors can contribute to financial stability.

Stock of Public Debt

The debt stock can affect financial stability through several channels. First, as shocks to the variables that determine the value of debt instruments can influence future fiscal costs, the debt stock can affect the government's balance sheet. In this regard, debt sustainability analysis should be conducted and results closely monitored, in order to spot future solvency problems. High levels of debt should also trigger policies for mitigating possible higher inflation rates and, in some extreme cases, deriving restructuring schemes. In particular, if debt is too high, the sovereign's credibility becomes less ensured in the eyes of international investors, which could result in higher volatility caused by difficulties in refinancing government debt, which in turn could trigger wider financial instability.

Second, a higher stock of public debt entails a higher probability of affecting the prices of financial assets, correspondingly influencing the soundness of the financial sector balance sheet. This impact will depend not only on the amount but also on the structure of the assets held by financial institutions.

The current stock of debt is often a consequence of past monetary and fiscal policies. It is not under the control of debt managers or part of their responsibilities but rather an important input to their mandate. Debt managers must make several decisions within these constraints that can affect financial stability. In general, the higher the debt stock, the greater the impact of such decisions.

Debt Structure and Composition

Different sources of vulnerabilities may arise from the debt profile, depending primarily on the debt structure (the composition of debt instruments and their maturities) (Bolle, Rother, and Hakobyan 2006). Inappropriate debt structures could become channels or sources of vulnerabilities to the real economy and the financial system (Borensztein and others 2004). The debt structure should pose low risk, not only for the government but also for markets. The literature has focused on two sources of vulnerabilities, foreign currency–denominated liabilities and the short maturity of liabilities (Papaioannu 2009; for a brief overview of the literature, see Guscina 2008).

Inappropriate debt structures can lead to higher interest payments. In general, lower-cost debt structures (such as the excessive use of foreign currency–denominated debt) are subject to higher risk in the event of an unexpected shock. In the past, many emerging market countries, especially in Latin America, relied heavily on the issuance of instruments linked to the exchange rate. Mexico's case during 1994 is a good example. At the end of 1994, the Tesobonos (domestic bonds linked to the U.S. dollar) represented almost the entire stock of domestic debt, up from just 4 percent a year earlier. This increase alarmed international investors. At the end of 1994, the domestic currency was devalued. The devaluation led to a significant increase in the debt stock and consequently to significant financial instability. Not long afterward, Mexico's financial instability spread to the region. This episode is a clear example of how a poor debt structure can have adverse financial consequences (Jeanneau and Verdia 2005). After the crisis many Latin American countries improved the composition of their debt and developed their domestic debt markets, in order to become less vulnerable to debt-related shocks (figure 15.2), a pattern also seen in Asia after the financial crisis that hit that region.

The change in the composition of domestic public debt between 1995 and 2008 clearly indicates efforts by Latin American countries to improve their debt profile (figure 15.3). They did so by reducing their debt exposure through the issuance of fewer exchange-rate-linked and more inflation-linked bonds, which tend to be of longer maturity. These strategies aimed not only to reduce the foreign exchange risk but also to reduce refinancing risk.

It is possible that sound debt management choices were rendered feasible by salutary changes in macroeconomic policy regimes taken in an external environment conducive to economic recovery and growth (figure 15.4). Where these policy changes were robust to domestic and external business cycle shocks, changes in debt structure proved to be beneficial to macroeconomic-financial stability in the longer run. In other cases, debt management efforts alone were unable to substitute for weaknesses in the policy framework to cope with cyclical shocks.

Brazil phased out exchange-rate bonds, considerably reducing exchange rate risks; for the past several years, it has tried to use floating-rate bonds and inflation-linked bonds to increase the average maturity of the debt

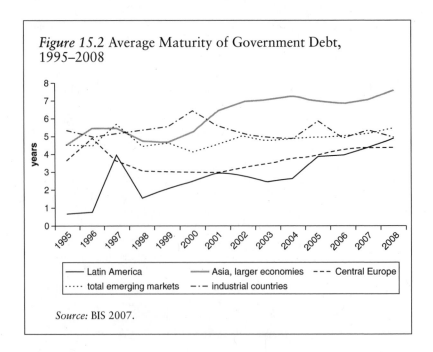

Figure 15.2 Average Maturity of Government Debt, 1995–2008

Source: BIS 2007.

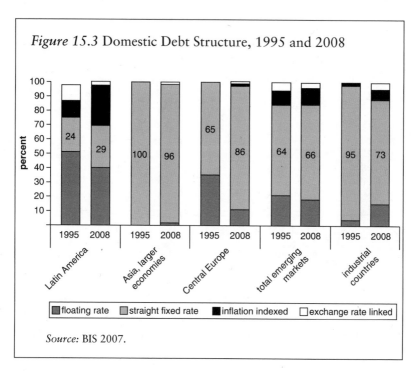

Figure 15.3 Domestic Debt Structure, 1995 and 2008

Source: BIS 2007.

while attempting to increase the share of fixed-rate instruments in the debt portfolio. The government also strengthened debt management capacity, through improvements in the institutional framework; establishment of regular contact with different market segments, particularly pension funds; and adoption of measures to increase liquid.

Mexico underwent similar changes to improve its debt structure starting in early 2000, enhancing its resilience to crises. The measures undertaken aimed at moving toward domestic financing of fiscal deficits, lengthening the maturity structure of the public debt portfolio, and developing a liquid yield curve for domestic debt. These objectives were accompanied by a policy to increase predictability and transparency of debt issuance and to introduce a market-making scheme for government instruments.

To underscore the importance of macroeconomic stability and policy frameworks in rendering feasible sound strategic choices in debt management, we also looked at developments in Mexico starting in 1995. Mexico changed its nominal framework in response to the 1994 crisis, moving from a pegged exchange rate anchor to a floating peso with price stability anchored by an inflation-targeting arrangement. Stable exchange and inflation rates, and a high and stable domestic savings rate, were probably important ingredients in a secular lowering of nominal bond yields, which allowed for a lengthening of the maturity profile and growing issuance in domestic currency. These

Figure 15.4 Macroeconomic Developments in Brazil, Mexico, and Turkey, 2002–10

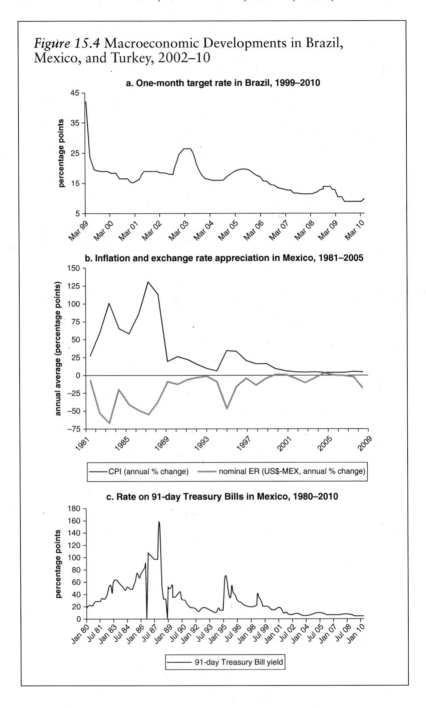

Figure 15.4 (continued)

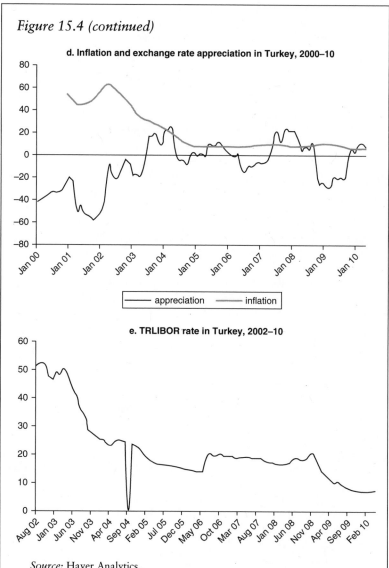

d. Inflation and exchange rate appreciation in Turkey, 2000–10

appreciation   inflation

e. TRLIBOR rate in Turkey, 2002–10

Source: Haver Analytics.

Note: SELIC is an interest rate derived by the average of one-day market rates for the Brazilian market. CPI = consumer price index; ER = exchange rate; TRLIBOR = Turkish Lira Reference Interest Rate.

changes reduced refinancing risk for the government and correspondingly extension and reinvestment risk for investors.

In Turkey crisis-triggered retooling of policies on debt management enhanced resilience to financial shocks. Turkey's public balance sheet was severely weakened as a result of the banking and exchange rate crises in 2001. The bailing out of the banking sector, through the issuance of (foreign exchange–linked) government bonds led to a surge in public debt, a shortening of maturities, and greater exposure to foreign currency risks. In the aftermath of the crisis, reducing the risks from high public debt became a necessary condition for ensuring financial stability. Prudent debt management, against the backdrop of strong fiscal and growth performance, contributed to the improvement in the country's sovereign balance sheet and prospects for financial stability.

Although a virtuous combination of tight fiscal policy, falling interest rates, and strong economic growth helped reduce debt ratios, the Turkish authorities also took advantage of the favorable macroeconomic tailwind to improve the debt structure, reduce risks, and increase financial stability, including through reductions in the level and volatility of interest rates (figure 15.5). For example, foreign currency–indexed domestic debt was halved between 2002 and 2006, from 32 percent to 16 percent, significantly reducing sovereign debt exposure to exchange rate risk. The fixed-rate share of domestic debt over the same period increased from 25 percent to more than 40 percent, and the share of short-term debt declined to less than 5 percent of total debt in mid-2006, down from more than 20 percent four years earlier.

In general, debt structures that rely heavily on short-term instruments are sources of vulnerability, because short average maturities entail high rollover and refinancing risk. In such cases, an increase in interest rates can have an adverse fiscal impact. Debt structures that are too short or allow for bumps in the maturity profile can potentially generate confidence crises, fueled by investors' concerns that the government will not have sufficient funds to redeem maturing bonds when they fall due. Depending on the extent of these fears, they could translate into lower demand for the country's instruments in auctions, thus triggering a self-fulfilling prophecy.

It is the debt manager's responsibility to design policies and schemes that reduce these risks. This could be done by preemptively building large cash buffers, ensuring efficient coordination with cash-management policies, and, at times, absorbing the higher cost of prefunding liability tranches maturing in the near future in order to extinguish the risk of a market call on solvency at the point of redemption.

The debt structure can also impose impediments to the exercise of monetary policy. Short-term or floating-rate instruments, for instance, tend to reduce the wealth effect needed for monetary policy to be effective. If this is the case, a much stronger increase in interest rates will be needed in order to generate the same impact on the level of inflation, thus having a much higher impact on the economy.

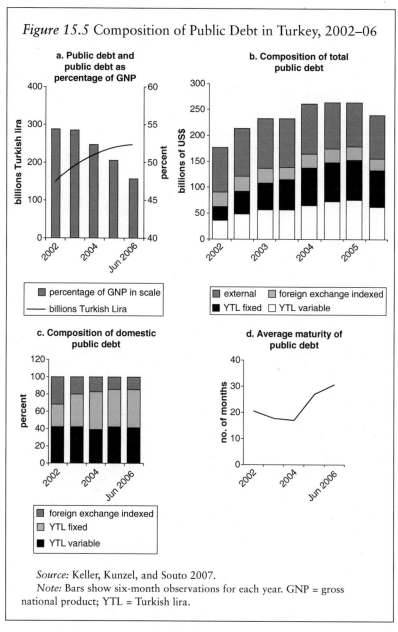

Figure 15.5 Composition of Public Debt in Turkey, 2002–06

Source: Keller, Kunzel, and Souto 2007.
Note: Bars show six-month observations for each year. GNP = gross national product; YTL = Turkish lira.

Debt managers of countries at different levels of development (for example, Brazil, Iceland, Mexico, the United Kingdom, and the United States) are relying on the issuance of inflation-linked bonds for their funding needs. Exchange-rate bonds have proven to be riskier and sometimes deleterious to financial stability, and short-term bonds represent higher refinancing risk. Inflation-linked bonds tend to increase the average maturity of debt without increasing the exchange-rate risks faced by debt managers. The use of this bond is also an approach to making the best use of the investor base, as some holders of debt are keen on holding this kind of instrument. However, inflation-linked bonds can increase the level of indexation in the economy, leading to higher inflation rates. Debt managers should undertake a careful assessment of such strategies, which can affect the economic performance of the country.

Investor Base

From the point of view of the debt manager, an ideal debt structure could be a fixed-rate, long-term bond portfolio. How would such a debt profile look from the investor side?

Financial institutions typically hold a significant share of public debt in most countries. Debt managers must recognize that their actions can have a very major impact on the balance sheets of these institutions. Moreover, given the usually high level of interdependence of financial institutions, the effects can have potential systemic implications. This impact is relevant not only when discussing possible sovereign liability management and debt-restructuring operations but also when thinking about the targeted composition of the debt.

Short-term debt involves higher refinancing risk, which could pose a higher risk to the financial stability of the country. However, longer-term debt may represent higher value at risk (VaR) for the debt holder. Fixed-rate bonds pose less risk to the government but may represent a higher risk to the investor. If individual investors, in search of higher profits, increase their exposure to interest rate risk and there is a hike in interest rates, the market as a whole may suffer, because the unwinding of positions by some institutions may trigger VaR thresholds for others (for a good discussion of this topic for India, see Sy 2005). Debt managers should be aware of and try to monitor this risk.

This risk is particularly relevant for many emerging market countries, whose debt structure is still undergoing structural improvements. In these cases the pace at which the debt composition shifts toward more fixed-rate instruments and longer maturities should be carefully assessed. In Brazil debt managers regularly monitor measures such as DV01[5] and the VaR of the market, which provide warnings of potential distress that the market could face if interest rates rise or volatility increases. This information can be essential for assessing the implications of implementing specific strategies.

In India, for example, historically low interest rates in the first half of the decade generated concerns that if and when rates rise, the position of financial institutions (heavily positioned with fixed-rate instruments) could represent problems to their balance sheets (Sy 2005). To combat this situation, during the same period, the government increased issuance of floating-rate bonds. As a result, the share of floating-rate bonds in gross market borrowing rose from 16 percent in 2003–04 to 29 percent in 2004–05.

As the investor base usually comprises banks, mutual funds, pension funds, and foreign and retail investors, debt managers must strike the right balance between meeting the specific needs of each of these groups of investors and reducing the costs to the government. Doing so entails better matching of each group of the investor base liability profile while avoiding too much market segmentation through different instruments.

Debt managers should not take the investor base for granted. Instead, they can play a preemptive role in developing the investor base further, by issuing instruments targeted at a specific group of investors and by working on increasing a specific group's participation in the debt or in particular instruments. Debt managers often issue inflation-linked bonds to satisfy demand by pension funds, for example. Brazil has traditionally attracted foreign investors for a small proportion of its domestic debt issues whose maturity structures are concentrated at the short end of the curve. A strategy was subsequently devised to issue longer-term domestic currency bonds in the international markets, create a reference point for interest rates in the domestic currency, and tap these maturities in the domestic market.

As this process moved along, it was expected that international investors would become more interested in holding domestic debt securities. Because foreign investors are usually less risk averse and tend to hold longer-term instruments, the inclusion of foreign investors in the investor base can reduce vulnerabilities associated with public debt. However, countries with a high concentration of foreign investors are more susceptible to financial crises, given that such investors are less committed to these assets. It is therefore important to find the best balance between these factors and to come up with an appropriate share of foreign investors. If their share is too low, the country may not be taking advantage of potential benefits from a diversification in the investor base. If it is too high, the country could become vulnerable.

These examples show the sensitivity of debt management policies to financial institutions' balance sheets and financial stability. These policies call for a careful design of the instruments issued to the market; they also point to the importance of a diversified investor-base structure. Different groups of investors with different risk appetites and liability structures tend to react to new information in different ways. A diversified investor base can therefore reduce the impact of shocks. For instance, longer-term investors (such as pension funds) can reduce the impact of possible interest rate increases on the market by increasing their holdings of longer-term instruments.

Overall, from the investors' point of view, the best instruments are those that better match their liability profile, given their return-risk characteristics.

However, these instruments may not be consistent with debt managers' preferred portfolio. Striking the right balance between these conflicting objectives should be part of debt managers' discretionary decision making.

Debt Capital Market Structure

Developing a domestic debt market is an important element in the development process of a country. The functioning of the financial system depends crucially on the instruments that facilitate its operations and activities. Among the prerequisites for a well-functioning financial system are efficient liquid markets. Illiquid markets are subject to abrupt falls in asset prices, which could lead to substantial losses for financial institutions. Promoting liquidity for debt instruments should thus be an important element in the debt managers' mandate.

When implementing their strategies, debt managers should think about proper ways to facilitate bond liquidity. Doing so would not only reduce costs for the issuer, it would also enhance the efficiency of capital markets (Crocket 2008). For these reasons, it has become accepted best practice to issue benchmark securities, which are critical to creating liquid securities.

The issuance of benchmark instruments enables the establishment of an efficient "risk-free" yield curve, which can serve as a reference point for pricing other instruments issued by financial enterprises or corporations. If corporates can issue their own instruments, they rely less on direct bank intermediation, thus reducing systemic risks stemming from the financial sector.[6]

Low-risk benchmark instruments can serve as efficient collateral for operations in the financial market. The existence of well-priced collaterals can reduce the transaction risk of institutions, which can use these instruments to offset credit risk. In the absence of these instruments, loans would be more expensive, issued in smaller volumes, or both. As a stakeholder in the financial system, debt management authorities should actively participate in debates on the regulatory scheme and try to affect the rules in ways that improve the effectiveness of debt management policy and ultimately strengthen financial stability.

Institutional Aspects

Institutional aspects also play an important role in enhancing a country's financial stability. These aspects relate to coordination schemes with other policies, the legal framework, and communications with relevant stakeholders.

Proper coordination between debt management and monetary policy tends to result in better signaling of government intentions and increase transparency. Because monetary and debt management policies coexist in the same market, it is crucial to ensure good coordination mechanisms. In many countries, lack of proper coordination has resulted in competing auctions and market confusion regarding the true signals of monetary policy. Similarly, poor coordination with cash management can increase refinancing risks, if the availability of funds at short notice is at risk.

Another important aspect that should not be neglected is the structure of the legal framework for debt management. An inadequate legal framework can lead to debt management structures that are too rigid (for example, structures that do not allow debt managers to buy or sell instruments at a price different from par or set budget limitations on specific types of instruments).

Communications with market participants need to strike the proper balance between transparency and flexibility. Striking such a balance can decrease costs over the medium term and minimize volatility in the market, if communications avoid sending mixed signals to the market. Debt strategies that are not properly communicated, are not transparent, or present abrupt changes in direction can result in constant shifts in the investor's portfolio. Under such conditions, investors cannot hold positions based on a medium-term view; instead, they have to keep changing instruments based on rumors and perceptions, which increases their risk and the costs to the government. Cross-country experience shows that predictable and transparent debt management strategies tend to result in lower costs and less volatile markets.

Qualified staff are also important. Lack of expertise may lead a country to fail to understand all of the links to financial stability, potentially incurring higher risks.

Relevance of Debt Management for Various Groups of Countries

In many developing economies, where debt capital markets are not yet fully structured, there may not be scope for issuing government bonds. In these cases debt is made up mainly of loans and nontraded securities, held largely by banks or suppliers. Often there is no secondary market in which securities are traded. Where a yield curve is defined, it could serve as a reference for pricing other financial assets in the economy. In the absence of traded bonds, central banks cannot rely on nontraded instruments for monetary policy operations. They must adopt more direct mechanisms. Therefore, the absence of traded debt instruments may lead to suboptimal monetary policy.

The existence of relatively developed debt markets could inhibit monetary financing of the deficit, which can itself be a source of vulnerability. Countries with less developed debt markets tend to face weaknesses related to the monetary link between debt management and financial stability. Therefore, developing the local debt market is a basic step that countries should take to achieve financial stability. The development of local markets is a necessary but not sufficient condition for financial stability, as evidenced in recent episodes in developed market economies.[7]

For many emerging market countries, all the channels mentioned above are broadly relevant. Their debt structures have not yet reached a steady-state level, implying fiscal risks, suboptimal monetary policies, or both. Moreover, the investor base is not sufficiently diversified, making volatility in bond prices higher than would otherwise be the case.

Developed markets usually do not encounter the problems mentioned above, and debt management does not face the same constraints as in less mature markets. However, debt and debt management have become more relevant for this group of countries. The sharp increase in the stock of sovereign debt in many mature economies since 2008 has made it a particularly pressing issue. Many of the points raised above will have to be addressed.

In some developed countries with high levels of government debt, the investor base could be a source of vulnerability. In these cases, a fall in bond prices coupled with an unwillingness of counterparties to buy these bonds can lead to liquidity or even solvency problems. In an environment of increased stock of debt and reduced appetite for government securities, another potential problem is the increase in refinancing risk (caused by the rise in solvency/liquidity risks), which can raise funding costs significantly. The framework presented above can be useful for these countries in assessing the level of debt, its composition, the structure of the investor base, and relevant institutional aspects.

Risk Mitigation Policies

When debt markets become unstable and financial stability is endangered by their behavior, debt managers can play an important role in smoothing market distortions. During the recent global financial crisis, for example, debt managers in developed markets made dealership rules more flexible in an effort to relieve the pressure on banks' balance sheets. In many emerging market countries, governments have intervened in the bond market through different auction mechanisms to stabilize bond prices. In Brazil, for example, during a period of turbulence in 2008, foreign investors sold off bonds in the domestic market. This action triggered sales orders by other investors, leading to a sharp increase in yields (figure 15.6). Debt managers intervened by conducting simultaneous buy and sell auctions, which were successful in stabilizing yields immediately. Investors' perception that debt managers would not allow a sharp depreciation of its liabilities played an important role in stabilizing the bond market and preventing external turbulence to spread and undermine domestic financial stability.

Figure 15.6 Buy and Sell Auctions in Brazil, 2006 and 2008

Source: Brazilian National Treasury.

Kumhof and Tanner (2005) note that debt managers are more careful in dealing with debt defaults or debt devaluations than the academic literature indicates, because they consider the impact of their decisions on financial system stability. Debt management remains extremely relevant when a debt restructuring or debt default is considered. In cases where the government will need funding to go forward, the outcome of such a deal is crucial: badly conducted debt management could impair the government's ability to keep raising money efficiently in the markets. In cases of debt restructuring, it is imperative for debt managers to provide assessments on a broad range of topics, such as instruments to be issued and exchanged, haircut levels, and timing of operations.

In Uruguay the broadly voluntary nature of the 2003 debt restructuring succeeded in affecting investors only mildly. As a result, the restructuring did not significantly damage Uruguay's ability to raise funds in the market. Indeed, the government was able to access international markets for new funding in October 2003, only five months after the restructuring was completed. Debt management helped ensure that the process of restoring financial stability was smooth.

The experience with Jamaica's debt restructuring was similar. In the recent past, Jamaica faced severe debt sustainability problems, and many investors considered default imminent. Default would have triggered significant losses to the financial system, which was dominated by securities dealers heavily exposed to domestic debt. The authorities therefore opted for a solution that would not only reduce fiscal costs without putting too much pressure on financial institutions but would also ensure market accessibility.[8]

Houben, Kakes, and Schinasi (2004) suggest some tools to address financial stability for each of the following three phases: prevention (implementing existing policies to safeguard financial stability), remedial action (implementing preemptive measures to reduce emerging risks to financial stability), and resolution (reactive policy interventions aimed at restoring financial stability). Debt management has a role to play at each stage (table 15.1).

Table 15.1 Debt Management Channels to Financial Stability

Channel	Preemptive policy	Risk mitigation policy mechanisms
Stock of debt	Issue low-cost, low-risk instruments	Debt buybacks, debt exchanges
Profile of debt	Issue low-cost, low-risk instruments	Exchange auctions, derivatives
Investor base	Diversify investor base; monitor investor base risk indicators and adapt appropriate strategy	Debt buybacks, exchange auctions, investors relations program
Debt market structure	Issue benchmark securities; establish appropriate primary dealer and market-maker structure; coordinate with regulatory bodies; put in place appropriate legal framework; craft debt market development strategy	Changes in legal framework and debt strategy
Institutional aspects	Coordinate with monetary policy and cash-management policy; maintain good communication channels; adopt a well-thought-out program, taking into account international practices and domestic idiosyncrasies and constraints	

Source: Authors.

Concluding Remarks

Inappropriate debt structures and poor debt management can greatly inhibit a sovereign's ability to ensure financial stability by affecting investors' country risk perception and exacerbating pressures on financial institutions' balance sheets, incomes, and capital reserves. Some of these effects appear evident in the recent crisis episodes, during which relatively poor public debt portfolio initial positions in some countries adversely affected both economic performance and financial stability.

Sound debt management strategies can be instrumental in ensuring financial stability, by creating a liability structure for public debt that sustains low levels of refinancing risk for the sovereign throughout the business cycle and by securing the sovereign's ability to issue the necessary volume of debt at a reasonable cost in a downswing. Debt managers have a broad range of responsibilities, including formulating and implementing the strategy; determining the instruments that will be offered to the market and their timing; and handling institutional matters and interaction with investors, taking into account investors' risk constraints and appetites at every point in time, all of which affect financial stability.

In addition, an often overlooked contribution of a sound debt management strategy is the efficacy of tactical liability management operations, in which debt managers credibly intervene in domestic debt markets in emergency situations and quickly rebuild investor confidence. The low level of market development in most developing countries, the still vulnerable structures of debt in many emerging markets, and the rise in debt levels in a number of developed economies make sound sovereign debt management even more challenging for global financial stability in the future, particularly given the higher global funding pressures. Understanding the risks and the channels of their transmission to financial stability is an essential element of formulating appropriate policies for strengthening domestic and international financial stability.

Notes

This chapter is based on an ongoing study by the authors on the 2007–09 global economic and financial crisis, cross-country experiences with debt liability–management operations, and their implications for public sector balance sheets and financial stability. The views expressed in this chapter are those of the authors and should not be attributed to the International Monetary Fund, its Executive Board, or its management.

1. Some studies examine the contribution of the use of (public) debt as a strategic component of policy directed at increasing the level and pace of economic growth. For example, Abbas and Christensen (2007) develop a model that shows that moderate levels of debt can increase growth and higher levels can undermine it. They conclude that if domestic debt is marketable and part of it is held outside the banking system, it can contribute to economic growth.

2. Liquidity is often also ensured by allowing domestic debt to be used as collateral at the central bank's lending window.

3. Much as in strategic asset allocation, risk hedging entails picking a portfolio across asset classes whose returns exhibit negative or weak correlation properties.

4. In addition to indicating the increased need for issuance in developed market economies following the recent global financial crisis, this pattern reflects the phenomenon of global imbalances. On the sovereign asset side, such imbalances are captured by burgeoning levels of central bank foreign exchange reserves and sovereign wealth fund asset bases in a number of emerging markets.

5. DV01 is a measure that captures the change in the value of the asset or portfolio based on a change of 1 basis point in the interest rate.

6. The extensive reliance of Asian corporates on funding to local financial institutions in the 1990s has often been cited as a major factor contributing to the Asian financial crisis of 1997–99.

7. In general, there is no simple causality between the stage of financial market development and financial stability.

8. The government used the call option feature of the old bonds to induce investors to exchange those higher coupon–bearing instruments for new bonds with lower coupons.

References

Abbas, S. M., and J. E. Christensen. 2007. "The Role of Domestic Debt Markets in Economic Growth: An Empirical Investigation for Low-Income Countries and Emerging Markets." IMF Working Paper 07/127, International Monetary Fund, Washington, DC.

Allen, M., C. Rosenberg, C. Keller, B. Setser, and N. Roubino. 2002. "A Balance Sheet Approach to Financial Crisis." IMF Working Paper 02/210, International Monetary Fund, Washington, DC.

BIS (Bank for International Settlements). 2007. "Financial Stability and Local Currency Bond Markets." CGFS Paper 28, Committee on the Global Financial System, Basel, Switzerland.

Bolle, M., B. Rother, and I. Hakobyan. 2006. "The Level and Composition of Public Sector Debt in Emerging Market Crises." IMF Working Paper 06/186, International Monetary Fund, Washington, DC.

Borensztein, E., M. Chamon, O. Jeanne, P. Mauro, and J. Zettelmeyer. 2004. "Sovereign Debt Structure for Crisis Prevention." IMF Occasional Paper 237, International Monetary Fund, Washington, DC.

Crocket, A. 2008. "Market Liquidity and Financial Stability." *Financial Stability Review*. Special Issue on Liquidity 11 (February), Banque de France, Paris.

Guscina, A. 2008. "Impact of Macroeconomic, Political, and Institutional Factors on the Structure of Government Debt in Emerging Market Countries." IMF Working Paper 08/205, International Monetary Fund, Washington, DC.

Houben, A., J. Kakes, and G. Schinasi. 2004. "Toward a Framework for Safeguarding Financial Stability." IMF Working Paper 04/101, International Monetary Fund, Washington, DC.

Jeanne, O., and A. Guscina. 2006. "Government Debt in Emerging Market Countries: A New Data Set." IMF Working Paper 06/98, International Monetary Fund, Washington, DC.

Jeanneau, S., and C. P. Verdia. 2005. "Reducing Financial Vulnerability: The Development of the Domestic Government Bond Market in Mexico." *BIS Quarterly Review* (December): 95–107.

Keller, C., P. Kunzel, and Marcos Souto. 2007. "Measuring Sovereign Risk in Turkey: An Application of the Contingent Claims." IMF Working Paper WP/07/23, International Monetary Fund, Washington, DC.

Krugman, P. 1979. "A Model of Balance of Payments Crisis." *Journal of Money, Credit, and Banking* 11: 311–25.

Kumhof, M., and E. Tanner. 2005. "Government Debt: A Key Role in Financial Intermediation." IMF Working Paper 05/57, International Monetary Fund, Washington, DC.

Papaioannou, M. 2009. "Exchange Rate Risk Measurement and Management Issues and Approaches for Public Debt Managers." *South-Eastern Europe Journal of Economics* 7 (1): 7–34.

Peiris, S. 2010. "Foreign Participation in Emerging Markets' Local Currency Bond Markets." IMF Working Paper 10/88, International Monetary Fund, Washington, DC.

Reinhart, C., and K. Rogoff. 2009. *This Time Is Different: Eight Centuries of Financial Folly*. Princeton, NJ: Princeton University Press.

Rosenberg, Christoph, Ioannis Halikias, Brett House, Christian Keller, Jens Nystedt, Alexander Pitt, and Brad Setser. 2005. *Debt-Related Vulnerabilities and Financial Crises: An Application of the Balance Sheet Approach to Emerging Market Countries*. IMF Occasional Paper 240. Washington, DC: International Monetary Fund.

Schinasi, G. 2004. "Defining Financial Stability." IMF Working Paper 04/187, International Monetary Fund, Washington, DC.

Sy, A. 2005. "Managing the Interest Rate Risk of Indian Banks' Government Securities Holdings." IMF Working Paper 05/78, International Monetary Fund, Washington, DC.

16

Public Debt Management in Emerging Market Economies: Has This Time Been Different?

Phillip R. D. Anderson, Anderson Caputo Silva, and Antonio Velandia-Rubiano

The global financial crisis of 2008–09 was the worst the world has seen since the 1930s in both intensity and global reach. Emerging market countries were not immune: at the height of the crisis, the Emerging Markets Bond Index Global (EMBIG) saw an increase in spread of more than 700 basis points from its low point in June 2007, and international capital markets were effectively closed to issuers for several months. Yet despite the severity of the global crisis, it did not result in an emerging market sovereign debt crisis of the type seen in the 1990s and early 2000s.

This chapter reviews the reasons why the impact of the global crisis on emerging markets was so much milder than it was in earlier episodes and examines the responses of debt management officials in emerging markets to the rapidly changing market environment they faced.[1] The first section outlines the outcomes of macroeconomic policy and changes in the composition of public debt over the decade beginning in 2000. It shows that a virtuous circle of improved macroeconomic fundamentals, reduced public debt levels, and more effective management of risk in public debt portfolios provided most countries with the resilience to ride out the crisis and adjust borrowing plans to cope with adverse market conditions. The second section reviews the impact on access to finance during the peak of market dislocation. The third section, based on the results of a survey conducted by the authors, examines how debt managers in emerging markets responded to the crisis.[2] The last section draws some lessons from the crisis for future macroeconomic policy and public debt management strategies.

Crisis Preparedness in Emerging Markets

Emerging markets enjoyed an unprecedented period during which both strong macroeconomic fundamentals and a benign global economic environment increased the scope for implementation of debt strategies that could reduce their risk to shocks. As a result, debt managers in most emerging market economies were able to improve their debt portfolios.

Historically, an unfortunate combination of weak macroeconomic fundamentals and debt management practices had exacerbated the impact of previous economic crises and downturns. This time was different.

In order to gauge the sea change in the macroeconomic scenario and how it influenced debt management practices, we start by illustrating the significant shift observed in four macroeconomic dimensions: fiscal accounts, monetary policy, growth, and external accounts. The contrast between the first years of the new century and the three years that preceded the crisis (2005–07) is striking.[3]

Fiscal accounts improved remarkably in emerging markets, with Latin America showing the sharpest changes. As a percentage of GDP, governments' primary balances were overwhelmingly positive or becoming positive during this period, and overall budget balances, as a percentage of GDP, improved steadily across all regions (figure 16.1). These improvements were crucial in boosting investor confidence that emerging markets could be better positioned to adopt countercyclical policies should conditions change—although few would imagine the sweeping global recession that was about to come.

Monetary policy in emerging markets experienced a period of increased credibility, given that inflation remained relatively stable at historically low levels, despite occasional pressures from commodity prices. Greater price stability and positive expectations in emerging markets helped boost confidence in longer-term bonds, including government bonds. In many countries, especially those that had historically been plagued by volatile and high inflation levels, this scenario paved the way for interest rate cuts, the development of local currency yield curves, and the lengthening of the average time to maturity of domestic government debt (as discussed below).

Most emerging markets enjoyed a long period during which fiscal indicators, interest rates, and GDP growth—the key determinants of debt to GDP ratios—improved, leading to a robust downward trend in debt to GDP ratios in virtually all regions (figures 16.2). Between 2000 and 2008, reductions in the debt to GDP ratios were particularly sharp in Sub-Saharan Africa and Central and Eastern Europe. Between 2005 and

Figure 16.1 Primary and Overall Balance as a Percentage of GDP, by Region, 2000–09

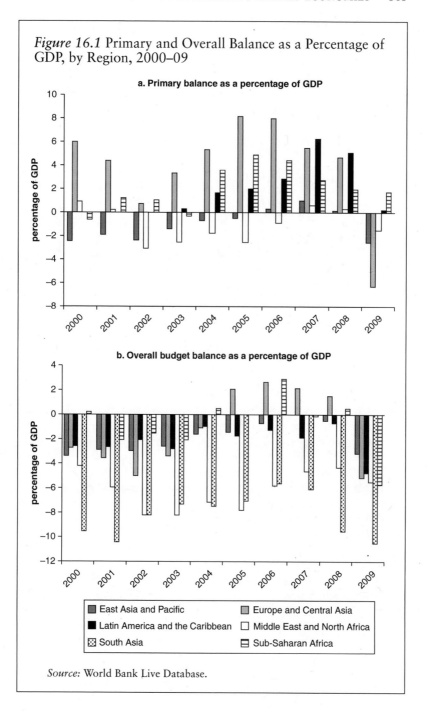

Source: World Bank Live Database.

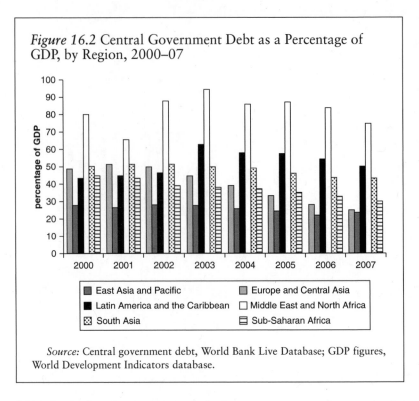

Figure 16.2 Central Government Debt as a Percentage of GDP, by Region, 2000–07

Legend:
- ■ East Asia and Pacific
- ■ Latin America and the Caribbean
- ⊠ South Asia
- ■ Europe and Central Asia
- □ Middle East and North Africa
- ▤ Sub-Saharan Africa

Source: Central government debt, World Bank Live Database; GDP figures, World Development Indicators database.

2008, Latin America experienced the largest percentage decrease in the average debt to GDP ratio. Out of our sample of 24 emerging markets, 6 countries showed reductions of about 5 percent in the debt to GDP ratio, 11 experienced reductions greater than 20 percent, and only 7 had higher ratios by the end of 2008 than in 2000.

Improvements in emerging markets' external accounts reflected these countries' falling debt levels and diminishing vulnerability to shocks and reversals in capital flows (figure 16.3). External account improvements were driven by cyclical factors that led to extremely high international liquidity conditions, but proactive policies to reduce debt vulnerabilities (for example, buybacks of external debt and a shift to funding in local markets) were highly instrumental in the rapid pace of change in external debt vulnerability indicators. This marked reduction in vulnerability represented a structural change in some economies to break out of a negative shock cycle experienced several times in the past, when pressures on the currency and increased risk aversion had a strong first-order impact on fiscal and debt sustainability indicators.

The 24 countries that are the focus of this chapter experienced generally positive trends; some other middle-income countries did not take advantage of the "good times" to strengthen their macroeconomic aggregates

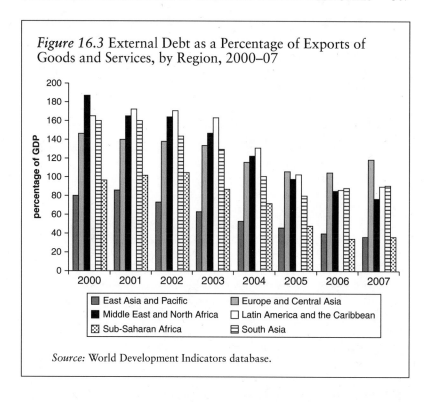

Figure 16.3 External Debt as a Percentage of Exports of Goods and Services, by Region, 2000–07

Source: World Development Indicators database.

and reduce the vulnerabilities to external shocks. In the Eastern Caribbean, for example, primary fiscal deficits combined with natural disasters and slow growth resulted in a continued buildup of public debt, reaching limits that raise sustainability concerns.[4] In Eastern Europe, Ukraine failed to correct external and fiscal imbalances, which, combined with the fragility of its banking sector, increased the exposure of the private sector to reversals of capital flows. The performance of these countries underscores the need to take advantage of the benign phase of the cycle to address debt problems, as once a crisis hits the options for action quickly narrow.[5]

On the back of healthier macroeconomic fundamentals and a benign external environment, debt managers engineered a significant transformation of government debt portfolios. They reduced exposures to changes in exchange and interest rates by focusing on domestic debt financing, including a reduction in floating-rate bonds. The sustained increase in the share of domestic debt helped mitigate the dependence from external funding sources and the exposure to currency risk. More important, the structure of domestic debt itself experienced a significant transformation, as government authorities embarked on market development programs that allowed debt managers to extend the average life of domestic debt, partly by issuing long-term fixed-rate instruments.[6] The progress attained in the past decade partly freed debt managers in emerging markets from choosing between long-term fixed-rate instruments denominated in foreign currency and short-term instruments in local currency. This traditional trade-off represents a choice between currency risk and interest rate risk.

Exposure to Foreign Currency Borrowing

The 34 countries that defaulted or rescheduled their external debt between 1980 and 2000 illustrate that excessive foreign currency borrowing weakens a country's financial stability by exposing it to sudden stops of capital flows or drastic declines in the value of the local currency (Reinhart and Rogoff 2009).[7] In several emerging markets, dependence on the international capital markets resulted in liquidity crises when these markets closed and governments were unable to roll over their foreign currency obligations. Emerging markets also experienced episodes of massive devaluations; when combined with high debt levels, these devaluations caused debt-servicing costs to represent such large shares of revenues that governments were unwilling to meet their obligations with external creditors. To some extent, the strengthening of the government debt portfolios could be interpreted as a debt manager's policy response to the external debt crises experienced in the 1980s and 1990s.

Most emerging market governments made significant progress in reducing the exposure of government finances to foreign borrowing—some to the point of becoming net foreign currency creditors.[8] This can be seen in the evolution of the net foreign currency debt, calculated as the gross government foreign currency debt minus international reserves. Two of the four most indebted countries in 2001, Brazil and the Russian Federation, had become net creditors by 2009 (figure 16.4). Mexico and Turkey had reduced their combined net foreign exchange debt from $123 billion in 2001 to $45 billion in 2009. Most impressive is the case of China, which experienced a fivefold increase in its international reserves, from about $200 billion in 2001 to more than $2 trillion in 2009 while contracting its foreign exchange debt from $49 billion to $35 billion.

Although international reserves may also be compromised by a high level of private external debt, there is no question that their accumulation dramatically reduced the overall exposure of the emerging markets group studied here.[9] In our sample of emerging markets, the weighted average of the ratio of total external debt to international reserves dropped from 3.5 in 2001 to 1.2 in 2009 (figure 16.5). The steadily declining trend over the decade was only slightly reversed by the global financial crisis in 2008.

The accumulation of international reserves played a major role in reducing the overall short foreign currency position in emerging markets. A significant shift in the currency composition of government debt portfolios was also an important contributor. The reduction in foreign currency

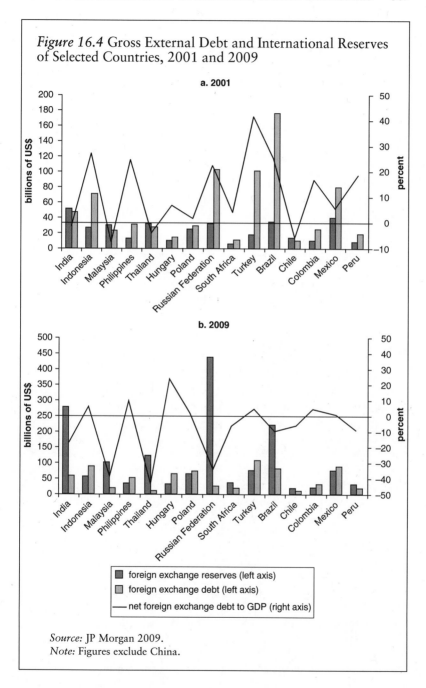

Figure 16.4 Gross External Debt and International Reserves of Selected Countries, 2001 and 2009

Source: JP Morgan 2009.
Note: Figures exclude China.

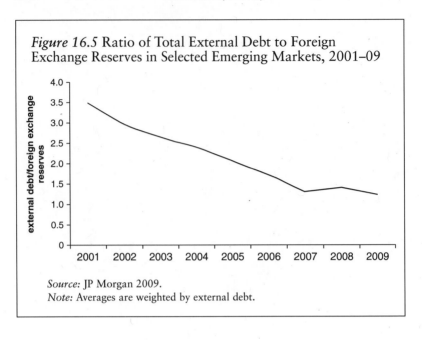

Figure 16.5 Ratio of Total External Debt to Foreign Exchange Reserves in Selected Emerging Markets, 2001–09

Source: JP Morgan 2009.
Note: Averages are weighted by external debt.

debt was achieved thanks to a parallel increase in domestic debt. The (weighted) average ratio of external to domestic debt for selected emerging markets dropped steadily, from 0.75 times in 2000 to 0.22 times in 2009 (figure 16.6).[10] The share of external debt declined across all regions; it was most impressive in Europe and Latin America. In Europe the external to domestic debt ratio plummeted monotonically, from 2.58 in 2000 to 0.58 in 2009. In Latin America, the ratio increased in 2001 and 2002 because of the financial turmoil in Brazil,[11] and increased foreign borrowing combined with a devaluation in Colombia, but the weighted average fell from more than 1.0 in 2002 to 0.2 in 2009.[12] Changes were also significant in Asia, where the (weighted) ratio fell from 0.5 to 0.15.

The relatively swift adjustment in the structure of the debt stock was possible thanks to the implementation of a series of liability management operations that altered the structure of the existing debt stock. In all regions, debt managers prepaid international bonds, multilateral and bilateral debt, or both, through buybacks or exchanges. In addition, for the first time ever, Brazil, Colombia, the Arab Republic of Egypt, and Uruguay issued global bonds denominated in local currencies in the international capital markets. Even if the contribution of these securities to the transformation of the composition of the government debt portfolios was marginal (except for Uruguay), these issuances led to a questioning of the "original sin hypothesis" and opened a new financing channel to

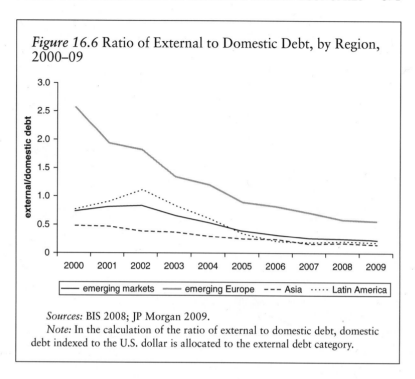

Figure 16.6 Ratio of External to Domestic Debt, by Region, 2000–09

Sources: BIS 2008; JP Morgan 2009.
Note: In the calculation of the ratio of external to domestic debt, domestic debt indexed to the U.S. dollar is allocated to the external debt category.

debt managers (Eichengreen and Hausmann 1999). For Brazil this channel allowed the government to issue fixed-rate securities in reais at longer maturities than those placed in local markets, creating a valuable reference for the gradual extension of the curve domestically (as discussed in more detail in the next section).

The reduction of foreign exchange exposure is also confirmed by the structure of outstanding securities issued by emerging markets reported in the quarterly statistics of the Bank for International Settlements (BIS).[13] According to the BIS, international outstanding bonds and notes issued by emerging market governments as a proportion of their total issuance dropped from more than 30 percent in 1998 to about 10 percent in 2009 (figure 16.7). This ratio varied widely across regions. In Asia securities issued in foreign markets traditionally accounted for less than 7 percent of the total; in Latin America, until 2002 more than half of the outstanding securities were issued in the international capital markets. The declining trend in the ratio for emerging markets was offset by Asia, whose stock of domestic securities in 2009 was five times that of Latin America and 2.5 times that of Europe. Indeed, the relatively low and stable share of international securities in Asia (1–3 percent) is in startling contrast to

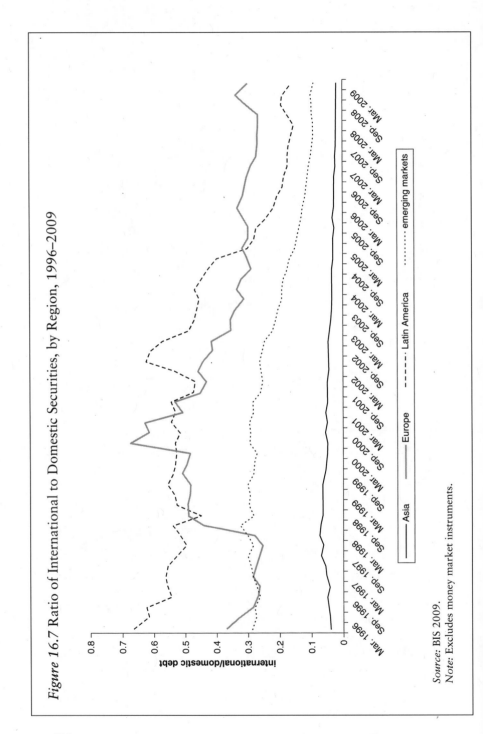

Figure 16.7 Ratio of International to Domestic Securities, by Region, 1996–2009

Source: BIS 2009.
Note: Excludes money market instruments.

Latin America, where the ratio dropped from more than 60 percent in 2002 to 17 percent in 2009. In Europe international securities, which represented 37 percent of the total in 1996, represented almost 70 percent by September 2000, driven by Russian foreign borrowing, before plummeting to 30 percent in 2009.

Transformation of the Domestic Debt Portfolio

Domestic debt portfolios in emerging markets went through major shifts in composition and maturity in the years that preceded the crisis, reducing the exposure of these countries to shifts in the economic cycle and market sentiment. These shifts occurred under several constraints that have affected many emerging markets for several years. More stable and sounder macroeconomic policies, together with reforms in the pension and insurance industries, changed the investor base, which had consisted almost exclusively of commercial banks. Holdings of domestic institutional investors grew steadily. Pension funds became the second-largest group of investors in emerging markets, with a strong presence in Chile, Colombia, Malaysia, and Uruguay. Insurance companies also became increasingly important, holding significant shares of debt in Hungary, India, and Poland.[14] Foreign investors played a major role in Brazil and Mexico, where they showed significant appetite for local currency long-term fixed-rate instruments. These changes loosened the constraints that had forced debt managers to focus on short-term or index-linked instruments.

The most noticeable shift was the decline in the (weighted) ratio of floating and short-term to fixed-rate debt, which fell from 2.0 in 2000 to 0.70 in 2009 (figure 16.8). The drop represented a substantial reduction in the exposure to interest rate risk. The spike in 2002 was caused by the setback in Brazil, where debt managers were forced to resort to floating or short-term securities as speculation on unfriendly market policies of the potential new government caused turmoil in the financial markets. When Brazil is taken out of the sample, the ratio shows a steady and significant decline, from 1.31 to 0.13. Brazil and Mexico, the two most indebted countries in the region, improved substantially after 2003. Progress was also impressive in Europe, where the ratio plummeted from almost 2.0 to 0.5. The indicator is less meaningful in Asia, because only Indonesia issued floating or short-term paper in significant volumes. It reduced its ratio of floating to fixed-rate debt from 1.7 in 2002 to 0.3 in 2009.

This shift in the composition of nominal debt brought about a significant increase in the average life of the portfolio, which reduced government exposure to refinancing risk. The average life of domestic debt portfolios rose steadily between 2000 and 2007, partly because of the success many emerging markets had in issuing longer-term instruments. For the first time, several countries were able to auction fixed-rate local

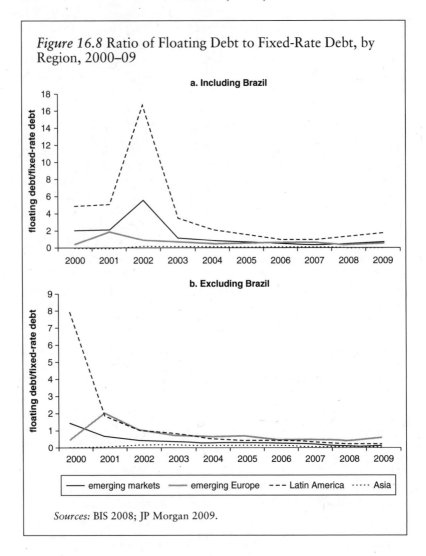

Figure 16.8 Ratio of Floating Debt to Fixed-Rate Debt, by Region, 2000–09

Sources: BIS 2008; JP Morgan 2009.

currency instruments at maturities of 10 years or longer. The most impressive progress was achieved in Latin America, where average life more than tripled, from 1.3 years in 2000 to 4.0 years in 2009. Asia gained almost three years, increasing the average life of its debt from 6.7 to 9.4 years. Europe gained eight months, increasing the average life of its debt from 2.4 to 3.1 years (figure 16.9).

Another trend in the structure of domestic debt over the past decade is the increasing importance of inflation-linked debt (figure 16.10). Although

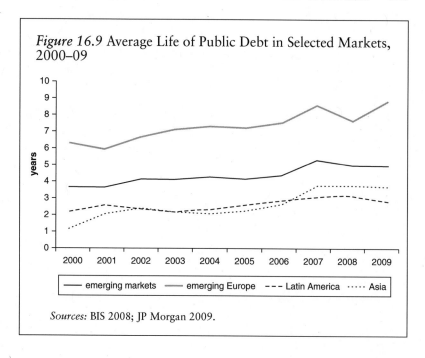

Figure 16.9 Average Life of Public Debt in Selected Markets, 2000–09

Sources: BIS 2008; JP Morgan 2009.

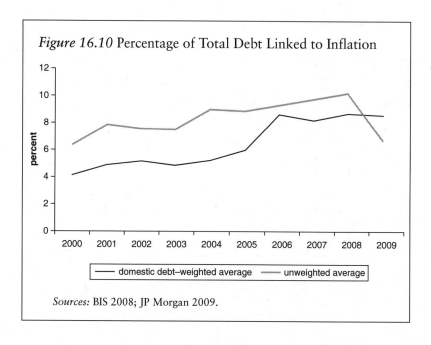

Figure 16.10 Percentage of Total Debt Linked to Inflation

Sources: BIS 2008; JP Morgan 2009.

these instruments are not used, or have low weights, in most emerging market portfolios, a number of countries introduced them as an alternative to nominal fixed-rate instruments to extend maturities and reduce currency and rollover risk.[15] Some countries also issue inflation-linked debt to reach an optimal debt portfolio, combining these instruments with fixed-rate securities. In South Africa, for instance, inflation-linked securities, which did not exist in 2000, represented 16 percent of the portfolio in 2009. Brazil increased its share of inflation-linked debt from 6 percent to 22 percent over the same period. In Turkey, which started using these instruments in 2006, they accounted for 10 percent of the portfolio by 2009. Inflation linkers have found strong demand from pension funds and nonresidents. This is good news, as the literature on government debt provides support for some use of inflation-indexed debt, because much of the government's revenues (which service the debt) are real in nature (Barrow 1997; Campbell and Shiller 1996).

Between 2000 and 2009, only four countries in the sample (Brazil, Chile, Colombia, and Turkey) issued domestic debt linked to foreign exchange. Brazil, which in 2000 had 22.5 percent of its portfolio in dollar-linked instruments, stopped issuing such instruments in 2002. In Chile and Colombia, foreign exchange–linked debt was eliminated from the portfolio by 2009, after reaching significant levels at the beginning of the decade. Turkey brought down its share of foreign exchange–linked debt from 35 percent in 2001 to 6 percent in 2009. These shifts were important in improving the composition of the debt portfolio in these countries. Most emerging markets in the sample, however, did not use this type of instrument during the period of analysis.

In sum, emerging markets arrived at the global financial crisis with government debt portfolios that were more resilient to shifts in the economic cycle and market sentiment than they had been. The increase in the share of domestic debt reduced the exposure to exchange-rate shocks and the vulnerability to sudden stops in capital flows. The lengthening of maturities in local currency instruments opened new alternatives for debt managers, who no longer had to choose between foreign currency and interest rate risk. Possibly the most important achievement in this area was the diversification of funding sources. Governments significantly reduced their dependence on bank financing. The evolution of the financial system, pension and insurance reforms, the growth of the mutual funds industry, and the increasing presence of foreign investors changed the investor map, creating new demand for long-term fixed-rate securities.

Development of the financial sector cannot be achieved quickly; it is the result of concerted and deliberate policy actions over a period of years. At the same time, decisions to borrow more in local currency at longer maturities usually require the acceptance of higher interest costs in the short run, in order to reduce risk. These realities underscore the strength of policy making in most emerging markets over the past decade.

The Crisis: What Happened in Emerging Markets?

Despite the improvement in macroeconomic and debt indicators in the years preceding the crisis, serious doubts remained concerning emerging markets' capacity to withstand shocks. These economies had not yet been tested by an environment of increased risk aversion and reduced appetite for their assets, which could be provoked by turbulence in the financial markets and prospects of an economic downturn. Strong skepticism persisted on how resilient emerging market economies really were to shifts in market sentiment.

Previous crises had been traumatic: poor debt structures exacerbated the impact of economic shocks. During these events, the world got used to seeing economic shocks leading to a vicious cycle of increased risk aversion to emerging market assets, strong capital outflows, abrupt currency depreciation, and a major negative impact on debt ratios and fiscal indicators— all reinforcing risk aversion and concerns about debt sustainability.

What most observers did not expect was the magnitude of the test that was about to come, in the form of the greatest financial-economic crisis since the Great Depression. Initially, the impact on emerging markets was mild, but it intensified significantly in the aftermath of the Lehman Brothers bankruptcy on September 15, 2008. The negligible effect of the crisis on emerging markets before Lehman's insolvency brought to the spotlight the debate over whether these economies had "decoupled" from events in the economies of the advanced countries A few months later, the answer was unequivocal: a widespread financial crisis had led to massive deleveraging and capital outflows across the world.

Debt managers saw funding conditions in international capital markets deteriorate suddenly, with generalized spikes in the spreads on five-year emerging market credit default swaps and on the Emerging Markets Bond Index Global (EMBIG) sovereigns (figure 16.11). These spreads peaked in October 2008. Sri Lanka's EMBIG spread reached 1,471 basis points, and Indonesia's five-year credit default swap spread reached 900 basis points, the sharpest increases that month among the 24 countries sampled. Since then these spreads have been falling almost homogeneously, to reach pre-crisis levels by the end of 2009.[16]

Emerging market external debt issuance stalled for months, as a consequence of increased risk aversion and higher borrowing costs (figure 16.12). International capital markets reopened only after Mexico's $2 billion issuance of a 10-year global bond in December 2008. That issuance was followed by placements by Brazil, Colombia, Turkey, and the Philippines in January 2009, as well as other issuances that eventually brought emerging market issuance back to reasonable levels.

Significant capital outflows from most emerging markets increased the challenge to debt managers, especially in countries still dependent

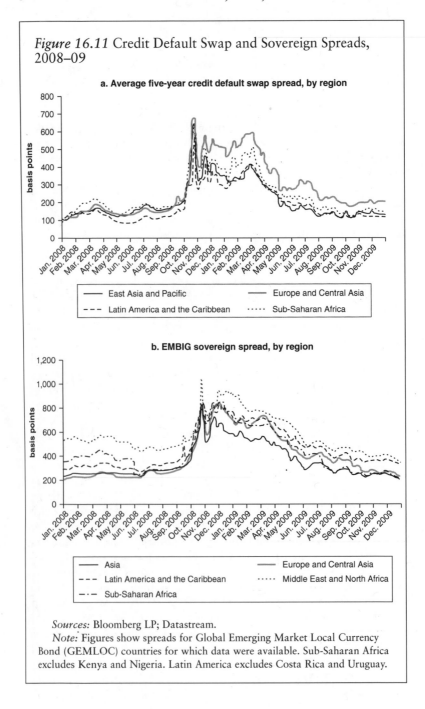

Figure 16.11 Credit Default Swap and Sovereign Spreads, 2008–09

a. Average five-year credit default swap spread, by region

b. EMBIG sovereign spread, by region

Sources: Bloomberg LP; Datastream.

Note: Figures show spreads for Global Emerging Market Local Currency Bond (GEMLOC) countries for which data were available. Sub-Saharan Africa excludes Kenya and Nigeria. Latin America excludes Costa Rica and Uruguay.

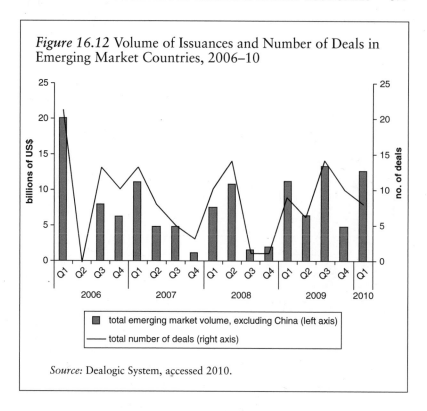

Figure 16.12 Volume of Issuances and Number of Deals in Emerging Market Countries, 2006–10

Source: Dealogic System, accessed 2010.

on external funding (figure 16.13). The strong and positive capital flows observed in 2007 fell drastically in 2008, influenced by the abrupt reversal in flows in the last months of that year. Europe and Sub-Saharan Africa witnessed some of the sharpest reversals in portfolio flows in the fourth quarter of 2008. Closed international capital markets and stronger imbalances on external accounts forced many countries to beef up borrowing from multilaterals.

The impact on emerging market local currency bond yields was also significant, but it moved yields in contrasting directions across countries in the first few months after September 15, 2008. In most cases, yields either increased or fell sharply (figure 16.14). Flight to quality, prospects for reduced economic activity, and consequent monetary policy easing were among the main factors driving yields down. These trends prevailed in emerging Asia, with the exceptions of Indonesia and Sri Lanka, where domestic bond rates declined right from the start of the crises, albeit much less than in mature markets. Deleveraging and increased uncertainty and risk aversion (as reflected in credit default swaps and EMBIG spreads)

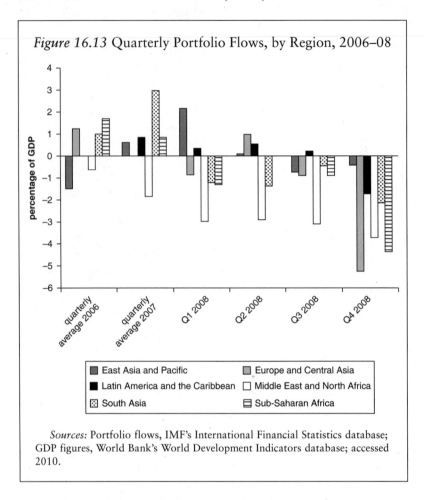

Figure 16.13 Quarterly Portfolio Flows, by Region, 2006–08

Legend:
- East Asia and Pacific
- Europe and Central Asia
- Latin America and the Caribbean
- Middle East and North Africa
- South Asia
- Sub-Saharan Africa

Sources: Portfolio flows, IMF's International Financial Statistics database; GDP figures, World Bank's World Development Indicators database; accessed 2010.

caused sell-offs in many markets, pushing yields up. These factors may dominate, especially shortly after a significant shock, when uncertainty is more acute and some groups of investors, such as emerging market bond funds, abruptly change their portfolios (figure 16.15).[17] This was the case in most countries in Latin America and Europe, where yields increased until October or November, when they started declining in close correlation with the EMBI.

The longer-term effect on local yields was more homogeneous: a generalized reduction consistent with monetary policy response and the economic downturn. Although some countries reacted more swiftly than others, central banks across the globe reduced policy rates over time, especially in 2009. With deleveraging losing its steam and emerging markets regaining the confidence of investors, yields declined in most

Figure 16.14 Index of Generic 10-Year Government Bond Yields in Selected Countries, 2008–09

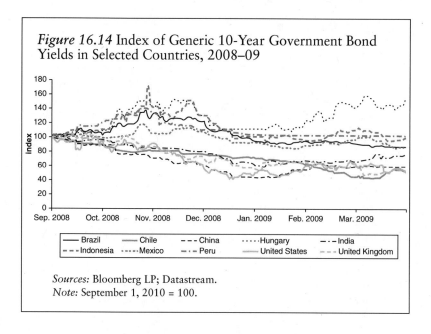

Sources: Bloomberg LP; Datastream.
Note: September 1, 2010 = 100.

Figure 16.15 Net Bond Flows, by Region, 2008–09

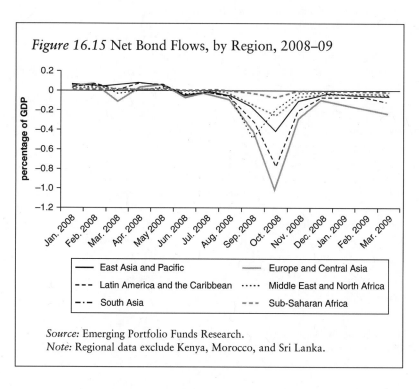

Source: Emerging Portfolio Funds Research.
Note: Regional data exclude Kenya, Morocco, and Sri Lanka.

countries to levels below those observed before the Lehman collapse in September 2008.

Unlike the impact on market rates and capital flows, the impact of the crisis on fiscal accounts was gradual and hit most emerging market economies mainly in 2009. The global financial crisis transmitted to emerging markets mainly through the contraction of capital inflows and exports. As most high-income countries plunged into the worst financial-economic crisis since the Great Depression, growth in emerging markets slowed from 7.8 percent in 2007 to 5.1 percent in 2008 and 0.8 percent in 2009, and government revenues contracted sharply.[18] A countercyclical policy aimed at soothing the impact of the crisis left a fiscal gap that widened in 2009. The size of the gap varied greatly in the emerging markets surveyed. As expected, because of the greater dependency on inflows and economic activity in the European Union, the fiscal gap was larger in Central and Eastern Europe and smaller in Asia and Latin America.

Borrowing requirements in the surveyed emerging markets expanded, but this time emerging markets were better prepared to handle the shock. In Romania and Turkey, where the crisis impact was stronger, borrowing requirements tripled in 2009.[19] In most Latin American and Asian countries, debt managers had to fund no more than 1.5 times the sums raised in 2008. The task was nonetheless challenging, given that during the third and fourth quarters of 2008 the international capital markets were effectively closed and domestic market conditions in most emerging market countries had deteriorated. The apparent success with which debt managers were able to meet the additional borrowing demands may reflect the facts that debt portfolios were less dependent on foreign borrowing and the increase in the primary deficit was limited. In addition the external markets, which were closed for nearly five months, reopened with foreign interest rates at historic lows, as monetary policy in the G-7 was aggressively expansionary.

This situation contrasts sharply with that of industrial countries, where deep deficits developed and debt to GDP ratios rose rapidly. The implementation of large bailout packages to keep the financial system afloat and the recession that followed the virtual paralysis of domestic credit and the burst of the real estate bubble brought about a dramatic increase in fiscal deficits and the borrowing requirements of these governments.[20]

Response to the Crisis by Debt Managers in Emerging Markets

The global financial crisis extended the role played by debt managers beyond meeting the unexpected borrowing requirements; their actions affected the effectiveness of the policy response to the crisis. In several countries, debt managers were asked to raise additional funding for the implementation of vital fiscal stimulus packages in an environment of investor retrenchment. Moreover, they had to do so in a manner that contributed to the stability of the domestic financial market, which had been shaken by the flight of foreign investors and strong risk aversion. In this delicate environment, decision makers needed to carefully weigh the potential impact on interest rates, the fiscal space taken by debt-servicing costs, investors' response, and the overall effect on the financial markets.

Debt managers' response to the crisis varied from country to country, depending on the instruments available and their experience working in a new adverse environment. The global financial crisis tested debt managers' flexibility to adapt their borrowing strategies after macroeconomic and market fundamentals shifted dramatically.[21]

Debt managers in the sample of selected emerging markets responded in three main ways: by reducing pressure on the market by filling part of the funding gap through other mechanisms, by adapting the funding program to shifts in the demand for government paper, and by implementing liability management operations to support the market. Each of these types of responses is examined below.

Reducing Pressure on the Market by Using Other Financing Mechanisms

Actions aimed at reducing pressure on the market by raising part of the funding needs by other means included three mechanisms: channeling the excess liquidity available within the public sector; using nonmarket funding sources, such as multilaterals; and expanding the investor base by using new debt instruments and distribution channels. Most countries reduced or delayed borrowing from the private sector by using liquid resources within the public sector. The use of cash reserves allowed the authorities in Peru to stay out of the market and effectively borrow less than originally planned (Peru does not have an official target for cash reserves). In Uruguay the authorities avoided borrowing from market sources by taking on loans from multilaterals to close the financing gap and reconstitute the liquidity cushion. In 2005 it adopted a prefunding policy that established that at any point in time, cash reserves should cover the financing needs of the next 12 months (Ministry of Finance 2009). Colombia borrowed $1.8 billion in 2008 and $3.8 billion in 2009 to build up its liquidity position. Central banks in Egypt, Hungary, Indonesia, and Mexico were permitted to buy government bonds, which buffered the fall in bond prices. In some countries with less developed local markets, the central bank extended credit lines to the government.

Emerging market debt managers also stepped up their borrowing from multilaterals. Hungary received substantial resources from the International Monetary Fund (IMF) to deal with the stabilization of the financial sector. Indonesia used contingent funding from multilateral and bilateral entities to backstop its borrowing needs. Peru used contingent credit lines contracted with the World Bank. Romania met a substantial part of its borrowing program with resources from the IMF, the European Commission, and the World Bank. The substantial increase in the demand for multilateral loans put significant pressure on the capacity of these multilateral institutions to expand their lending programs. The World Bank responded by increasing its 2009 lending volume to almost three times the volume projected before the crisis.[22]

Some emerging markets started or expanded retail debt programs or tried new debt instruments in an effort to diversify funding sources and tap segments of investors not explored before. Although this route was marginal compared with the first two mechanisms, it was worth exploring in some countries. Hungary introduced a new three-year instrument linked to the consumer price index (CPI) for the retail market. Indonesia aggressively expanded its retail program, introduced *Sharia*-compliant *sukuk* market instruments, and launched a Samurai bond. Turkey introduced new revenue-indexed bonds and CPI linkers for the wholesale market.

Revising Funding Programs in Response to Shifts in Demand for Government Paper

The loss of appetite for emerging market government bonds forced debt managers to modify funding strategies while dealing with the ongoing interest rate and refinancing shocks. In response to the outflow of funds by foreign—and in some cases even local institutional—investors out of emerging market governments, debt managers suspended issuance in the international capital markets and concentrated the bulk of the issuance program in the shortest tenors and floaters, for which demand from commercial banks was greater.

Emerging market issuance in the international capital markets came to a virtual stop in the third and fourth quarters of 2008. Activity recovered strongly in 2009, following the aggressive expansionary monetary policies of the G-7.

Market conditions also deteriorated in most local markets, and most countries suspended or reduced the auctions of local currency medium-term fixed-rate securities. The impact of the crisis in this regard was worst in Hungary, Turkey, Poland, and Romania, in all of which the local currency debt market for medium- and long-term paper came to a virtual halt. Peru postponed its auctions of local currency securities and relied on large cash reserves. Brazil and Mexico dramatically reduced the issuance of fixed-rate paper during the crisis. Indonesia and Morocco reacted in the same way, although the impact there was less severe. In South Africa and Central and Eastern Europe, the impact of the foreign investor sell-off was probably more important than elsewhere, because nonresidents traditionally hold a significant share of local currency government securities and capital mobility is higher than in Latin America or Asia.

In some countries the sell-off of local currency medium-term fixed-rate securities by foreign investors was compensated for in part by institutional investors. In Brazil, Colombia, and Peru, pension funds absorbed part of the excess supply of medium- to long-term paper, making the switch to floating/short-term securities less pronounced. In contrast, in Central and Eastern Europe, even institutional investors shifted their preference to foreign currency or short-duration local currency assets, leaving banks to absorb most of the excess supply of government securities.

To offset the decline in demand for medium-term paper, some countries switched to Treasury Bills. The most notable case was probably Hungary, whose funding plans relied almost exclusively on T-bills during the eight months surrounding the crisis. Over the same period, Poland doubled its T-bill share, from 6 percent to 12 percent; Romania significantly increased its T-bill volume and introduced one- and three-month securities; and South Africa tripled its issuance of T-bills.

Other emerging markets switched funding from fixed-rate instruments to floating-rate ones. Brazil reduced its target of fixed-rate paper after the crisis hit and increased the target for floating-rate paper. Turkey increased the issuance of both shorter-term and floating-rate paper.

As a result of these changes in funding policy, most countries reduced the average time to maturity. However, given the relatively short duration of the intense phase of the financial crisis and the fact that emerging markets regained normal access by mid-2009, most of the reductions in average maturity were small, short-lived, or both. Brazil, Mexico, and Poland experienced small reductions in the average life of their portfolios. Hungary reduced the average time to maturity by 0.6 year, going from 2.7 years in September 2008 to 2.1 years in July 2009. Turkey reduced the average maturity of its portfolio from 34 months in 2007 to 32 months in 2008 but recovered in 2009 to 35 months.

Implementing Liability Management Operations to Support the Market

Liability management techniques such as buybacks and exchanges proved to be powerful tools to help stabilize markets. Many debt managers found that these transactions reduced market pressure and played a catalytic role in adjusting the debt structure to the changing characteristics of the demand profile.

Hungary, Indonesia, and Mexico used buybacks to alleviate sell-off pressures, enhance liquidity, and improve the pricing of liquid instruments. As securities were bought back for cash, these operations provided much-needed liquidity relief to investors and helped contain sell-off pressures, especially on illiquid securities.[23] In Hungary, for example, a large-scale bond buyback program of about $2.5 billion was launched in the second quarter of 2009 because of the significant sell-off by foreign investors and weak demand for local bonds. The program was successful, enabling Hungary's debt agency to restart regular bond auctions in April 2009. Indonesia helped stabilize prices by conducting buybacks and switches of short-term instruments, providing good price references when market liquidity was weak.[24] Mexico implemented buyback auctions of selected medium- and long-term securities to enhance their liquidity. Poland used switches to stabilize the market by redeeming illiquid bonds in exchange for more liquid securities. During the crisis, Poland replaced illiquid long-term CPI–indexed bonds and floating-rate notes with more liquid instruments in order to stabilize the market.

An innovative approach that seems to be working well is the simultaneous buy and sell auctions used by Brazil. At the peak of the crisis, the Brazilian Treasury conducted this type of auction for some long-term securities. These auctions provide reliable buy and sell price parameters at a time when references in the secondary markets are weak or nonexistent. Price discovery usually requires a sequence of two to three auctions for each instrument. Brazil had already tested simultaneous auctions during recent periods of turbulence and found that they did a better job of stabilizing markets than did pure buyback auctions.

Countries implemented debt managers' responses to the crisis in different ways. Some were forced to revisit and adjust their debt management strategies; others, which had looser or more directional guidelines, could operate within the prevailing policy framework.

Countries with strategies expressed as formal targets for managing risk were forced to review their strategies during the crisis. Brazil, which has annual targets for the composition of the debt portfolio, reviewed its targets, opening up more space for floating-rate paper and reducing the target for fixed-rate debt. The Brazilian debt management office saw this adjustment as a temporary setback and reversed it after the situation normalized. Hungary and Poland reviewed their strategies to include a higher share for foreign currency debt in the years to come, at least until some of their multilateral loans mature.

In contrast, countries in which debt management strategies are expressed as broad directional targets for certain risk indicators did not need to undertake formal reviews of their strategies. Although most countries formally acknowledged the increase in funding requirements, not all revised their policy frameworks, with debt managers continuing to operate under the prevailing one. Poland's broad bands for local currency risk indicators did not require revision during the crisis. The directional targets in Mexico and Turkey did not need to be reviewed, although both countries slowed their progress in reducing risk in their debt portfolios.

Concluding Remarks

The impact of the global financial crisis on the 24 countries considered in this chapter, as well as the responses by their public debt managers, provides a number of positive lessons for policy makers and international financial institutions. First, sound and well-coordinated macroeconomic policy during the years before the crisis, which led to much-improved fundamentals, served as a buffer and positioned emerging markets for quicker recovery. Although the improvement in macroeconomic fundamentals could in part be attributed to a very benign (cyclical) environment, driven by ample global liquidity and a strong risk appetite by investors, explicit policy choices by emerging market decision makers enabled them to capitalize on this environment and reduce their vulnerability. Some of the main measures implemented were improved fiscal policy, accumulation of foreign reserves, controlled inflation, and consequent reduction in public debt to GDP ratios.

Prudent public debt management with a focus on containing risks in debt portfolios also strengthened resilience to the crisis. Policies that reduced foreign exchange exposure, extended the maturity of domestic debt, reduced reliance on floating-rate instruments, and diversified funding sources were particularly important. In contrast to many previous events, the impact of the events of 2008 and 2009 on government budgets was muted by the reduced level of foreign exchange exposure (and in some cases attainment of a net foreign exchange asset position).

Both sound and well-coordinated macroeconomic policy and prudent debt management before the crisis provided public debt managers with room to maneuver when the crisis hit. Governments were able to delay borrowing, use nonmarket sources of funding, and introduce a range of measures to continue borrowing in their domestic securities markets. In this way, when markets were suffering severe risk aversion to the point of dysfunction, governments had the capacity to absorb some risk and contribute to the stabilization and recovery of local markets.

The availability and quick disbursement of multilateral funding were critical in cases where international capital markets were closed and investors in domestic government securities withdrew from the market. Contingent credit lines proved extremely useful, and debt managers learned how valuable these options became. The massive increase in demand for multilateral loans revealed the limited capacity that multilateral institutions have to offset a significant reversal of private capital flows, however.

Countries with larger and more developed domestic bond markets tended to be less affected by the crisis. In some of these countries, even during the worst of the crisis, capital flew to government securities, mirroring the market movements experienced in the United States, Europe, and Japan. Although some time elapsed before interest rates came back to precrisis levels, most other countries were able to satisfy their funding needs in the domestic market.

The crisis highlighted the degree to which the capacity of public debt managers in the surveyed countries has improved in the past decade. In a number of countries, debt managers were able to quickly employ a range of measures (liability management techniques, the use of cash reserves, quick adjustment of debt strategies, and so forth) that helped governments weather the turbulence in financial markets and implement appropriate countercyclical fiscal policies. This outcome underscores the need for governments to ensure that finance ministries and debt offices are appropriately resourced and staffed.

The 24 countries considered in this chapter account for the majority of people living in emerging markets (and about 60 percent of the world's population). In a number of other countries, the financial crisis has had a greater negative impact on market access and funding costs. Most of these countries went into the crisis with poor fiscal positions, debt sustainability concerns, unresolved debt renegotiations, or some form of political deadlock that affected their ability to effectively manage macroeconomic policy. Their predicament underscores the need to take advantage of the benign phase of the cycle to address debt problems, as once a crisis hits, the options for action quickly shrink.

Notwithstanding the positive developments that most emerging markets enjoyed between June 2009 and March 2010, the period ahead presents more risks than usual, for several reasons. First, high-income countries have huge borrowing requirements (in 2009 their net marketable securities issuance was estimated at more than seven times that of 2007 [OECD 2009]), which will create strong competition for capital and potential market instability. Second, by its very nature, the process of phasing out extraordinarily supportive monetary policy increases risk. Moves in this direction are likely to result in increased market volatility as "carry trades," put in place to profit from very low short-term interest rates, are unwound. Monetary tightening must be carefully timed, in order to avoid increasing inflationary expectations on the one hand or cutting off the economic recovery and financial sector recuperation on the other. Opinions on the strength and durability of the global recovery differ; there remains a sizable risk that a faltering recovery would put pressure on the borrowing needs of most governments.

Given this outlook, it is important that policy makers in emerging markets maintain the prudent approach to macroeconomic management that has served them well over the past decade. The specific policy measures will depend on individual country circumstances. For countries with weaker fiscal positions, the recovery of growth presents an opportunity to reduce debt to GDP ratios by reversing the fiscal accommodation implemented to mitigate the impact of the global crisis. For countries with greater fiscal buffers and significant external surpluses, the emphasis should be on stimulating domestic demand and allowing exchange rates to adjust while maintaining vigilance over inflationary expectations. At the same time, debt managers in emerging market countries are well advised to maintain preparedness for market dislocations and to continue to seek opportunities to contain risk in public debt portfolios at levels that will ensure that fiscal policy is not jeopardized if disaster strikes again.

Notes

1. This chapter does not examine the impact of the financial crisis on low-income countries, because the focus is on the first-round financial impact during September 2008–April 2009, when their lack of integration into global financial markets to a large extent buffered them from impact. Transmission occurred later, through the real sector, as trade and remittances declined.

2. Surveys were sent to 24 countries: Brazil, Chile, China, Colombia, Costa Rica, the Arab Republic of Egypt, Hungary, India, Indonesia, Kenya, Malaysia, Mexico, Morocco, Nigeria, Peru, the Philippines, Poland, Romania, the Russian Federation, South Africa, Sri Lanka, Thailand, Turkey, and Uruguay. Fourteen of these countries—Brazil, Colombia, Egypt, Hungary, Indonesia, Kenya, Mexico, Morocco, Peru, Poland, Romania, South Africa, Turkey, and Uruguay—responded. Debt managers from the 24 countries were surveyed about the main impacts of the crisis on their funding needs and their access to the domestic and international capital markets. The survey also asked about changes in debt management strategies and operational responses to deal with the crisis, such as the use of cash reserves, alternative funding mechanisms, and liability management techniques.

3. Changes in fiscal and monetary policies, external accounts, and economic growth are highly interrelated. Disentangling exogenous and endogenous drivers of such variations is beyond the scope of our analysis.

4. The average debt to GDP ratio of the eight most indebted Caribbean Community (CARICOM) countries passed the 100 percent threshold in 2009.

5. These countries were the exceptions; the ones covered in the sample contain the majority of the world's population.

6. A common denominator of the transformation of the domestic debt markets in emerging markets was the expansion and growth of the local investor base, especially nonbank financial institutions, most notably pension funds, but also insurance companies and mutual funds. Foreign investors also played a major role in countries such as Brazil and Mexico, where they showed a significant appetite for local-currency long-term fixed-rate instruments.

7. The number of defaults was 15 in Latin America, 11 in Africa, 4 in Asia, and 4 in Europe. In Latin America, four countries defaulted or rescheduled three times during that period.

8. Full analysis of the exposure of the government financial position to foreign currency borrowing requires complete information on government stocks and flows. Because of data limitations, this chapter ignores cash flows and assumes that the main government stocks are government debt and the international reserves of the central bank.

9. The implementation of more flexible foreign exchange regimes in many emerging markets also contributed to reducing their exposure to shocks and facilitated adjustments in the external accounts.

10. The unweighted ratio fell steadily, from 1.44 to 0.77, over the same period.

11. The turmoil was created by a strong market reaction against the increasing probability of the left-wing candidate winning the presidential elections in 2002.

12. Unweighted averages are not used for the regions because in small samples, countries with low debt stocks and high ratios (for example, Chile) distort the mean. The trends in unweighted averages indicate the same structural changes.

13. The sample included in figure 16.7 tracks the same countries tracked by BIS for domestic and international securities (see http://www.bis.org/statistics/secstats. htm). The ratio of international to domestic securities slightly overestimates the ratio of foreign to local currency because of the issuance of local currency bonds in the international capital markets.

14. The IMF *Global Financial Stability Report* of April 2006 documented the structural changes in the domestic base of investors in emerging markets, identifying the increased relevance of institutional investors as one of the key factors behind the improvements in the profile of emerging market government debt.

15. Uruguay, for instance, has indicated that it has relied on inflation-linked instruments to shift from foreign exchange to local currency debt.

16. Hungary and Poland are exceptions, reaching their peak five-year credit default swap spreads for 2008–09 in late February and early March 2009. The extent of the problems of the financial system in both countries extended the period of relatively wide and widening spreads.

17. Emerging Portfolio Funds Research (EPFR) tracks net capital flows to a country through bond funds. Net capital flows from bond funds are computed by determining the change in bond fund assets over a period, weighted by the percentage of the fund allocated to a particular country during that period.

18. Growth in the G-7 economies (France, Canada, Germany, Italy, Japan, the United Kingdom, and the United States) fell from 2.5 percent in 2007 to 0.1 percent in 2008 and –3.5 percent in 2009, triggering the slowdown in emerging market country growth.

19. In Hungary the agreements with the IMF and the European Union forced a fiscal adjustment which kept the government deficit within relatively narrow bands.

20. Financial rescue programs in industrial countries are estimated to have cost 13.2 percent of GDP (Cecchetti, Mohanty, and Zampolli 2009).

21. Romania is the most striking example. At the beginning of 2009, projections forecast GDP growth of 2.9 percent and a deficit of 2.0 percent of GDP. By the end of the year, GDP had contracted by 7.0 percent, and the deficit had risen to 7.2 percent of GDP.

22. The increase in lending was one of the reasons why the World Bank sought an increase in capital from its shareholders.

23. Most countries financed buybacks with cash reserves or short-term funding or through their regular auctions of more liquid instruments.

24. Switches are most frequently used to reduce debt fragmentation, consolidate large-size benchmarks, and manage refinancing risk. Brazil and South Africa have also used them for these purposes.

References

Barro, Robert J. 1997. "Optimal Management of Indexed and Nominal Debt." NBER Working Paper 6197, National Bureau of Economic Research, Cambridge, MA.

BIS (Bank for International Settlements). 2008. "Financial Stability and Local Currency Bond Markets." *BIS Quarterly Review* December.

————. 2009. *BIS Quarterly Review*. December.

Campbell, J. Y., and R. J. Shiller. 1996. *A Scorecard for Indexed Government Debt.* Chicago: University of Chicago Press.

Cecchetti, Stephen G., M. S. Mohanty, and Fabrizio Zampolli. 2009. *The Future of Public Debt: Prospects and Implications.* Bank for International Settlements, Basel, Switzerland.

Eichengreen, B., and R. Hausmann. 1999. "Exchange Rates and Financial Fragility." In *New Challenges for Monetary Policy.* Proceedings of a symposium sponsored by the Federal Reserve Bank of Kansas City, Kansas City, MO.

IMF (International Monetary Fund). 2006. *Global Financial Stability Report: Market Developments and Issues.* April. Washington, DC.

————. International Financial Statistics database. Washington, DC.

JPMorgan. 2009. *Emerging Markets Debt and Fiscal Indicators.* New York.

Ministry of Finance, Uruguay. 2009. *Uruguay Debt Report.* July. Montevideo.

OECD (Organisation for Economic Co-operation and Development). 2009. "The Surge in Borrowing Needs of OECD Governments: Revised Estimates for 2009 and 2010 Outlook." *Financial Market Trends* 2009 (2), Paris.

Reinhart, Carmen, and Kenneth Rogoff. 2009. *This Time Is Different: Eight Centuries of Financial Folly.* Princeton, NJ: Princeton University Press.

World Bank. World Development Indicators database. Washington, DC: World Bank.

17

Crisis Preparedness and Debt Management in Low-Income Countries: Strengthening Institutions and Policy Frameworks

Dana Weist, Eriko Togo, Abha Prasad, and William O'Boyle

In the wake of the financial crisis of 2008–09, a number of governments in both developed and developing countries undertook massive fiscal and monetary interventions in order to stave off a systemwide financial and economic collapse. The magnitude of the public liabilities incurred as a result of this unprecedented, albeit necessary, government action and the consequences of exiting from the projected high-debt scenario have themselves become a major source of concern about a future crisis (Braga 2010). Indeed, history has shown that public borrowing accelerates markedly and systematically ahead of a sovereign debt crisis (Reinhart and Rogoff 2010). The International Monetary Fund (IMF) projects that government debt to GDP ratios will rise to 85 percent in Group of 20 (G-20) countries by 2014 as a result of the crisis, up from 62 percent in 2007 (IMF 2009).[1] However, G-20 countries, with stronger institutions and policies, are better equipped to deal with pressures of this kind. Among more vulnerable developing countries, especially low-income, the ability to manage their public debt burdens through a crisis of this magnitude is far from assured.

Empirical evidence supports the view that strong public debt management institutions and policies have played a critical role in mitigating the effects of the financial crisis in middle-income countries (see chapter 16). To some extent, the same could be said for low-income countries, albeit for different reasons. In middle-income countries, positive policy action led to risk reductions in their debt portfolios in the years leading up to the crisis. In low-income countries, creditor relations have historically been dominated by the official sector on the external front. In many (but not all) cases, a captive investor base on the domestic front helped prevent debt portfolios from becoming sources of financial vulnerability. The current environment will be particularly challenging for debt managers in low-income countries because financing options, from official as well as private sources, that were available to them before the crisis may no longer be available or may now have very different cost and risk characteristics. The new challenges that have emerged since 2008 call for a reevaluation of debt management strategies, focusing on the assessment and mitigation of potential risk.

Although the acute phase of the crisis is over, many pitfalls remain, foremost among them the potential for a new sovereign debt crisis (figure 17.1). The precrisis picture in low-income countries was one of optimism. Debt relief through the Heavily Indebted Poor Countries (HIPC) Initiative and the

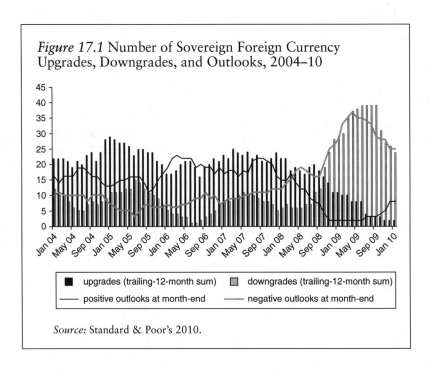

Figure 17.1 Number of Sovereign Foreign Currency Upgrades, Downgrades, and Outlooks, 2004–10

Legend:
- upgrades (trailing-12-month sum)
- downgrades (trailing-12-month sum)
- positive outlooks at month-end
- negative outlooks at month-end

Source: Standard & Poor's 2010.

Multilateral Debt Relief Initiative (MDRI) gave countries new fiscal space and renewed the potential for economic growth, which induced new creditors with more stringent terms to engage with low-income countries in both international and domestic markets.

As conditions in the international capital markets deteriorated, many such plans have been put on hold, as a new reality has set in. The longer-term trend shows declining access to donor funding as low-income countries move up the development ladder. Flows may be drying up even faster than previously projected given the severity of the financial crisis on sovereign balance sheets in donor countries. Such a shift in donor flows can accelerate the need for low-income countries to borrow on commercial terms, which could rapidly increase the exposure of their debt portfolios to financial risks if not managed prudently. These developments reinforce the importance of establishing strong institutions and policies.

Despite recognition of the need for such institutional strengthening, debt management performance in low-income countries has stagnated or even deteriorated in recent years, as measured by the CPIA Debt Policy Indicator (World Bank 2006). In light of this, it is important to assess the priority areas for improving debt management performance in a way that is tailored to country-specific circumstances and stages of development. For countries without the necessary legal and institutional framework to support effective debt management, the focus must be on identifying and addressing these weaknesses. For countries that have the institutional underpinnings of a functional debt management framework in place, the focus should be on building capacity to develop medium- to long-term debt management strategies that examine the cost-risk trade-offs in order to safeguard future debt sustainability. This is particularly important in preparing for future crises, as low-income countries gradually accumulate increasingly complex public debt portfolios that combine a wider array of financial instruments from both public and private creditors.

It is in this context that this chapter examines the application of two global public goods in low-income countries, the Debt Management Performance Assessment (DeMPA) and the Medium-Term Debt Management Strategy (MTDS) tools.[2] Drawing upon results from the application of these tools between 2007 and 2009 provides valuable information to policy makers and other stakeholders on the development of sound public debt management practices and analytical capacity.

A 2006 World Bank/IMF analysis of public debt management in low-income countries provided the empirical justification for the need to improve debt management capacity in low-income countries (World Bank and IMF 2006). It showed that debt management policy and high indebtedness are significantly related in low-income countries. This chapter builds on those results by identifying specific shortcomings in debt management in low-income countries and providing the basis for targeted reform programs to increase debt management performance.

A large body of literature exists on the importance of debt management in developing countries as well as on the links between debt management and financial crises (see Anderson and Togo 2009; Jaimovich and Panizza 2006; Melecky 2007; Panizza 2008; World Bank 2009a; World Bank and IMF 2003). This chapter builds on this literature by looking at new data that identify vulnerabilities and highlights areas for improvement.

The chapter is organized as follows. The next section gives a brief overview of the crisis, paying particular attention to its effects on low-income countries. The second section looks at the unique challenges developing countries, particularly low-income countries, face with regard to debt management. The third section focuses on the results of the DeMPA and MTDS tools and what they say about the current state of debt management in low-income countries. It identifies priority areas for improvement and highlights potential pitfalls in the current environment. The last section provides some concluding remarks.

The Global Financial Crisis and Developing Countries

The global financial and economic crisis of 2008–09 has significantly altered the economic landscape for developing countries. The effects of the crisis have been diverse, a function of both developmental and structural factors. Many Eastern European economies that were highly integrated with and reliant on Western European capital markets were hard hit by financial contagion and the sudden stop in capital flows. In contrast, low-income countries, with financial sectors that were largely not integrated with the global markets, were insulated from the financial market contagion that spread from developed economies. They were, however, severely affected by the decline in exports and falling commodity prices. As a result, developing countries now face a new and more precarious postcrisis environment, the major consequence of which will be potential reductions in trend growth over the medium term (figure 17.2).

With the exception of some large emerging markets that came into the crises with strong fundamentals and large external surpluses, capital inflows have declined sharply for most developing countries. For example, although China, India, and Indonesia have recovered to their precrisis levels, the rest of developing Asia has not (figure 17.3). Similarly, Central and Eastern Europe, which has larger current account deficits and greater reliance on foreign capital, saw private flows decline to below 2005 levels in 2009 (figure 17.4).

Despite these declines, the financing needs of developing countries have not fallen (figure 17.5). Overall, net private capital flows to developing countries in 2009 are estimated to have fallen by $795 billion relative to their 2007 peak; total external financing needs, measured by current account deficits and maturing private debt, are $1.2 trillion. Low-income

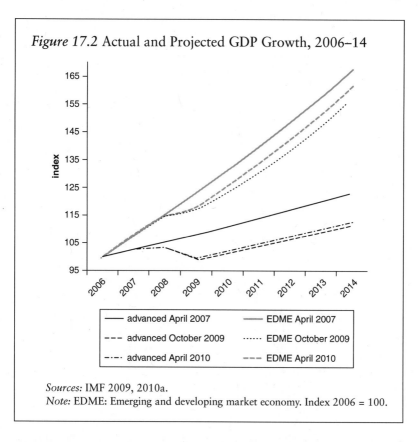

Figure 17.2 Actual and Projected GDP Growth, 2006–14

Sources: IMF 2009, 2010a.
Note: EDME: Emerging and developing market economy. Index 2006 = 100.

countries will suffer the most from this decline, as their already low 2.6 percent of total private capital flows is projected to fall to almost zero in 2010. Although small in absolute terms, these flows represent a significant share of national income, investment, and budgetary support. Their loss will have a severe impact on the ability of low-income countries to meet their financing needs in the short to medium term (World Bank 2010a). Countries eligible for soft loans and grants from the International Development Association (IDA) may require as much as $35 billion–$50 billion in additional funding in 2010 just to maintain 2008 program levels, on top of the resources necessary to fund additional demands created by the crisis (World Bank and IMF 2009c).

Tighter regulation in high-income countries and the need for multinational banks to conserve capital will also impede foreign bank lending in developing countries. In some regions growing participation by foreign banks in domestic financial systems supported the rapid rise in domestic financial intermediation. Indeed, the expansion in domestic credit in

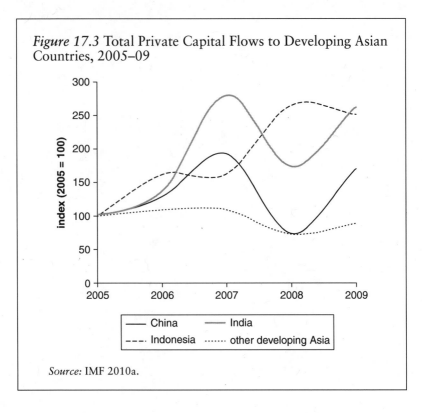

Figure 17.3 Total Private Capital Flows to Developing Asian
Countries, 2005–09

Source: IMF 2010a.

developing countries was directly related to GDP growth and the extent to
which foreign banks increased their market shares (figure 17.6). Foreign
direct investment (FDI) is usually less volatile and should be less affected
by the crisis than debt or equity flows. However, parent firms will face
higher capital costs, which are likely to reduce their ability to finance
individual projects. The real-side consequences of such a decline could be
serious, because FDI represents an important share of fixed investment
in developing regions, particularly in low-income countries (figure 17.7).
Remittances, another important and resilient source of capital for low-
income countries, have declined sharply (figure 17.8) and are not projected
to regain their precrisis levels until 2012 (Mohapatra and Ratha 2010).

The longer-run effects of the decline in capital flows are serious for
low-income countries, particularly because deficiencies in domestic intermediation systems are likely to prevent them from compensating for a
reduced foreign presence. However, low-income countries are not without
a potential remedy, particularly regarding improvement in their policies,
institutions, and the overall regulatory environment. Recent empirical
work shows that the inefficiencies in domestic financial sectors greatly
influence borrowing costs in developing countries (World Bank 2010a).

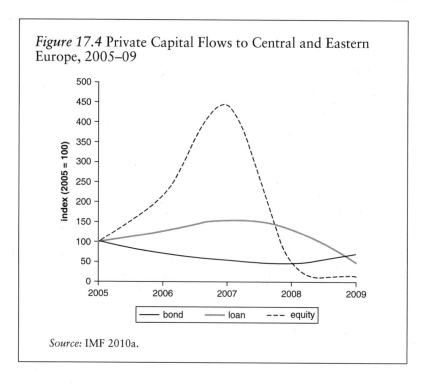

Figure 17.4 Private Capital Flows to Central and Eastern Europe, 2005–09

Source: IMF 2010a.

Improvements in policies and institutions governing the financial sector can thus significantly boost domestic financial intermediation to an extent that could outweigh the potential negative impact of higher global risk premiums, offsetting some of the long-term effects of the financial crisis.[3]

Faced with a less active external financing system, the authorities in developing countries must take steps to improve public debt management practices, including efforts to develop domestic debt markets, and to build the institutional capacity necessary to adapt to changes in the international financial environment to cushion the effects of exogenous shocks. Such improvements will decrease market perceptions of risk and increase cost efficiency, mitigating the effects of less favorable external financial conditions. Such improvements will also help reduce vulnerability to future crises.

Debt Management, the Crisis, and Low-Income Countries

Effective debt management covers such issues as ensuring effective policies and procedures for undertaking borrowings through external and domestic markets; designing and implementing a medium-term debt management

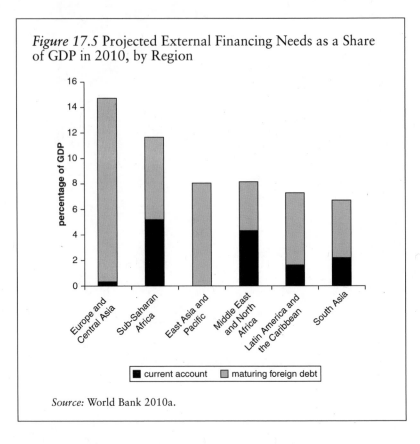

Figure 17.5 Projected External Financing Needs as a Share of GDP in 2010, by Region

Source: World Bank 2010a.

strategy; and putting in place effective systems for administration, analysis, and reporting of debt data (World Bank 2009a, 2009b). In times of crisis, sovereigns' access to resources, particularly through external markets, is stressed. There is thus an urgent need for prudent and effective debt management strategies, policies, and procedures to stave off and mitigate vulnerabilities at such times.

Low-income countries face limited choices with regard to debt management. Their internal challenges lie in developing adequate capacity to manage public debt effectively, particularly in establishing institutional and governance arrangements and developing analytical capabilities. Their choices are significantly more limited with respect to the sources and instruments they can access to meet their financing needs (figure 17.9).

The creditor composition and concessionality of the debt portfolio also differ markedly in low- and middle-income countries (figure 17.10). Multilateral and official bilateral creditors make up more than 95 percent of the public and publicly guaranteed external debt held by low-income

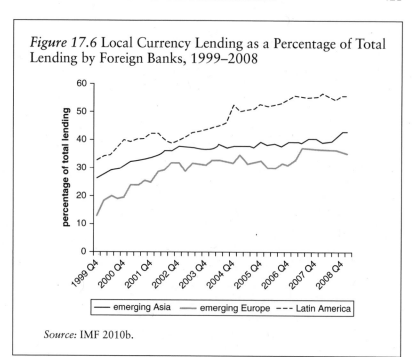

Figure 17.6 Local Currency Lending as a Percentage of Total Lending by Foreign Banks, 1999–2008

Source: IMF 2010b.

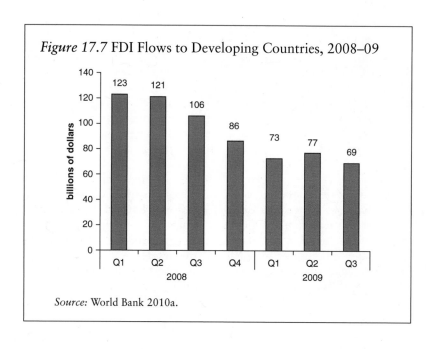

Figure 17.7 FDI Flows to Developing Countries, 2008–09

Source: World Bank 2010a.

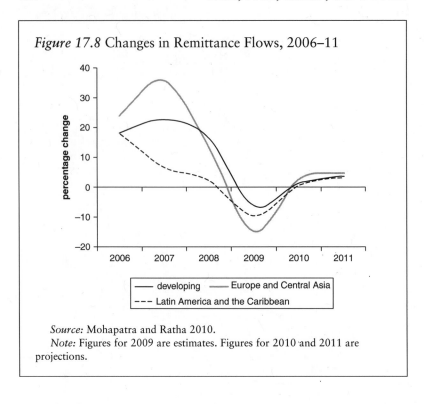

Figure 17.8 Changes in Remittance Flows, 2006–11

Source: Mohapatra and Ratha 2010.
Note: Figures for 2009 are estimates. Figures for 2010 and 2011 are projections.

countries. More than 90 percent of this debt is contracted on concessional terms, with below-market interest rates and long maturity periods. Largely fixed-rate concessional sources of funding limit exposure to interest rate risk, but the consequent exposure to currency risk has been significant. By contrast, one-third of the public external debt stock in middle-income countries is made up of commercial credits. The combination of commercial debt and nonconcessional financing provided by bilateral and multilateral institutions implies that more than half of middle-income country debt is contracted on nonconcessional terms.

Traditionally, the typical strategy for low-income countries has been to maximize concessional debt. Such a strategy minimizes debt-servicing costs, leading to a lower risk of debt distress and improved debt sustainability. It also results in significant exchange rate risk (figure 17.11). In many low-income countries, the mix of external and domestic financing is not a choice but rather a function of the international donor community's willingness and ability to provide external financing, with domestic financing used as a residual to close the funding gap. The characteristics of donor funding can be highly advantageous, but when the mix of external and domestic debt financing is not a domestic policy choice, the scope for

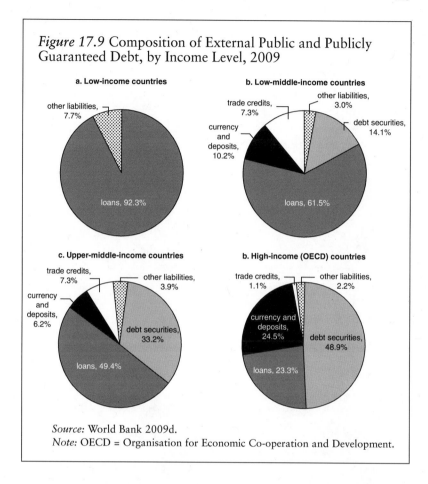

Figure 17.9 Composition of External Public and Publicly Guaranteed Debt, by Income Level, 2009

Source: World Bank 2009d.
Note: OECD = Organisation for Economic Co-operation and Development.

effective and independent policy making is constrained. Focusing solely on external sources of funding can also lead to the neglect of domestic debt market development, an important alternative that provides additional degrees of freedom, often with lower transaction costs, to the debt manager. This alternative is especially important when access to external financing has been reduced.

The current environment is particularly challenging for debt managers in low-income countries because the financing options that were available in 2007 now have very different cost and risk characteristics. Analysis of the crisis effects on donor financing illustrates the large extent to which donor country aid declines in the years after a banking crisis, posing a significant risk to fiscal and debt sustainability in low-income countries.

Aid flows from crisis-affected donor countries can decrease significantly for a decade or more postcrisis (figure 17.12). This volatile and changing

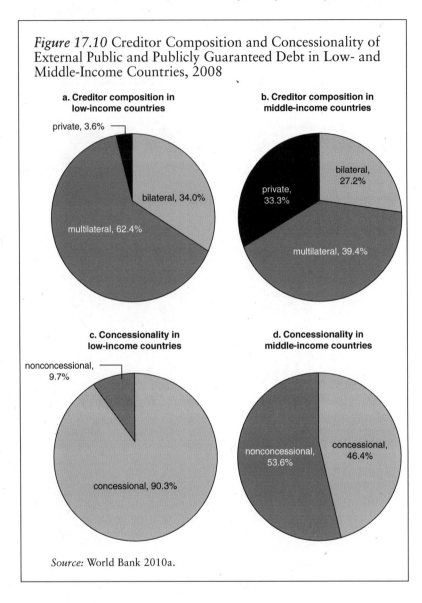

Figure 17.10 Creditor Composition and Concessionality of External Public and Publicly Guaranteed Debt in Low- and Middle-Income Countries, 2008

a. Creditor composition in low-income countries

private, 3.6%
bilateral, 34.0%
multilateral, 62.4%

b. Creditor composition in middle-income countries

bilateral, 27.2%
private, 33.3%
multilateral, 39.4%

c. Concessionality in low-income countries

nonconcessional, 9.7%
concessional, 90.3%

d. Concessionality in middle-income countries

nonconcessional, 53.6%
concessional, 46.4%

Source: World Bank 2010a.

outlook for debt markets, creditors, and donors highlights the importance of developing and maintaining a diverse range of financing sources and a resilient source of domestic savings to absorb shortfalls in external financing. Low-income countries are constrained, however, in that the scope to substitute external concessional sources with domestic savings is severely

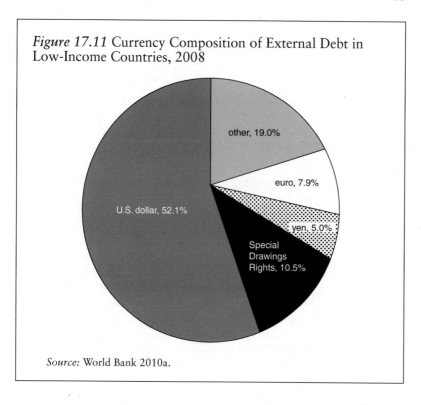

Figure 17.11 Currency Composition of External Debt in Low-Income Countries, 2008

other, 19.0%

euro, 7.9%

U.S. dollar, 52.1%

yen, 5.0%

Special Drawings Rights, 10.5%

Source: World Bank 2010a.

limited because of the state of domestic market development or the lack of a viable domestic market, as in the case of small states. (See chapter 8 for an analysis of the evolution of domestic debt in small states.)

Debt managers could undertake a simple analysis to determine the relative advantages and disadvantages of accessing external versus domestic debt. The analysis compares the forward exchange rate at time t using implied real interest rates with the forward exchange rate using real interest rates (table 17.1). This analysis gives the debt manager two different theoretical rates. In theory, the forward exchange rate gives the rate at which there should be no preference between contracting external or domestic debt. If using the implied rates translates into a larger depreciation needed to reach the equilibrium point, the bias is toward external debt because under the implied scenario, the external option is less expensive than the domestic alternative. The message is twofold. First, because of concessionality, low-income countries prefer to maximize concessional debt (see countries C and G). However, the bias toward concessional debt is not always as large and such debt is not as cost-effective as many assume (see countries A and E). In some cases, despite donor concessionality, contracting domestic

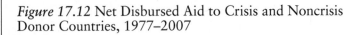

Figure 17.12 Net Disbursed Aid to Crisis and Noncrisis
Donor Countries, 1977–2007

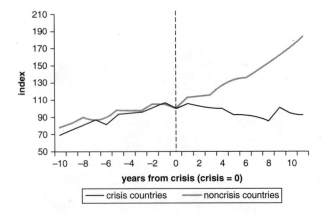

Source: Dang, Knack, and Rogers 2009.
Note: Vertical dashed line shows year of crisis, when index value is 100.
Data do not include the Republic of Korea, which became a donor only in
1990.

debt may be more advantageous because of negative real implied domestic
interest rates (see countries B, D, and F). Countries with a bias toward
domestic debt, or a mild bias toward external debt, can also use such an
analysis to support decisions to further develop domestic markets. Identification of this trade-off highlights the importance of developing the requisite
analytical capacity in debt management offices.

The DeMPA and MTDS Analytical Tools

Although debt-restructuring and debt relief initiatives have greatly benefited heavily indebted countries in putting them back on the track of debt
sustainability, they do not address the cause of debt distress, particularly
in the face of crises. In 2003 the World Bank and IMF published *Guidelines for Public Debt Management,* to help reduce developing-country
vulnerability to international financial shocks. Despite growing recognition of the benefits of debt management, measures of debt management
performance have not shown improvement in low-income countries. In
fact, debt management, as measured by the Country Policy and Institutional Assessment (CPIA) Debt Policy Indicator, has shown marginal
deterioration in recent years, falling from 3.32 in 2005 to 3.28 in 2006

Table *17.1* Analysis of External/Domestic Debt Bias
(percent, except where otherwise indicated)

Variable	Country						
	A	*B*	*C*	*D*	*E*	*F*	*G*
Real interest rate	7.80	-0.40	0.80	7.50	5.59	10.30	-4.10
External real interest rate	2.90	2.90	2.90	2.90	2.90	2.90	2.90
Implied domestic real interest rate on government debt	3.40	-3.10	7.00	-0.40	2.20	6.40	-3.60
Implied external real interest rate on government debt	-2.84	0.80	-0.10	-0.20	-1.80	-0.40	2.00
Forward foreign exchange rate at real rates (LCU/$)	71.87	6.61	67.76	3,913.20	1,227.57	11.14	110.44
Forward foreign exchange at implied rates (LCU/$)	73.01	6.56	74.09	3,738.15	1,245.04	11.10	125.38
Percentage point difference in forward rate (positive = external debt bias)	1.58	-0.68	9.34	-4.47	1.42	-0.34	13.53

Source: Authors' calculations based on sample of seven countries in which DeMPA and MTDS analysis was performed. U.S. real interest rates and inflation rates are used for the external scenario; cross-rates are not considered.

Note: LCU = local currency unit.

and 2007. This deterioration is important because the quality of debt management and the probability of becoming heavily indebted (that is, having a present value of debt to exports ratio of 150 percent) are closely related in low-income countries. Probit regression analysis of the relationship between a country's CPIA debt management score and its probability of becoming a HIPC shows that an increase in the quality of debt management equivalent to a one-point increase in the CPIA Debt Policy Indicator reduces the probability of a low-income country having an unsustainable debt burden by 25 percent (see annex table 17A.1 for probit results) (World Bank 2006). These finding are reinforced by a wider body of empirical work that finds strong linkages between debt distress and institutional quality (Kraay and Nehru 2006; Reinhart, Rogoff, and Sevastano 2003). An important conclusion from this analysis is that although the HIPC Initiative and the MDRI have reduced debt burden indicators, there is a continued need to improve debt management capacity and institutions in low-income countries in order to reduce the risk of debt distress.

The DeMPA

The DeMPA is a benchmarking exercise that assesses a country's debt management strengths and weaknesses. It examines the institutional underpinnings of government debt management practice and procedures through a comprehensive set of 15 debt performance indicators that cover the full range of government debt management operations. It also assesses the overall environment in which these operations are conducted. The DeMPA aims to measure government debt management performance and capture the elements recognized as indispensable to achieving sound debt management practice. An important facet of the tool is the emphasis it puts on debt management processes and capacity, both of which are required for effective debt management.

The DeMPA emphasizes meeting the minimum requirements on all measures (that is, receiving scores of at least C).[4] Doing so indicates that a country possesses the adequate institutions and capacity to carry out essential debt management functions effectively. Failure to meet the minimum requirements signals an area for priority attention and reform. The results of a DeMPA can help guide the design of sequenced and actionable reform programs, facilitate the monitoring of performance over time, and enhance donor harmonization based on a common understanding of priorities.[5]

Early results from the DeMPA exercise are useful in identifying priority areas for debt management reform across countries.[6] Indicators for which fewer than 10 countries in the sample met the minimum requirements are identified by the inner circle in figure 17.13. Low-income countries underperform lower-middle-income countries across nearly every indicator, although the patterns for the two groups of countries are broadly similar (figure 17.14).

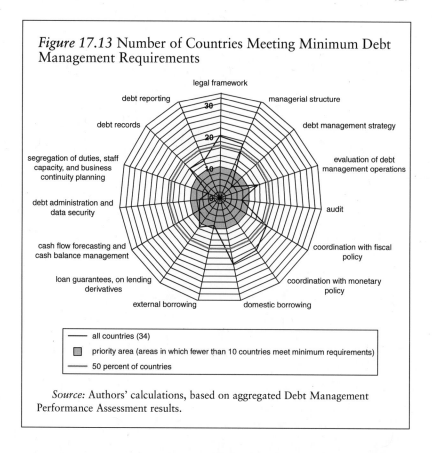

Figure 17.13 Number of Countries Meeting Minimum Debt Management Requirements

Source: Authors' calculations, based on aggregated Debt Management Performance Assessment results.

Priority areas for reform are areas in which fewer than 10 countries met minimum requirements (table 17.2). See annex figure 17A.1 for a detailed breakdown of priority areas.[7] They include the following areas:

• Medium-term debt management strategies
• Performance audits of debt management activities, processes, and operations
• Procedures for analyzing and documenting external borrowing .
• Cash management practices
• Administration, record keeping, and reporting of debt data
• Operational risk management.

Areas in which half of the countries met the minimum requirements under the DeMPA framework relate to the legal framework, managerial structure, coordination with fiscal and monetary policy, and policies and procedures for domestic borrowing.

Figure 17.14 Percentage of Countries Meeting Minimum
Requirements, by Income Group

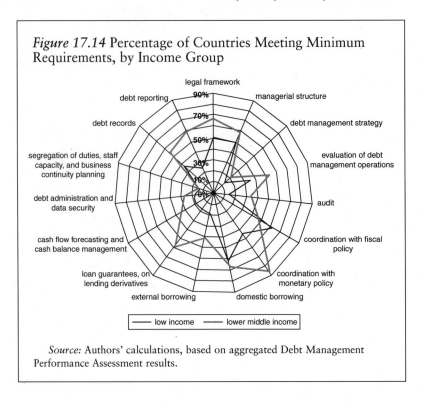

Source: Authors' calculations, based on aggregated Debt Management
Performance Assessment results.

The positive results can be explained by the fact that several countries
assessed during this round of the DeMPA were from regional monetary
unions, where central banks usually managed domestic debt. These central
banks were well versed in the Bank for International Settlements procedures and outreach activities on such issues, which explained the higher
scores on monetary policy indicators and procedures for domestic borrowing. Scores on the fiscal policy interactions are explained by the fact that
several countries were post–HIPC Initiative and Poverty Reduction and
Growth Facility (PRGF) countries, with effective medium-term fiscal and
expenditure frameworks in place.

Effective coordination with macroeconomic policies was compromised
by the fact that the policies and procedures for external borrowings were
lacking in several respects. Scores within this indicator reflect a low degree
of assessment of the most beneficial/cost-effective borrowing terms and
conditions and a general absence of documented procedures for borrowing in foreign markets. These findings are particularly worrisome because
a number of the countries in the sample have expressed interest in issuing
in international capital markets once the financial turbulence settles. Most
countries have effective legal frameworks that underpin borrowing, but

Table 17.2 Priority Areas for Improvement

Area	Number of countries not meeting minimum requirements	Percentage of total
Debt management strategy		
Quality of debt management strategy documents	29	85.3
Decision-making process, updating, and publication of debt management strategy	11	32.4
Audit		
Frequency of internal and external audit on debt management activities, policies, and operations, as well as publication of external audit	27	79.4
Degree of commitment to address outcomes of internal and external audits	4	11.8
External borrowing		
Assessment of most beneficial/cost-effective borrowing terms and conditions	25	73.5
Availability and quality of documented procedures for borrowing in foreign markets	28	82.4
Availability and degree of involvement of legal advisers	13	38.2
Cash flow forecasting and cash balance management		
Effectiveness of forecasting aggregate level of cash balances in government bank account	27	79.4
Effectiveness of managing aggregate level of cash balances in government bank account, including integration with domestic borrowing program	25	73.5
Where debt management entity operates its own bank accounts, frequency of reconciliation of these bank accounts	6	17.6

(continued next page)

Table 17.2 (continued)

Area	Number of countries not meeting minimum requirements	Percentage of total
Debt administration and data security		
Availability and quality of documented procedures for processing of debt service	26	76.5
Availability and quality of documented procedures for debt data recording and validation, as well as storing of agreements and debt administration	28	82.4
Availability and quality of documented procedures for controlling access to central government debt recording, management system, and payment system	26	76.5
Frequency and off-site secure storage of debt recording and management system backups	25	73.5
Segregation of duties, staff capacity, and business continuity		
Segregation of duties for some key functions, as well as presence of a risk-monitoring and compliance function	28	82.4
Staff capacity and human resource management	26	76.5
Presence of operational risk management plan, including continuity and disaster recovery arrangements	29	85.3

Source: Authors' calculations, based on aggregated DeMPA results.

accountability and transparency are lacking, as regular performance audits have not been undertaken.

A surprising area of deficiency is debt records and reporting: despite several years of technical assistance and the availability of off-the-shelf software, less than half of the countries met the required criteria. Anecdotal evidence suggests that loss of key trained staff, lack of transfer of skills among staff, and lack of documented procedures are the main reasons for poor performance. In several countries, public sector policies mandate rotation of staff. Better incentives by the private sector for skilled debt managers lure away key personnel. Both factors result in loss of key skill sets, resulting in slippages that require starting all over again. This problem is compounded by fundamental weaknesses inherent in most debt offices, such as the lack of procedure manuals and documented work processes that would mitigate gaps when key staff are transferred or leave.

Cash management is rudimentary across the assessed countries. Most countries have a large number of bank accounts, at times driven by donor insistence. In many countries, information on the aggregate level of cash balances is not available or monitored, and cash is neither invested nor integrated within the domestic debt borrowing program. In some countries, although several government accounts were flush with liquidity, the government still borrowed, incurring interest costs while earning no returns on surpluses. The DeMPA findings reveal a lack of analytical capacity to forecast cash flows and manage cash balances across several countries, along with the lack of single treasury accounts that could enable sovereigns to better manage costs.

Operational risk management practices were either absent or inadequate across countries.[8] Only one-quarter of countries met the minimum requirements for debt administration and data security, and only 6 percent demonstrated effective practice for aspects relating to segregation of duties, staff capacity, and business continuity. The sovereign debt portfolio is usually the largest in the country; mitigating the risk of fraud, human error, and market risk is critical given the high value of the transactions involved and the potential consequences of substantial financial loss as well as the severe reputational and political risks associated with operational error or failure. Deficiencies on this front are compounded by the lack of accurate and secure debt records and transparent and regular reporting.

The results suggest the need for increased technical assistance and strengthening in these areas, coupled with the procedures and institutional arrangements necessary to maintain a functioning debt management program. Administration, documentation, and monitoring and evaluation also need to improve.

The Medium-Term Debt Management Strategy

Taking a more strategic approach to evaluating financing choices requires greater integration of the formulation of debt management strategy and broader macroeconomic management. As its name suggests, the Medium-Term Debt Management Strategy (MTDS) provides a framework for formulating and implementing a debt management strategy over the medium term, typically a three- to five-year horizon.[9] It focuses primarily on determining the appropriate composition of the debt portfolio. The MTDS is useful for illustrating the trade-offs between cost and risk associated with different debt management strategies and for managing the risk exposure embedded in a debt portfolio, in particular the potential variation in debt-servicing costs because of exogenous developments and their budgetary impact.

The first step in developing an MTDS is to articulate the country's debt management objectives and scope.[10] Ideally, debt management objectives are stated in terms of meeting the government's financing needs in accordance with its cost and risk preferences. Extending the maturity profile of the domestic portfolio and developing the domestic debt market are common secondary objectives over the medium term. Most of the sample countries lack clarity in their objectives for managing their debt. When examining alternative strategy options, the debt manager needs to know whether the government is willing to assume higher costs to reduce risk or achieve other goals, such as developing the domestic debt market.

In most countries in the sample, governments follow an informal debt management strategy that is neither explicitly approved by the minister of finance nor based on an analysis of cost and risk. For low-income countries, this informal strategy has sought to maximize concessional borrowing. On the domestic front, the strategy has been to reduce refinancing risk, as the share of short-term debt in total domestic debt has been high in many countries. These informal strategies have typically been developed heuristically, which is important even when deriving a strategy based on quantitative analysis.

As a reflection of the existing debt management strategy, the debt portfolio in most of the sample countries was dominated by official sector concessional financing. However, the proportion of external to domestic debt and the relative depth and breadth of the domestic markets varied widely (table 17.3). Countries that received HIPC Initiative, MDRI, and other external debt relief experienced an instantaneous transformation of the portfolio composition toward a greater share of domestic debt (figure 17.15). As a result, foreign exchange exposure was reduced dramatically, although in most countries where an MTDS had been adopted, the share of external debt in the total portfolio still exceeded 50 percent.

As the share of domestic debt has grown, refinancing risks have become more acute. The contrast between the average time to maturity of domestic and external debt in all countries is stark. Going forward, the extent to which the domestic debt market development agenda is advanced will determine the pace at which the domestic share of total debt can be increased. The share of variable rate debt in the total debt portfolio tends to be low in

Table 17.3 Key Risk Indicators of Existing Debt Portfolio in Six Sample Countries
(percent, except where otherwise indicated)

Item	A	B	C	D	E	F
Outstanding debt to GDP ratio	48	71	23	33	43	12
Exchange rate risk						
Share of domestic debt in total debt	46	42	36	29	51	58
Refinancing risk						
Average time to maturity domestic debt (years)	1.6	3.9	1.0	5.3	4.3	2.7
Average time to maturity external debt (years)	16.2	15.8	12.5	20.6	11.5	10.9
Share of total domestic debt maturing in next 12 months	38	21	54	12	39	33
Interest rate risk						
Share of fixed-rate debt in total debt	95	99	79	100	100	98
Average time to maturity total debt (years)	8.6	10.9	8.4	14.7	7.7	5.9
Share of total debt that will refix interest rate in next 12 months	39	11	56	9	25	24

Source: Authors' calculations, based on sample of countries using the Medium-Term Debt Management Strategy.

low-income countries, pointing to minimal interest rate exposure. Analysis of the debt portfolio highlights the need to reduce exchange rate risk in the external debt portfolio and refinance exposure in the domestic portfolio.

The MTDS is forward looking. It is useful for evaluating the cost and risk consequence of new borrowing, particularly in the context of the changing financial landscape facing low-income country governments today. With the rapid increase in borrowing requirements in the aftermath of the global crisis and the need to finance scaled-up development expenditures to promote desired growth, the need to broaden and diversify sources of financing has become very important. In most of the sample countries, concessional borrowing has been maximized. The question is how to finance additional needs that cannot be met through concessional loans. In some countries, nontraditional bilateral lenders are emerging as important sources of finance, though their terms vary significantly from country to country. Countries at the upper end of the low-income country spectrum are exploring the possibility of becoming International Bank for Reconstruction and

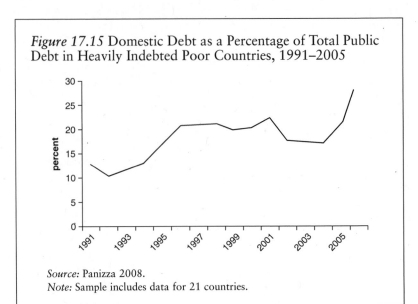

Figure 17.15 Domestic Debt as a Percentage of Total Public Debt in Heavily Indebted Poor Countries, 1991–2005

Source: Panizza 2008.
Note: Sample includes data for 21 countries.

Development (IBRD) blend countries.[11] In almost all of the sample MTDS countries, international issuance of bonds is being discussed.

Countries have deepened and broadened their domestic debt markets to different degrees. In some countries, the closed capital account has meant that foreign investors and foreign banks have not been competing in the domestic financial system. A closed capital account has allowed governments to tap domestic savings that were captive within their borders at low or negative real interest rates. It may keep markets shallow, however, and it tends to limit absorptive capacity for future increases in domestic debt issuance.

Where pension reforms have not dealt with underfunded defined-benefit schemes for public and private employees, domestic absorptive capacity of long-term debt is limited and represents a significant contingent liability for the government. Other countries with open capital accounts have been aggressively courting foreign investors. Pension and capital market reforms have helped deepen the domestic debt market, contributing to the growth of the domestic investor base.

Countries in the sample have been affected by the recent financial crisis through the real sector: the slowdown in developed-countries' economies has led to a dramatic reduction in export volumes and prices, as well as a fall in tourist receipts and remittances. Although import prices have also declined, the decline has not been enough to compensate for the reduction in exports, and external imbalances are expected to continue to deteriorate in the near term.

The resources to finance the current account deficit have been curtailed as private capital inflows have slowed, putting pressure on the exchange rate, reducing international reserves, and decreasing the import cover ratio. The fiscal position has also weakened, because the crisis has reduced government revenue collection and privatization receipts and expenditure has increased to counterbalance the effects of the recession. In some countries, significant uncertainty exists regarding the potential extent of contingent liabilities, particularly in the form of guarantees to parastatals, which constitute an important part of public debt. Donor inflows will also likely decline as a result of the worsening fiscal position of bilateral partners.

The sample countries vary in their ability to soften the effects of the crisis. Some of the commodities-exporting countries implemented countercyclical fiscal policy; because they had accumulated reserves, they were well placed to cushion the impact of the crisis. Other countries had capital control policies in place, which insulated them from the sudden stop of capital inflows and rush in outflows.

Many countries also experienced supply shocks, as headline inflation is often dominated by food and fuel prices. Some mix of nominal fixed-rate debt and inflation-indexed debt will help mitigate the effects of uncertainty of these events. From the perspective of the MTDS, the analysis suggests a bias toward borrowing in domestic currency to mitigate foreign exchange exposure given external vulnerabilities and low reserve levels. Achieving low and stable inflation will be essential to the success of domestic capital market development.

Two cost-risk measures are typically assessed in the MTDS analysis: the interest payments to GDP ratio and the nominal debt to GDP ratio. Conflicting results could emerge from using the different measures. The cost and risk measure of the interest payments to GDP ratio highlights the vulnerability of the budget to variations in interest payment projections. In the sample of low-income countries, without exception the interest cost of a strategy that maximizes concessional borrowing dominates other strategies, with the low cost reflecting highly concessional interest rates and the low risk reflecting the slight variations from the baseline as a result of the low absolute level of interest payment.[12] Strategies that pursue larger shares of domestic debt will have higher costs and risks according to this measure. The higher risk of the domestic debt is explained by the fact that higher-cost domestic financing replaces lower-cost external financing, which leads to higher absolute cost and risk levels.[13]

Cost and risk measured in terms of the debt to GDP ratio display a range of results across the sample countries. This measure assesses the vulnerability in terms of debt sustainability created by the path taken by alternative debt management strategies. In countries in which the domestic debt market was severely constrained and commanded a high premium, external concessional borrowing continued to outperform domestic borrowing in terms of cost and risk. Although the interest rates associated with external borrowing typically have lower coupon rates than those on domestic borrowing, in cases in which interest rates in the domestic debt market were more moderate and assumptions projected an important baseline exchange rate depreciation, the results showed a trade-off between a strategy that had a higher share of domestic debt (with higher cost and lower risk) and a strategy that had a higher share of external debt (with lower cost and higher risk). In such cases, the interest payments on the depreciated (that is, higher domestic currency equivalent) principal value can be higher than the interest payments on domestic debt, rendering domestic debt cheaper than external debt. Similarly, risk may be higher for external debt if the deviation in interest cost on the depreciated principal is greater than the deviation on the domestic interest cost as a result of interest rate shocks or a depreciation shock. Without exception, exchange rate shocks dominated the risk outcome (relative to interest rate shocks) for the debt to GDP measure, as this shock affects not only interest cost but also principal valuation.

In addition, the results of the MTDS are highly country specific and depend on the characteristics of the existing debt portfolio, the assumptions about baseline future exchange and interest rate projections, and the shock scenarios and macroeconomic projections that drive the pricing assumptions. For this reason, monitoring other risk indicators is crucial. For example, it is difficult to gauge the implications of refinancing risk from the cost and risk analysis. Closely examining and comparing the principal repayment schedule at the end of the time horizon for different debt management strategies, as well as comparing the average time to maturity and the percentage of debt maturing in a particular year, may identify an uncomfortable level of refinancing risk that may have resulted from a strategy that appeared to be attractive from a cost-risk perspective.

The main risk to debt sustainability arising from debt composition derives from exchange rate risk. However, given the relatively short maturities of domestic debt compared with external debt, there is a need for an aggressive domestic issuance strategy just to maintain the current domestic to external currency mix in the portfolio. If this debt is allowed to mature according to its principal repayment schedule, after three years external debt will have barely matured, with just 1–18 percent of the original debt reaching maturity (table 17.4). In contrast, domestic debt will have matured substantially, with 40–100 percent of the original debt having matured after three years. Of the total original debt, 63–85 percent will still be outstanding. Together with indicators such as average time to maturity, this measure indicates the length of time it takes to transform the existing debt portfolio. The fact that it takes longer to

Table 17.4 Percentage of Domestic and External Debt
Outstanding after Three Years in Selected MTDS Countries

Country	Domestic debt	External debt
A	39	99
B	54	91
C	0	82
D	59	96
E	44	84

Source: Authors' calculations.
Note: MTDS = Medium-Term Debt Management Strategy.

transform a portfolio can be advantageous, as it means that the portfolio is subject to lower refinancing risk. If, however, the existing debt is risky—for example, if it is heavily foreign currency denominated—the country will have to live with this risk for an extended period. In the absence of swaps, changing the debt composition can be achieved only marginally over time, as existing debt matures and new debt is contracted to finance the budget deficit.

In an environment of increasing deficits and infrastructure investment needs that will raise the new financing requirement, the implication of this analysis is that debt structures can quickly evolve. Unless a prudent debt management strategy is in place, the public debt portfolio can quickly become riskier. As countries increasingly evaluate nonconcessional sources of financing, including the option of issuance in the international capital market, assessing the risk consequence of such borrowing on the overall portfolio becomes increasingly acute.

Nonconcessional Borrowing

Many low-income countries seek to reduce donor dependence because donor financing can be volatile and unpredictable, the use of funds is often tied to specific project-related expenditures, and doing business with multilateral institutions can involve high transaction costs. But moving to the international capital markets adds to financing volatility while raising costs. Turning to such nonconcessional sources also fails to address exchange rate and refinancing risks and is subject to international credit cycles. Moving to domestic financing has merit in that it eliminates exchange rate risk, but doing so can add to refinancing risk and increase interest cost. For some small low-income economies, there may not be the investor base to support a viable government bond market.

Given the large social and infrastructure needs in many countries, additional inflows can be a welcome development, particularly where domestic resources are insufficient. Access to new sources of financing can also improve the scope for actively managing risk in the public debt portfolio, by offering greater scope to change the currency exposure of the portfolio to tailor it to the country's export revenue streams, for example. However, the diversification of financing sources is likely to be achieved at the expense of higher debt-servicing costs and potentially higher refinancing and interest rate risks. Greater foreign investor interest also increases the scope for domestic debt to play a more active role in the portfolio, because increased availability of resources in domestic currency can facilitate the extension of the tenor of domestic debt.

The management of nonconcessional debt poses new challenges and could increase the risk that low-income countries will accumulate unsustainable debt burdens, however. The buildup of nonconcessional external debt can place a heavy debt-servicing burden on low-income countries. If debt management units lack the capacity to undertake a credible forward-looking debt sustainability analysis, borrowing strategies may not be aligned with long-term servicing capacity, and imprudent borrowing may result.

Even a modest amount of nonconcessional borrowing can significantly increase debt-servicing costs. Despite the relatively modest amount of nonconcessional debt stock in 2007 (the latest year for which data are available), debt service on nonconcessional debt in several countries represented a large portion of total debt service (figure 17.16). In Ethiopia, Ghana, Myanmar, Uzbekistan, and Zimbabwe, for example, nonconcessional debt service made up the majority of total debt service. The availability of nonconcessional financing has increased the urgency to build capacity to develop and implement credible debt management strategies, so that governments can make informed borrowing decisions to manage their debt portfolios.

Concluding Remarks

Sound debt management practices play a critical role in preventing and mitigating financial crises in both low- and middle-income countries. The challenges are particularly great in low-income countries, which lack economic diversification, deep financial markets, and sufficient endowments of institutional and human capital with which to prepare for and respond to crises.

The first step in addressing debt management performance is to assess the strengths and weaknesses in a country's current framework. The DeMPA was designed to identify these weaknesses and provide

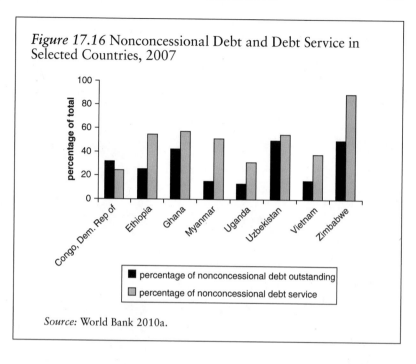

Figure 17.16 Nonconcessional Debt and Debt Service in Selected Countries, 2007

Source: World Bank 2010a.

benchmarks for reform. Preliminary assessment of its results shows that developing countries need to strengthen crucial areas of debt management, particularly the capacity to assess cost-risk trade-offs in their public debt portfolios. The MTDS is an important tool for addressing this issue. An effective MTDS illustrates the cost-risk trade-offs of a variety of strategies within a country's debt management framework. Reducing these costs and risks, while providing flexibility to achieve long-term objectives, will lead to stronger public balance sheets and increased resilience against future shocks.

Given the uncertainty of the current environment and the evolution of debt levels and interest rates worldwide, it remains to be seen whether vulnerable low-income countries will be able to effectively manage their debt. Although this uncertainty and uncertainty surrounding the outcome of the financial crisis remain, one concrete lesson to be drawn from recent experience is that strengthening debt management capacity in developing countries, particularly low-income countries, will be an indispensable tool in preventing and mitigating crisis effects now and in the future.

Annex

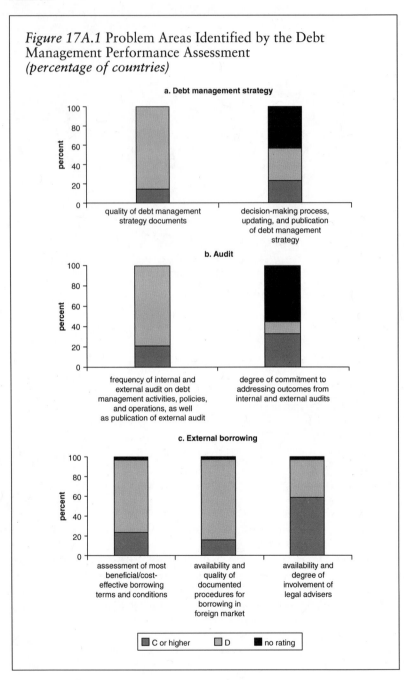

Figure 17A.1 Problem Areas Identified by the Debt
Management Performance Assessment
(percentage of countries)

Figure 17A.1 (continued)

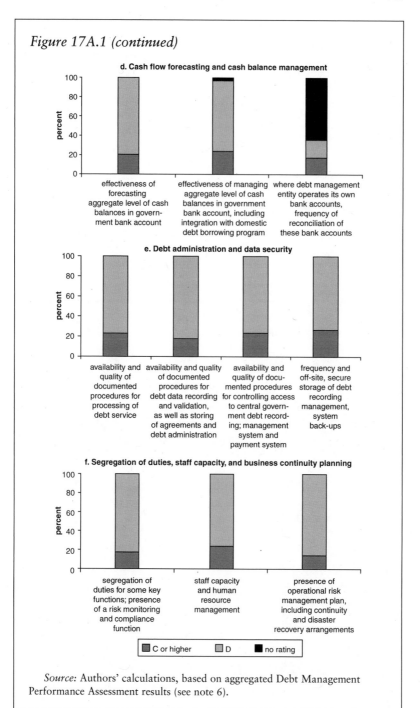

Source: Authors' calculations, based on aggregated Debt Management Performance Assessment results (see note 6).

Table 17A.1 Quality of Debt Management and HIPC Eligibility

Variable	I	II	III	IV	V	VI	VII
Net present value of debt/GDP	0.23***	0.19***	0.28***	0.12**	0.19***	0.11***	0.61***
	2.56	*2.85*	*2.64*	*2.09*	*2.89*	*2.83*	*3.03*
Income	-0.28***	-0.24***	-0.30***	-0.22***	-0.24***	-0.25***	-0.43***
	5.74	*5.51*	*5.73*	*5.80*	*5.41*	*4.59*	*5.25*
CPIA debt management		-0.32***		-0.25**	-0.32**	-0.48***	-0.71***
		2.65		*2.51*	*2.54*	*3.60*	*3.41*
CPIA			0.04				
			0.72				
Growth 1985–95				-0.38***			
				2.89			
Growth in volume 1985–95					-0.12		
					0.08		
Number of observations	102	102	100	102	102	101	82
Pseudo-R^2	0.56	0.60	0.57	0.66	0.60	0.56	0.60
Wald	38.12	36.38	40.28	36.51	36.80	21.92	37.94
Year	1995	1995	1995	1995	1995	1990	1985

Source: Authors' calculations and World Bank 2006.
Note: Marginal effects dF/dx reported. Absolute value of t-statistics in italics. Dependent variable: binary variable = 1 if the country is eligible for HIPC relief and = 0 if not (48 eligible countries). Income is the log of real per capita income denominated in U.S. dollars. All errors are robust standard errors correcting for heteroskedasticity. CPIA = Country Policy and Institutional Assessment; HIPC = Heavily Indebted Poor Countries.
* Significant at the 10% level; **Significant at the 5% level; ***Significant at the 1% level.

Notes

1. In fact, the rise in debt levels comes uniquely from the developed countries in the G-20, whose general government debt levels are predicted to rise from 78.2 percent in 2007 to 118.4 percent in 2014.

2. The DeMPA was developed by the World Bank; the MTDS was developed jointly by the Bank and the IMF. Both tools were developed through a broad consultative process that sought suggestions and inputs from client countries and providers of international technical assistance that are active in the field.

3. A World Bank study (2010) shows that an average annual decline in interest spreads of 25 basis points could increase long-term potential output by 13 percent, increasing potential average annual output growth by 0.3 percent.

4. DeMPA indicators are scored on a scale from A to D. A score of C or higher indicates that the minimum requirements for effective debt management have been met; a D indicates that these requirements have not been met.

5. See World Bank (2009a) for a complete list of DeMPA indicators and sub-indicators. DeMPA material and a list of country implementations can be found at www.worldbank.org/debt.

6. The analysis is based on the results of 34 assessments conducted between November 2007 and December 2009.

7. This in no way implies that other areas are less important for reforms, simply that few countries met minimum requirements at the time of this study.

8. A factor in the comparative neglect of this area of public debt management in low-income countries could well be that most borrowers access multilateral and bilateral sources of finance. Operational risk is mitigated in these cases, because the lending institutions have strong fiduciary safeguards in place (although this is clearly not sound practice, as the borrower should be able to independently verify and manage the risk). This could well be a reason for the low priority bestowed on this critical area in several low-income countries and an explanatory factor for the low DeMPA scores.

9. The MTDS consists of a toolkit to assist governments in analyzing and developing an MTDS, taking into account macroeconomic and market environments.

10. For the framework for developing an MTDS, see World Bank and IMF (2009a). Quantitative analysis is not necessary to put a good MTDS in place. If countries followed the Guidance Note and assess the various considerations to derive candidate strategies, they can develop an acceptable set of strategies for consideration by policy makers. Even if some outcomes are obvious, it is useful to explicitly quantify the cost and risk consequences of a particular strategy to understand the opportunity cost of adopting inefficient financing strategies. It is also useful to explicitly quantify the marginal cost of developing the domestic debt market, if this is an explicit objective.

11. See http://data.worldbank.org/about/country-classifications for borrowing options of IDA/IBRD Blend status.

12. Loans from the International Development Association (IDA) and the African Development Bank have zero interest rate risk, as interest rates are fixed at 0.75 percent, regardless of market conditions. Interest rate risk arises only from the nonconcessional borrowing incurred after countries reach the limit on concessional debt.

13. Substitution of a 2 percent external loan coming due by a 10 percent domestic loan would result in an increase in interest cost of 8 percent. Domestic debt would also be riskier because of the higher absolute level of interest payments and the higher interest rate shock applied to the domestic interest rate relative to

the foreign interest rate (say, a 2 percent shock for a domestic interest rate and a 1 percent shock for the foreign interest rate).

References

Anderson, P., and E. Togo. 2009. *Government Debt Management in Low-Income Countries*. Washington, DC: World Bank.

Braga, C. A. 2010. "The Great Recession and International Policy Coordination." Paper presented at the Reserve Bank of India Conference, Mumbai, February 12–13, 2010.

Dang, H.-A., S. Knack, and H. Rogers. 2009. "International Aid and Financial Crisis in Donor Countries." Policy Research Working Paper 5162, World Bank, Washington, DC.

IMF (International Monetary Fund). 2009. "The State of Public Finances." Fiscal Affairs Department, Washington, DC.

———. 2010a. *Financial Stability Report*. Washington, DC: International Monetary Fund.

———. 2010b. *World Economic Outlook*. Washington, DC: International Monetary Fund.

Jaimovich, D., and U. Panizza. 2006. *Public Debt around the World: A New Dataset of Central Government Debt*. Inter-American Development Bank, Washington, DC.

Kraay, A., and V. Nehru. 2006. "When Is External Debt Sustainable?" *World Bank Economic Review* 20(3): 341–65.

Melecky, M. 2007. "A Cross-Country Analysis of Public Debt Management Strategies." Policy Research Working Paper 4287, World Bank, Washington, DC.

Mohapatra, S., and D. Ratha. 2010. *Impact of the Global Financial Crisis on Migration and Remittances*. Washington, DC: World Bank.

Panizza, U. 2008. *Domestic and External Public Debt in Developing Countries*. New York: United Nations Conference on Trade and Development.

Reinhart, C. M., and R. Rogoff. 2010. "From Financial Crash to Debt Crisis." NBER Working Paper 15795, National Bureau of Economic Research, Cambridge, MA.

Reinhart, C., K. Rogoff, and M. Savastano. 2003. *Debt Intolerance*. Cambridge, MA: National Bureau of Economic Research.

Standard & Poor's. 2010. *Sovereign Rating and Country T&C Assessment Histories*. New York.

World Bank. 2006. "Public Debt Management in Low-Income Countries." Background paper for joint World Bank/IMF report "Strengthening Debt Management Practices: Lessons from Country Experiences." Economic Policy and Debt Department (PRMED), World Bank, Washington, DC.

———. 2009a. "Managing Public Debt: Formulating Strategies and Strengthening Institutional Capacity." World Bank, Washington, DC.

———. 2009b. *Guide to the Debt Management Performance Assessment (DeMPA) Tool*. Economic Policy and Debt Department (PRMED), Washington, DC.

———. 2009c. *Protecting Progress: The Challenge Facing Low-Income Countries in the Global Recession*. Poverty Reduction and Economic Management Network (PRMVP), Washington, DC.

———. 2009d. *Quarterly External Debt Statistics*. Washington, DC.

———. 2010a. Development Data Platform database; accessed April 2010.

———. 2010b. *Global Economic Prospects*. Washington, DC: World Bank.

World Bank and IMF (International Monetary Fund). 2003. *Guidelines for Public Debt Management*. Washington, DC: World Bank and IMF.

———. 2006. *Strengthening Debt Management Practices: Lessons from Country Experiences*. Washington, DC.

———. 2009a. *Developing a Medium Term Debt Management Strategy (MTDS): Guidance Note for Country Authorities*. Economic Policy and Debt Department (PRMED), Washington, DC.

18

Public Debt Management and Sovereign Risk during the Worst Financial Crisis on Record: Experiences and Lessons from the OECD Area

Hans J. Blommestein

This chapter reviews the experiences of Organisation for Economic Co-operation and Development (OECD) countries with public debt management during the worst financial crisis on record, the 2007–09 global financial crisis. It shows that the unprecedented global shock created local banking crises before setting the stage for a surge in government deficits and (contingent) liabilities. The rapid acceleration in sovereign borrowing needs was boosted by the fiscal response to concerns about the possibility of a severe economic slump. The resulting increase in sovereign risk created market concerns about an imminent or actual local sovereign debt and financial crisis in some OECD countries. The mutation into an actual sovereign debt crisis has revived concerns about renewed threats to the private financial intermediary system, including the interbanking market.

The origin, severity, and global nature of the financial shock and its aftermath made the 2007–09 crisis different from previous crises. Skillful debt management will need to be part of the overall macroeconomic exit strategy in order to contain the acceleration in sovereign risk, mitigate possible contagion dangers, and ensure the overall consistency of the macroeconomic policy mix. A credible exit strategy is also needed to control overly negative market sentiments and uncertainties surrounding sovereign credit risk that could lead again to dysfunctional markets.

OECD debt managers reported a softening of demand at some auctions, leading to postponed, failed, or canceled auctions and distortions in primary markets. Tougher issuance conditions as well as conditions of overall financial instability (which affect the functioning of primary dealers) are the principal reasons why existing issuance procedures, primary dealer arrangements, and portfolio management strategies have not always worked as efficiently as they did before the global financial crisis. Because they did not, sovereign issuers had to operate in circumstances that were at times unprecedented.

Signs of serious liquidity pressures were also present in secondary markets. A direct response to tougher issuance conditions by debt management offices (DMOs) in the OECD area included the implementation of changes in existing issuance procedures and policies. This type of policy response may have led to somewhat greater diversity of primary market arrangements and portfolio management procedures (for a detailed overview, see Blommestein 2009a).

The responses to the financial crisis—and, later, the economic crisis—resulted in a rapid increase in budget deficits and sovereign debt. These developments are likely to affect longer-term interest rates, with an adverse impact on the real sector ("crowding out"). The increase in sovereign risk, upward pressure on interest rates, and the resulting risk of crowding out put the spotlight on the importance of the overall macroeconomic exit strategy. Over time a return to a prudent medium-term fiscal strategy is an essential element of any credible exit strategy to bring debt-service costs, sovereign risk, and contagion pressures under control. A more comprehensive balance sheet definition of sovereign risk is urgently needed to help policy makers better assess the outlook for sovereign risk. There is also a need for closer (domestic and international) cooperation (including information exchange) by debt managers, fiscal authorities, and monetary policy makers.

This chapter is organized as follows. The next section examines the origin and impact of the global financial shock and its aftermath. The following section analyzes the policy challenges and responses to the crisis, including exit challenges and changes in borrowing strategies in OECD countries. The last section provides some concluding remarks.

Impact of the Global Financial Crisis

The origin, scope, severity, and global nature of the financial shock and its aftermath made the 2007–09 crisis different from previous crises. This unprecedented global shock created local banking crises before setting the stage for a surge in government deficits and (contingent) liabilities. The rapid acceleration in sovereign borrowing needs was boosted by public support for the financial sector and the fiscal response to concerns about the possibility of a depression-like economic slump.

Increase in Short-Term Government Issuance

At the peak of the financial crisis—following the collapse of Lehman Brothers on September 15, 2008—markets in private financial paper froze. The private financial intermediary system almost completely collapsed during the panic of 2008 (Warsh 2010). Measured by the degree of collapse of short-term financial markets, the 2008 global financial crisis is the most severe crisis on record. As Alan Greenspan (2010, p. 18) notes, "Evaporation of the global supply of short-term credits within hours or days of the Lehman failure is . . . without historical precedent."

This near-collapse of the financial intermediation system triggered unprecedented public support operations. Liquidity support by central banks (often in cooperation with DMOs) replaced or shored up short-term private markets, and capital injections by treasuries in the form of cash (such as the Troubled Asset Relief Program [TARP]) added billions to bank equity. Several DMOs in the OECD had to raise funds on very short notice for capital injections or recapitalization operations of nationalized insolvent banks. These injections of public funds represented a signal that OECD governments were standing behind the liabilities of the entire banking system, creating massive implicit contingent government liabilities. Governments also introduced guarantees for bonds issued by private banks, creating explicit contingent government liabilities.

In sum, financial support operations contributed strongly to the surge in issuance by OECD governments of both conventional and contingent liabilities. These operations by debt managers and other financial officials were instrumental in transforming banking crises and frozen market problems into increases in sovereign risk. In the absence of a credible medium-term fiscal exit strategy, such a policy may have set the stage for new bouts of financial market turbulence, this time triggered by a sovereign debt crisis.

The explosion in the supply of public debt happened at a time when even sovereign issuers were experiencing liquidity problems in their secondary markets. Moreover, in several markets interbank trading (almost) disappeared, affecting the market-making capabilities of primary dealers and transforming quote-driven markets into order-driven ones (an example includes the Hungarian market). In addition, several governments had to face increased competition not only from other sovereigns but also from bank bonds guaranteed by their own government.

Despite these liquidity problems and uncertainty about counterparty risk, even at the peak of the crisis, in 2008, primary markets for government paper continued to function reasonably well, even in countries facing major local banking crises. However, in countries with extreme market turmoil, for some time operations were restricted to Treasury Bill issuance, and Treasury Bond auctions were suspended. In almost all OECD markets, the issuance of short-term debt increased significantly (figure 18.1). As an additional response to the crisis, many OECD primary markets introduced changes in issuance procedures and techniques.

Higher Budget Deficits

Borrowing needs have increased rapidly in response to the soaring costs of financial support schemes, other crisis-related expenditures, and recession-induced declines in tax revenues and increases in government expenditures. As a result, in 2010 many OECD governments were expecting significant increases in budget deficits.

Amidst a highly uncertain economic outlook with increasing budget deficits (figure 18.2), gross borrowing needs of OECD governments increased explosively: by 2010 they were estimated to have reached almost $16 trillion in 2009, up from an earlier estimate of about $12 trillion. Projections for 2010 show borrowing stabilizing at about $16 trillion (Blommestein and Gok 2009).

Many OECD governments faced a significant increase in expected deficits in 2010 because of the fiscal fallout of a recession that was worse than first anticipated and the financial consequences of resolving banking crises. In 2010 the OECD areawide fiscal deficit is projected to peak at a postwar high of about 8.25 percent of GDP (OECD 2009a). Delegates

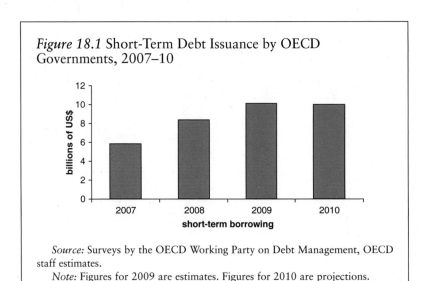

Figure 18.1 Short-Term Debt Issuance by OECD Governments, 2007–10

Source: Surveys by the OECD Working Party on Debt Management, OECD staff estimates.

Note: Figures for 2009 are estimates. Figures for 2010 are projections.

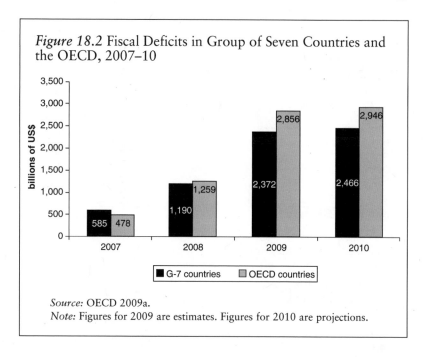

Figure 18.2 Fiscal Deficits in Group of Seven Countries and the OECD, 2007–10

Source: OECD 2009a.
Note: Figures for 2009 are estimates. Figures for 2010 are projections.

from the OECD Working Party on Public Debt Management confirmed that many DMOs in the OECD area (as well as outside it) are confronting dramatically increased borrowing needs.[1]

As a result, sovereign issuers all over the world are facing increased competition in raising funds from markets, leading to higher expected borrowing costs. A looming additional challenge is the risk that when the recovery gains traction, competition for savings will increase. If this occurs, yields will rise (figure 18.3).

Systemic Market Absorption Problems and Increasing "Crowding Out"

Issuance conditions have worsened in some markets. To date, however, less successful auctions can best be interpreted as "single market events" rather than unambiguous evidence of systemic market absorption problems (Blommestein 2009b). The future trend could be more challenging for the execution of borrowing programs, however, given that rising issuance is occurring hand in hand with increasing overall debt levels (figure 18.4).

Fiscal policy, government borrowing programs, and the resulting higher public debt are also likely to affect longer-term interest rates. These

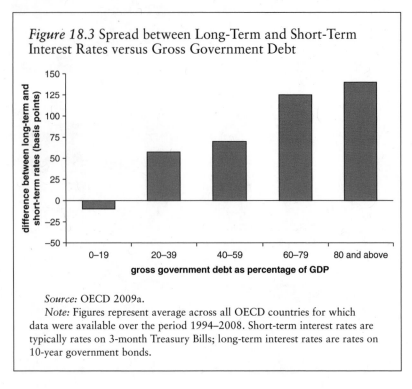

Figure 18.3 Spread between Long-Term and Short-Term Interest Rates versus Gross Government Debt

Source: OECD 2009a.
Note: Figures represent average across all OECD countries for which data were available over the period 1994–2008. Short-term interest rates are typically rates on 3-month Treasury Bills; long-term interest rates are rates on 10-year government bonds.

financial market developments are projected to have an adverse impact on the real sector by crowding out private demand and production through higher (expected) borrowing costs.[2] As of May 2010, this crowding-out effect remained muted: the savings rates of households and companies were relatively high in most OECD countries. Over time, however, when the recovery gains further strength, this situation is likely to change.

Larger Government Debt and Interest Payments

The rapid and massive surge in government issuance can be expected to push the prices of sovereign debt down and yields (further) up. The issuance challenges for many DMOs are compounded by increasing debt levels—a trend already visible before the crisis.

Debt levels in the United States, the Euro Area, and Japan have risen sharply since the peak of the crisis in 2008 (see figure 18.4). Total OECD area central government debt is projected to reach almost $32 trillion at the end of 2010 (OECD staff estimates). The surge in sovereign borrowing needs may drive up real longer-term interest rates (figure 18.5).

Empirical estimates of the impact of higher debt on interest rates differ considerably. Studies report estimates of an increase of (nominal) public

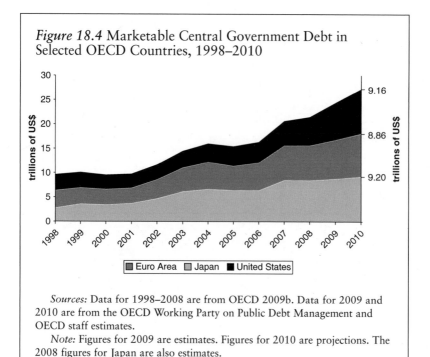

Figure 18.4 Marketable Central Government Debt in Selected OECD Countries, 1998–2010

Sources: Data for 1998–2008 are from OECD 2009b. Data for 2009 and 2010 are from the OECD Working Party on Public Debt Management and OECD staff estimates.

Note: Figures for 2009 are estimates. Figures for 2010 are projections. The 2008 figures for Japan are also estimates.

debt of 1 percent of GDP on higher (nominal or real) long-term interest rates ranging from less than 1 to 32 basis points. There is also evidence of a nonlinear relationship between debt and interest rates. The strong increase in outstanding debt and higher long-term interest rates in OECD countries also imply higher interest expenditures (figure 18.6).

Responding to the Global Crisis

OECD debt managers reported a softening of demand at some auctions. In almost all markets, the issuance of short-term debt increased significantly. As an additional response to the crisis, and to the tougher issuance conditions that resulted from the crisis, DMOs introduced changes in issuance procedures and techniques in primary markets.

Exit Challenges

Tougher issuance conditions and the risk of crowding out put the spotlight on the importance of a proper fiscal and monetary exit strategy

456   BLOMMESTEIN

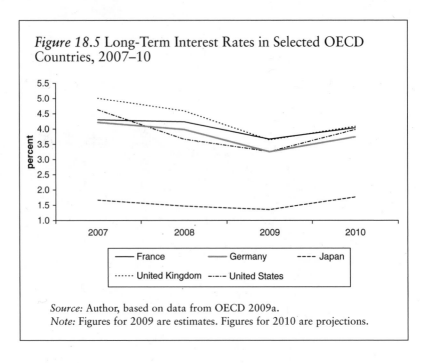

Figure 18.5 Long-Term Interest Rates in Selected OECD Countries, 2007–10

Source: Author, based on data from OECD 2009a.
Note: Figures for 2009 are estimates. Figures for 2010 are projections.

and better communication channels between DMOs and the monetary and fiscal authorities. Sovereign debt managers, with the support of sound fiscal consolidation policies, need to prepare and implement timely and credible medium-term exit strategies (Blommestein 2009b). Although skillful adjustments of the debt management strategy, discussed below, could potentially reduce government borrowing costs, sound public debt management is not a perfect substitute for sound fiscal policy. Over time a return to a prudent medium-term fiscal strategy is an essential element of any credible exit strategy to bring debt service costs under control.

The sovereign risk outlook is usually defined in terms of a traditional debt sustainability framework in which risk is a function of the country's primary balance (influenced by fiscal adjustment strategies) as well as interactions between economic growth and the average cost of funding (Blommestein 2010). This definition fits most of the emerging market crises during the 1980s and 1990s. Since the fall of Lehman, crisis-related interactions have led to an unprecedented expansion in sovereign balance sheets and a sharp increase in off-balance sheet items such as contingent liabilities. These developments warrant a redefinition of sovereign risk, with greater emphasis on a sovereign balance sheet approach together with reliable information on off-balance sheet items such as guarantees and outstanding derivatives positions (Blommestein, Guzzo, and Holland forthcoming). An additional complication is the need to avoid or mitigate

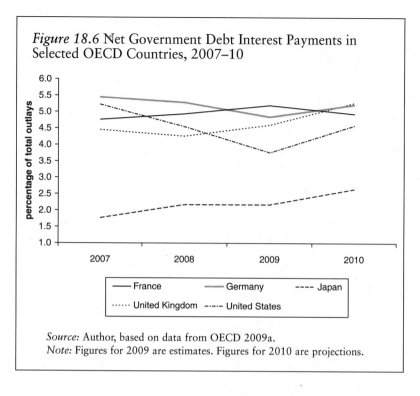

Figure 18.6 Net Government Debt Interest Payments in
Selected OECD Countries, 2007–10

Source: Author, based on data from OECD 2009a.
Note: Figures for 2009 are estimates. Figures for 2010 are projections.

possible market stress related to the higher real interest rates associated
with the central bank's exit strategy (Blommestein 2009b). To that end,
it is important that the (future) shift to a tighter monetary policy be
carefully implemented in terms of the timing and sequencing of the different exit measures taken by the monetary authorities. Because debt
managers are financing historically high (and still increasing) budget
deficits, it is important that DMOs and central banks keep each other
informed about policy moves that may have significant market impacts
(Blommestein 2009b).

Changes in Borrowing Strategies

OECD debt managers underline four important influences of the ongoing
financial and economic crisis on borrowing strategies:

- The borrowing requirements in many OECD countries have increased
  significantly in response to bailout operations and other crisis-induced
  expenditures (figure 18.7). Borrowing needs also increased through
  additional knock-on effects of the recession on expenditures and lower
  tax revenues.

- Liquidity conditions tightened initially, and market participants all over the world became much more risk averse, leading to an increase in the demand for safe assets by many categories of investors.
- Policy responses by central banks (through both conventional and nonconventional measures) and governments (with DMOs playing an important supporting role) improved liquidity conditions significantly.
- In countries that experienced extreme turmoil, for some time borrowing operations were restricted to Treasury Bill issuance and Treasury Bond auctions were suspended.

These influences forced debt managers to change or modify their borrowing strategies by holding more frequent auctions, shortening maturities, increasing foreign liabilities,[3] and issuing a different mix of instruments, made up of more short-term debt, notably bills[4] (figure 18.8). As a result, the response to crisis-induced uncertainty resulted in somewhat more opportunistic issuance programs.

Tighter issuance conditions are compounded by increasing debt levels. OECD governments with low debt levels and modest borrowing requirements (or fiscal surpluses) are in a much more comfortable situation than countries with higher debt levels. Countries with high and quickly climbing outstanding stocks of debt will face additional issuance challenges, which in turn may induce changes in borrowing strategies.

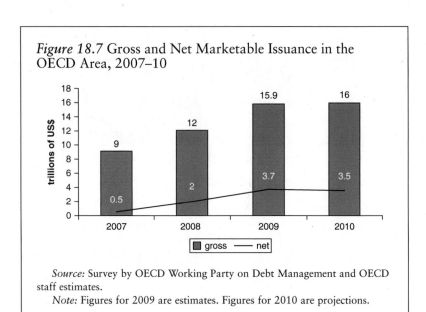

Figure 18.7 Gross and Net Marketable Issuance in the OECD Area, 2007–10

Source: Survey by OECD Working Party on Debt Management and OECD staff estimates.

Note: Figures for 2009 are estimates. Figures for 2010 are projections.

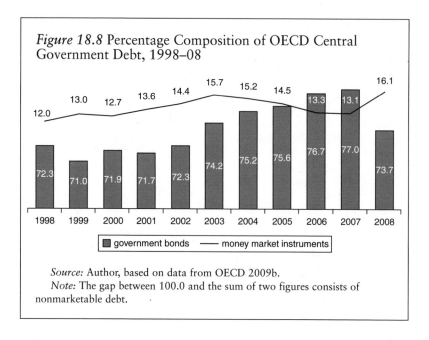

Figure 18.8 Percentage Composition of OECD Central Government Debt, 1998–08

Source: Author, based on data from OECD 2009b.
Note: The gap between 100.0 and the sum of two figures consists of nonmarketable debt.

Responses to the Surge in Borrowing Needs

The surge in borrowing needs has worsened issuance conditions, with some OECD debt managers reporting liquidity pressures in secondary markets and sometimes weak demand and distortions in primary markets. Delegates from the OECD Working Party on Public Debt Management confirm that responses to much higher borrowing requirements and concerns about possible market absorption problems included changes in issuance methods (including more flexible auctions, the introduction of auction fees, and the use of distribution methods other than auctions, such as syndication, Dutch direct auction procedures, and private placement) and changes in optimal sovereign portfolios (driven by new benchmarks that place greater emphasis on short-term paper and a reformulated cost-risk trade-off).

In response to liquidity pressures, rising borrowing requirements, and tougher issuance conditions, many DMOs made major changes to issuance procedures and the conditions for using existing systems and techniques (table 18.1). The risk-averse behavior of investors forced debt managers to modify their fundraising strategies. There are reports of increasing interest in the use of syndication, which has the potential to rapidly achieve a very high initial outstanding volume of issues with better placing certainty than auctions. The use of syndication may increase liquidity and reduce borrowing costs. Syndication also has potential downsides,

Table 18.1 Changes in OECD Issuing Procedures and
Instruments in Response to the Global Crisis

Country	Change
Australia	More flexible auction calendars Issuance of inflation-indexed bonds recommenced in second half of 2009 to broaden investor base; first issuance was through syndicated offering. Subsequent issuance of inflation-indexed bonds planned through single-price auctions. Auctions for all nominal debt are through the multiple-price format.
Austria	More emphasis on investor relations
Belgium	Tap sales for long-term debt Increased placement of medium-term euro notes
Canada	Reintroduction of three-year maturity Reduction in regular buy-back program but maintenance of switch operations on long end to support market liquidity Introduction of additional benchmarks for two- and five-year sectors
Denmark	Use of private placement in foreign markets in 2008 Termination of Treasury-bill program in 2008 Greater use of auctions in lieu of tap sales
Finland	Diversification of funding sources Greater emphasis on investor relations More coordination with primary dealers Higher syndication fees Active use of demand-supply windows
France	Increased flexibility for better matching demand Issuance of off-the-run bonds since second half of 2007
Germany	Use of tap sales for long-term debt More frequent auctions
Greece	Beginning in 2009, auctions of Treasury bills adopted single-price format Syndication for all types of bonds and reopenings
Hungary	More flexible auction calendar (biweekly bond auctions with dates but without tenors in calendars) More flexibility in amounts offered Introduction of top-up auctions (noncompetitive subscription) and auction fees More frequent use of reopenings of off-the-run bonds and buy-back auctions Planned introduction of exchange auctions Introduction of direct, regular meetings with institutional investors

Table 18.1 (continued)

Country	Change
Iceland	Single-price auctions (for long-term bonds) used together with multiple-price auctions
Ireland	Syndication added as funding tool Auctions for short-term debt
Italy	More flexible procedures Increase in range of offered amounts for on-the-run bonds Possibility of offering additional off-the-run bonds as response to highly volatile market conditions Adjustment of auction pricing mechanism for nominal bonds, linkers, and floaters (issuer discretionally sets total allocated volume within previously announced range) Participants in T-bill (Buoni Ordinari del Tesoro [BOT]) auctions required to submit bids in terms of yield Modification of method for calculating share in auctions Range of maturity of bonds sold to primary dealers at noncompetitive prices extended Introduction of reopenings of old bonds
Korea, Rep. of	Single-price format of auctions changed to multiple-price format in September 2009 Introduction of conversion offers
Mexico	Use of tap issues for short- and long-term bonds
Netherlands	Increased frequency of bond auctions (of off-the-run bonds) Extended repo and commercial paper facilities (longer maturity, extra foreign currency issuance) Extended Treasury-bill programs
New Zealand	Introduction of new long-term bond Use of tap issues for short-term debt Monitoring of foreign markets for attractive foreign borrowing opportunities Introduction of new "reverse tap tender" facility
Norway	Only single-price auctions now used
Slovak Republic	Contemplation of direct selling and buybacks in secondary market, underwriting auctions (single price based on price discovery through syndication), buybacks, and exchange auctions
Turkey	Revenue-indexed bonds introduced to broaden investor base
United Kingdom	Mini-tenders introduced in October 2008 as more flexible supplementary distribution method alongside core auctions program DMO using syndicated offerings to supplement its auction program Introduction of postauction option facility

Source: Responses to 2009 Survey of the OECD Working Party on Public Debt Management.

however, such as more limited reach among potential buyers, the presence of more risk-averse investors than dealers participating in auctions, and higher intermediation costs.

Many DMOs are operating more frequent auctions, whose schedules have become more flexible and opportunistic. The maturity of debt has become shorter, and there is growing use of foreign currency liabilities.

These changes create some risks. As debt managers become more opportunistic, issuance programs are becoming less predictable—something that may not be desirable in the long term. DMOs emphasize that they will continue to operate a transparent debt management framework supported by adopting a strong communication policy. Transparency and predictability remain instrumental in reducing the type of market noise that can unnecessarily increase borrowing costs.

Concluding Remarks

DMOs responded to dramatically increased borrowing requirements and concerns about possible market absorption problems in several ways. Responses included changes in issuance methods (including more flexible auctions, the introduction of auction fees, and the use of distribution methods other than auctions such as syndication); adoption of Dutch direct auction procedures and private placement; and changes in optimal sovereign portfolios (driven by new benchmarks with a greater emphasis on short-term paper and a reformulated cost-risk trade-off).

Although fundraising strategies have become more flexible and somewhat more opportunistic, OECD debt managers remain committed to maintaining a transparent debt management framework in order to minimize medium-term borrowing costs. This policy perspective is a necessary condition to maintain uninterrupted access by sovereign borrowers to markets.

The immediate crisis response by OECD DMOs was fairly successful. But the situation can deteriorate rapidly beyond a market comfort level,[5] as evidenced by the sharp increase in Greek borrowing costs in April–May 2010 and contagion risk. In view of looming serious fiscal problems and sovereign risk, not only in Greece but in several OECD governments, the importance of a credible medium-term fiscal outlook has increased. The Greek experience demonstrates the importance of sound crisis management (including sending clear policy messages and maintaining good communication channels with the market) and a credible fiscal outlook. Especially during crisis periods, markets need the comfort or deterrence of policy actions that reduce noise, increase the signal, or both.

By themselves, debt and deficit levels as a percentage of GDP cannot be used to predict the onset and subsequent dynamics of debt crises, because they conceal important structural differences across countries that have important (sometimes nonlinear) impacts on the sustainability of government debt (examples include growth potential, the degree of domestic institutional savings, home bias of investors, and fiscal capacity). A more thorough assessment also requires taking into account the (expected) real costs of the 2007–09 banking crises. Several studies demonstrate that the real costs of systemic banking problems have been growing since the 1970s and exceed those of currency crises (Bordo and others 2001).[6] These higher costs increase the chance that a banking crisis will mutate into a sovereign debt crisis (Candelon and Palm 2010). Reinhart and Rogoff (2008) estimate that on average, the stock of sovereign debt almost doubled three years after the banking crisis. The increase in sovereign risk, the risk of crowding out, and the tightening of issuance conditions put the spotlight on the importance of a proper fiscal and monetary exit strategy. Sovereign debt managers, with the essential support of sound fiscal consolidation policies, need to prepare and implement a timely and credible medium-term exit strategy. A credible exit strategy is also needed to control overly negative market sentiments and uncertainties about sovereign credit risk that could lead to dysfunctionalities at the short end of markets. Better communication channels among DMOs, the monetary and fiscal authorities, and markets are essential, especially during periods of financial fragility and perceptions of higher sovereign risk.

Crisis-induced policy responses since the collapse of Lehman have led to an unprecedented expansion in sovereign balance sheets and a sharp increase in off–balance sheet items such as contingent liabilities. These developments necessitate a redefinition of sovereign risk when assessing the sovereign risk outlook. Measures of sovereign risk should fully reflect key vulnerabilities on sovereign balance sheets associated with financial liabilities and assets (for a detailed analysis, see Blommestein 2006 and Blommestein and Koc 2008). These broader risk measures require an integrated approach to sovereign risk management, with greater emphasis on a sovereign balance sheet approach while taking into account reliable information on off–balance sheet items, such as guarantees, and outstanding derivative positions, such as swaps.

Notes

The author is indebted to Ms. Eylem Vayvada Derya (on secondment from the Turkish Treasury) for excellent statistical assistance.

1. The policy information in this chapter is based on OECD surveys of delegates of the Working Party on Public Debt Management, public information from official sources, and OECD (2009a, 2009b).

2. This reasoning implies rejection of the Ricardian equivalence hypothesis. An earlier period of widespread deficits (the 1980s) prompted a vigorous (sometimes almost ideological) debate about the effect of fiscal policy on interest rates. Chinn and Frankel (2003, p. 2) thought this debate would have been settled by now

in the direction of "rejecting Ricardian equivalence as a practical description of the real world," a conclusion also drawn by Gale and Orszag (2003). Other analysts strongly disagree with this conclusion.

3. Many DMOs are using currency swaps to eliminate the risks associated with the resulting foreign currency exposure.

4. In times of extreme risk aversion and high uncertainty, governments use short-term issuance to raise extra funds at short notice while providing liquid and secure instruments to the market.

5. To an important degree, this comfort level is arbitrary (or subjective) and therefore hard or impossible to predict. This perspective on crisis situations reflects the insight that a debt sustainability framework cannot be used to predict the "real time" onset and evolution of a sovereign debt crisis. Moreover, markets are prone to under- and overshooting as well as bubbles.

6. A key finding of Bordo and others is that the average banking crisis is followed by a 4.1 percent fall in real output growth and a recession lasting two years.

References

Blommestein, H. J. 2006. "Government Balance Sheet Risk Management." In *Government Debt Management: New Trends and Challenges,* ed. M. Williamson. London: Central Banking Publications.

———. 2009a. "Responding to the Crisis: Changes in OECD Primary Market Procedures and Portfolio Risk Management." *OECD Journal: Financial Market Trends* 2: 191–206.

———. 2009b. "State Borrowing and Exit Policies Create a New Set of Challenges." *Financial Times,* December 17.

———. 2010. "Outlook for Markets and Risks from the Perspective of Sovereign Issuers." Paper presented at the Financial Round Table of the OECD Committee on Financial Markets, Paris, April 15.

Blommestein, H. J., and Arzu Gok. 2009. "The Surge in Borrowing Needs of OECD Governments: Revised Estimates for 2009 and 2010 Outlook." *OECD Journal: Financial Market Trends* 2: 177–89.

Blommestein, H. J., and Fatos Koc. 2008. "Sovereign Asset and Liability Management: Practical Steps towards Integrated Risk Management." *Forum Financier/ Revue Bancaire et Financière* 6–7: 360–69.

Blommestein, Hans J., Vincenzo Guzzo, and Allison Holland. 2010. "Debt Markets: Policy Challenges in the Post-Crisis Landscape." *OECD Journal: Financial Market Trends* 2010 (1).

Bordo M. D., B. Eichengreen, D. Klingenbiel, and M. S. Martinez Peria. 2001. "Is the Crisis Problem Growing More Severe?" *Economic Policy* 32 (January): 51–82.

Candelon, B., and F. C. Palm. 2010. "Banking and Debt Crises in Europe: The Dangerous Liaisons?" *The Economist* 158 (1): 80–99.

Chinn, M., and J. Frankel. 2003. "The Euro Area and World Interest Rates." Paper presented at the Centre for Economic Policy Research/European Banking Center annual conference "The Euro Area as an Economic Entity," Eltville, Germany, September 12–13.

Gale, W. G., and P. R. Orszag. 2003. "The Economic Effects of Long-Term Fiscal Discipline." Urban-Brookings Tax Policy Center Discussion Paper 8, Brookings Institution, Washington, DC.

Greenspan, A. 2010. "The Crisis." *Brookings Papers on Economic Activity*, Spring: 1–49.

OECD (Organisation for Economic Co-operation and Development). 2009a. *OECD Economic Outlook No. 86* (Preliminary Edition). Paris: OECD.

———. 2009b. *OECD Central Government Debt, Statistical Yearbook 1999–2008.* Paris: OECD.

Reinhart, C. M., and K. S. Rogoff. 2008. "The Forgotten History of Domestic Debt." NBER Working Paper 13946, National Bureau of Economic Research, Cambridge, MA.

Warsh, K. 2010. *An Ode to Independence.* March 26. Shadow Open Market Committee, New York.

Index

Boxes, figures, notes, and tables are indicated by b, f, n, and t, respectively.

A

accountability and transparency
  DeMPA analysis of low-income
    countries, 433
  in OECD countries, 462
  subnational debt, 280–81
adjustment conditionality,
    ILLR, 337
adjustment facility, ILLR,
    340–41
Admati, Anat R., 311
administrative versus
    administrative approaches
    to subnational insolvency,
    284–85
Africa. *See* IDA-only African
    countries; Middle East
    and North Africa;
    Sub-Saharan Africa;
    specific countries
African Development Bank,
    255–56, 296, 445*n*12
Aggarwal, Vinod K., 305
Ahmed, Faisal, xix, 9, 357
Akaike information criterion, 54
Albert, J., 60
Alesina, Alberto, 309
Allen, M., 358
Anderson, Phillip R. D., xix,
    10, 383

Angola, 31
Antigua and Barbuda, 209
Arab Republic of Egypt. *See* Egypt,
    Arab Republic of
arbitration
  NGO proposals, 320
  tribunal proposal. *See* tribunal
    for sovereign debt
Argentina
  debt restructuring mechanisms
    and financial crisis in,
    245–46
  deflation during financial
    crisis in, 231, 233–35,
    235f
  external debt relative to GDP,
    2002–07, 175, 192*n*4
  fiscal rules implemented in,
    192*n*3
  inflation rates, 2002–07, 175
  macroeconomic space in,
    177, 184
  medium-term challenges and
    adjustment strategies,
    187, 188
  sovereign bond spreads in, 180
  subnational debt in, 274
Armenia, 31
ASEAN (Association of Southeast
    Asian Nations), 192*n*9

467

trade sanctions and sovereign
default, 244
transparency. *See* accountability
and transparency
tribunal for sovereign debt, 8–9,
317–29
advantages of, 320
binding nature of decisions,
323–24
concept of, 319–20
creation and composition of,
320–22
deficiencies of current ad hoc
system, 317–19
financing and support for, 326
governing law, 324–25
intercreditor equity in, 323–24
jurisdiction and competence,
322–24
location of, 319
mediation preceding, 326
representation of creditors
before, 325
triggering mechanisms, 324
Trichet, Jean-Claude, 318
Troubled Asset Relief Program
(TARP), 451
Trust Indenture Act (U.S.), 267n17
trust instruments, English versus
U.S., 254, 267n17
Tunisia, 43n1
Turkey
debt composition and structure
in, 369f, 370, 371f, 396
debt managers' response to
global crisis in, 404,
405, 406
external debt, 125n1, 397
foreign currency borrowing,
388, 396
GDP growth in, 181
global financial crisis, effects of,
397, 402
history of debt crises in, 20
inflation rates, 2002–07, 175
inflation targeting in, 192n3
macroeconomic space in, 177

medium-term challenges and
adjustment strategies,
186, 187, 188, 193n14
nonlinear crisis events
in, 43n1

U

Ukraine
credit as share of GDP in, 175
external and fiscal imbalances,
failure to correct, 387
external debt relative to GDP,
2002–07, 175
GDP, external debt as percentage
of, 182
GDP growth in, 181
inflation rates, 2002–07, 175
macroeconomic space in,
176–77, 184
medium-term challenges and
adjustment strategies,
187, 188
Naftogaz debt restructuring in,
125n2
new debt stress events,
2008–09, 31
sovereign bond spreads
in, 180
uncoordinated creditors, 306–9
uncoordinated debtors, 309–10
United Kingdom
English trust deeds versus U.S.
trust indentures, 254,
267n17
inflation-linked bonds, 371
rise of sovereign debt in, 2
subnational debt in, 279
United Nations and tribunal
proposal, 321, 325,
326–27
United Nations Commission on
International Trade Law
(UNCITRAL), 325
United Nations Conference on
Trade and Development
(UNCTAD), 259, 260